INCREASING READING EFFICIENCY

seek the ideas behind the words

READING EFFICIENCY

INCREASING READING EFFICIENCY

FOURTH EDITION

LYLE L. MILLER

Professor
Guidance and Counselor Education

Director
Uniwyo Reading Research Center

University of Wyoming

HOLT, RINEHART AND WINSTON

New York   Chicago   San Francisco   Atlanta   Dallas   Montreal   Toronto   London   Sydney

Library of Congress Cataloging in Publication Data

Miller, Lyle L.
    Increasing reading efficiency.

    Bibliography: p.
    1. Developmental reading. I. Title.
LB1050.53.M54   1977   428'.4'.3   76–19051
ISBN: 0–03–089932–X

ACKNOWLEDGMENTS

"Anger." Reprinted from the December 1966 *News Release* of the American Medical Association by permission of the director of Magazine Relations.

Furman Bisher, "Island in the Sun." Reprinted from the Winter 1966–1967 issue of *Adventure Road* magazine by permission of the editor.

Cliff Bosley, "Man and the Synthetic Age." Reprinted from the December 1965 issue of *Wyoming Wildlife* by permission of the editor.

Tim Britt, "Szzzzzzz." Reprinted from the May 1967 issue of *Wyoming Wildlife* by permission of the editor.

Admiral Arleigh Burke, "Freedom Demands Self-discipline." Reprinted by permission of the author from the February 1966 edition of *Scouting* magazine, published by the Boy Scouts of America.

R. C. Burkholder, "Sludge Slough." Reprinted from the November 1973 issue of *Wyoming Wildlife* by permission of the editor.

Don Cannalte, "The Rockies' Riotous Ski Festivals." Reprinted from the January 1967 edition of the United Airlines' *Mainliner* magazine by permission of the author.

The *Changing Times* Staff, "Safer Ways to Drive at Night." Excerpted by permission from *Changing Times*, the Kiplinger magazine, March 1967 issue. Copyright 1967 by the Kiplinger Washington Editors, Inc., 1729 H Street, N.W., Washington, D.C. 20006.

Alexander K. Ciesielski, "Totems under Siege." Copyright 1975 by the National Wildlife Federation. Reprinted from the August–September 1975 issue of *National Wildlife* Magazine by permission of the editors.

Dennis J. Cipnic, "New Life in the Old Quarter." Reprinted from the Winter 1966–1967 issue of *Adventure Road* magazine by permission of the editor.

"Edison and Electricity." Reprinted from a pamphlet of the same name by permission of the General Electric Company.

Thomas I. Emerson, "Bill of Rights." Reprinted with permission from *Public Affairs Pamphlet*, No. 489, Copyright © 1964 by the Public Affairs Committee, Inc.

"Emotions within the Family." Reprinted from the 1967 pamphlet of the Metropolitan Life Insurance Company by permission of the publishers.

Glen Evans, "Crusader in the Pine Barrens." Reprinted from the November 1974 issue of *Dynamic Maturity* by permission of the editor and the author.

"Free and Responsible People." Excerpted from an article in the November 1975 issue of *The Royal Bank of Canada Monthly Letter* by permission of the editor.

"French at the Fork," *Friends*, February 1974. Reprinted by permission of *Friends* Magazine, Ceco Publishing Company.

Lon Garrison, "The Lady at the Bell." Reprinted from the May–June 1967 issue of *Conservation Volunteer* by permission of the editor.

Paul H. Gnadt, "Winning Isn't Enough." Reprinted from the December 1973 issue of *Listen* by permission of the editor.

"Guidelines to Efficiency." Reprinted from excerpts from the January 1974 issue of *The Royal Bank of Canada Monthly Letter* by permission of the editor.

Marvin Harris, "The Myth of the Sacred Cow." Reprinted from the March 1967 issue of *Natural History* by permission of the editorial secretary.

Roger Hart, "Wooded Wonderland." Reprinted from the November 1973 issue of *Natural History* by permission of the editorial secretary.

Pennfield Jensen, "A Student Manifesto." Reprinted from the April 1970 issue of *Natural History* by permission of the editorial secretary.

Bel Kaufman, "Letter to a Dead Teacher." Reprinted from the March–April 1975 issue of *Today's Education* by permission of the executive editor and the author.

Dick Kirkpatrick, "The Guns That Went West" (adapted from the technical data by James E. Serven). Copyright 1966 by National Wildlife Federation. Reprinted from the October–November 1966 issue of *National Wildlife* Magazine by permission of the editors.

——, "High Soars the Eagle." Copyright 1963 by the National Wildlife Federation. Reprinted from the January 1963 issue of *National Wildlife* Magazine by permission of the editors.

Theodore Lesley, "Egmont Key." Reprinted from the May 1, 1973, issue of the *Congressional Record*.

William McCormack, "Faculty Travel Abroad." Reprinted from the April 1972 issue of the *School and Society* magazine by permission of the editor.

Russell McKee, "John Muir." Reprinted from the November–December 1966 edition of the *Colorado Outdoors* magazine by permission of the publications chief.

Stephen P. Maran, "Missing Matter." Excerpted from an article in the January 1976 issue of *Natural History* by permission of the editorial secretary.

Donna Martinez, "Curse of the Pharaohs." Reprinted from an original article of the Uniwyo Reading Research Center by permission of the director.

——, "Three Black Executives." Reprinted from an original article of the Uniwyo Reading Research Center by permission of the director.

Hon. Lee Metcalf, "The Future of the Oceans." Reprinted from the December 8, 1974, issue of the *Congressional Record*.

PREFACE

Ecology and efficiency

Our extensive concern for ecology, conservation, and recycling of resources certainly emphasizes our national recognition of the tremendous waste that has accompanied many of our advances in technology. Recycling is not a new concept to some of us who can still remember the Great Depression years and the days when we reused everything we could as many times as we could because we simply could not afford to replace it. Our choice was often recycling or doing without. One of the basic lessons of the 1930s was to get maximum effective use of all of our physical resources.

As a boy growing up in that period, I became concerned about one very important resource that simply could not be recycled—our time! Personal experience with the sudden death of a close boyhood friend reinforced the concern about the irrevocable passage of time and the undetermined supply of time available to any one of us.

These concerns led to the preparation of an entry in the National IBM Essay Contest on the topic "The Value of Time in Education." Some of the ideas expressed must have been challenging and innovative, because the essay won the State Award. But the profound effect was that the work on the essay started me on an extensive search for more effective ways to use time wisely, and for ways to get more done in less time. For me, the concept of *efficiency* had been born. It was to grow rapidly and to influence much of my personal and professional behavior in the following years. But the emphasis on *quality* of work always took priority over any emphasis on speed alone.

Many years later, when a small group of students approached me and asked me to help them learn to read faster, I certainly did not anticipate the interesting and challenging project I was undertaking. Little did I dream that most of my professional reading and research time henceforth would be devoted to the task of helping people read faster and better.

Certainly, I laid no claim to being a reading expert; if anything, I was a real skeptic about speed reading programs. I was concerned with effective study skills in my capacity as a study skills instructor, and I was concerned with helping young people define and resolve their problems in my role as a counselor. These two perspectives made the question of speed reading a challenging one. Could speed be achieved without losing quality of achievement? Could one be a fast reader and a good reader at the same time?

Resources and research

I soon found that there were few, if any, experts and only very limited source materials on any developmental reading programs beyond the sixth grade level. Today there is significantly more material, but still a shortage of people who claim to be experts in the field. So much of the reading process goes on in the eye and the brain that no one can really observe or study the real reading process to learn answers about it. All one can do is to observe behavior and record data in such a way that, bit by bit, one adds to knowledge and contributes to the improvement of methods and materials for the developmental reading program. I never expect to become an expert on reading, but I certainly have learned a great deal about the process and do know considerably more than I would have thought possible twenty-five years ago. More than any other thing, I have been impressed greatly by the observed behavior of young people who have discovered previously undreamed-of potential for learning through their experience in a developmental reading laboratory.

Needs and purpose

In an age of automation, space labs, and color TV, we may take for granted some of our basic concepts of communication. Instantaneous communication of ideas through radio, television, international Telstar relays, and constantly improving modern telephone services literally has brought the world into our living room. There can be no doubt that we depend extensively on *looking* and *listening* to keep us informed today. In the midst of all of these modern developments, however, we find reports of increasing circulation of magazines, continuous publication of new books, expanding library facilities, and an ever-increasing volume of printed material being circulated through the mail. In our high-speed world of electronic and atomic wonders, we still find that *reading* is our most fundamental process of interpersonal communication.

With our rapidly expanding field of human knowledge, reading ability has become one of the most important factors of success in many fields today. This is true of busy doctors or lawyers keeping up with recent developments through their professional journals, of the modern scientists analyzing the work of others through their research papers, of the business executive reading market reports and correspondence, and of the housewife seeking relaxation and relief from her daily problems through reading her favorite magazine. Reading is especially important to conscientious students who are trying to grasp an understanding of the many new concepts in their chosen curriculum. All of them need to read. More important, however, is the fact that all of them need to read *quickly* and *efficiently*.

Colleges are aware of the reading problems of young adults and are attempting to deal with these problems. Remedial reading programs have been available for many years to help the student with specific reading difficulties or deficiencies. Developmental reading programs have expanded rapidly in recent years, however, with a focus on the needs and problems of the "average" or "good" readers, who need to read more in less time.

Few readers have been able to avoid the pressures of the faster pace of living and learning and the parallel need to read more effectively. Efficient habits of reading are of value to any reader, and many college reading centers have engaged in extensive research on this problem. The first edition of *Increasing Reading Efficiency* (24)[1] was the product of such research in the Study Skills Center and the Reading Research Center at the University of Wyoming. Extensive use of the workbook in many colleges and adult reading programs since then has confirmed the value of this approach to developmental reading.

Experimental work in many high schools and universities has shown that few students are reading at speeds that even begin to approach their real reading capabilities. Although some universities and colleges still place the stress on remedial reading, many instructors in study skills programs have come to feel that this emphasis is misleading, for it tends to discourage many students from participating in reading training programs because they feel that they already have normal reading habits. Experience has shown, however, that

reading training can help any person who has a sincere desire for self-improvement. Therefore, this manual has been developed primarily as a basic drill series for group reading practice. Those individuals who need specific remedial help usually can secure this assistance in addition to this group training. Those who are interested primarily in increasing reading efficiency may devote extra time to practice on longer reading exercises such as those provided in *Maintaining Reading Efficiency* (25).

Letters from many teachers and students who have used *Increasing Reading Efficiency* in many parts of the United States and abroad have convinced the author that this pattern of reading exercises has been of real practical value to thousands of high school and college students and adults. Its popularity led to the development of a companion volume, *Developing Reading Efficiency* (23), which has the same basic pattern of organization but which is focused on the reading needs of students in grades seven through ten, and of *Personalizing Reading Efficiency* (27) for the upper high school years. For further reading practice with longer standardized materials, the supplementary volume, *Maintaining Reading Efficiency* (25) was developed. A manual for teachers was developed later and published under the title *Teaching Efficient Reading Skills* (29). These publications are now distributed by Burgess Publishing Company, Minneapolis, Minnesota 55435. A collection of *Maintaining Reading Efficiency Tests* for pretesting and posttesting is distributed by Developmental Reading Distributors, Laramie, Wyoming 82070.

In attempting a revision of *Increasing Reading Efficiency*, therefore, the author has been careful to preserve the basic format and exercise sequence. The changes in this edition include the restandardization and replacement of about 60 percent of the exercises in Series V, VI, VII, and VIII in order to update materials and provide a better content balance. With these changes, the fourth edition of *Increasing Reading Efficiency* should continue to provide outstanding service in developmental reading programs for many years to come.

Use of the workbook

Although this workbook may be used for self-improvement practice in individual cases, it was designed primarily for use with small groups of readers, where competition within the group may serve as a psychological motivation for increased proficiency in the drill exercises. With a planned supervision that stresses both self-improvement and competition with other readers, most group members will be pleasantly surprised by the improvement they can make in a series of reading classes. It is not unusual for many students in a group to double or triple reading efficiency if they make a sincere effort to do so.

[1]All reference numbers refer to the numbered selected references on p. 27.

Sources of inspiration

In developing this manual, the author is indebted to several sources for ideas and inspirations. In these reading workbooks he has attempted to incorporate some of the best of the ideas on developmental reading and of effective study. First of all, Dr. Francis P. Robinson (40) stimulated his interest in the field of study skills and reading needs of college students. Although many authors contributed to his understanding of the reading process, the author was most impressed by the concepts and basic reading drill sequences developed by Stroud and Ammons (47). The criticisms of hundreds of students in study skills classes and of dozens of graduate students throughout the past decade have contributed to the expansion and polishing of these ideas.

The inspiration of Oscar Causey and his work with a series of National Reading Conferences at Fort Worth, Texas (9 and 10), throughout the late 1950s was of tremendous significance. Answers were obtained to many questions about reading through the research efforts of a number of graduate students at the University of Wyoming throughout the years, as they selected some aspect of reading as a focus for their graduate' theses. These included Jeanne Taylor, James Gordon Shaw, Kristen Solberg, Robert A. C. Jones, Dudley Sykes, Paul Koziey, Martin Faber, Ed Johnson, Tom Marshall, Russell Washburn, and many others.

Many authors and publishers have been extremely generous in granting permission to use their materials and to revise these materials slightly when necessary to develop them into standard reading exercises. Those whose materials appear in this final revision are acknowledged by the credit line on the article, and on page iv, but many others had been just as gracious in granting permission to use their material in developing the wide range of potential reading exercises from which the final sets were selected. Many of their exercises have been used extensively in the Study Skills classes at the University of Wyoming.

The necessity for standard lengths of articles and balance of reading difficulty determined the final choice of exercises included in this book; but without the encouragement from *all* those who granted permission to use their materials in this way, this workbook would not have been possible.

Many suggestions and evaluative comments have come from teachers who have used the workbook in their classes. Many reading specialists and developmental reading teachers throughout the country have contributed to the evaluation and to the revisions of the whole series of workbooks. All of their help is, of course, reflected in this new edition. Special thanks should go to the following reviewers for their valuable critiques of the last edition and for their suggestions for improvements to be made in the present one: Marion Axford, Bakersfield Community College; Marjorie Durling, West Virginia Community College; Charles Hadley, director of research, Colorado Springs Public School System; Conner Hall, University of Texas; Christine Payne, West Virginia Community College; Alfred Snap, district coordinator of instruction, Mt. Prospect, Illinois, Public School System; and Russell Washburn, Ritenour Senior High School, Overland, Missouri.

Special recognition should be given to staff members in the Reading Research Center at the University of Wyoming for their contributions in developing new materials. Especially deserving of credit for this revision are Nelda Hernandez, Mary Connors, Mary Warren, Larry Zeitner, Connie Holt, Mary Ellen Latham, Lisa Nelms, Sarah Peterson, and Betty Ramsey.

Above all, I am most appreciative of the inspiration of my two children, Tom and Patty, who participated in experimental reading groups and spoke freely of student reactions, and to my wife, Grace M. Miller, who has been a partner in the long-term development of the whole Reading Efficiency series. Without her patient understanding, continued support, encouragement, and hours of diligent labor on the manuscript, I would have been unable to complete this revision of *Increasing Reading Efficiency*.

L. L. M.

Laramie, Wyoming
January 1977

CONTENTS

INCREASING READING EFFICIENCY

seek the ideas behind the words

READING EFFICIENCY

TO THE TEACHER

Survival

With the release of this fourth edition, *Increasing Reading Efficiency* will have survived for more than twenty years in the academic marketplace. During this period, it has had a profound impact on the lives and reading habits of many thousands of individuals. By increasing their reading efficiency, they have been able to live much fuller lives and to engage in many more activities than would have been possible otherwise. Many of them have found a great deal more pleasure in reading and have come to recognize reading as one of the important keys to success in their lives. The strongest supporters of the continued use of this book are those individuals who have had a positive personal experience in the way that it can improve their individual perception and retention of verbal symbols.

In that period of time, *Increasing Reading Efficiency* has been used by several hundred teachers in public schools, colleges, and adult education programs. Many of these teachers have written back to the author to share student reactions and to make suggestions for improvement. With the benefit of those suggestions, each revision has reflected some improvements over the earlier editions.

Although it was originally designed as an instrument for use primarily with study skill groups at a college level, it has proved to be practical at many other levels and in many other types of group and individual situations. It has been a useful tool of many teachers with differing perspectives and purposes.

For those who have been behaviorally oriented, it has provided a carefully structured sequence of drill materials designed to bring about specific modifications of basic reading behavior. Such changes can be functionally defined and carefully measured to reflect the individual's attainment of his goals and expectations.

For those more interested in the affective aspects of learning, the materials have provided a basis for bringing about attitudinal change about reading, study skills, and personal responsibility. Many teachers comment on the value of the suggestions and the application of reading skills to practical needs. Changes in self-concept often seem to be significant outcomes of the development of flexibility in reading skills. Flexible reading habits lead to broader interests and make it more possible for students to become involved at greater depths in those things that are of real interest and challenge to them.

The practical use of this book seems to range from its use as *the* basic workbook in some groups or classes on reading improvement to simple application of a single student. In the first case, it seems to serve as the basic instrument for specific behavioral change in reading habits in a sixteen- to twenty-hour structured program of carefully planned and supervised reading experiences. On the other end of the scale is its use by an individual student who purchases a single copy at the bookstore for his own program of self-structured self-improvement. Between these two extremes are many other variations of functional use in the classroom or reading resource center.

Within a wide range of experimentation and critical examination, the earlier editions of *Increasing Reading Efficiency* seem to have proved the continuing value of this material sufficiently to justify further refinement and revision in this fourth edition.

Demands for reading efficiency

The constantly increasing explosion of knowledge and the resultant publication of increasing numbers of challenging and stimulating books and periodical articles have made good reading a key to a wide range of vicarious experiences. The success of so many highly advertised commercial reading programs seems to be ample evidence that many people want to read better and faster. It has been a concern of this author for many years that public schools and colleges have not been more responsive to these needs. Surely, our schools could offer all of the best characteristics of most of the commercial reading programs at a fraction of the costs being charged for them.

A focal point of attention for this author for the past twenty-five years has been the development of appropriate instructional materials for developmental reading programs with the hope that these materials might at least provide a sound basis for personal development of reading skills in a variety of settings.

A family of reading efficiency books

The popularity of *Increasing Reading Efficiency* (24),[1] first published by Holt, Rinehart and Winston in 1956 and now in its fourth edition, has demonstrated the value of such materials for college students and adults. Subsequently, a companion volume, *Developing Reading Efficiency* (23), was published by Burgess Publishing Company and has been equally effective for younger students in grades seven through ten.

[1] All reference numbers refer to the numbered selected references on p. 27.

More recently, a third workbook, *Personalizing Reading Efficiency* (27) has been published by Burgess Publishing Company in 1976. With structure comparable to the other two books, this one is designed specifically for the upper high school years. It is a condensed version with only half as many exercises as the other two and planned specifically for classroom use without the exercises for suggested outside practice.

A fourth workbook, *Maintaining Reading Efficiency* (25) has been designed to provide practice in the application of flexible reading skills over longer periods of time. This book and other tests, pacing tapes, and related study skills materials are available from Developmental Reading Distributors, 1944 Sheridan, Laramie, Wyoming 82070.

Resources for teachers

One reaction of teachers using the earlier editions of *Increasing Reading Efficiency* was that materials for teachers should be included *in the workbook itself,* rather than in a separate teachers manual. They also suggested that the teachers' section should be expanded to cover several basic points of concern to the teacher. In response to those suggestions, this brief section for teachers has been developed, and sets of answer keys arranged on perforated pages for easy removal have been included at the back of the workbook.

Teachers who desire more specific suggestions on methods and materials for teaching developmental reading are encouraged to secure the more comprehensive manual for teachers, *Teaching Efficient Reading Skills* (29), published by Burgess Publishing Company, Minneapolis, Minnesota.

Purpose of the workbook

Increasing Reading Efficiency was originally designed to promote the mutual development of reading speed and reading comprehension through carefully controlled group activity. Although the author has since received abundant evidence of effective and highly gratifying use of the workbook by individuals and in individualized settings in reading clinics, he still emphasizes that the materials were intended primarily for use in groups, where competition with oneself and with others in the group tends to provide parallel patterns for psychological motivation. The author is firmly convinced that this dual competitive pattern, supported by a teacher who can provide a system of both group and individual motivation, provides a stimulus more appropriate than any specific pattern of mechanical or machine-oriented motivation.

With a primary goal of increasing rate along with a maintenance or improvement of comprehen-sion skill, other aspects such as vocabulary improvement and critical reading skills are of secondary importance in the overall structure of the book. With full recognition of the basic importance of higher level study skills, analytical reading, critical reading, and vocabulary development, one must recognize that any attempt to expand this book to include comprehensive coverage of all of these points would result in an extremely bulky and expensive volume and would represent a sacrifice of some currently established and meaningful sequence of exercises. Teachers seeking these other types of emphasis are encouraged to consider other appropriate materials on the market.

In summary, then, this material was designed primarily for use in groups under supervision of an able teacher who can motivate people to reach beyond their current grasp. It was designed also for use with young adults and mature individuals who have mastered the basic development of language skills. Teachers of younger or less mature groups are urged to consider the use of *Developing Reading Efficiency* (23). Consideration might also be given to the shorter collection of materials at a slightly lower interest and vocabulary level. This collection is available from Burgess Publishing Company under the title *Personalizing Reading Efficiency* (27).

The concept of reading efficiency

Although both rate of reading and comprehension are recognized as important aspects of reading ability, neither one is stressed in itself. Instead, this author places the stress on a combination of the two factors that he calls *reading efficiency*. This measures what might be called a "rate of understanding." Reading efficiency is computed by multiplying the rate (in words per minute) by the comprehension score (percentage of correct answers on tested material). This yields a "words-per-minute" figure that serves as a measure of the amount of material understood during a minute of time. Although one recognizes that ideas cannot be measured accurately in "words per minute," this stress on efficiency does seem to overcome some of the concern over comprehension loss in the early stages of reading improvement.

Early experimentation in the University of Wyoming Study Skills Center revealed that students seemed to attain lower comprehension scores for a period of time immediately after having successfully increased their reading rate. Consequently, much thought has been given to the provision of training exercises designed to bring about increases in *both* rate and comprehension. After years of observation and comparison, however, research seems to show that most students can make very substantial increases in rate with no significant loss in comprehension.

During the years in which *Increasing Reading Efficiency* has been used in the Study Skills Center, group evaluations have revealed an increase in both rate and comprehension on comparable standardized tests administered at the beginning and end of the ten-week training period. *Maintaining Reading Efficiency Tests* (26) are published by Developmental Reading Distributors, Laramie, Wyoming 82070. With five different forms, these tests can be used effectively for such pre- and postcomparisons. Also available from the same source is the *Reading Pacing Tape*, which can be used for individual pacing, or can be used with the group to free the teacher for more careful observation of individual behavior during reading activities. Simultaneous improvement of rate and comprehension results from a careful integration of speed reading skills and higher level study skills.

This can be accomplished by introducing students to techniques of self-recitation, reading for ideas, and recognition of textbook clues. The materials in this workbook are organized in such a way that the effectiveness of this approach is easy to illustrate to the students.

Do not expect these characteristics

No one book on developmental reading can be all things to all people. Therefore, one should consider some of the things that this book is *not! It is not a "speed-reading" workbook.* The author believes that teachers should deal cautiously with the idea of "speed" in reading. The gullible public often is given the idea that all reading difficulties are essentially speed problems. The recent flood of commercial materials and programs implies that improvement in reading rate will evolve miracles. At its very best, the situation oversimplifies what may be a serious problem. A slow reading rate may very easily be a symptom of other reading difficulties, such as weaknesses in basic word recognition, interpretation skills, study skills, or even more serious physiological problems; or it may be a problem of attitude toward school and learning. The author already has indicated his concern for a balanced approach and for supervision by a teacher who can be observant of, and sensitive to, symptoms of other problems.

It is not a remedial workbook. The materials are designed for older adolescents and adults who have already mastered basic language skills. Many other good materials are available on the market that emphasize basic language skills and remedial techniques.

It is not primarily a vocabulary builder. Vocabulary training is assumed as an essential supplementary activity. Exercises in this book allow for the basic identification of some potential vocabulary problems, but practice on vocabulary improvement is a matter of individual emphasis. The author would recommend a supplemental practice book such as *Basic Vocabulary Skills* by Davis (11) or *Developing Vocabulary Skills* by Joffe (17).

It is not a book for reading improvement through concentrated applied practice. This book involves much basic drill material. For those who prefer direct practice in reading content-oriented materials, the author would recommend *Maintaining Reading Efficiency* (25).

Basic concepts of reading

One of the confusing points to students and teachers alike is the absence of a universal definition of the term *reading*. Consequently, many people are writing and talking about *reading* and not meaning the same thing. Let us first explore the much quoted statement that no one can possibly read at a rate of more than 800 words per minute. This statement evidently is based on the following steps of logic:

1. Readers identify and recognize visual material only during eye pauses or fixations.
2. Research indicates that the average adult reader can recognize clearly only 1.1 words during such a fixation and that the most able readers seldom recognize over 2.7 word per fixation or stop.
3. Efficient readers require at least a one-fifth second duration to recognize any symbols during any stop.
4. Efficient readers, therefore, cannot hope to make more than five stops per second.
5. Therefore, it can be mathematically calculated that the very efficient reader who can see 2.7 words per fixation and who makes five stops per second will be able to read only 810 words per minute.

Thus the 800 words per minute maximum is established—based on a concept of *deliberate reading* that is defined as the act in which the reader *contacts all of the words visually and strives for complete comprehension*. Of course, this does not discount the fact that people can "skim" or "scan" at much more rapid rates, but to the "purist" this is *not* reading. For those with more practical interests, however, questions exist about all but the first step in the logic outlined above.

If the many demands for varied types of reading in modern society are considered, one can see why most teachers and students find acceptance of such an extreme definition impractical. But no other definition has been accepted universally. Therefore, each author should feel an obligation to make clear his own concepts of the term. As used in this book, the term *reading* means *that process of communica-*

tion of ideas from one person to another through the medium of writing or printing. More concisely, the purpose of reading is seen as *seeking the ideas behind the words.*

Within this definition, skimming and scanning can be viewed as effective types of the total reading program, and the concept of reading rates beyond 800 words per minute is much more understandable and acceptable.

Basic points of reference

Any development of materials is dependent on concepts developed for other purposes. Materials in this book are dependent for meaning on two basic concepts in addition to the "reading efficiency" concept previously described.

The basic vocabulary around which reading exercises in Series I, II, and III are built is the *Teacher's Word Book of 30,000 Words* (50) developed by E. L. Thorndike in 1944. Considering the publication date, one can see that many words of recent vintage are not included. The scope of these exercises is somewhat limited, therefore, by the basic word list. The author is unaware, however, of any more recent word list composed by a comparable authority.

The measurement of reading difficulty in all exercises in Series V through VII has been accomplished through the use of the Flesch formula (12). Although limited to only two basic factors, sentence length and syllable count per hundred words, this has been viewed for many years as the most efficient measure of reading difficulty for adult materials. Although it has been criticized widely by teachers of English, no one seems to have come forth with any better tool to serve the same purpose. So, with due recognition to its obvious limitations, this author has used it as the best available instrument for establishing some standardization of the relative difficulty of exercise material.

Development of the reading exercises

Of basic importance to the exercises in this manual is a provision for increasing eye span and for establishing rhythmic eye movements. Also basic is the need to increase rate of mental perception of what is read and so reduce the eye fixation time. These exercises were planned to provide training for these purposes. In addition, the difficulty of the exercises has been standardized sufficiently to allow comparisons between similar exercises in sequences of gradually increasing difficulty.

Standardization of the materials

One of the major difficulties a few years ago in evaluating the results of a training program in developmental reading was the lack of standardized materials. The materials used in this book are now standardized as much as possible in order to make exercises comparable.

In Series I and II, answer frequency per column has been standardized, so that in each exercise the right answer will occur five times in each column.

In Series I and II, all key words occur in Thorndike's list of 10,000 most frequently used words (49), and all words in the answer columns occur in Thorndike's list of 30,000 most frequently used words (50). Therefore, these exercises may serve also as vocabulary drills for high school or college students.

In the phrase and sentence meaning drills, the key words have been checked against the same word list. These exercises have been arranged in an order of gradually increasing length and difficulty.

The paragraph reading material in Series V, VI, and VII has all been reduced to standardized lengths so that rates may be obtained from tables. This material has been rated by the Flesch formula (12) and has been arranged in order of increasing difficulty— from fifth grade through the upper college level, with most of the material falling in the range of the upper high school years.

Arrangement of materials

Although these materials are arranged by groups in the sequence believed to be most advantageous, the groups are designed for some overlapping in class practice. For example, practice on "word meaning" exercises should be started when the class is only about 30 percent through the "word recognition" section. This overlapping in the four basic groups of exercises provides better continuity. The "idea reading," "exploratory reading," and "study reading" drills should be started at least by the second period of training and should be used regularly thereafter.

If time is limited, the odd-numbered exercises may be used for individual practice and the even-numbered ones for group work. If time permits, however, all the exercises may be used for group practice.

The purpose and method of procedure for each set of exercises is given immediately preceding that set of exercises. These include "Suggestions" for students to think about. Students should be encouraged to read these before they start the series, and then to go back and review the suggestions again after having done one or two exercises in the series.

Progress Charts are provided on page 297–305 for maintaining daily records of reading progress during the period of training. Keeping this daily progress chart is an important aspect of self-motivation. Teachers should clarify the use of these *progress charts* very early in the program and should check frequently to see if students understand and use these to set goals for self-improvement.

Types of exercises

The first exercises are designed primarily as speed exercises. In Series I, the major emphasis should be on the establishment of rhythmic eye movements and increased eye span. In Series II, understanding is emphasized, and most readers will slow down. Each error indicates a possible misunderstanding of these words that may serve as reading blocks. The key word obviously may be a problem as well as the one marked in error. But the correct answer that was overlooked also may be a clue to a vocabulary problem. Hence students should be encouraged to develop vocabulary lists, and to study words missed to increase vocabulary.

Series III continues this stress on understanding but deals with groups of words and emphasizes increased eye span and the grasping of ideas rather than words. In this sequence, stress is put on gradual increase of eye span in both a horizontal and a vertical direction.

Series IV concentrates on rapid scanning of basic ideas in a sentence.

Series V provides practice in high-speed reading for basic ideas. The tests on these materials consist of two questions relating only to basic thoughts or ideas in the material. Here both rapid reading and correct understanding are important. The questions are of the same type for each exercise. Questions are designed to pick up recurrent thoughts, basic themes, or overall purpose in the article. The primary purpose of this series, however, is to emphasize the development of high-speed reading with minimal emphasis on comprehension.

Series VI places stress on more accurate reading for short periods of time. Here again, the tests follow similar patterns for each exercise; but, in this case, they require more attention to detailed ideas and facts presented in the material.

Series VII demonstrates an application of the Self-Recitation technique and does much to give students definite evidence of the values of this study technique. It is designed to help them develop habits of *thinking* as they read. The exercises are matched with those in Series VI for readability, length, and type of questions asked; but here the reader is required to stop, think, and answer at intervals as he goes along.

Series VIII provides some initial practice in critical thinking and is designed to help develop an inquiring and critical mind. A series of short excerpts from undisclosed sources is presented with basic questions for consideration. Keys reveal the sources and purposes.

Sequence of exercises

This book can be used for reading improvement in many types of training groups. In general, the writer recommends a ten-week training period to provide time for additional practice and application. A five-week training period has been demonstrated to be less satisfactory but still productive. Periods shorter than five weeks may have limited carry-over value.

As an illustration of a procedure for the overlapping of exercises—for college students or adults—one might consider the sequence used in the Extension Classes at the University of Wyoming. The pattern shown on page 333 is that used in a class that meets once weekly for one-and-a-half to two-hour sessions.

During the last half of the course, workbook practice should be supplemented by longer reading exercises from current materials or from standardized ten-minute reading exercises. The supplementary workbook *Maintaining Reading Efficiency* (25) provides a collection of standardized reading exercises appropriate for this purpose.

Motivation

Experience has shown that giving the exercises in overlapping sequence usually proves stimulating to the students. All exercises should be clocked by a stopwatch, and the time, in seconds, should be called out for each student as he finishes. Frequently a "pacing" technique of calling out five-second or ten-second intervals helps to keep up the motivation, especially if the group exhibits signs of fatigue. The *Reading Pacing Tape* mentioned earlier provides a standard pattern of pacing at five-second intervals for a ten-minute period with appropriate instructions. Many teachers find these tapes helpful for general classroom use with a reading class or for check-out to individuals who want to practice under some pressure outside the class.

The instructor must be alert constantly to provide encouragement and motivation, not only to the group as a whole, but to individual students as well. In addition to the pacing techniques mentioned before, one should suggest goals. For example, in Series I, one can suggest that most students should be able to finish in 30 seconds or less. In Series V, the instructor can suggest that all students should strive to complete these exercises in 60 seconds or less. Accuracy in setting realistic goals in different exercises depends upon the developmental pattern of any particular group as well as the teacher's experience with the materials. Students always should be urged to improve their own scores. Encouraging competition with other specific members of the group also is effective in many cases.

Watching the fastest reader and calling a finishing time a few seconds before he is through help to keep him working at a maximum. Calling time intervals a few times after the slowest reader has finished may help him to avoid feeling that the whole class was waiting for him. If one or two slow readers hold up the whole class to the point that others are getting restless, however, something may need to be done to help both the individuals and the class. Rather than keep the whole group waiting, individual assignments can be made for slow readers. For example, one might ask them to complete only half an exercise. Extremely slow readers who retard the whole group should be removed from the group if possible and given individual help.

Emphasis should be placed on keeping individual progress graphs up-to-date and encouraging students to compare results of the trends in their reading improvements. During the period between exercises, the staff member should circulate among the readers and provide individual encouragement.

If reading machines are available, a class demonstration with two or three class members may be an effective way of demonstrating to some skeptical individuals what their potential for eye movement really is. Thus, they may be stimulated to increase their self-motivation.

Scoring of questions

Series I is self-scoring because identical words are to be selected. Keys are scoring the other exercises are presented on pages 317–332. These keys are grouped according to odd and even numbers in case the teacher wishes to make one set available to students for their own scoring. In the completion questions, individual teachers should use their judgment in accepting "equivalent terms" for full or half credit.

These perforated key pages may be left in the book for self-scoring or may be removed by the teacher to discourage advance study. Many teachers prefer to leave the keys for the odd-numbered exercises in the book and to remove the even-numbered keys for standardized testing in class.

Variations in use

Many teachers have reported a wide range of application of *Increasing Reading Efficiency* and *Developing Reading Efficiency* in their classes. Innovative experimentation with different combinations or different sequences of exercises may produce better results. The author is always interested in hearing from teachers who have developed new and interesting ways to use these materials.

TO THE READER

Can you spare the time?

Do you have the time to do what you want to, or are you running a little behind schedule? Have you missed any deadlines lately? Do you sometimes get desperate and wonder if you can keep up the pace in this fast-moving world?

Can you survive?

Every day thousands of students are facing the decision to drop out of school before graduating. On the college scene, only four out of every ten students who start ever attain their academic goals. In the daily routine, thousands of individuals lose their jobs because they can not do all that their employers 100 expect. Often the problems is one of verbal communication. Frustration and failure lead many people into depression that may result in hospitalization or even suicide. How are you keeping up with all the conflicting expectations of family, friends, teachers, supervisors, employers, and community responsibilities?

Life in an exploding society

Survival is complicated by the rapid change that you encounter all around you. No previous generation faced the problems that confront you today. *The population explosion* has created many problems of competition for jobs, high unemployment, and increasing demands for flexibility in placement. *The knowledge explosion* overwhelms many by the 200 mere quantitative aspects. The world body of knowledge now doubles every six or seven years. Last year over 1,000 books per day were published. *The technology explosion* has plunged our world into a super industrial revolution. Over 90 percent of *all* scientific inventions have been developed within the last twenty years, most of them since you were born! Within your lifetime there has been more technological progress than the world has seen in 50,000 years. Culture changes faster than individuals can adjust. Many fall by the wayside. How good are *your* survival skills?

Could you use a time-stretcher? 300

Do you reach the end of the day with unfinished tasks regretfully laid aside? Do you wish sometimes that you had just an extra hour or so in order to finish important tasks? Do you really have time to read the newspapers, magazines, and other recreational materials you would enjoy? Like many others, you may find that at least one third of your time is required for reading of some kind. At the same time, you probably recognize that your reading habits are not adequate to meet these demands, and you may

400 become depressed when you can not keep the pace and complete the amount of reading you feel that you should.

No one has developed a "time-stretcher" to lengthen your days for you, but for years many educators have studied the problem of slow reading habits. Research since World War II, however, has led to many improvements in techniques and has encouraged new approaches to the problem of developmental reading. Reading centers today are using many techniques and group exercise materials that represent great advances over those used twenty years ago.

Developmental reading services are now available to many high school and college students and adults. Many participants in these classes have made 500 astonishing improvements in reading skill without any serious loss in comprehension. Thus one is able to do, in five hours, the reading that once took ten hours. Many individuals have increased their reading efficiency much more than this. Saving these five hours for other activities can give you the "time-stretcher" of which you may have dreamed.

One reading authority once computed that the saving in time required to do all the reading in the nation, computed at only 50 cents per hour, would be more than five billion dollars if every American 600 over fifteen years of age were given reading training for at least a month (7).[1] Many industrial concerns have recognized this potential saving of manpower and have subsidized reading programs for their employees with very gratifying results. Many students have found free time for greater enjoyment of their school activities by registering for classes in developmental reading. What benefits could you obtain if you were to double your reading efficiency? Would that help you to survive?

Are you ready to be exposed to a program to increase your reading speed? Some individuals who have become faster readers have not necessarily be- 700 come better readers. If you have difficulty understanding what you read now, you will not be helped by learning to misunderstand faster. If you have a very inadequate vocabulary, you will not be helped to learn to skip any faster through unknown or vaguely defined words. In either case, you have the challenge of developing some basic skills and knowledge before you really can benefit from a developmental reading program. But first, let us explore a few attitudes you may have about reading.

---

[1] All reference numbers refer to the numbered selected references on p. 27, with the second number, if any, identifying the page number.

Exploding some myths

Before going further in your exploration of the $\overset{800}{\leftarrow}$ reading process, you should consider some of the myths that students often use to rationalize their failure to improve their reading skills.

1. *No one can really read over 800 words per minute.* They can quote many authorities, especially those who have been critical of some of the commercial reading programs in recent decades. This statement is based on an analysis of typical eye movement patterns and typical eye fixations. If one accepts a definition of reading that involves an *actual eye contact with every word* in the material, then this limitation of 800 words is a fairly accurate statement. Most people $\overset{900}{\leftarrow}$ use the term *reading* in a much broader sense, however. Reading is a communication skill used to *communicate ideas by means of the written or printed message.* In this sense, the upper limits of speed in communication have not been identified.

2. *Skimming and scanning are bad habits that I should avoid.* Again this is based on a misinterpretation of the critics of speed reading. Within the broader concept of reading, these skills are very valuable and essential aspects of efficient reading and effective study.

3. *My comprehension will drop if I read fast or skim.* $\overset{1000}{\leftarrow}$ There is no foundation in research to support this. Raygor and Schick (39, 29) made the following comment after an extensive review of research: "It is relatively easy for most people to make very significant increases in the rate at which they read without any loss in reading comprehension."

4. *Machines are necessary to improve my speed.* This idea is perpetuated by salesmen for some media companies, but again Raygor and Schick (39, 29) report: ". . . experimental studies have shown no difference between the various methods and, in fact, have shown no advantage for any of the devices over the use of the book." $\overset{1100}{\leftarrow}$

5. *My eyes won't let me read fast.* With the exception of a very few persons with severe physiological handicaps, research has shown that most people have the potential in the brain and the eyes to function at much higher levels of reading than they have ever tried.

6. *It is wrong to skip passages in reading.* This is an old-fashioned idea still perpetuated by some teachers and guaranteed to make reading a deadly dull experience. All modern concepts of reading and study skills stress the importance of being selective and using judgment in deciding what to $\overset{1200}{\leftarrow}$ read and the extent of detail needed.

7. *I must read every word to get meaning.* Many words are necessary to sentence structure or to an author's style, but are not essential in the com- $\overset{1700}{\rightarrow}$ munication of the basic ideas. Good readers learn to seek out those words that convey meaning and give minimal attention to many supporting words.

Set your own goals

You should realize, however, that your ability to increase your speed and comprehension significantly depends upon many variables—intelligence, physiological and psychological traits, general background of knowledge, motivation, previous reading, $\overset{1300}{\rightarrow}$ experience, diligence in doing recommended practice, and general attitude toward reading and toward the reading group with which you work. No one can predict how much you will improve from the pretest to the posttest. People love to quote "averages" or outstanding achievements that seem dramatic, but there always are individuals all along the scale. Only you can determine your own achievement!

You must recognize also that there is no one speed of reading that you attain and maintain. There are many speeds that must vary with the nature of the reading activity and with your own familiarity $\overset{1400}{\rightarrow}$ with the materials. You should have a purpose in mind as you read. This purpose should help you understand more and remember better. The purpose is a determining factor in *how* you read. You may have many good and logical reasons for reading, but, at any one time, you should know *why* you are reading *that* particular material in *that* particular way.

Different people cannot and should not read at the same rate. You establish your own unique patterns of reading. You probably will be able to achieve a significant improvement by using these materials, but it takes a lot of self-discipline, hard $\overset{1500}{\rightarrow}$ work, and often monotonous practice to replace old reading habits with new, more effective ones.

When you finish this work, you should be able to identify substantial personal growth. Whatever your measured rate at that time, you should have achieved the flexibility of at least *four* rates. Your slower rate will be the one to use when you have to pay close attention to detail for later retention. You can have another (about twice that fast) when you read for relaxation.

When you skim for new ideas, you can go about four times as fast as your slower rate; and when you $\overset{1600}{\rightarrow}$ scan to locate specific material for specific purposes, your rate may be much higher.

Much more could be said about the reading process before you start your program, but perhaps a few suggestions and ideas thrown in along the way will be more helpful. At least some students who used this material before thought so! On the introductory pages for each new series of exercises, you will find "suggestion" sections. May I suggest that you read these again *after* you have done the first few exercises. In that way we can "keep in touch" as you $\overset{1700}{\rightarrow}$ read your way through the workbook.

I
How Do We Read?

Good reading is a key to new information and ideas. It opens the door to many opportunities to enrich your life. Your reading skills are essential aspects of self-preservation in a dynamic society. You probably place great importance on becoming a successful reader.

But what are the characteristics of successful readers? You might say that they are the ones who keep up with their fair share of the millions of words of printed material that is created in the world each day. This means that they are able to keep up with all of their personal and professional correspondence and to keep informed on significant developments ⇐100 in their society from skimming newspapers and news magazines. They must find the time to deal with their daily mail and to keep up on developments in their business or professional field through many specialized professional publications. For a balanced life, they also find time for reading for pleasure in areas of their own personal interests.

For most students, success in reading those materials essential to all of their academic course work is merely a preparation for the challenge of the deluge of reading materials they will face when they leave the academic field and go out into the world of work. ⇐200

Even if your plans do not include intense specialization for a professional field of work, you will still find that successful reading is an essential for coping with many daily problems in the modern world. Operating instructions for cars, boats, machines, appliances, and household equipment are a challenge to everyone. Unless you can read application forms, insurance policies, sales contracts, and employee memos effectively, you may miss many of the opportunities for personal improvement and protection open to you. You also may find yourself vulnerable to many unscrupulous salesmen or promoters. You have a real stake in your long-term ⇐300 effectiveness as a successful reader. You may find it very helpful to give some thought to how you became the kind of reader you now are, and to how you can move toward a higher level of success in your own reading.

Good reading involves not one skill, but many. Although some individuals can increase their rate of reading without specific training, few can improve—without such help—their comprehension, analytical skill, judgment, skimming and scanning skills, and the technique of adjusting their habits of reading to their purpose and the nature of the material. These ⇐400 skills require thorough understanding of the reading process and practice in a carefully planned program.

The first fact that must be recognized is that your present reading habits are the result of your early experiences in learning to read and your continuing experiences in reading over a period of years. These habits, practiced for many years, are hard to break. You may encounter many feelings of insecurity while you are in the process of substituting new habits for old. Therefore, you should give some attention to how you may have developed some of your 500→ present reading habits.

Development of reading habits

Many articles in popular periodicals have criticized public schools and current methods of teaching reading. You should be cautious in placing the blame for your habits on the schools you attended, however, and should consider several other factors that have affected your own particular reading habits. Consider the following factors and see which of them may have had an effect on your habits of reading:

1. Reading is not demonstrable as are speaking, walking, or problem solving. It is impossible to *show* someone how you *read*. It involves recognition of many symbols that have no meaning in themselves and that must be combined in innumerable combinations in order to convey meaning to others. The visible eye movements and fixations are only a small part of the total reading process involving a continuous invisible mental process.

2. The irregular supply of well-qualified developmental reading teachers in the last few decades has resulted in the assignment to reading classes of many teachers who possessed only limited interest, desire, or skill in the teaching of reading. Such teachers may have overlooked individual needs and problems in reading development. Unintentionally, they may have reinforced some negative self-concepts and created negative attitudes toward reading. Such teachers may have stressed reading every word, oral reading, vocalizing, and enunciating every syllable. Overemphasis on such factors may make some students feel guilty about any attempts to develop efficient silent reading skills. Under these circumstances, many young people continue to pass through our school systems

without developing a sound pattern of basic reading skills.

3. Schools have been developing better methods of teaching. The children in elementary schools today are getting better basic training in reading than their parents in the past. Many teachers now have greater understanding of the factors of reading and of the learning problems of the $\overset{800}{\leftarrow}$ $\overset{1200}{\rightarrow}$ individual student. In all periods, however, some schools have developed programs that are more effective than those in other schools.

4. We have come through a period of conflicting philosophy about the basic approach to reading. Some teachers insisted that the "phonics" approach of sounding out syllables was the best method. Others were completely dedicated to the "sight reading" approach of recognizing words as units of meaning and developing a vocabulary by visual association. As a result, we had a great variation between different schools and even between teachers in the same school, with a resulting confusion on the part $\overset{900}{\leftarrow}$ $\overset{1300}{\rightarrow}$ of the students. Fortunately, today most of our elementary teachers are recognizing that both "sight reading" and "phonics" have a place in developing reading skills. Unfortunately, they still are not in complete agreement on the best combination or sequence of application of these two ideas.

5. Our population has become increasingly mobile, and, as a consequence, many children do not follow the planned sequence of courses in a single school, but attend many schools during their elementary years. Thus they may miss a basic part of their reading instruction because it has not yet been reached in one school, but $\overset{1000}{\leftarrow}$ has already been covered in another school to which they transfer.

6. Overcrowded schools, in many instances, contributed to poor reading because the problems of the individual student were overlooked and the teaching was directed toward the assumed average of the class. Better schools attempt to discover individual problems in reading through testing programs and observation, and try to provide special attention for slow readers by means of remedial reading classes.

7. Specific instruction in reading has placed emphasis on oral reading, and limited attention has been given to helping the student discover various techniques to be used in silent reading. $\overset{1100}{\leftarrow}$ Consequently, some people have carried oral reading habits into silent reading practice.

8. Instruction in reading skills often is terminated after the fourth or fifth grade. It was assumed by both teachers and parents that, having mastered the basic skills of reading, the student $\overset{1600}{\rightarrow}$ could make the adaptations of those skills to the different reading needs he would face later. Unfortunately, many individuals made few adaptations, and many adults today try to read adult-level materials, using reading skills appropriate for a fifth-grade level of reading.

9. Many students who feel that they are poor readers really are expressing an attitude rather than a limitation in skill. At some time, they may have had a very frustrating experience in a reading program, and they may still continue to carry bad feelings about reading that make them feel inadequate in facing current reading problems.

10. Many adolescents and adults avoid activities involving reading because they are self-conscious about some reading problems. As a consequence, lack of practice has made their existing habits even more ineffective.

The process of reading

A second important fact to recognize is that we do not read while our eyes are moving. Just as the motion picture is made up of many still pictures flashed before us rapidly, so our reading is a series of visual impressions carried to our brain in a rapid sequence. We stop for each glance and then move on for another glance at another word or phrase. Reading rate, then, is a combination of the amount we see at each glance, the length of time we hesitate for each eye fixation, and the speed with which the eye can move and focus on another unit of material.

The first of these factors is referred to as *eye* $\overset{1400}{\rightarrow}$ *span*—the quantity of reading material one can see at one glance. For some people this may be a single word; for others, one complete phrase; and for others, still larger units of thought. For the very rapid reader, this may be several lines or a paragraph.

The second factor is closely related to the thinking process. It is referred to as a *rate of perception*. How long does it take to register the impression of what you see and to transmit it to your brain, and how long does it take the brain to inter- $\overset{1500}{\rightarrow}$ pret what was seen? Unless one has had an injury resulting in damage to brain tissue, he probably is capable of a great deal of acceleration in this thinking process.

The third factor of rate is that of eye movement in shifting from one point of focus to another. This is primarily a physical factor requiring the acceleration of rhythmic habits of eye movement.

The average individual is not aware of his complex pattern of reading habits and, therefore, makes little effort to coordinate the factors affecting his reading efficiency. Recognition of various types of reading and adjustment of reading habits to the $\overset{1600}{\rightarrow}$ type and purpose of specific reading assignments are essential. Most individuals have developed a rather limited range of reading efficiency, however, and therefore have little leeway in adjusting to different types.

One of the greatest contributions of a reading program is that of increasing the ceiling on reading speed. As one increases this upper limit of reading speed, of course, he also increases his range of reading efficiency and develops greater flexibility in his reading habits. By focusing attention on reading habits and placing an individual in a position where he is stimulated to operate at his maximum, teachers find that most persons are capable of reading at least 1700 twice as fast as they had been doing. Thus the normal adult who may be reading at a rate of about 250 words per minute actually may be capable of reading 500 words per minute or more if properly stimulated. With practice and concentrated personal effort, this individual may learn to read at 750 to 900 words per minute. Many individuals have made even greater improvements; reading class records reflect many persons who have read 2,000 or 3,000 words per minute. Some reading centers have reported individuals who have achieved rates as high as 50,000 1800 words per minute on certain types of material. The potential maximum reading speed of any individual is unknown. The possibilities for any normal adult seem to be limited only by his own interest and his determination to improve. Only *you* can determine just how fast you can read, but you can be assured that you should be able at least to double or triple your present reading rate and perhaps to achieve much more than that.

How do we read faster?

Slow readers may possess any one or a combination of poor reading habits. Most of these habits 1900 can be changed by recognizing the factors involved in the habit. Glance over the list of poor reading habits below and see which ones may apply to you; then consider what you might do to change these habits.

Vocalizing. Sounding out each word as if you were reading aloud slows you down to a snail's pace. This may be only a mental pronunciation process, but frequently it is accompanied by the moving of the lips as you read. If you do this, try placing your finger tightly on your lips as you read until you have broken the habit of lip movement. Once the lip 2000 action is broken, you will find it easier to push yourself to faster rates where mental vocalization decreases considerably.

Word-by-word reading. Looking at one word at a time to be sure you understand it may obscure the overall meaning of the sentence or paragraph. Remember the old adage about the man who could not see the forest because of the trees. To break yourself of this habit, try reading for ideas instead of words. Try to grasp whole phrases in a glance and sense their meaning.

Word blocking. Stopping to worry about an 2100 unfamiliar word breaks the rhythm of your reading and makes you lose the trend of thought or miss some of the main ideas. If you do this often, you probably have a poor vocabulary and need to work intensively on building up a greater understanding of commonly used words. In many instances, you can find the meaning of a certain word in the context, however, if you will just keep reading with an emphasis on ideas instead of words. Later on, after you have finished reading, you can go back and check the dictionary for some of the words that 2200 troubled you. After looking them up, think about their meaning and try to use them several times in conversation or writing that same day. This will fix the meaning in your mind. But do not let new words upset you and make you feel self-conscious. Most people encounter new words in their reading and take them in stride, identifying their meaning from other words or phrases with which they are associated.

Number attraction. Some readers come to a complete stop every time they reach a number. They seem to want to study it carefully as if it were a completely different concept of communication. Un-2300 less you are studying thoroughly for detailed content, dates, and quantitative ideas, you should try to generalize the numerical idea into verbal symbols such as "many" or "few," "long ago," "recently," "next year," or similar clues that will help in getting general ideas from the material.

Word analysis. Stopping to analyze a strange word as to its origin, structure, prefixes, and suffixes may be a sound vocabulary building exercise, but it destroys the trend of thought in reading and may lead to many false impressions, as meanings of many 2400 words vary with the context in which they are used. We must look for the larger ideas. *Seek the ideas behind the words.*

Monotonous plodding. Keeping the same pace of reading in all materials, from light fiction to heavy study, is tiresome. You need flexibility in reading habits. Let yourself go on some reading materials and do not worry about comprehension. You are missing much of the enjoyment of recreational reading by applying to it the same type of reading used for study. Learn to adjust your rate to the type of material and the purpose for reading it. Good readers 2500 may read at a very slow rate if they want detailed understanding, but read at a rate of several thousand words per minute on fiction, light correspondence, and other materials they are reading for main ideas or for recreation.

Finger following. Following a line of print with a finger or with a guide of some kind always slows down the reading process because fingers can not move as fast as eyes. To break this habit, keep both hands in your lap if reading at a desk, or hold the book in both hands. Rely solely on your eyes to follow the printed page.

Head swinging. Moving the head from side 2600← to side as one reads is much more laborious than moving the eyes. In addition to slowing down reading, this increased muscular activity will hasten fatigue. If you have this habit, try holding your head firmly in place with your hands and force your eyes to do the moving until the habit is broken.

Clue blindness. Like the driver who is too busy watching the road to see the signposts that direct him to his destination, many readers become too involved in word reading to notice such things as headings, subtitles, styles of type, listings, illustrations, introductions, and summaries. These all are 2700← important clues put in by the author to help you understand his concept of what is important. Try looking through some materials, reading only the headings and the ideas set off by a different style of type or by listings, and see how much you can really get from these clues alone. Use the introductory paragraphs and lead sentences as clues to organization and the summary statement as a review of material read. Try to develop the ability to glance over some material and get an understanding of the author's style and the types of signposts he has 2800← erected for you.

Backtracking. Going back to reread words or phrases is an indication that you doubt your own ability to pick out the important material. It slows you down a great deal because you are constantly thinking back instead of looking ahead to spot new ideas. Consequently, you miss ideas until you have gone past them, and then you have to go back to pick them up. The more you backtrack, the more necessary backtracking becomes to you. Try to concentrate on reading everything *only once.* You will be surprised to find that you get an overall under- 2900← standing of it without the mental underlining.

Rereading. Closely associated with backtracking is the habit of going back to read the whole assignment over again to be sure you understand it. Studies have shown that rereading is a fairly ineffective method of reviewing immediately after study (34). If you concentrate on doing a good job of reading in the first place, a few minutes of thinking about what you have read will be far more valuable than rereading. Try laying the reading material aside after you have finished it and thinking over what you have read. This not only will develop a better under- 3000← standing of the material, but also will serve as an aid to remembering it later.

Daydreaming. Allowing your attention to wander to other things while you read leaves you with the feeling of having covered pages but having no knowledge of what you have read. To overcome this, you must develop the ability to concentrate on one thing at a time. This matter of concentration is complex and will be discussed in detail in Sections III and IV.

Programs for improvement

Unless a person has a serious physical or mental handicap, none of the habits mentioned above 3100→ is serious. All can be overcome with concentrated practice. Thousands of people have overcome them and established flexible reading habits that enable them to read several times more efficiently than they did before. Some individuals find that bifocal glasses limit their reading speed. Usually, this problem can be overcome by changing to reading glasses.

Colleges and businesses have come to realize the benefits that can be obtained by providing a training situation in which individuals can be motivated to achieve such changes of reading habits. Such reading programs try to force the individual to read 3200→ faster by applying pressure of various kinds.

Some training centers rely heavily upon mechanical devices such as the reading films, tachistoscopic devices, flash cards, reading-rate controllers, and reading accelerators of various types. Some use these devices for group work; others provide them for individual practice. The reading center in your vicinity may have one or more of these types of training devices with which you can practice if you are interested in them.

Other centers rely largely upon group drill methods and the psychological pressure of competition within the group as a motivating device. In such situations, the instructor usually will use pacing techniques 3300→ and a great deal of urging to get students to read faster.

Regardless of the program, much of the progress depends upon the motivation of the individual. Unless you really want to improve your reading and are willing to try out new ideas in an attempt to break old habits, you will gain but little from the experience. If you really want to improve and will try new approaches to reading, the possibilities seem unlimited for your improvement in reading rate.

How do we understand more of what we read?

All of the techniques discussed above are designed 3400→ primarily to increase rate of reading, but reading is a complex process, of which the rate is only one factor. In this workbook, emphasis is placed upon *reading efficiency,* which is a combination of factors. In order to understand this term, we should first define clearly what is meant in this book by certain other terms, such as rate and comprehension.

Rate of reading is a numerical expression of the amount of material covered in a unit of time. It is expressed in words per minute. Thus a normal adult reading rate of 250 means that a normal adult should be able to cover 250 words of the material he is reading each minute. ⇄ 3500

Just covering words or pages would mean little if you did not grasp some meaning from what you read. Comprehension, therefore, is an essential factor in good reading. Let us stress, however, that perfect comprehension is not the ideal of good reading, for perfect comprehension would be almost synonymous with memorization of the material, and this is seldom essential. The degree of understanding is measured more commonly in terms of the understanding of the main ideas and basic facts expressed in the reading. In some reading, it is more important to get a fairly thorough knowledge of these facts than in others. ⇄ 3600 Therefore, comprehension also should be flexible and should be adjusted to the type of material read and the purpose of reading. One hundred percent comprehension is seldom needed unless one is memorizing material. For most reading, a 60 to 80 percent comprehension is adequate. For light recreational reading, detailed comprehension is even less important. In studying, you should be concerned with more detailed comprehension, but should not depend on reading alone. Here you need to use a balanced study approach that will make use of other techniques of understanding and remembering material. These ⇄ 3700 will be discussed in detail in Section IV.

One of the most important factors in improving comprehension is that of having a purpose for reading. This purpose must be personalized to be effective. Mere reading of material because an instructor assigns it is not sufficient. You, personally, must see some reason for reading the material and must be looking for something in the material read. There are several ways of developing this personal interest.

First of all, you should *think* before starting to read. Think about the subject matter covered in the material. What do you already know about it? What ⇄ 3800 would you like to know about it? What do you know about the person who wrote the article? Is the author an authority? Is he or she well known for personal prejudice on this subject? Will the presentation be biased? Can you depend on statements being accurate and complete, or is the author likely to try to persuade you in certain ways by presenting only partial facts or distorting views of the problem? These are just some of the questions which you should ask yourself before starting to read, but thinking about them will help to establish a good mental attitude ⇄ 3900 toward reading the article with interest and concentration.

After having spent a few seconds in thinking before starting to read, glance over the article quickly to look for clues. The headings and boldface print will tell you the direction that the article will take in presenting the ideas. This helps prepare you to recognize important points as they are presented.

A third point in helping improve concentration and retention of material is to concentrate on small units, one at a time. Intense concentration on the →4000 portion between two headings with a slight pause to rest your eyes and think about the material before going on to the next section will provide relaxation as well as help to organize your thinking.

Take a few seconds after each unit, and a longer time at the end of the reading period, to think over what you have read and to fix a mental impression. This will help you to retain that impression for a longer period of time. In short, an alternation of reading and thinking provides a greater comprehension of what is read.

In order to measure comprehension, you must →4100 be tested in some way to see how much you remember of what was read. Comprehension usually is expressed numerically as a percentage score. *The comprehension score is the percent of questions answered correctly in a test on the material read.* A good reader should be able to score at least 60 to 80 percent on such a test, depending on the number of questions asked and the amount of detail involved in the questions.

What is reading efficiency?

Many students, in trying to increase their reading rate, become disturbed when their comprehension drops. Others trying hard to improve →4200 comprehension slow down in an attempt to get better understanding. Many reading teachers have found that the faster readers often secure better comprehension scores than the slower readers. Similarly, they find that, at the end of a reading training program, students often read at several times their original rate with comprehension as great as or greater than they did before starting training. Although most of them go through a period of decreased comprehension while they are working hard on increasing rate, they find that, as they become adjusted to reading at a faster rate, they are able to build up their comprehension again.

→4300 Neither rate nor comprehension really gives us the complete picture of reading skills. Reading at a rapid rate is of little value if you understand very little of what you have read. On the other hand, reading with a high degree of comprehension is of little value if you never have time to read all the material you are expected to cover. The most important factor is *neither* the speed at which you read *nor* the amount you can remember of what you read, but a combination of these: *the amount you can read and remember* per unit of time. In an attempt to ← 4400 express this factor and place an emphasis on the importance of this combination of skills, we use the term *reading efficiency* to represent the amount of material comprehended per minute of reading time. Efficiency is computed by taking the product of the *rate* of reading (expressed in words per minute) and the *comprehension* score (expressed as the percent of correct answers on a test over the material). *Efficiency,* then, is a numerical expression of rate of effective reading represented in words per minute. Let us compare the following sequence of scores to see how this works.

	1st test	2d test	3d test	4th test
Rate	150	200	400	600
Comprehension	80	70	60	70
Efficiency	120	140	240	420

If this individual were to consider only the decreasing comprehension scores during practice, he might become discouraged and stop pushing his rate improvement. By stressing the efficiency score instead of rate or comprehension, he gets a better picture of his real progress, however; and although his final comprehension score is still below his initial one, his efficiency score gives a better picture of the amount of material he can grasp in a unit of study time. This individual probably would find that he was accom- ← 4600 plishing at least three times as much work in his periods of reading as was possible before, and the slight difference in comprehension could be offset by other techniques of remembering.

Throughout this book, stress will be placed upon the efficiency scores on reading exercises because efficiency seems the best expression of the effectiveness of reading habits.

Conditions for improvement

In this chapter you have been urged to explore some new possibilities for reading improvement, recognizing some of the bad habits that may slow you down, some of the factors that influence these reading habits, and some of the terms used to describe the ← 4700 results of reading habits. We have presented the idea that anyone is capable of improving his reading efficiency unless prevented from doing so by physical or mental handicaps. The question remains: How can *you* improve your reading efficiency? Three conditions are needed to make satisfactory progress in the improvement of reading efficiency.

First of all, you must be convinced that you want to become a better reader. You must be willing to put in several hours of hard and sometimes monotonous work in reading practice. You must be 4800 → willing to face the problems of being compared with others, of competing with others, and of working under pressure that may be irritating. You must be willing to cast aside established habits in order to try new ones. You need to be convinced that the time to be saved in the future, when more satisfactory reading habits have been established, is worth the sacrifice of several hours of your time now. If you can see the long-range value and are willing to work, your possibilities of improvement are practically unlimited.

Second, you will need to work with appropriate 4900 → materials from which comparisons can be made to determine improvement. Unless the exercises you use are of comparable difficulty, misunderstanding and discouragement may follow. Unless all sets of questions are made up in comparable forms, your comprehension scores may vary because of the difficulty of the test rather than your degree of understanding. There will be a better chance of progress if you work from a workbook that has been standardized and that has comparable tests. The materials used in this workbook represent the results of many years of experimentation and revision in order to develop the best possible sequences of exercises. Note that all 5000 → exercises are graded with a readability score. These scores are determined by the application of the Flesch formula (12) to the material. Exercises are arranged in a gradually ascending order of difficulty so that, as you learn to read faster, you also learn to read material of a little greater difficulty.

Finally, you must feel a sense of progress and satisfaction. Using your scores from one exercise to set goals for the next one will help sustain your motivation. You must compare results of today with those of yesterday and then set higher goals for 5100 → tomorrow. The reading progress charts in this book help you to do that. They are organized in such a way that you can compare results on any particular exercise with others in that series, or with different types of exercises. Keeping your reading graphs up-to-date will help you to get an overall view of progress in increasing your reading efficiency. The extent of your growth in effective reading skills will depend upon your desire, your attitude, and your concentration.

A combination of motivation, concentration, and comprehension should lead you to a deeper level of understanding and to more effective retention of 5200 → the materials you read.

← 4500   4900 →

II
Kinds of Reading

Recognize types of reading

If you want to evaluate your success as an effective reader, you might look at your ability to adjust your reading to the different types of materials and to your different purposes in reading. The greater the range of reading efficiency you have, the greater possibilities you have to judge what types of reading skills are most appropriate for what materials. Limited space in this workbook prevents the presentation of detailed analysis of the various types of reading and their application. However, a brief consideration of some of the major types of reading may help you to understand your present reading habits 100 and your reactions to some of the work you will do in this book.

Purpose for reading

Some authors see only two major classifications for your purpose for reading. Either you are reading for ideas or reading for facts. Either of these purposes has specific implications for you. These may be reviewed in considerable detail in two pairs of books: *Reading for Ideas* (35) and *Reading for Facts* (34) by Pauk and Wilson, or *Reading for the Main Idea* (37) and *Reading for Significant Facts* (38) by Alton Raygor.

In addition to these major classifications, one 200 might add the purpose of "light" reading for entertainment and that of "heavy" reading for aesthetic appreciation of style, content, or philosophy. This type of reading involves a combination of intense concentration and uninterrupted contemplation that is not readily measured in terms of rate or comprehension.

Regardless of your basic purpose in reading, you constantly should use reading as a channel to improve vocabulary. Some good resources to help you improve your process of vocabulary development are *Basic Vocabulary Skills* by Davis (11), *Developing Vocabulary Skills* by Joffe (17), and *The Teacher's Word Book of 30,000 Words* by Thorndike 300 (50).

Skimming and scanning

These two terms are used interchangeably by many writers. They are denounced as inappropriate labels for reading by many critics of speed reading. Some writers refer to these activities as "semi-reading" skills. Many writers in the developmental reading field do recognize them as types of reading that have very significant meaning in the total reading process. They feel that these types are essential to the total development of flexible and efficient reading skills.

Both techniques involve reading by the "sign-posts"—the clues set up by the author. By using 400 these you can learn to skip materials that are not of immediate interest to you and to locate more quickly those that you really wish to read in detail. Most textbooks are organized to make intelligent skimming possible. All devices such as chapter titles, sectional headings, **boldface** or *italicized* type, and underlining are clues to help you with this technique. Take time to think before you start to read, and get a good idea of just what you are looking for. Then clues can save a great deal of reading time by leading you 500 right to the sections in which you are interested. This allows you to skip over the rest.

In recent years, some writers have attempted to establish a difference between the two terms. There is no general agreement on this distinction, however. Emphasis on scanning as a search for main ideas and on skimming as a search for specific facts or details is presented by both Norman (33) and Pickett (36). They are presented in exactly the opposite pattern by Adams (1), Maxwell (22), and Thomas and Robinson (48). This latter position seems to be more widely accepted, however. It will be used in this 600 publication. *Skimming* is that technique of rapid reading designed to identify the major ideas and relationships discussed in an article. *Scanning* is that technique used to locate and utilize specific facts or ideas related to a predetermined goal. Both skills require preplanning and intense concentration to be effective.

Skimming is the basic first step in the well-known SQ4R method of study discussed in Section IV. Skimming also can be very effective as a preliminary step to reading something more thoroughly. It gives an overview of what you can expect in the material.

Scanning is a essential aspect of any search for 700 specific information. Use it in sources such as telephone books, encyclopedias, dictionaries, or general reference sources. It also is an essential aspect of the self-recitation study technique, which emphasizes reading to seek answers to predicted questions.

Idea reading

Idea reading extends use of skimming techniques beyond the heading into the content paragraphs. It involves more comprehensive coverage of total word content, but in a highly selective fashion. It is essential in many types of business and professional reading as well as in much incidental and recreational reading. The basic meaning of many published articles could be condensed into a few simple statements.

This reading for the main ideas is a technique 800← of rapid reading in which the eyes move rapidly. They catch large phrases at each glance and register with the brain only the most significant words or ideas in those phrases. Successful idea reading is perhaps one of the most difficult types of reading to master. It is also one of the most efficient. One can develop extremely rapid rates of reading with it. It means being familiar with the makeup of the English language as a means of communication. Rapid recognition of key sentences, illustrative words and phrases, and the skeletal structure of the sentence is 900← essential to discovering the basic meaning. Idea reading means making quick decisions as to the relative importance of different sentences and paragraphs as you read. It means quick recognition of the author's clues and rapid association with ideas you already understand that relate to this material.

Exploratory reading

Exploratory reading, or general content reading, involves more detail than the two types mentioned before. This type of approach is appropriate for longer articles in magazines, for descriptive literature, and for light fiction. It may be used for similar reading in which you wish to pick up a better under- 1000← standing of some new ideas. You should use this technique on many outside references in which you wish to find background material, but in which you will not be tested for detail. Emphasis here should be placed on recognizing and understanding main ideas more thoroughly. You should relate them to other ideas in the article or to previous knowledge of the subject.

Study reading

Study reading is a type in which you must get a maximum understanding of the main ideas and their relationships. This is the type you must apply to your textbooks. You may apply it to contracts, legal papers, technical manuals, instructions, and other similar materials. Here you frequently deal with materials that you must read and understand 1100← now and also remember for future use.

Clues are important. A preliminary scanning may be quite helpful. The actual reading process, however, needs to be an alternating activity between reading for ideas and thinking about those ideas. The actual reading process itself may be quite rapid, but greater skill must be developed in thinking and organizing the ideas for long-term retention. Many different study skills must be used to supplement the reading process. These are discussed in more detail in Section IV.

Critical reading

Another type of reading that must sometimes 1200→ be applied wisely is that of critical reading. You may find a certain article that tends to stir you to action. You may feel you should write to your congressman or rush downtown to buy some new and indispensable household appliance. Then you should stop and consider what you have read more carefully. Many periodical articles, books, and advertising materials are loaded with carefully worded propaganda devices. These are designed to sway your opinion or to sell you on some particular idea or product. Be careful that a rapid reading of the main ideas does not lead to false conclusions.

To apply techniques of critical reading, you 1300→ should go back and consider carefully what you know about the source of the reading material. What are the possible biases or ulterior motives that its publisher or author may have? You also should consider what you know about the author's background experience and potential knowledge of the subject. You should watch the reading material for inconsistent logic or false analogies. Particularly important is an awareness of emotionally loaded words that appeal to basic emotions. With experience, you soon can learn to spot some of these types of appeals through quick scanning for the clues the author 1400→ provides. Then you can beware of these techniques before beginning to read. In any reading, you should frequently ask yourself: "What is the author trying to make me believe and why?"

Analytical reading

Certain sections of study materials require a much more thorough type of reading than those mentioned before. Mathematical theorems and problems, scientific formulas and certain definitive statements of key ideas require careful attention to each word and to its relative importance. You must approach such reading with a questioning mind, seeking complete clarification. You can learn to recognize such passages and to slow your reading 1500→ pace to deal with such sections more adequately.

Identify and adjust

By learning to recognize different types of reading and to judge what types of reading skills to apply to them, you may become more effective in your overall use of reading time. Streamline your reading activities to meet the needs of the time and the material to be read. Such judgment can be developed only from practice. This workbook will provide an opportunity to practice several types of reading, but you must apply the principles of efficient reading to the materials that you read every day if 1600→ you hope to maintain really efficient reading habits.

III
Is Reading Enough?

Reading is what *you* make it. You can make your reading hard work, or you can make it an exciting adventure. It can be drudgery or relaxation. From the previous chapters you should have developed a better understanding of *how* you read, and *why* you read that way. You understand *how* you can control further development in your reading skills to make them more effective for you. Your eyes and your brain have the potential to make reading skills work in any way you desire.

Only you can determine the ultimate effectiveness of your reading skills. But a word of caution is perhaps appropriate.

Overdependency on reading

No one would question that reading is essential to personal development. Too many persons jump to the conclusion, however, that reading is the *only* respectable approach to learning. They tend to depend *entirely* on reading for gaining new ideas and for understanding them. They frequently consider audiovisual devices as mere recreational gadgets of momentary interest but of little lasting value. Such persons may completely ignore the possibilities of note making from speeches, conferences, seminars, and telephone conversations as an effective technique. They often consider note making in conjunction with reading as too much extra work.

Extreme dependency on reading may make you fearful of any techniques that might lower your reading comprehension even temporarily. This fear is the basis of much hesitancy in learning.

You may be afraid that if you develop faster rates of reading, you will lose some comprehension accuracy. Research shows that this is not a matter for concern (33). Most people are able to make very significant increases in their reading rates without any significant loss in comprehension. Many fast readers maintain comprehension levels much higher than the average for their age or grade.

But reading still has its limitations in comparison with some other means of communicating ideas. For most people, reading is one of the slower techniques of picking up ideas. A picture sometimes can convey as much information in one glance as several pages of descriptive literature could do. The oral statement often can be made to convey much more meaning than the same statement in print. The speaker can do this through the changes of tone or inflection and the verbal stress on certain words.

Identification with the author

One way to get more understanding from the printed page is to seek a better understanding of authors as unique individuals. Find out more about who they are and what they have done. Use the title page or introductory comments to try to get a feel for their attitudes and enthusiasms. Try to visualize these authors as persons like yourself. They want to express themselves clearly to you, but they need your help to do it effectively. As you read, try to identify their attitudes, interests, and biases. Watch for their use of tone and inference. Study how they use words and figurative language to individualize their presentations. Seek evidence of their use of critical judgment. Watch for evidence of their distinction between fact, fiction, and personal opinion. Seek help if you need assistance in developing these skills of personal identification with the author. You can find many detailed suggestions in *Developing Reading Versatility* by Adams (1) or in *Reading for Ideas* by Pauk and Wilson (35).

Some supplements to reading

One reason some people feel so self-conscious about their reading may be that they are too dependent upon it. They may fail to associate it adequately with other means of communication. Think about some of the techniques that can be used to enrich its meaning.

Listening involves skills often overlooked and ignored. A speaker uses many "signposts" just as the writer does. He or she uses introductions and summaries during which you should be thinking. Relate what you hear to what you already understand. Changes of tone, pitch, and rate of speaking are used to emphasize certain points. Speakers use lead statements as headings to new topics. They frequently list or itemize points they think are important. The listener who is alert to these clues can learn a great deal during these concentrated periods of listening.

Thinking is the conscious process by which you try to control some of the activities of your brain. Thinking seems to be a very rapid, continuous process that may or may not be in tune with your reading or listening activities. Because thinking seems to go on at a speed so much greater than reading or listening, you must make a special effort to achieve some congruence in these activities.

Perhaps your thinking process can be focused on three phases of learning activity. First is the recognition of facts that are significant to you for some reason. Second is the fusing of your understanding of the purpose, function, and specific relationships of these facts with your existing knowledge. Third is the classification and filing away in the brain for future application and use.

Learning may be enhanced by a three-stage classification system. First, you identify the general topic of the author. What or who is he or she writing [800] about? Next, what special area within that topic is the focus of this unit of reading? Finally, what attitudes is the author expressing about this special area of this topic? Such an approach may help you in seeing relationships and achieving long-term retention of significant information.

Note making is a very important technique for the busy students. By relying on brief notes, you can relieve the stress of detailed mental comprehension of many minute facts of temporary importance. Brief, well-organized notes taken on important reading assignments provide an excellent basis for review at [900] a later time. An important aspect of good notes, however, is that they are *made* in the writer's own words rather than *taken* as a few random excerpts from the speaker's terminology (6).

Self-recitation of important points helps to keep them in mind. This process of predicting questions to which answers must be found requires occasional pauses to think over what is being read. The questions posed serve as a goal for reading. The pauses for thinking provide brief relaxation for the eyes.

Frequent review of important materials is an invaluable aid in remembering and will make later [1000] rereading unnecessary. Well-organized notes are a much more effective basis for review than reliance on rereading or on skimming again the material originally read on the subject.

Improving comprehension

In the previous chapter, reference was made to several techniques that might be used to improve comprehension. These are all supplementary techniques not actually a part of the reading process itself but closely related to it. At this time, let us consider more carefully the actual steps involved in these activities.

Orienting oneself to the reading assignment

Most efficient individuals operate on some sort of schedule. They plan a certain time of day for [1100] reading. By having regular times for certain types of reading work, they get into habits of thinking about these things at regular periods. This helps to establish a "mood" for reading. This can be intensified by

taking a few minutes to survey the reading to be done, to arrange it according to importance, and to anticipate the questions that must be answered in the reading.

Getting the overall view

In the consideration of any particular item of reading, rapid skimming of pages looking for key ideas will set up general idea goals to be attained. This will make the task more meaningful.

Reading to find answers to questions

In the preview of the material, you will recognize several main topics. As you approach each topic, try to pose questions for yourself to give you a purpose for reading. You will find that looking for [1200] answers does much to focus your interest more sharply. This helps you attain faster rates of reading.

Visualizing and making associations

As you pause, at intervals, try to form a mental picture of the things about which you have been reading. Relate the ideas to something you already know and understand. Establishing associations with known facts will provide a more thorough understanding.

Making notes from materials read

If you are reading to organize material for a speech or a report or if you want some deails for later use, take some notes *in your own words* during [1300] your pauses. Brief notes with personalized expression help you to organize verbal concepts more clearly. These notes should have more lasting meaning for you. If you have difficulty concentrating on important material, making notes forces you to think about it.

Reviewing

Use some time *regularly* to think over materials read during the previous few days and to pull together the important ideas from various sources. This is an invaluable supplement to the reading process. Ideas picked up from very rapid reading can be fixed more firmly in your mind for later use.

In summary

These techniques will serve to strengthen your [1400] comprehension of what you read. They will make it easier for you to relax. They will allow you to read at a maximum rate without fear of losing comprehension. The time you save in rapid reading should provide an opportunity to use some of these techniques so important to remembering ideas and their [1450] relationships.

IV
A Program for Effective Study

The ideas in the previous sections are basic to any sound program of study. You need to develop sound habits of study if you hope to live a balanced life and to survive in the competitive academic world today. You must provide time for both academic requirements and social opportunities. Many colleges are attempting to help students establish such habits by the provision of classes in "Study Skill Techniques." Such courses recognize reading as one aspect of study, but also point out that efficient reading *alone* is not enough to meet the competition of college classes today. 100

Let us look at some of the factors that are important in study. We might consider them by asking five questions about effective study:
What? Who? Where? When? How?

What is effective study?

Many students, even some of those who receive good grades regularly, spend a great deal more time in study than is necessary. These students have developed study techniques that are laborious and time-consuming. Other students put in many hours in study, but seem to get little out of the time spent. They frequently complain about difficulties in certain courses, and the only remedy they can think of is to spend more time on that subject. In both circum- 200 stances the students probably are ignoring some basic principles about fatigue and span of interest. Instead of spending *more time* in study, they need to make *better use of the time* they do spend. You need to get the most possible good out of each hour spent on a course. This is what is meant by *effective study*. If you have effective study habits, you will spend *less* time on the same material and will understand it better than one who has not learned effective methods.

Whose responsibility?

In high school, parents and teachers usually try 300 to encourage study habits by providing certain times and places for study, and by trying to reduce possible interruptions. As you grow older, however, you find yourself more "on your own." Especially at college you will find that no one seems to exert much effort to *make* you study. By now you are supposed to be mature enough to realize that study is essential to success in school. One very important aspect of maturity is the personal assumption of responsibility

for control of your time. Achieving freedom from control by others implies developing greater self-control and exercising self-discipline. Therefore, it is 400 your responsibility to see that you provide adequate time for study. Other school activities will place many demands on you, and you will find it easy to devote to them time that should be given to study.

Some students realize too late that they have been neglecting their studies and try desperately to cram all their study and review into the last few days before examinations. When they fail the exams, they frequently rationalize and blame the instructor, their roommates, or someone else for their inability to keep up with the requirements of the course. With 500 the keen competition present in college, poor study habits can undermine the entire enjoyment of a college program. An early recognition of this could save much unhappiness.

If you wish to improve your academic record, you must assume the responsibility *yourself* for keeping up-to-date in all your school work. The sooner you accept this responsibility seriously, the more likely you are to succeed in your school program. Specific suggestions to help you establish better study habits are given on the following pages.

Where to study?

Some students are able to study almost anywhere. While walking or resting, they may be men- 600 tally organizing ideas. Many students, however, do not have this ability to concentrate in the midst of other activity. Even when seated at a study desk, you may find other ideas creeping into your mind to keep you from thinking about the school work waiting to be done. You may find it helpful to consider some of the factors that *you can* control to make that study desk a more effective place to work.

Auditory distractions usually can be controlled by selecting as quiet a place as possible. You can reduce, to some extent, distraction from outside 700 noises. This may mean working out arrangements for study hours with your roommate and making an agreement not to have guests in the room during certain hours. If you find yourself unable to eliminate these distractions in your own room, then consider the scheduling of study hours in the library, where the atmosphere is kept as quiet as possible. Another possibility is the use of a vacant classroom for those free periods between classes.

19

Some students find that a radio or stereo set playing continuous music and set at a minimal volume creates a sound barrier sufficient to block out the variety of outside distracting noises. By careful ⁸⁰⁰ selection of the station or of recordings, you can establish a stable sound background to which you can adjust and thus be protected from the uncontrolled sounds of your environment. In doing this, however, you need to keep your volume low enough to avoid creating sound distractions for others who work near you.

Visual distractions frequently are present without being recognized. The picture of a friend on your desk may take you off on a chain of pleasant memories every time you glance at it; the souvenir ash tray you picked up on your vacation trip last summer ⁹⁰⁰ may recall many pleasant experiences; the colorful new sport jacket you wore to the last ball game may revive the excitement and competition you enjoyed then; the letter you got from home yesterday may start you worrying about the situation at home; the advertising on the desk blotter may stir thoughts of the good times you could have if you only followed the suggestions printed there. The curling smoke from the cigarette in your ash tray may attract your attention and lead your thoughts astray. These and many other items frequently found on study desks may lead you to many minutes of daydreaming ¹⁰⁰⁰ during the hours when you *think* you have been studying.

One of the first essentials in improving the place of study is to clear the desk of as many of these diverting influences as you can. If possible, the study desk should be cleared of everything except the textbook you are studying at the moment and the necessary papers and pencils for taking notes.

Next, consider what disturbing items lie in your range of vision as you sit at your desk. Consider carefully any objects that lie in the area of distraction. To do this, check the *angle of distraction* from ¹¹⁰⁰ your study desk. Any object falling within a 60-degree angle on either side of the forward view from your desk is likely to interfere with your concentration. Mirrors are especially disturbing as they expand the area of distraction to include a reflected area as well as the actual one. How many things in your room fall within this range? What do they make you think about? To improve your concentration you would be wise to move your desk so that the space included in this area of distraction is at a minimum and so that most of the wall surfaces ¹²⁰⁰ included are blank. Ideally, then, a study desk should be placed in a corner, and the wall above it should be kept clear of distracting influences.

Lighting is also an important factor in concentration. Eye strain and general fatigue are the logical results of poor lighting. Do not depend on a single overhead light. You need a good desk lamp that will provide indirect lighting in your working area. Desk lamps that cause a glare on the books and papers should be avoided. In addition to a good study lamp ¹³⁰⁰ on the desk, some other light in the room is needed to prevent sharp contrasts between a brightly lighted desk and a dark room. Extreme contrasts make the eyes tire more rapidly. A combination of a good, indirect desk lamp and an overhead light is considered ideal for effective study conditions.

Ventilation and temperature are important, too. There should be some provision for fresh air without a draft. If you cannot work with a window open, make a point of airing out the study room once a day. A warm room develops drowsiness and makes studying difficult. Usually, you can study best ¹⁴⁰⁰ in a room that is slightly cooler than the normal living room temperature.

Avoid physical relaxation when trying to study. If you pick the easy chair or the bed as a place to study, do not expect to be able to concentrate very long. By relaxing physically, you invite mental relaxation as well. A good straight chair at a study desk is the ideal location for effective study.

Having one place for study *and study only* is important. If you study at the same place that you play games, do your nails, write your letters, or plan ¹⁵⁰⁰ dance programs, you will find it more difficult to get to work. If, however, you use one desk exclusively for studying, you will find it natural to start concentrating when you sit there.

You can control the environment in which you try to study. Do not blame others for distractions. Take time to check out your study area, and do some reorganization to make it an atmosphere more conducive to effective study.

When to study?

Your school program is one of your most important obligations and requires more time than you are likely to give to it without careful planning. The ¹⁶⁰⁰ best protection against late assignments and the necessity for "cramming" is to budget your time as you go along and to plan a proper balance between work, study, and recreational activities. One of the best ways to do this is to use a *Time Budget Sheet*. A sample *Time Budget Sheet* is shown on pages 23 and 24. Copies of these usually can be obtained through your school bookstore. The success of such a time budget will depend on how carefully you plan it and use it. Several points should be considered. The suggestions on the back of the *Time Budget* ¹⁷⁰⁰ *Sheet* are worthy of careful consideration. Read them thoughtfully; think about their meaning to you. Discuss them with your advisor or with a counselor if you need help in applying them to your own planning.

How to study?

Probably no two students study in exactly the same way. You have learned certain techniques that seem easiest for you. If these techniques bring you understanding of the materials with a minimum expenditure of time, then you are probably satisfied with these study habits. If, however, you feel that you are not getting the desired results or that your methods are too time-consuming, then you should *1800←* consider a change. If your present study habits are leading only to poor grades and discouragement, they should be discarded and replaced by a new set that may lead to more effective use of your time.

Many students fail to make effective use of new techniques of study because they are unwilling to give up the old techniques, even though these older ones have not produced the desired results. Often it is necessary to *unlearn* poor work habits before you can establish good ones. If you wish to develop a greater efficiency in your study, you must be willing *1900←* to release some old habits in favor of some new ones.

Space in this book does not allow a detailed discussion of many of the techniques of study. You will find references on study skills in your library or your bookstore. For detailed suggestions on note making, you may read *Learning More by Effective Study* by Charles and Dorothy Bird (6). For specific suggestions on classroom and examination skills, you will find *Effective Study* by F. P. Robinson (40) very helpful. For detailed information on the preparation of reports and term papers, you can find assistance in *The Research Paper* by Hook and *2000←* Gaver (16). *Tips to Improve Personal Study Skills,* prepared by the New York State Personnel and Guidance Association (31), is a concise pamphlet—an excellent reference to keep in your notebook. Other good books with detailed suggestions to improve study habits are *A Time to Learn* by Bandt, Meara, and Schmidt (4) and *Study Skills* by Carmen and Adams (8).

Three major techniques presented by Francis P. Robinson in his book *Effective Study* (40) have proved to be so helpful to many college students that they merit a presentation here. These techniques *2100←* provide an excellent means of establishing important ideas in one's mind and retaining them. These may be identified as the three "S.R." techniques because these letters can be used as memory clues for all three techniques. All three require a high level of personal self-discipline and planning. Only you can make them work for you. In brief, these techniques may be applied as follows:

A. **Self-Recitation.** Ask questions of yourself as *2600→* you study and as you review. Be alert at all times to the questions suggested about major ideas, and

2200→ try to read for answers to them. In reviewing, ask yourself questions, and see if you can answer them; then check your answers against your notes. In studying for exams, try to predict the questions that the instructor may ask, and be prepared for these questions in the examination.

B. **Spaced Review.** Review briefly immediately after study; then review again within a week. Each week, schedule review periods where you can review all the material presented thus far in the course. These brief weekly reviews will reduce the necessity for any last-minute cramming before examinations.

C. **The SQ3R Method,** originated by Robinson (40), frequently has been referred to as the *2300→* SQ4R Method for purposes of clarification. The following explanation of the six steps of this method has been presented by Miller and Seeman (30).

The SQ4R method of study

1. **Survey.** Glance over the headings in the chapter to see the few big points that will be developed. This survey should take only a few seconds and will show the several core ideas around which the discussion will be developed. This preview will prepare you for more effective study of the details in the following steps.

2. **Question.** Turn the first heading into a question. This should arouse your curiosity and thus aid *2400→* comprehension. It will help to bring to mind information that you already know. In this way, your understanding of that section will be increased. The question will make the important points stand out.

3. **Read.** Read to answer the question. Make this an active search for the answer. You will find that your eyes tend to move more rapidly over the material, slighting the unimportant or explanatory details while noting the important points.

4. **Recite.** Try to recite the answer to your question without looking at the book. Use your own words, *2500→* and think of an example. If you can do this, you know what is in the book; if you cannot, glance over the section again. If you jot down "cue" phrases in outline form as you do this, you will have an excellent basis for later review and study.

5. **Repeat.** Repeat steps 2, 3, and 4 on each succeeding section. Turn the next heading into a question, read to answer that question, and recite the answer by jotting down "cue" phrases in an outline. Read in this way until the lesson is completed.

6. **Review.** Look back over your notes to get a bird's-eye view of the points and their relationships. Check your memory as to the content by

reciting on the major subpoints under each heading. This checking of your memory can be done by covering up the notes and trying to recall the main points, then exposing each major point and trying to recall the subpoints listed under it. Save these notes for later use in *Spaced Review* activity.

SQ4R applied to problem solving

A modification of the SQ4R Method to apply to mathematical-type reading that involves problem solving might be summarized as follows:

1. **Survey.** Look over the problems to see what types of logic they require and what basic formulas will 2700 ← be used. Try to make associations with practical situations in which similar problems might be encountered.
2. **Question.** Looking at the first problem, think through it to be sure you understand what is the unknown factor which you are to find and what are the known facts with which you can work.
3. **Solve.** Work through the problem to find the unknown factor.
4. **Check.** Substitute the answer you have found for the unknown in the original statement and see if it makes sense. Check through the basic formula to see if it balances with this value. 2800 ←
5. **Repeat.** Apply steps 2, 3, and 4 to each successive problem in the assignment.
6. **Review.** Check over the whole assignment again to be sure you have completed all the assigned work and that your answers were reasonable. Be sure you understand the purpose of such exer- 3100 → cises, and try to think of practical applications of principles involved in the problems.

Concentrate on end results

The application of these three "S.R." techniques will free you from much of the tension associated with trying to get thorough comprehension from the reading alone. Frequently, students depend 2900 → on one reading of the material to grasp its entire content. The methods outlined above decrease the stress on detailed comprehension in initial reading. They provide other study techniques—skimming, questioning, reciting, and reviewing—to develop the understanding of material. This frees you to read as rapidly as possible with a major emphasis on *seeking the ideas behind the words*.

Improving comprehension requires a constant awareness of your own goals and a sensitivity to the ideas and organization of the author.

As you develop this technique of rapid reading, you usually will find that comprehension will improve 3000 → also. But more important than either is the efficiency of reading—that is, the amount you understand per unit of study time. By increasing the efficiency of the initial reading, you can find time for the other techniques, which will help build a more permanent comprehension of the whole body of material. More than that, a combination of efficient reading with effective study techniques should enable you to get more studying done in less time. So you should have more time to spend on other things you want to do. This is your ultimate reward for exercising self-control of your own study habits and environment.

TIME BUDGET SHEET

COLLEGE FORM

Prepared by
Lyle L. Miller
UNIVERSITY OF WYOMING

Self - Recitation
S R
STUDY
PROGRAM
Speed Review
SQ4R Method

Name _____

(Study the suggestions on the back before making out budget)

	MON	TUES	WED	THUR	FRI	SAT	SUN	TOTAL
12 - 2					SEX	SEX		
2 - 4					SEX	SEX		
4 - 6					SEX	SEX		
6 - 7								
7 - 8								
8 - 9								
9 - 10								
10 - 11								
11 - 12								
12 - 1								
1 - 2								
2 - 3								
3 - 4								
4 - 5								
5 - 6								
6 - 7								
7 - 8								
8 - 9								
9 - 10								
10 - 12								
CLASS								
STUDY								
TOTAL								

S P A C E D   R E V I E W

SELF-RECITATION

SURVEY   QUESTION   READ   RECITE   REPEAT: QRR   REVIEW

These three evening plans interchangeable

Original Copyright: 1955 by Lyle L. Miller; Revised Edition Copyright: 1969

SOME HINTS ON PLANNING A BETTER TIME SCHEDULE

Lyle L. Miller

Professor of Guidance and Counselor Education, University of Wyoming

The effectiveness of your time schedule will depend on the care with which **you** plan it. Careful consideration of these points will help you to make a schedule which **you** can control and which will **work for you.**

1. **Plan a schedule of balanced activities.** College life has many aspects which are very important to success. Some have fixed time requirements and some are flexible. Some of the most common which you must consider are:

FIXED:	eating	organizations	classes	church	work
FLEXIBLE:	sleeping	personal affairs	recreation	relaxation	study

2. **Plan enough time in studying to do justice to each subject.** Most college classes are planned to require about three hours work per week per credit in the course. By multiplying your credit load by three you can get a good idea of the time you should provide for studying. Of course, if you are a slow reader, or have other study deficiencies, you may need to plan more time in order to meet the competition of colleges classes.

3. **Study at a regular time and in a regular place.** Establishing habits of study is extremely important. Knowing what you are going to study, and when, saves a lot of time in making decisions and retracing your steps to get necessary materials, etc. Avoid generalizations in your schedule such as "STUDY." Commit yourself more definitely to "STUDY HISTORY" or "STUDY CHEMISTRY" at certain regular hours.

4. **Study as soon after your lecture class as possible.** One hour spent soon after class will do as much good in developing an understanding of materials as several hours a few days later. Review lecture notes while they are still fresh in your mind. Start assignments while your memory of the assignment is still accurate.

5. **Utilize odd hours during the day for studying.** The scattered one-hour or two-hour free periods between classes are easily wasted. Planning and establishing habits of using them for studying for the class just finished will result in free time for recreation or activities at other times in the week.

6. **Limit your blocks of study time to no more than 2 hours on any one course at one time.** After 1½ to 2 hours of study you begin to tire rapidly and your ability to concentrate decreases rapidly. Taking a break and then switching to studying some other course will provide the change necessary to keep up your efficiency.

7. **Trade time—don't steal it.** When unexpected events arise that take up time you had planned to study, decide immediately where you can find the time to make up the study missed and adjust your schedule for that week. Note the three weekend evenings. Most students can afford no more than two of them for recreation, but may wish to use different evenings on different weeks. This "trading agreement" provides for committing one night to study, but rotating it as recreational possibilities vary.

8. **Provide for spaced review.** A regular weekly period when you will review the work in each of your courses will help to keep you up to date. This review should be cumulative, covering briefly all the work done thus far in the quarter. Such reviews will reduce the need for "cramming" later.

9. **Practice self-recitation as a device for increasing memory.** Organize your notes in a question and answer form and think in terms of questions and answers about the main ideas of the material as you review weekly. When preparing for exams, try to predict the questions the instructor may ask.

10. **Keep carefully organized notes on both lectures and assignments.** Good notes are one of the best bases for review. Watch for key ideas in lectures and try to express them in your own words in your notes. Watch for headings and bold face type in your reading to give you clues of main ideas for your notes. Take down careful notes as to exactly what assignments are made and when they are due.

11. **Always try to improve your study efficiency.** The SQ4R method of study is a very sound approach to improving comprehension. Details on this method can be found in the library in Chapter IV of "Increasing Reading Efficiency," published by Holt, Rinehart, and Winston, New York City 10017 or in Chapter IV of "Developing Reading Efficiency," published by Burgess Publishing Co., Minneapolis, Minnesota 55415.

Publisher:

DEVELOPMENTAL READING DISTRIBUTORS

1944 Sheridan Ave.
Laramie, Wyoming
82070

V
Using This Workbook

The exercises in this workbook have been grouped according to types, each of which plays a distinct part in the development of more efficient reading habits.

Series I
Word recognition exercises

Word recognition exercises are designed to accelerate rate and to establish some rhythmic patterns of eye movement. As you proceed through these exercises, you will find yourself dealing with longer words. Here you will have an opportunity to break the habit of syllabication and to learn to pick up longer words at a single glance.

Series II
Word meaning exercises

Word meaning exercises, involve you in thinking processes as you are expected to identify synonyms at a rapid pace. The arrangement is the same as before, except that you now must think about word meanings. In addition to eye span and rhythmic eye movements, the factor of rate of perception has been added. Because all of the words used in these exercises have been taken from Thorndike's list (49) of the 30,000 most frequently used words in our vocabulary, these exercises also serve to point up potential weaknesses in your vocabulary list, which may need study. Any words missed here should be placed on a vocabulary list and studied carefully so that they will not remain as stumbling blocks to your reading.

Series III
Phrase meaning exercises

The third series introduces phrases and is designed primarily to increase eye span. At the same time, you continue to practice on rhythmic eye movements and perception of meaning under time pressure. These are exercises in which you should begin to sense an improvement in rate of reading as you learn to pick up several words at one glance. These exercises begin with short phrases and gradually build up in length until the last few exercises are composed of phrases of several words.

Series IV
Sentence meaning exercises

The fourth series consists of exercises in recognition of sentence meaning. Here increased eye span is further stressed, and, in addition, you are expected to recognize the key words that provide meaning for a sentence. This is basic training for the idea-type of reading, in which you strip the sentences of their verbal padding to pick up the basic ideas. This series provides basic training in quick recognition of key ideas, which is essential to developing your skills in skimming for new ideas or scanning to pick up specific content.

Series V
Idea reading exercises

Series V is made up of short articles from which you are to pick up the main ideas or basic themes as quickly as possible. On these you should apply your techniques of *idea reading* to attain maximum rates with only a general comprehension of the more basic ideas being presented. Primary emphasis in this series is on the extension of your upper limits in reading rate.

Series VI
Exploratory reading exercises

The sixth series is composed of readings of longer length and greater complexity. They provide practice in *exploratory reading*. In these exercises you develop skill in reading at a fairly rapid rate, while concentrating for greater detail in terms of general content and ideas, rather than specific facts.

Series VII
Study reading exercises

Here you must stop and *think* to answer questions at intervals in your reading. The basic purpose is to demonstrate how rapidly material can be covered even when you take time out for thinking and answering questions. Although not an exact duplication of the *study* reading, in which you develop idea outlines, these drills will provide an objective comparison of this type of reading. You can develop skills in reading shorter units more intensively and in interrupting your reading with short periods of thinking and note making. These exercises provide opportunities for application of alternating patterns of studying: think . . . read . . . think . . . write . . . think . . . read . . . think . . . write . . . and so forth.

Series VIII
Critical thinking exercises

Here you must think critically about all of the materials presented to you. Exercises are identified only by a number, and you have to try to detect the purpose and intent, author bias or propaganda, and attempt at emotional appeal. Emphasis here is not on rate, but on the quality of your thinking skill in dealing with unidentified material.

Computing scores and recording progress

700
←

On each exercise throughout the book, you are to record time, rate, comprehension, and efficiency. Tables are provided for looking up your reading rates. Each exercise refers you to the table for rates for that exercise.

Keys for scoring exercises are located in the back of the workbook. After computing the comprehension and efficiency scores, you should compare these with scores on other exercises to determine your progress. Progress charts are provided on page 297 of this book to record your scores on each

reading exercise. Keeping these progress charts up-to-date will help motivate you to try for continued improvement. Supplementary reading from longer exercises, such as those in *Maintaining Reading Efficiency* (25), will help you to establish more effective reading habits.

800
→

On the page preceding each series of exercises, you will find instructions and illustrations of the type of work to be done in that series and further suggestions about the purpose and use of that material.

Setting personal goals

As you move through each series, you can help motivate yourself by setting goals of consistent improvement. Before starting a new exercise, look back at the time on the previous one in that series, and try to cut your time a little bit.

900
→

You probably will find that your comprehension scores remain fairly constant as you increase your rate gradually. Errors in comprehension should be used to help expand your vocabulary. You *will not* automatically increase your comprehension by slowing down. Avoid the tendency to read more slowly whenever comprehension scores drop. Instead, go back and try to understand *why* you missed the specific items.

Effective use of these exercises should enable you to increase your reading speed at the same time that you are increasing your vocabulary and improv-

1000
→

ing your skill in concentration.

VI
Selected References

1. Adams, W. Royce. *Developing Reading Versatility,* 2d ed. New York: Holt, Rinehart and Winston, 1977.

2. Adams, W. Royce. *Increasing Reading Speed.* London: The Macmillan Company, 1969.

3. Bamman, Henry A.; Midori F. Hujama; and Delbert L. Prescott. *Free to Read.* San Francisco: Field Educational Publications, 1970.

4. Bandt, Phillip L.; Naomi M. Meara; and Lyle D. Schmidt. *A Time to Learn.* New York: Holt, Rinehart and Winston, 1974.

5. Bieda, Margaret R., and Vinola S. Woodward. *Realizing Reading Potential.* New York: Holt, Rinehart and Winston, 1971.

6. Bird, Charles, and Dorothy M. Bird. *Learning More by Effective Study.* New York: Appleton-Century-Crofts, 1945.

7. Brown, James I. *Efficient Reading.* Boston: D. C. Heath and Company, 1952, 1965.

8. Carman, Robert A., and W. Royce Adams. *Study Skills.* New York: John Wiley & Sons, 1972.

9. Causey, Oscar S., ed. *Exploring the Levels of College Reading Programs.* Ft. Worth, Tex.: Texas Christian University Press, 1956.

10. Causey, Oscar S. *The Reading Teacher's Reader.* New York: The Ronald Press Company, 1958.

11. Davis, Nancy B. *Basic Vocabulary Skills.* New York: McGraw-Hill Book Company, 1969.

12. Flesch, Rudolph. *The Art of Readable Writing.* New York: Harper & Row, Publishers, 1949.

13. Fry, Edward B. *Reading Drills for Speed and Comprehension.* Providence, R.I.: Jamestown Publishers, 1975.

14. Gerow, Joshua R., and R. Douglas Ling. *How to Succeed in College.* New York: Charles Scribner's Sons, 1975.

15. Hess, Karen M.; Robert E. Shafer; and Lanny E. Morreau. *Developing Reading Efficiency.* New York: John Wiley & Sons, 1975.

16. Hook, Lucyle, and Mary Virginia Gaver. *The Research Paper,* 4th ed. Englewood Cliffs, N.J.: Prentice-Hall, 1969.

17. Joffe, Irwin L. *Developing Vocabulary Skills.* Belmont, Calif.: Wadsworth Publishing Company, 1971.

18. Joffe, Irwin L. *Finding Main Ideas.* Belmont, Calif.: Wadsworth Publishing Company, 1970.

19. Joffe, Irwin L. *Opportunity for Skillful Reading.* Belmont, Calif.: Wadsworth Publishing Company, 1970.

20. Locke, Edwin A. *A Guide to Effective Study.* New York: Springer Publishing Company, 1975.

21. McCorkle, R. M., and S. D. Dingus. *Rapid Reading.* Totawa, N.J.: Littlefield, Adams and Company, 1970.

22. Maxwell, Martha J. *Skimming and Scanning Improvement.* New York: McGraw-Hill Book Company, 1969.

23. Miller, Lyle L. *Developing Reading Efficiency.* Rev. ed. Minneapolis: Burgess Publishing Company, 1967, 1972.

24. Miller, Lyle L. *Increasing Reading Efficiency.* New York: Holt, Rinehart and Winston, 1956, 1964, 1970.

25. Miller, Lyle L. *Maintaining Reading Efficiency.* Rev. ed. Laramie, Wyo.: Developmental Reading Distributors, 1962, 1967, 1973.

26. Miller, Lyle L. *Maintaining Reading Efficiency Tests.* Laramie, Wyo.: Developmental Reading Distributors, 1967, 1970.

27. Miller, Lyle L. *Personalizing Reading Efficiency.* Minneapolis: Burgess Publishing Company, 1976.

28. Miller, Lyle L. *Speed Reading in the Seventies.* Educational Leadership, Vol. 30, No. 7, 623–627.

29. Miller, Lyle L. *Teaching Efficient Reading Skills.* Minneapolis: Burgess Publishing Company, 1972 (A revision of *Accelerating Growth in Reading Efficiency*).

30. Miller, Lyle L., and Alice Z. Seeman. *Guidebook for Prospective Teachers.* Columbus, Ohio: The Ohio State University Press, 1948.

31. New York State Personnel and Guidance Association. *Tips to Improve Personal Study Skills.* Albany, N.Y.: Delmar Publishers, 1968.

32. Nielsen, Duane M., and Howard F. Hjelm. *Reading and Career Education.* Newark, Delaware: International Reading Association, 1975.

33. Norman, Maxwell H. *Successful Reading: Key to Our Dynamic Society,* 2d ed. New York: Holt, Rinehart and Winston, 1975.

34. Pauk, Walter, and Josephine Wilson. *Reading for Facts.* New York: David McKay Company, 1974.

35. Pauk, Walter, and Josephine Wilson. *Reading for Ideas.* New York: David McKay Company, 1974.

36. Pickett, Thomas. *Guide to Efficient Reading.* Minneapolis: Burgess Publishing Company, 1969.

37. Raygor, Alton L. *Reading for the Main Idea.* New York: McGraw-Hill Book Company, 1969.

38. Raygor, Alton L. *Reading for Significant Facts.* New York: McGraw-Hill Book Company, 1970.

39. Raygor, Alton L., and George B. Schick. *Reading at Efficient Rates.* New York: McGraw-Hill Book Company, 1970.

40. Robinson, Francis P. *Effective Study.* New York: Harper & Row, Publishers, 1946, 1961, 1970.

41. Smith, Carl Bernard. *How to Read and Succeed.* New York: Essandess Special Editions, Div. of Simon & Schuster, 1964, 1967.

42. Solberg, Kristin B. "A Measurement of Readability of the Texts Used on the Freshman and Sophomore Level in 1952 and 1953." Doctoral dissertation. Laramie, Wyo.: University of Wyoming, 1953.

43. Spargo, Edward. *Selections from the Black.* Providence, R.I.: Jamestown Publishers, 1970.

44. Spargo, Edward. *Topics for the Restless.* Providence, R.I.: Jamestown Publishers, 1974.

45. Strang, Edward; James A. Giroux; and Livia J. Giroux. *Voices from the Bottom.* Providence, R.I.: Jamestown Publishers, 1972.

46. Strang, Ruth. *Guidance and the Treasury of Reading.* Newark, Del.: International Reading Association, 1969.

47. Stroud, James B., and Robert B. Ammons. *Improving Reading Ability.* New York: Appleton-Century-Crofts, 1949; 3d ed., 1970.

48. Thomas, Ellen Lamar, and H. Alan Robinson. *Improving Reading in Every Class.* Boston: Allyn and Bacon, 1972.

49. Thorndike, Edward L. *The Teacher's Word Book.* New York: Bureau of Publications, Teacher's College, Columbia University, 1921.

50. Thorndike, Edward L., and Irving Lorge. *The Teacher's Word Book of 30,000 Words.* New York: Bureau of Publications, Teachers College, Columbia University, 1944.

51. Zintz, Miles V. *The Reading Process.* Dubuque, Ia.: Wm. C. Brown Company Publishers, 1970.

SERIES I
Word Recognition Exercises

Instructions

Series I exercises are designed to help you establish rhythmic habits of eye movement. The exercises are of equal difficulty, and you should be able to reduce the time necessary to complete them quite rapidly. Keep practicing on them until you are able to complete an exercise in 20 seconds or less.

In these exercises are two columns of words, one with a single word and the other with five words. The first column contains the key word. On each line this key word is repeated somewhere among the five words in the other columns. You are to locate this identical word as rapidly as possible and underline or check it. Then you proceed to the next line and so on till you have finished. As soon as you have finished, raise your hand, and the instructor will give you your time in seconds. Record this time,

and look up your rate in the table on page 307. (Find your time in Column I, and then look in Column II for your rate.)

Next go back, and check your work to see if you have marked any words that were not identical with the key. Count your errors, and record them at the bottom of the exercise. Compute your comprehension by multiplying the number of correct answers by four (4). Compute your reading efficiency on this exercise by multiplying the rate you secured from the table by this comprehension score. Round off the efficiency score to the nearest whole number. Record both the rate and the efficiency on the Progress Chart for Word Recognition Exercises on page 297.

These exercises begin on page 31; rate tables are on page 307; progress charts, on page 297.

Example

22. six	six	hexagon	fix	kiss	sex
23. oxen	often	toxin	shown	oxen	boxes
24. rite X	kite	ritual	right	rate	rite
25. were	ware	we're	were	wear	went

Time 32 Sec.
No. Correct: 24
I-0

RATE (from table on page 307):   R. 281
COMPREHENSION (4% for each correct answer): (4×24) C. 96
EFFICIENCY (R × C): $(281 \times .96) = 269.76$ E. 270

Suggestions

Although the primary purpose of this type of reading exercise is to break up old habits of rigid use of eye muscles and to develop rapid rhythmic eye movements, there is also an aspect of logical reasoning and sound study skill application that you may begin to apply.

The practice of speeded recognition of exact duplicates in words tends to reduce the thinking process requirements and to allow one to concentrate on eye movements.

You might want to consider this as a game in quick recognition of symbols, however, and begin to apply some logical thinking to the activity. Man lives in a world of symbols and must learn to identify quickly a wide variety of items by size, shape, color, or location in relationship to other symbols. Thus we can "read" a highway sign by its shape long before we actually can see the words on it. We often can tell what brand of gasoline a station sells by the shape of its signs long before we can make out the

words on those signs. Symbols help us to select our food, clothing, and recreational activities. Words are only verbal symbols, and we learn to recognize and use many of them as such without question or without deep thought process.

If this were a game in which you had to find boxes of an appropriate shape to pack something in, you would apply many skills once developed to help you in early learning experiences. Size and shape would be most important to you in selection. Although you cannot read words while your eyes are moving, you can form some impressions of size and shape. If you have a particular size and shape in mind, a word will sometimes seem to stand out from a group for you. The secret is in knowing what you are looking for so you can recognize it when you find it!

Let us consider the word in the first column as a symbol that we need to pack in the right size box. If we study it carefully as to size, shape, and unique irregularities in form, then we have some idea of what we need to look for in our "box pile" in the other column. A quick scan eliminates several of our choices because they obviously are too large or too small. So we have only one or two that have possibilities and that we might look at more carefully. A quick glance is often enough to convince us that one will do or will not do, and we quickly narrow our choice to the specific one that will fit our key word exactly. When we find the box that fits it perfectly, we do not have to search further.

Even if we did not understand meaning of words, we could still play this matching game with verbal symbols. Let us consider the basic rules of the game:

1. Concentrate first on the key symbol to be matched. Form a visual image of its appearance, its size, shape, and specific characteristics. Know what you are looking for!
2. Scan the answer section quickly for possible matching materials. Sometimes the perfect match will stand out clearly and can be identified without detailed searching. If not, the scanning at least eliminates some choices that obviously do not fit.
3. Look individually at those most likely prospects identified in the scanning. Mentally match each one to your key, and discard it quickly if it does not fit.
4. Concentrate on your key symbol and matching it. Do not take time to study in detail all of the five choices. When you have found the match for the key symbol, *stop* your search. There is no point in looking at other empty boxes when you have already selected the right one for your key symbol.

Even simple exercises like these can be more than visual activity. Routine reading process is more than eye movement and word recognition. It can be a challenge to logical thinking as well. Time spent in thinking and establishing goals can pay off in quick identification and selection from the alternatives presented. Scanning as a rapid reading technique is effective only if you *think first* and have some idea you are seeking. You can use these exercises to help develop your goal-setting and scanning skills.

Reading can be fun if you think ahead and plan as you read.

Exercise I-1

1. beech   beast   beach   beetle   write   <u>beech</u>

2. civil   meat   civilian   <u>civil</u>   evil   civic

3. desist   desire   <u>desist</u>   design   resist   shoe

4. fabric   fabulous   fabricate   ruining   <u>fabric</u>   fable

5. gun   <u>gun</u>   foil   gum   sun   gunnery

6. supple   supply   support   supplicate   minister   <u>supple</u>

7. miner   concern   <u>miner</u>   diner   mine   mineral

8. pebble   <u>pebble</u>   peddle   treble   medal   flout

9. redden   fish   reddish   gladden   <u>redden</u>   ratify

10. shrub   grub   tangle   <u>shrub</u>   scrub   rub

11. talcum   vacuum   <u>talcum</u>   annoy   welcome   falcon

12. unveil   bewail   unwieldy   object   sail   <u>unveil</u>

13. begot   forgot   begone   beget   <u>begot</u>   friend

14. clasp   <u>clasp</u>   head   clap   chap   class

15. cheat   cheapen   photo   <u>cheat</u>   check   chess

16. deer   dear   beard   dare   ever   <u>deer</u>

17. hadn't   haven't   <u>hadn't</u>   haddock   sign   aren't

18. meed   <u>meed</u>   rose   need   seed   mean

19. minus   minute   plus   case   <u>minus</u>   minor

20. peg   leg   pug   <u>peg</u>   few   pig

21. refer   reference   confer   dealt   defer   <u>refer</u>

22. random   <u>random</u>   ranger   ransom   rankle   medal

23. tape   tap   <u>tape</u>   stun   taper   ape

24. six   <u>six</u>   kiss   hexagon   sexton   sex

25. we're   ware   let's   <u>we're</u>   were   we've

Time __35__ Sec.   **RATE (from table on page 307):**   R. _257_

No. Correct: __25__   **COMPREHENSION (4% for each correct answer):**   C. _100_

I–1   **EFFICIENCY (R × C):**   E. _____

Record on Progress Chart on page 297

start

31

Exercise I-2

1. adopt   adapt   <u>adopt</u>   arrange   clot   adoption

2. belle   bell   bowl   peal   <u>belle</u>   belt

3. blight   light   oblige   punch   <u>blight</u>   blind

4. devout   devour   vault   <u>devout</u>   bout   about

5. farce   face   false   race   rigid   <u>farce</u>

6. hammer   hamper   stammer   <u>hammer</u>   midst   pound

7. job   syne   <u>job</u>   bog   jog   sob

8. he'd   held   she's   he   <u>he'd</u>   would

9. per   <u>per</u>   par   stir   pet   pert

10. pillar   pillage   pillow   <u>pillar</u>   pill   coarse

11. smelt   felt   rode   smell   melt   <u>smelt</u>

12. thine   time   <u>thine</u>   forest   thing   thin

13. he'll   she   hell   held   <u>he'll</u>   we'll

14. bent   <u>bent</u>   broad   scent   regard   tent

15. closet   cabinet   closed   tabby   clothes   <u>closet</u>

16. mud   muddy   dumb   <u>mud</u>   cud   muddle

17. fatal   <u>fatal</u>   futile   fated   frost   total

18. hap   hop   joy   hole   haste   <u>hap</u>

19. jolly   jelly   <u>jolly</u>   holly   haste   jam

20. mitten   hidden   smite   <u>mitten</u>   often   more

21. pirate   pistol   piracy   pilot   <u>pirate</u>   rate

22. sneak   ratify   <u>sneak</u>   neat   snake   sneer

23. sinful   fully   almost   sinister   awful   <u>sinful</u>

24. teeth   beneath   teem   aback   <u>teeth</u>   tee

25. villa   <u>villa</u>   void   silly   tell   house

Time 30 Sec.

No. Correct: 25

I-2

RATE (from table on page 307):

COMPREHENSION (4% for each correct answer):

EFFICIENCY (R × C):

R. _____

C. _____

E. _____

Record on Progress Chart on page 297

Exercise I-3

1. abuse   bruise   cord   <u>abuse</u>   bus   about

2. betake   <u>betake</u>   take   better   trace   rush

3. germ   fish   stern   worm   <u>germ</u>   gem

4. dilute   delude   dirt   <u>dilute</u>   rain   dish

5. scrap   bandy   scrip   rap   <u>scrap</u>   scrape

6. harlot   hauteur   <u>harlot</u>   lot   harlequin   marry

7. jumble   mumble   gore   jungle   rumble   <u>jumble</u>

8. stud   <u>stud</u>   study   extra   stub   studio

9. attain   sustain   rock   <u>attain</u>   attend   attach

10. cast   caste   fast   casting   true   <u>cast</u>

11. cycle   bicycle   <u>cycle</u>   master   cymbal   cyclist

12. gilt   silt   gild   gift   <u>gilt</u>   silk

13. pulp   <u>pulp</u>   pulse   pup   pulpit   town

14. beyond   below   <u>beyond</u>   yonder   frost   bead

15. cog   <u>cog</u>   fog   cogent   many   got

16. dirt   skirt   funny   ditty   dirge   <u>dirt</u>

17. felon   simple   fell   long   <u>felon</u>   felt

18. hast   last   <u>hast</u>   masque   haste   aster

19. jury   hurry   junk   <u>jury</u>   juror   fix

20. monkey   <u>monkey</u>   key   money   monarchy   skunk

21. style   mess   study   stile   stylish   <u>style</u>

22. remove   remodel   remnant   <u>remove</u>   move   take

23. wager   bet   wages   wag   <u>wager</u>   wagon

24. ten   tend   <u>ten</u>   bend   fen   ace

25. volume   rescue   voluntary   voluble   luminous   <u>volume</u>

Time _30_ Sec.   **RATE (from table on page 307):**   R. _300_

No. Correct: _25_   **COMPREHENSION (4% for each correct answer):**   C. _100_

I–3   **EFFICIENCY (R × C):**   E. _____

Record on Progress Chart on page 297

–5 sec

Exercise I-4

1. awe   stop   <u>awe</u>   aware   awake   await

2. bog   log   bogus   <u>bog</u>   affix   dog

3. eschew   escort   shrew   screw   topped   <u>eschew</u>

4. ditch   ditty   <u>ditch</u>   witch   mansion   itch

5. flash   moral   flak   <u>flash</u>   lash   flask

6. herd   curd   heard   hero   <u>herd</u>   bird

7. massy   <u>massy</u>   stock   massive   mash   master

8. sultan   pending   sulk   sulky   sultry   <u>sultan</u>

9. plane   true   pane   <u>plane</u>   lane   plain

10. babe   baboon   babble   mercy   <u>babe</u>   baby

11. sober   sobering   <u>sober</u>   bolder   cold   sob

12. etch   <u>etch</u>   civil   etc.   catching   catch

13. goody   good   scorch   <u>goodly</u>   goodman   goody

14. bonny   sonny   bondage   <u>bonny</u>   risk   bone

15. racer   <u>racer</u>   race   eraser   south   tracer

16. dizzy   discreet   forth   divulge   <u>dizzy</u>   fuzzy

17. fleece   maximum   <u>fleece</u>   flee   fleet   feet

18. sunny   summon   summary   verbal   sunken   <u>sunny</u>

19. lard   <u>lard</u>   land   lord   hard   roll

20. muster   mustard   <u>muster</u>   accede   must   master

21. wean   wear   bean   luxury   weak   <u>wean</u>

22. revery   <u>revery</u>   revere   message   very   review

23. solder   rescue   older   <u>solder</u>   soldier   sold

24. thump   thumb   under   hum   hump   <u>thump</u>

25. weekly   meekly   weak   week   <u>weekly</u>   read

Time __33__ Sec.

No. Correct: __24__

I-4

RATE (from table on page 307):   R. _____

COMPREHENSION (4% for each correct answer):   C. _____

EFFICIENCY (R ✕ C):   E. _____

Record on Progress Chart on page 297

Exercise I-5

1. anybody   <u>anybody</u>   mixing   anywhere   anyhow   nobody

2. bumble   twist   bundle   <u>bumble</u>   bungle   bumblebee

3. cottage   cotton   phrase   pottage   <u>cottage</u>   cot

4. easily   eagerly   <u>easily</u>   easy   surgery   ease

5. freight   yearling   freighter   eight   free   <u>freight</u>

6. hurtful   <u>hurtful</u>   saddles   healthful   hurt   hurry

7. liver   livid   <u>livery</u>   liver   live   candy

8. notebook   cookbook   pawning   note   <u>notebook</u>   noted

9. prelate   preach   prelude   township   <u>prelate</u>   precede

10. saber   safer   sable   sober   wing   <u>saber</u>

11. stag   staff   vain   <u>stag</u>   stage   tag

12. trespass   tress   <u>trespass</u>   clocking   trestle   trespasser

13. appall   <u>appall</u>   appeal   apparel   misery   appear

14. burner   force   burn   bureau   <u>burner</u>   bunker

15. couple   coupled   reserve   couplet   coupe   <u>couple</u>

16. eddy   edify   <u>eddy</u>   yank   edge   edit

17. frighten   fright   hairpin   freighter   afraid   <u>frighten</u>

18. iceberg   ice   iceboat   <u>iceberg</u>   cooking   icebox

19. lock   <u>lock</u>   locker   idle   loch   local

20. novice   sucker   <u>novice</u>   novel   novelist   novelty

21. sailboat   iceboat   macaroni   <u>sailboat</u>   sailor   soil

22. staple   <u>staple</u>   mixture   stable   table   fable

23. triumph   triumphant   <u>triumph</u>   mulberry   trial   triumphal

24. worry   hurry   stock   worldly   scurry   <u>worry</u>

25. preservation   presentation   preservative   journalistic   <u>preservation</u>   reservation

---

Time 30 Sec.

No. Correct: 23

I-5

RATE (from table on page 307):   R. _____

COMPREHENSION (4% for each correct answer):   C. _____

EFFICIENCY (R × C):   E. _____

Record on Progress Chart on page 297

Exercise I–6

1. action   faction   <u>action</u>   fact   act   actor

2. colt   coax   volt   <u>colt</u>   cotton   mother

3. discord   disclose   cord   discourage   <u>discord</u>   office

4. feud   turn   <u>feud</u>   feudal   futile   rude

5. hawthorn   <u>hawthorn</u>   hawk   hauser   fording   thorn

6. kettle   mettle   kernel   <u>kettle</u>   ketch   morning

7. mope   mop   hope   scope   rather   <u>mope</u>

8. repine   sent   <u>repine</u>   repose   pine   reprove

9. sled   led   slowed   lead   <u>sled</u>   moist

10. theater   <u>theater</u>   thaw   heater   theatrical   fooling

11. adieu   mess   die   <u>adieu</u>   adjure   address

12. blank   blast   lower   blink   last   <u>blank</u>

13. disguise   disgust   nesting   dish   guise   <u>disguise</u>

14. fifteen   sixteen   purple   fifth   <u>fifteen</u>   teens

15. heap   leap   <u>heap</u>   heart   heaven   chair

16. kindred   kindness   slacks   hindered   kind   <u>kindred</u>

17. mosquito   moss   faintly   <u>mosquito</u>   quite   mosque

18. picker   lost   <u>picker</u>   picnic   ticker   pick

19. repulse   <u>repulse</u>   repulsive   repel   pulse   gauntlet

20. sling   slang   sing   <u>sling</u>   slink   force

21. therein   therefore   in   fiddle   <u>therein</u>   wherein

22. wampum   wanton   wander   pumice   course   <u>wampum</u>

23. comforter   <u>comforter</u>   blanket   fixture   comfort   fort

24. philosophic   philosophy   microscopic   physiology   <u>philosophic</u>   earnestness

25. birthright   <u>birthright</u>   daintiness   right   birthplace   birthday

Time __ Sec.

No. Correct: 25

I–6

RATE (from table on page 307):

COMPREHENSION (4% for each correct answer):

EFFICIENCY (R × C):

R. _____

C. _____

E. _____

Record on Progress Chart on page 297

Exercise I–7

1. brand   <u>brand</u>   ran   branch   student   brandy

2. doz.   mature   dozen   <u>doz.</u>   buzz   oz.

3. foolish   cool   keelson   fooling   foot   <u>foolish</u>

4. holder   hole   <u>holder</u>   letter   hold   older

5. ledge   led   ledger   perform   <u>ledge</u>   edge

6. necklace   necktie   neck   <u>necklace</u>   marauder   lace

7. polite   <u>polite</u>   politic   light   polish   depart

8. rite   dully   <u>rite</u>   right   kite   ritual

9. spade   valve   space   paid   span   <u>spade</u>

10. alphabet   alkali   <u>alphabet</u>   faintness   allegation   alpha

11. breath   <u>breath</u>   breather   council   beneath   breast

12. drawback   drawer   heading   back   draw   <u>drawback</u>

13. fore   mat   four   ore   <u>fore</u>   forty

14. honest   modest   hornet   <u>honest</u>   honey   punch

15. leisure   <u>leisure</u>   pairing   leisurely   composure   sure

16. Negro   shirk   Negroid   neglect   neither   <u>Negro</u>

17. pony   pond   <u>pony</u>   pooh   puny   smug

18. robe   robes   oboe   toxin   rob   <u>robe</u>

19. special   <u>special</u>   serial   perfect   facial   specify

20. tonight   tonic   versus   <u>tonight</u>   tone   night

21. whoever   whatever   whom   twenty   <u>whoever</u>   who

22. constancy   horseback   constraint   constant   <u>constancy</u>   fancy

23. tolerable   rabble   tolerate   <u>tolerable</u>   review   total

24. consecration   journalistic   <u>consecration</u>   consecrate   conservation   secret

25. allowable   masterful   allows   <u>allowable</u>   lowly   allot

---

Time _30_ Sec.   **RATE (from table on page 307):**   R. _____

No. Correct: _24_   **COMPREHENSION (4% for each correct answer):**   C. _____

I–7   **EFFICIENCY (R × C):**   E. _____

Record on Progress Chart on page 297

Exercise I–8

1. audience   auditor   audible   quadrant   <u>audience</u>   audibly

2. caught   casual   <u>caught</u>   caucus   fish   cauldron

3. damn   <u>damn</u>   dame   prince   dam   damp

4. entrails   entrance   trails   <u>entrails</u>   jackass   entreat

5. glassful   <u>glassful</u>   grateful   locality   glass   glassware

6. inflict   inflame   gossip   afflict   <u>inflict</u>   influx

7. mare   care   <u>mare</u>   halter   hare   margin

8. purity   <u>purify</u>   jurist   pure   destroy   purity

9. subtle   suckle   subtlety   snatch   <u>subtle</u>   subtly

10. celery   <u>celery</u>   celebrity   celebrate   salary   plant

11. daring   dare   punch   darning   darling   <u>daring</u>

12. epitaph   <u>epitaph</u>   epistle   epithet   rating   epoch

13. glory   gory   lorry   <u>glory</u>   gloria   grate

14. initial   initiate   <u>initial</u>   milestone   initiative   inimical

15. marrow   fact   maroon   tomorrow   <u>marrow</u>   marry

16. oven   <u>oven</u>   make   oxen   oval   <u>oven</u>

17. quake   quack   fuse   <u>quake</u>   quick   wake

18. seemly   seemingly   <u>seemly</u>   seer   gaunt   see

19. universe   <u>universe</u>   union   occupancy   unit   universal

20. warmth   warmly   warm   warn   destiny   <u>warmth</u>

21. sufferance   suffrage   suffice   sufficient   <u>sufferance</u>   contacting

22. automobile   automotive   auto   <u>automobile</u>   plenteous   automatic

23. ungrateful   ungainly   <u>ungrateful</u>   originality   ungentle   grateful

24. secondary   stand   seclude   second   primary   <u>secondary</u>

25. outlandish   outlaw   land   <u>outlandish</u>   moldboard   outlive

Time 31 Sec.   **RATE** (from table on page 307):   R. 291

No. Correct: 24   **COMPREHENSION** (4% for each correct answer):   C. 96

I–8   **EFFICIENCY** (R ✕ C):   E. 278

Record on Progress Chart on page 297

Exercise I-9

1. angry   angry   finish   anger   angel   argue

2. brownie   brow   brownie   browse   brown   courage

3. coo   cook   coax   cue   coo   rue

4. duration   durable   horseman   duration   during   curable

5. fountain   fountain   foundation   neither   fount   fountainhead

6. howl   cowl   fowl   record   jowl   howl

7. lilac   lilt   prime   like   lilac   lily

8. nobility   section   nobility   nobody   mobility   noble

9. pounce   pour   pound   sphinx   pouch   pounce

10. ruby   ruby   rubber   rubble   silk   rub

11. spouse   next   souse   spouse   spoil   spout

12. annual   courage   annul   annuity   annual   annually

13. bud   bed   bud   lion   budget   buddy

14. core   corn   cork   core   corner   each

15. dwindle   dwindle   study   dwell   wind   dwarf

16. linoleum   linseed   scorch   linnet   linden   linoleum

17. noontide   noodle   midnight   noontide   eventide   noonday

18. preacher   preacher   preamble   preaching   tombstone   reach

19. rump   such   rumple   lump   rump   rummage

20. spun   vale   spun   spurn   spur   pun

21. trash   rash   track   trash   paper   trace

22. woke   wolf   walk   kink   wake   woke

23. humankind   mankind   humankind   human   disgust   humane

24. framework   housework   stronghold   frame   framework   franchise

25. transfigure   horseradish   transfer   torment   transfix   transfigure

---

Time _31_ Sec.

No. Correct: _23_

I-9

RATE (from table on page 307):

COMPREHENSION (4% for each correct answer):

EFFICIENCY (R × C):

R. _____

C. _____

E. _____

Exercise I–10

1. ambition   ambiguity   <u>ambition</u>   ambitious   hurrying   amble

2. brighten   <u>brighten</u>   gauntlet   bright   bring   light

3. drip   hook   <u>drift</u>   dribble   <u>drip</u>   trip

4. forgave   forgive   genus   <u>forage</u>   gave   <u>forgave</u>

5. hornet   horn   <u>hornet</u>   honest   figure   horse

6. level   <u>level</u>   lever   shelve   levy   levee

7. portal   port   gouge   postal   <u>portal</u>   portage

8. romp   <u>romp</u>   rump   purple   roam   jump

9. sphere   horrible   <u>sphere</u>   spherical   sphinx   here

10. tortoise   tortuous   torpedo   tortoise   famous   torture

11. ample   <u>amble</u>   sample   future   amplify   <u>ample</u>

12. broaden   board   secure   road   <u>broaden</u>   broad

13. forsook   forsooth   riding   force   forsake   <u>forsook</u>

14. hostile   occupant   hostel   host   <u>hostile</u>   fierce

15. lid   fly   lie   lied   <u>did</u>   <u>lid</u>

16. nickel   nasty   <u>nickel</u>   fickle   sickle   nick

17. postage   hostage   comment   postal   age   <u>postage</u>

18. rosette   rosary   phrase   <u>rosette</u>   rosy   rosin

19. spite   cache   spit   pit   spite   <u>spice</u>

20. trace   ~~trace~~   train   track   race   traceable

21. windy   kindly   <u>windy</u>   window   wind   winch

22. drunkenness   <u>drunkenness</u>   militarism   drunk   drinking   sunken

23. contradict   contridiction   letterhead   <u>contradict</u>   contractor   contraction

24. nevertheless   nevermore   insistently   <u>nevertheless</u>   unless   never

25. contemplation   contemptuous   temptation   <u>contemplation</u>   content   hieroglyphic

---

Time **29** Sec.   RATE (from table on page 307):   R. **310**

No. Correct: **20**   COMPREHENSION (4% for each correct answer):   C. **80**

I–10   EFFICIENCY (R × C):   E. **248**

Record on Progress Chart on page 297

3.1
8
248

Exercise I-11

1. aisle   air   ailment   first   isle   <u>aisle</u>

2. bosom   handsome   ran   boss   <u>bosom</u>   some

3. domestic   enthusiastic   rolling   dome   <u>domestic</u>   mystic

4. flop   <u>flop</u>   lop   flow   float   ruler

5. hillock   capsize   <u>hilltop</u>   bullock   hill   hillock

6. lava   lavatory   <u>lava</u>   have   lave   mason

7. nameless   <u>nameless</u>   namesake   blameless   name   decorous

8. plow   plod   slow   <u>plow</u>   plot   too

9. riches   muse   ditches   rickety   <u>riches</u>   rice

10. somewhat   eighteen   what   some   somewhere   <u>somewhat</u>

11. timber   <u>timber</u>   eager   limber   time   climber

12. alert   ale   <u>alert</u>   avert   ascent   mercy

13. bouquet   shortly   <u>bouquet</u>   boast   croquet   book

14. dost   pretty   does   <u>dost</u>   lost   dust

15. fluid   <u>fluid</u>   flush   lurid   remain   fluent

16. lea   leaf   <u>lea</u>   leeward   smug   leave

17. nativity   horse   activity   <u>nativity</u>   native   naive

18. sorry   sorrow   <u>sorry</u>   morrow   sore   today

19. tip   in   lip   <u>tip</u>   top   tipple

20. whenever   topple   <u>whichever</u>   whatever   whenever   ever

21. righteous   headache   <u>rightful</u>   rightly   cautious   righteous

22. pneumonia   <u>pneumonia</u>   moustache   ammonia   pneumatic   monetary

23. historian   historical   custodian   history   glycerin   <u>historian</u>

24. congenial   congressional   regional   gentile   <u>congenial</u>   feudalism

25. confession   <u>confusion</u>   tricking   confession   confess   confessed

---

Time __31__ Sec.   **RATE (from table on page 307):**   R. _____

No. Correct: __20__   **COMPREHENSION (4% for each correct answer):**   C. _____

I–11   **EFFICIENCY (R × C):**   E. _____

Record on Progress Chart on page 297

Exercise I–12

1. button   button   buttress   suit   buttons   butter

2. cowslip   bulls   coward   slip   cowboy   cowslip

3. fruitful   fruitless   looking   frugal   fruitful   fretful

4. illegal   ill   lawful   illicit   illegal   illness

5. loom   school   loom   loon   loan   look

6. oaken   oaken   type   oxen   oak   oakum

7. prick   prickly   medal   price   pick   prick

8. sample   noose   trample   sample   simple   ample

9. stave   starve   staves   staff   stave   perch

10. truant   truck   truant   ring   truculent   truce

11. arbor   scare   labor   arbor   ardor   arbiter

12. calamity   calcareous   calcite   disastrous   calculus   calamity

13. crash   crash   rash   crass   crater   smash

14. eldest   roost   elderly   oldest   eldest   elder

15. lovable   feasible   force   lovable   lovely   legible

16. obscure   cattle   cur   obscene   obscurity   obscure

17. printer   stark   prince   pint   printer   princely

18. sandy   sandal   sandy   sundry   task   sand

19. stem   stem   stern   stench   stencil   corset

20. tube   tubular   ebb   tube   tuck   tub

21. writhe   mate   whether   wither   with   writhe

22. immediate   immediate   occupancy   mediator   intermediate   immediately

23. fundamental   function   fundamental   prescription   mental   functional

24. efficient   posterior   efficient   proficient   efficacy   effigy

25. appreciation   apprentice   painstaking   appreciation   depreciation   appreciate

---

Time: 29 Sec.   RATE (from table on page 307):   R. 310

No. Correct: 23   COMPREHENSION (4% for each correct answer):   C. 92

I–12   EFFICIENCY (R × C):   E. 285

Record on Progress Chart on page 297

42

Exercise I–13

1. bawl   tour   bowl   bale   bald   bawl

2. chord   chord   foot   chore   choice   choral

3. denounce   announce   denounce   dense   punctual   denote

4. exploit   explicit   expect   sparse   exploit   exotic

5. groove   groove   groom   grove   root   salad

6. irrigate   irradiate   irritate   tragic   irrigate   obligate

7. mid   mild   vile   middle   mix   mid

8. pastry   paste   pastry   pantry   pastel   cord

9. shingle   shining   shingle   treaty   single   shingles

10. swim   taxi   swam   whim   swim   twin

11. variable   variable   varied   variance   variegated   messing

12. beaten   sweater   deaden   beater   mice   beaten

13. churl   church   more   churl   curdle   curl

14. deposit   despot   deposit   depot   withdraw   depose

15. extent   tent   extensive   intent   extent   opposite

16. itch   itch   rip   ache   scratch   etch

17. mild   supper   mold   mild   milk   mill

18. pattern   lantern   patty   patter   cushion   pattern

19. shorn   fork   short   shorn   shown   shun

20. vein   vain   vein   feign   veined   prose

21. wig   met   wag   wig   fig   fib

22. syndicate   syndicate   ringing   synthetic   symbol   mental

23. recognition   reception   reclamation   reckless   recognition   sanguinary

24. guarantee   warranty   guaranty   guardian   vicinity   guarantee

25. recapture   salutation   capture   recapture   recapitulate   rapture

---

Time_____Sec.   **RATE (from table on page 307):**   **R.** _____

No. Correct:_____   **COMPREHENSION (4% for each correct answer):**   **C.** _____

I–13   **EFFICIENCY (R ✕ C):**   **E.** _____

Record on Progress Chart on page 297

Exercise I-14

1. camera   cameo   camera   trust   camel   cam

2. creed   creed   creek   cried   creep   erase

3. elm   ton   elk   alms   emblem   elm

4. gad   gadfly   horse   gad   gadget   fad

5. lukewarm   lucrative   lukewarm   luckily   warm   vacancy

6. o'clock   since   ocean   occult   ooze   o'clock

7. product   product   vulgar   produce   prodigy   productive

8. satyr   satin   satisfy   satyr   satire   imply

9. stir   handle   stirrup   skin   stir   stare

10. turnip   turnpike   skip   turn   urn   turnip

11. arrogant   missing   arrogant   ignorant   arrow   arrogance

12. canned   canner   yacht   canned   cannon   canopy

13. criminal   crime   crimp   trucking   criminal   crimson

14. embody   embody   embellish   embattle   head   body

15. gallows   allows   gallows   gallon   gallop   truism

16. official   officiate   vicinity   officious   official   office

17. savory   serve   savor   crouch   savory   save

18. stork   full   stork   stark   store   tore

19. twill   aspic   twice   rill   twirl   twill

20. yoke   bore   yolk   yoke   woke   yogi

21. progressive   progressive   academical   program   aggressive   progress

22. luxuriant   screwing   luxury   sumptuous   luxurious   luxuriant

23. impossible   impose   finishing   impossible   improbable   probable

24. imperative   imperturbable   sticking   impertinent   imperative   imperfect

25. aristocratic   aristocratic   aristocracy   studiously   aristocrat   arithmetic

Time _____ Sec.   **RATE (from table on page 307):**   R. _____

No. Correct: _____   **COMPREHENSION (4% for each correct answer):**   C. _____

I–14   **EFFICIENCY (R × C):**   E. _____

Record on Progress Chart on page 297

Exercise I-15

1. bargain   bargain   sacking   margin   barge   bargainer

2. chest   quest   cheat   chest   chaste   slot

3. defy   deify   defied   deny   mild   defy

4. execute   executive   execute   occupant   excite   example

5. gravy   gravy   grow   gravity   grave   gravel

6. mention   mental   mansion   attention   mention   element

7. parch   parch   bib   porch   pouch   arch

8. ratify   rational   ratify   rectify   cart   railing

9. usurp   usher   bear   usury   usurp   us

10. bashful   bath   bashful   recount   baseball   basal

11. chill   chide   still   hill   magnify   chill

12. deliver   livery   signora   deliver   delirium   delay

13. mess   mull   table   mass   mess   message

14. readily   readiness   reading   salute   readily   ready

15. sheen   afraid   teen   shine   sheep   sheen

16. sweeper   sweeping   swim   sweeper   sweetly   treatise

17. vagabond   vagabond   thence   vagary   vagrant   vague

18. whilst   white   whittle   victim   whilst   while

19. intricate   phosphorus   intrigue   intricate   intrinsic   intimate

20. shapeless   shameless   happiness   quadrant   shiftless   shapeless

21. suspicious   roughness   suspension   suspicious   susceptible   suspicion

22. exhortation   exhortation   exhort   stronghold   exhilaration   exhibition

23. greenwood   tomahawk   greenback   greenhouse   reduced   greenwood

24. investment   inversion   investment   invention   invitation   vaccination

25. partaker   partition   partaker   particular   yearling   parted

---

Time_____Sec.   RATE (from table on page 307):   R. _____

No. Correct:_____   COMPREHENSION (4% for each correct answer):   C. _____

I-15   EFFICIENCY (R × C):   E. _____

Record on Progress Chart on page 297

Exercise I–16

1. ashore   fruit   shore   ashen   aside   ashore

2. caper   capes   near   caper   capital   caprice

3. crucify   crucify   crucible   cruise   dabble   crucifix

4. employ   employer   employ   capable   empower   employee

5. gas   gorge   gash   gasoline   gas   gasp

6. madman   madly   madness   dorsal   madame   madman

7. omen   omission   men   amen   omen   exit

8. scarlet   scarlet   scar   scarcity   scarcely   purple

9. ugly   win   fly   urge   glee   ugly

10. assent   assent   ascent   consent   assert   accede

11. carcass   dirge   canvass   confess   carcass   canvas

12. cube   cub   cubic   high   cube   tube

13. gem   germ   gem   gee   gin   force

14. string   strung   sting   coarse   string   ring

15. virtual   vital   virtual   eraser   virtuous   virulent

16. unceasing   uncertain   mechanize   increasing   cease   unceasing

17. property   frivolity   property   proper   prophet   propaganda

18. incense   incentive   incendiary   incense   license   courage

19. scientific   scientist   scientific   filler   science   terrific

20. magnify   sturdy   magnitude   magnificent   magnetic   magnify

21. encounter   encounter   encumber   counter   encourage   skirmish

22. prosperity   prospective   largeness   prosperity   prosperous   property

23. operation   operation   operator   observation   operate   inducement

24. incurable   curable   incumber   incurable   touring   incursion

25. strawberry   straw   blueberry   strawberry   raspberry   headstrong

---

Time 31 Sec.   RATE (from table on page 307):   R. 291

No. Correct: 21   COMPREHENSION (4% for each correct answer):   C. 84

I–16   EFFICIENCY (R X C):   E. 267

Record on Progress Chart on page 297

46

Exercise I-17

1. affront   affair   carding   affront   affect   front
2. certify   certify   risking   certain   certified   certificate
3. daybreak   daylight   daytime   schedule   break   daybreak
4. godlike   godlike   phrase   golden   godly   manlike
5. inquiry   inquisitor   inquiry   inquest   wailing   query
6. overseer   oversee   overseer   critic   over   overseas
7. quicken   question   battery   quickly   quick   quicken
8. reunion   review   fixing   reunite   union   reunion
9. deathbed   dearth   death   decadence   deathbed   deathless
10. mattock   haddock   mattress   buttocks   merry   mattock
11. conclude   include   conclusion   conclave   conclude   yearling
12. heroism   erosion   zealot   heroism   heroine   hero
13. playground   barometer   playing   playhouse   ground   playground
14. aggravate   aggravating   aggravate   wanderer   aggregate   grave
15. thriftless   thriftless   footlights   shiftless   thrift   thrive
16. murderous   vacantly   murky   murder   murderous   hideous
17. lamentation   legislation   lamenting   lamentation   undeveloped   lame
18. comprehend   comprehensive   tabernacle   hen   comprehend   compromise
19. unspeakable   doubtfully   unstable   speak   unspoiled   unspeakable
20. sepulcher   spectacle   sepulcher   entering   spectator   sepulchral
21. oxen   oxen   often   toxin   sown   box
22. inspector   instance   spectator   touring   inspector   inspire
23. chandelier   chant   chanticleer   chandelier   courtesy   chevalier
24. unpleasant   unpack   unpleasant   pleasant   unpaid   columnist
25. sensation   sensation   sensitive   sensual   busybody   compensation

Time_____Sec.	RATE (from table on page 307):	R. _____
No. Correct:_____	COMPREHENSION (4% for each correct answer):	C. _____
I–17	EFFICIENCY (R × C):	E. _____

Record on Progress Chart on page 297

Exercise I-18

1. carrion   carried   carrier   carriage   <u>carrion</u>   switch

2. engrave   <u>engrave</u>   engross   engraving   ruling   engage

3. coachman   mansion   coat   scarlet   <u>coachman</u>   man

4. orchard   <u>orchard</u>   orchestra   orchid   ordeal   pencil

5. prudent   prune   student   <u>prudence</u>   telephone   prudent

6. feature   creature   <u>feature</u>   feat   federal   academic

7. moisture   moist   mixture   <u>moisture</u>   peculiar   hoist

8. undergo   underground   false   underwent   <u>undergo</u>   undergone

9. sixpence   twopence   roofing   <u>sixpence</u>   sixteen   sextette

10. enormous   enough   enormity   immense   courage   <u>enormous</u>

11. tenement   tendency   sentiment   rudiment   <u>tenement</u>   extreme

12. manifest   manifold   manifesto   recorder   manipulate   <u>manifest</u>

13. scullion   stallion   <u>scullion</u>   meaning   scull   scuffle

14. perverse   <u>perverse</u>   perhaps   verse   pervert   rolling

15. skirmish   shrimp   skirt   rescue   <u>skirmish</u>   mission

16. accordingly   <u>accordingly</u>   cablegram   across   cross   accord

17. remainder   remain   <u>remainder</u>   extreme   rejoinder   schooling

18. perseverance   <u>perseverance</u>   pursue   persevere   ransoming   backwoods

19. undoubted   doubted   undo   undesirable   <u>undoubted</u>   prescribe

20. originate   oriental   crowning   origin   original   <u>originate</u>

21. inevitable   inequality   pensively   <u>inevitable</u>   ineffable   inexcusable

22. malicious   impromptu   malice   <u>malicious</u>   delicious   malignity

23. indignation   indignant   <u>indignation</u>   snatching   indigestion   indigenous

24. curiosity   currency   curio   pensively   <u>curiously</u>   curiosity

25. astronomy   astronomical   <u>astronomy</u>   astrology   noontide   astray

Time _33_ Sec.   RATE (from table on page 307):   R. _23_

No. Correct: _23_   COMPREHENSION (4% for each correct answer):   C. _92_

I–18   EFFICIENCY (R × C):   E. _241_

Record on Progress Chart on page 297

Exercise I–19

1. abandon   band   abuse   abandon   bandanna   backward

2. disperse   dispersion   disperse   dispel   identify   purse

3. mission   missive   permission   passion   sylvan   mission

4. silvery   silver   slavery   silvery   silvered   saunter

5. taxicab   cab   taxicab   toxin   ability   tropical

6. bluebell   blue   resting   bell   bluebell   blueberry

7. firmness   firmness   firm   first   foolishness   pacifism

8. laborer   excuse   laboratory   bore   laborer   labor

9. dictate   direct   detect   estate   roseate   dictate

10. perfume   perfume   refuse   perhaps   fuming   perfect

11. rejoice   quaint   rejoice   voice   join   revolve

12. thorough   finish   thought   thorough   though   borough

13. abominable   tabernacle   abandoned   abominable   fundamental   practically

14. adversity   adversity   adverse   folding   advisable   verse

15. financial   jealously   final   financial   facial   finance

16. watermelon   salutation   melon   waterfall   watermelon   water

17. responsible   responsive   quadrangle   response   sponsor   responsible

18. dissolution   soluble   dissuade   dissertation   occupancy   dissolution

19. compensate   comparison   compensate   compensation   necessary   pension

20. regardless   retard   regardless   homeless   relative   joyousness

21. resistance   resist   machination   resolute   assistance   resistance

22. mountaineer   maintain   kindergarten   mountain   mountaineer   mount

23. knighthood   knighthood   largeness   night   neighborhood   knight

24. clergyman   clergyman   candlelight   salesman   minister   accountant

25. commonwealth   common   commotion   hallucination   commonwealth   wealth

---

Time_____Sec.   RATE (from table on page 307):   R. _____

No. Correct:_____   COMPREHENSION (4% for each correct answer):   C. _____

I–19   EFFICIENCY (R × C):   E. _____

Record on Progress Chart on page 297

Exercise I-20

1. balance   balance   charge   balcony   balanced   lance

2. charity   chariot   cherish   charge   drift   charity

3. decisive   decision   decisive   exclude   declension   derisive

4. gradual   radiate   graduate   grad   invest   gradual

5. meantime   heading   meander   meanwhile   meantime   text

6. painter   painful   painter   headache   pointer   painted

7. raiment   railway   soldier   raiment   regiment   rainbow

8. janitor   janitor   jangle   jungle   sloppy   banister

9. verdict   convict   vindicative   predict   verdict   allow

10. bandage   occupant   band   bandanna   bandy   bandage

11. faithful   faithful   fitful   faithless   convince   fateful

12. insurance   insurance   insular   dressing   insure   insult

13. grandpa   grandma   grandpa   python   grandfather   father

14. servitude   service   servitude   servile   serve   vomiting

15. pancake   panacea   sturdy   pan   pancreas   pancake

16. uppermost   upper   insistence   uppermost   upraise   underneath

17. surgeon   surgery   surge   highland   surly   surgeon

18. witchcraft   witchery   feudalism   handicraft   witchcraft   craft

19. sideboard   sideways   headboard   sideboard   eighteen   boardwalk

20. vexation   sensation   vexation   fixation   vegetation   syllable

21. interchange   interchange   recharge   intercept   exchange   hydrophobia

22. destroyer   battleship   distraught   destine   destroyer   destroy

23. jeopardy   perfidy   jeopardize   leopard   jeopardy   schedule

24. examine   exaggerate   lobbying   examine   exasperate   example

25. everybody   everyone   frivolity   everybody   evermore   anybody

---

Time _____ Sec.

No. Correct: _____

I–20

RATE (from table on page 307):

COMPREHENSION (4% for each correct answer):

EFFICIENCY (R × C):

R. _____

C. _____

E. _____

Record on Progress Chart on page 297

SERIES II (ODD NUMBERS)

NO. 1	NO. 3	NO. 5	NO. 7	NO. 9
1. forehead	light	parched	trifle	crocodile
2. tease	support	inferior	obscure	stigma
3. bed	smell	hood	mark	devote
4. tranquillity	cupola	twist	port	salary
5. ice	fowl	economical	manservant	affection
6. sound	furnish	overlook	bent	lift
7. brisk	honor	prevent	rodents	discourse
8. dent	bare	goddess	dynamo	need
9. fine	cut	victim	remember	rule
10. tatter	wealthy	soothe	leg	danger
11. stick	ravage	song	vowed	vast
12. direction	slope	blemish	mist	sign
13. tired	stay	scribe	relieve	hum
14. mournful	degrade	stick	youthful	pretend
15. father	signal	scorch	yield	law
16. dash	postpone	bear	ball	hook
17. trip	avid	get	thigh	voice
18. score	anger	dress	costume	adorn
19. hotel	cage	chart	stately	power
20. powder	crazy	threat	enigmatic	form
21. heathen	ancient	pageant	drudge	verbal
22. craft	liable	headlong	penitence	bow
23. rare	scour	clean	criminal	pastoral
24. trap	dough	brace	seduction	chipmunk
25. dictator	daze	pure	eruption	shake

NO. 11	NO. 13	NO. 15	NO. 17	NO. 19
1. heard	shoeless	stir	terrify	indignantly
2. bovine	estimate	flower	benevolent	concerned
3. woman	cheat	truism	conclusion	convert
4. style	condone	distribute	forever	lasting
5. gaze	seriousness	pecuniary	mournful	cyclone
6. fever	drunk	weighty	killer	yet
7. limestone	intellectual	observe	recede	also
8. excursion	bundle	hill	hurtful	bias
9. clear	estimate	spoil	railroad	chickens
10. isolate	wise	oppose	subservient	litter
11. hidden	uncertainty	sully	replace	stainless
12. rude	escort	silent	rare	convey
13. nut	front	cascade	illiterate	feast
14. box	lift	rub	cutter	spine
15. limpidness	entrust	tuber	university	waterfall
16. mature	refuse	vicious	scholar	formal
17. starve	haze	serious	prolific	trap
18. shout	dully	liberty	sense	renounce
19. pitcher	infirm	throw	powerful	hellish
20. change	city	solitary	rural	stonework
21. endure	melancholy	incubator	region	disregard
22. ruin	taste	pretense	trellis	origin
23. pretense	soft	bone	trust	satisfy
24. distrust	tuft	ruler	fabric	stop
25. helpful	strength	diplomacy	distant	rational

317

SERIES III (ODD NUMBERS)

NO. 1

1. a precious stone
2. to say something
3. an opening for
4. divide evenly
5. quite happy
6. about medium
7. one fully grown
8. a violent wrong
9. to go ahead of
10. articulate sound
11. view critically
12. a rascal
13. rather meager
14. to lean down
15. to amuse
16. a big tree
17. for smelling
18. has mild temper
19. morning hymn
20. a search for game

NO. 3

1. physical vigor
2. even surface
3. scarcity of food
4. exhibiting envy
5. close at all times
6. to reveal openly
7. in great need
8. a cheerful person
9. true to life
10. a modest person
11. with promptness
12. quickness of action
13. lighter than water
14. made imperfectly
15. open to view
16. act of dominating
17. show preference
18. brought about by
19. to frighten suddenly
20. to set free

NO. 5

1. some incentive
2. to move ahead
3. man of decision
4. not using care
5. a sudden calamity
6. act of forgetting
7. the threshold
8. completely worthless
9. gain full meaning
10. no set price
11. show satisfaction
12. confirm the deed
13. to take turns
14. something odd
15. in all probability
16. on the offensive
17. make a thrust
18. a trivial matter
19. have no boundary
20. serve as a guide

NO. 7

1. a common junction
2. to bid farewell
3. eternal existence
4. act of liberation
5. keeping a secret
6. comes to an end
7. an exhibit of humor
8. in correct position
9. that which is beyond
10. being very busy
11. to fascinate
12. likely a quarrel
13. considerable amount
14. with promptness
15. regular procedure
16. a severe look
17. join in a group
18. absence of sound
19. honesty of mind
20. not completed

RATE TABLE FOR SERIES IV—SENTENCE MEANING

Look up your time (to the nearest 5 seconds) in Column I and read your rate in the Column under the appropriate exercise number. If your time is more or less than the limits of the table, or if you desire to compute your time more accurately to the exact second, divide the time (No. of seconds) into the "Division Constant" for that exercise.

Time	Exercise #1−6	Exercise #7−14	Exercise #15−20
# words	120	160	200
Division Constant	7200	9600	12,000
# seconds			
5	1440	1920	2400
10	720	960	1200
15	480	640	800
20	360	480	600
25	288	384	480
30	240	320	400
35	206	274	343
40	180	240	300
45	160	213	267
50	144	192	240
55	131	175	218
60	120	160	200
65	111	148	185
70	103	137	171
75	96	128	160
80	90	120	150
85	85	113	141
90	80	107	133
95	76	101	126
100	72	96	120
105	69	91	114
110	65	87	109
115	63	83	104
120	60	80	100
125	58	77	96
130	55	74	92
135	53	71	89
140	51	69	86
145	50	66	83
150	48	64	80
155	46	62	77
160	45	60	75
165	44	58	73
170	42	56	70
175	41	55	69

RATE TABLE FOR EXPLORATORY READING AND STUDY TYPE READING DRILLS
SERIES VI AND VII

Since all the exercises in Series VI and VII have been standardized to a length of 1350 words, rates for any of these exercises can be found by looking up the time in Column I of this table and reading the rate from Column II. Times are given at 5 second intervals. For an approximate time you may take the time figure nearest your actual time.

For any time figures beyond the limits of this table or between the intervals, the rate may be computed by dividing 81,000 by the time (*in seconds*).

I	II	I	II	I	II	I	II
5	16,200	105	771	305	266	505	160
6	13,500	110	736	310	261	510	159
7	11,571	115	704	315	257	515	157
8	10,125	120	675	320	253	520	156
9	9,000	125	648	325	249	525	154
10	8,100	130	623	330	245	530	153
11	7,333	135	600	335	242	535	151
12	6,750	140	579	340	238	540	150
13	6,231	145	559	345	235	545	149
14	5,786	150	540	350	231	550	147
15	5,400	155	523	355	228	555	146
16	5,063	160	506	360	225	560	145
17	4,765	165	491	365	222	565	143
18	4,500	170	476	370	219	570	142
19	4,263	175	463	375	216	575	141
20	4,050	180	450	380	213	580	140
21	3,857	185	438	385	210	585	138
22	3,667	190	426	390	208	590	137
23	3,522	195	415	395	205	595	136
24	3,375	200	405	400	203	600	135
25	3,240	205	395	405	200	605	134
26	3,116	210	386	410	198	610	133
27	3,000	215	377	415	195	615	132
28	2,893	220	368	420	193	620	131
29	2,793	225	360	425	191	625	130
30	2,700	230	352	430	188	630	129
35	2,314	235	345	435	186	635	128
40	2,025	240	338	440	184	640	127
45	1,800	245	331	445	182	645	126
50	1,620	250	324	450	180	650	125
55	1,473	255	318	455	178	655	124
60	1,350	260	312	460	176	660	123
65	1,246	265	306	465	174	665	122
70	1,157	270	300	470	172	670	121
75	1,080	275	295	475	171	675	120
80	1,012	280	289	480	169	680	119
85	953	285	284	485	167	685	118
90	900	290	279	490	165	690	117
95	853	295	275	495	164	695	117
100	810	300	270	500	162	700	116

RATE TABLES FOR SERIES V—IDEA READING DRILLS

Since all the exercises in this series have been standardized at 900 words, this table can be used for all 20 exercises. Look up your time (to the nearest second interval shown) in Column I and then read your rate from Column II. For an approximate rate, you may use the time figure nearest your actual time. For any time figures beyond the limits of this table, or between the intervals given, the actual rate may be computed by dividing 54,000 by the time *(in seconds)*.

I	II	I	II	I	II	I	II
5	10,800	45	1,200	205	263	405	133
6	9,000	46	1,173	210	257	410	131
7	7,710	47	1,149	215	251	415	130
8	6,750	48	1,125	220	245	420	129
9	6,000	49	1,102	225	240	425	127
10	5,400	50	1,080	230	235	430	125
11	4,909	51	1,059	235	230	435	124
12	4,500	52	1,038	240	225	440	123
13	4,153	53	1,019	245	220	445	121
14	3,857	54	1,000	250	216	450	120
15	3,600	55	982	255	212	455	119
16	3,375	60	900	260	208	460	118
17	3,176	65	831	265	204	465	116
18	3,000	70	771	270	200	470	115
19	2,842	75	720	275	196	475	114
20	2,700	80	675	280	192	480	113
21	2,571	85	635	285	189	485	111
22	2,454	90	600	290	186	490	110
23	2,348	95	568	295	183	495	109
24	2,250	100	540	300	180	500	108
25	2,160	105	514	305	177	505	107
26	2,077	110	491	310	174	510	106
27	2,000	115	469	315	171	515	105
28	1,929	120	450	320	169	520	104
29	1,862	125	432	325	166	525	103
30	1,800	130	415	330	163	530	102
31	1,742	135	400	335	161	535	101
32	1,688	140	386	340	159	540	100
33	1,636	145	372	345	156	545	99
34	1,588	150	360	350	154	550	98
35	1,543	155	349	355	152	555	97
36	1,500	160	338	360	150	560	96
37	1,460	165	327	365	148	565	96
38	1,421	170	318	370	146	570	95
39	1,385	175	309	375	144	575	94
40	1,350	180	300	380	142	580	93
41	1,317	185	292	385	140	585	92
42	1,286	190	284	390	138	590	91
43	1,256	195	277	395	136	595	91
44	1,227	200	270	400	135	600	90

RATE TABLE FOR SERIES III—PHRASE MEANING

Look up your time (to the nearest 5 seconds) in Column I and read your rate in the Column under the appropriate exercise number. If your time is more or less than the limits of the table, or if you desire to compute your time more accurately to the exact second, divide the time (No. of seconds) into the "Division Constant" for that exercise.

Time	Exercise #1-4	Exercise #5-8	Exercise #9-12	Exercise #13-16	Exercise #17-20
# words	300	350	400	500	600
Division Constant	18,000	21,000	24,000	30,000	36,000
# seconds					
5	3600	4200	4800	6000	7200
10	1800	2100	2400	3000	3600
15	1200	1400	1600	2000	2400
20	900	1050	1200	1500	1800
25	720	840	960	1200	1440
30	600	700	800	1000	1200
35	514	600	686	875	1029
40	456	525	600	750	900
45	400	467	533	667	800
50	360	420	480	600	720
55	327	382	436	545	655
60	300	350	400	500	600
65	277	323	369	462	554
70	257	300	343	429	514
75	240	280	320	400	480
80	225	263	300	375	450
85	212	247	282	353	424
90	200	233	267	333	400
95	189	221	253	316	379
100	180	210	240	300	360
105	171	200	229	286	343
110	164	191	218	273	327
115	157	183	209	261	313
120	150	175	200	256	300
125	144	168	192	240	288
130	138	162	185	231	277
135	133	156	178	222	267
140	129	150	171	214	257
145	124	145	166	207	248
150	120	140	160	200	240
155	116	135	155	194	232
160	113	131	150	188	225
165	109	127	145	182	218
170	106	124	141	176	212
175	103	120	137	171	206
180	100	117	133	167	200
185	97	114	130	162	195
190	95	111	126	158	189
195	92	108	123	154	185
200	90	105	120	150	180

Use for the word recognition drills and the word meaning drills.

Look up your time in Column I and read your rate in Column II.

I	II	I	II
1	9000	31	291
2	4500	32	281
3	3000	33	273
4	2250	34	265
5	1800	35	257
6	1500	36	250
7	1286	37	243
8	1125	38	237
9	1000	39	231
10	900	40	225
11	818	41	220
12	750	42	214
13	692	43	209
14	643	44	205
15	600	45	200
16	563	46	196
17	529	47	191
18	500	48	188
19	474	49	184
20	450	50	180
21	429	51	176
22	409	52	173
23	391	53	170
24	375	54	167
25	360	55	164
26	346	56	161
27	333	57	158
28	321	58	155
29	310	59	153
30	300	60	150

I	II	I	II	I	II
61	148	101	89	182-185	49
62	145	102	88	186-189	48
63	143	103-104	87	190-193	47
64	141	105	86	194-197	46
65	138	106	85	198-202	45
66	136	107	84	203-206	44
67	134	108-109	83	207-211	43
68	132	110	82	212-216	42
69	130	111	81	217-222	41
70	129	112-113	80	223-227	40
71	127	114	79	228-232	39
72	125	115-116	78	234-240	38
73	123	117	77	241-246	37
74	122	118-119	76	247-253	36
75	120	120	75	254-260	35
76	118	121-122	74	261-268	34
77	117	123-124	73	269-276	33
78	115	125	72	277-285	32
79	114	126-127	71	286-295	31
80	113	128-129	70	296-305	30
81	111	130-131	69	306-315	29
82	110	132-133	68	316-327	28
83	108	134-135	67	328-339	27
84	107	136-137	66	340-352	26
85	106	138-139	65	353-366	25
86	105	140-141	64	367-382	24
87	103	142-144	63	383-400	23
88	102	145-146	62	401-418	22
89	101	147-148	61	419-439	21
90	100	149-151	60	440-461	20
91	99	152-153	59	462-486	19
92	98	154-156	58	487-514	18
93	97	157-159	57	515-545	17
94	96	160-162	56	546-580	16
95	95	163-165	55	581-620	15
96	94	166-168	54	621-666	14
97	93	169-171	53	667-720	13
98	92	172-174	52	721-782	12
99	91	175-178	51	783-857	11
100	90	179-181	50	858-947	10

SERIES II
Word Meaning Exercises

Instructions

In these Series II exercises, the emphasis shifts to a rapid recognition of *meaning*. Here each key word is followed by five others, one of which means almost the same as the key word. This exercise is the first to give you practice in reading for meaning. Here you want to scan as rapidly as you can, looking for similar meanings.

The directions are the same as for the preceding exercise. Look at the key word in each line, and then find the one in the answers that has most nearly the same meaning. Underline or check that answer, and go on to each succeeding line as rapidly as possible. When you have finished, ask for your time, and look up your rate in the table on page 307. Use the keys on pages 317 and 325 to check your errors.

Find your number of errors and compute your comprehension by multiplying the number of correct answers by four (4). Compute your efficiency to the nearest whole number, and record scores on the Progress Chart on page 297.

Because these words are all among the 30,000 most frequently used words, you can use these exercises also as a check on your vocabulary. List all key words missed, all correct answers not underlined, and all words underlined in error on the vocabulary page; and look up their meaning. Try to study and to use these words until you have added them to your vocabulary.

These exercises begin on page 53; rate tables are on page 307; keys are on pages 317 and 325; progress charts, on page 297; vocabulary lists, on page 293.

Example

22. prefer		refer	preface	confer	peace	choose
23. dent	X	spent	bend	dens	split	dines
24. night	X	might	dark	nigh	blight	evil
25. film		haze	craze	limb ·	kiln	finest

Time 63 Sec.
No. Correct: 23
(Key on page 317)

RATE (from table on page 307):   R. 143
COMPREHENSION (4% for each correct answer) (4 × 23)   C. 92
EFFICIENCY (R × C): (143 × .92) = 131.56   E. 132

II–0   Words to be added to vocabulary list:

dent	night
split	dark
bend	blight

Suggestions

These exercises are much like the ones in the first series, but the same game does not apply because you have to know the *meaning* of the symbols in greater detail. Now you must recognize that symbols have various meanings and that your skill in playing the game depends on previous experience and knowledge.

Thinking about what you are doing is essential to success in these exercises, but to improve reading skills you must learn to think fast and effectively.

Many students waste time by doing unnecessary thinking that has no direct bearing on the rules of the game. Some dash off mentally in search of an answer without knowing what they are really looking for. Some become disturbed over the meaning of six

words when the instructions stress the importance of only *one* key word.

Again the logical thing to do is to concentrate on the *key* word before beginning the search for synonyms. Just studying its physical characteristics of size and shape is not appropriate this time though. You must add another dimension of meaning *to you*. If the key word has no meaning to you, there is no need to go on to the answer columns. You have found a word that you need to add to your vocabulary; and until you do, it has no value to you as a symbol or a tool. If the key word has no meaning to you, just check it as an error to add to your vocabulary list for further study, and move on quickly to the next line.

In most cases, the key word will have some meaning for you. It may have several meanings. You have to sort out the various meanings it might have and to project in your mind these various possibilities.

Armed with several possible synonyms, you are ready to scan the answer columns. You may recognize one of these synonyms immediately and be ready to go on to the next line. If you do not see any of them at once, you may need to go back to the key and think of other possible meanings. Again you may be faced with a new meaning for this word, which you will need to add to your vocabulary.

There is little reason for you to take each of the five choices in the answer column and think about each one intensively, however. In fact, you may never read some of these choices at all if you are able to identify quickly and confidently the match for the key word. If you know what you are looking for and then find it, you can stop and go on to the next line.

Do not be afraid of making errors. They are a natural part of the learning process. But each error can be a means of improving your understanding of the language and your reading skill. Look upon errors as a means of pinpointing ideas that need further study and application in your communicative skills.

Use your errors in this series as steps to learning. *Think* about the key words that bothered you, that you guessed at, and that you missed! All of these words in these exercises are common words in your native vocabulary. If you do not understand them, they may become barriers to effective communication.

This book is not intended as a workbook in vocabulary building, but there are many such publications available. Ask your teacher or your librarian to suggest good materials for vocabulary development. An analysis of errors made in these exercises might help to identify the kind of vocabulary help that you need most. Your directions suggest that for each word missed, you should add three words to your vocabulary check list.

But do not stop with just putting them on a list! Think about each one. Try to decide why you missed it. Review your earlier experiences with the word. Do you have any feelings about it? Have you avoided or resisted it for some reason? Do you really want to add it to your vocabulary?

Your vocabulary list can be a real help in specific vocabulary expansion, but it will require time and effort on your part to accomplish this. There are no magic tricks for sound vocabulary development, but these words will come up again in some unexpected time and place, and you will be more secure if you have mastered them.

Use your dictionary as a first step. Most of these words are in a standard college dictionary. If you do not have a copy of your own, you should get one, and you should use it regularly. If a word is not in your desk dictionary, go to the library and seek it out in the larger dictionary there.

Once you find it, look at all the possible meanings presented. You will probably find that your experience has exposed you to only a limited aspect of the total use of the word. Write down several of the synonyms of the word. Take notes on the basic definition and derivation of the word, and then consider the various extensions or modifications of the term.

Thinking about words is not enough. You need to use them in speech and writing to make them functional. Try using your newly found vocabulary in various ways.

Some people like to use library "cue cards" to help develop fluency with new words. Setting up the word on one side of a card and the definitions and synonyms on the back of the card provides a good practice card that can be carried in your pocket and used frequently until the word has become firmly set in your vocabulary.

Constructive thinking and planned vocabulary development can make reading more interesting and meaningful. Logical thinking on these exercises can help you set up goals in reading and become more selective in your skimming and scanning activities.

Developing skills in rapid recognition of similar ideas or recognition of new concepts will do much to help you become a more efficient reader and will save you many hours of time that you may now be spending on unnecessary reading.

Exercise II-1

1. brow   sow   forehead   now   bow   scow

2. bully   fully   pulley   gully   tulip   tease

3. cot   bed   rot   tot   bought   aught

4. ease   tranquillity   knees   difficulty   squeeze   sleep

5. freeze   lizard   job   ice   care   ire

6. noise   choice   mount   notice   source   sound

7. lively   lovely   brisk   liver   blithely   vile

8. notch   crotch   foam   gulch   dent   dotage

9. noble   head   bobble   fine   foal   hobo

10. rag   tatter   fag   tag   gag   bag

11. staff   raft   stick   laugh   quaff   show

12. trend   send   bend   tend   drench   direction

13. worn   born   sworn   mourn   tired   foreign

14. woeful   armful   mournful   artful   baleful   manful

15. dad   bad   cad   father   fad   gad

16. dart   dish   dash   disc   disk   cart

17. errand   trip   head   ferret   wand   tang

18. goal   foal   sole   soul   score   role

19. inn   fin   gin   hotel   skin   hinge

20. meal   feel   peal   peel   powder   seal

21. pagan   sage   fagot   patron   hag   heathen

22. raft   craft   draft   graft   abundance   aft

23. scant   rant   pant   rare   faint   banter

24. catch   match   adapt   crack   cattle   trap

25. tyrant   pirate   hydra   scour   dictator   dysentery

Time_____Sec.

No. Correct:_____
(key on page 317)

II–1

RATE (from table on page 307):

COMPREHENSION (4% for each correct answer):

EFFICIENCY (R × C):

R. _____

C. _____

E. _____

Record on Progress Chart on page 297

Exercise II–2

1. bed   fed   red   head   cot   bred

2. civil   devil   shrivel   swivel   level   polite

3. arise   mount   size   maize   nice   barge

4. fable   falsehood   table   stable   staple   gable

5. gum   bum   resin   sum   dumb   hum

6. jam   dam   damn   lamb   predicament   ham

7. mind   find   rind   memory   hind   bind

8. camel   dromedary   cancel   sample   trample   dame

9. weigh   weird   well   measure   sleigh   mellow

10. shroud   conceal   loud   crowd   bowed   proud

11. taint   contaminate   faint   quaint   saint   paint

12. verdant   aunt   veranda   pant   green   shank

13. amateur   sure   pure   cure   dabbler   lure

14. bribe   tribe   scribe   price   five   live

15. cone   phone   lone   roan   bone   shell

16. dogma   hog   bog   cog   doctrine   foggy

17. flit   hit   dart   kit   slit   bit

18. lucky   duchy   touchy   much   fudge   fortunate

19. lease   please   grease   contract   tease   peace

20. neat   heat   tidy   peat   beat   seat

21. pace   taste   gait   case   haste   chase

22. reside   beside   aside   decide   tide   dwell

23. slap   cap   map   slop   straight   pat

24. occur   fur   befall   sir   stir   burden

25. wallet   pallet   mallet   pocketbook   palate   palette

Time____Sec.

No. Correct:____
(key on page 325)

II–2

RATE (from table on page 307):

COMPREHENSION (4% for each correct answer):

EFFICIENCY (R × C):

R. 95

C. 65

E. 55

Record on Progress Chart on page 297

Exercise II-3

1. airy	light	dairy	diary	fairy	lira
2. back	lack	support	tack	sack	sac
3. stink	blink	smell	think	wink	summer
4. dome	cupola	come	foam	home	comb
5. turkey	turnkey	murky	slack	fowl	furl
6. yield	furnish	wield	sealed	reeled	field
7. laurel	honor	quarrel	sorrel	moral	haul
8. naked	sake	slaked	bare	baked	caked
9. plow	allow	plot	cut	how	slow
10. rich	pitch	wealthy	ditch	bit	wick
11. sack	back	ravage	lack	hack	rack
12. tilt	slope	lilt	silt	kilt	gilt
13. wait	fate	date	rate	stay	saith
14. abase	erase	degrade	taste	case	dash
15. beckon	reckon	second	hexagon	seclude	signal
16. defer	confer	refer	postpone	affair	peevish
17. eager	beaver	meager	lever	agent	avid
18. fury	flurry	jury	brewery	aura	anger
19. pen	few	threw	hew	cage	cession
20. mad	bad	bade	crazy	fad	cad
21. olden	golden	stolen	den	ancient	alter
22. prone	phone	drone	gnome	liable	lone
23. rub	dub	tub	scour	tug	sub
24. paste	waste	waist	taste	dastardly	dough
25. trance	dance	enhance	glance	branch	daze

Time_____Sec.   RATE (from table on page 307):   R. _____

No. Correct:_____   COMPREHENSION (4% for each correct answer):   C. _____
(key on page 317)

II-3   EFFICIENCY (R × C):   E. _____

Record on Progress Chart on page 297

Exercise II-4

1. glance   lance   manse   glimpse   dance   enhance

2. quack   lack   rack   charlatan   back   cub

3. colony   call   loan   loon   sol   settlement

4. stile   style   file   aisle   (steps)   child

5. fetter   (hamper)   letter   debtor   hew   better

6. yell   yes   cry   bell   knock   yellow

7. keen   seen   sharp   bean   dean   lean

8. mop   pop   (sop)   cop   pout   flop

9. turban   (hat)   turbine   suburban   fat   ban

10. rack   backward   tack   jack   (afflict)   repeat

11. slayer   thrill   player   clay   killer   kitty

12. thaw   melt   haw   jaw   law   maw

13. wage   salary   adage   beige   cage   sage

14. amity   calamity   aim   absurdity   (friendship)   family

15. baby   fade   child   bake   lady   dabble

16. brief   grief   belief   sheaf   fief   short

17. dump   jump   drop   bump   chunk   dumb

18. fought   sought   aught   struggled   fault   ought

19. drill   fill   grill   bill   pill   (practice)

20. lit   ignited   fit   bit   kit   itch

21. horn   born   corn   mourn   morn   cornucopia

22. prefer   close   preamble   creditor   confer   choose

23. retort   resort   deport   (answer)   fort   aerial

24. spent   rent   exhausted   bent   cant   dent

25. tight   light   fight   taut   sight   night

Time _82_ Sec.

No. Correct: _17_
(key on page 325)

II–4

RATE (from table on page 307):

COMPREHENSION (4% for each correct answer):

EFFICIENCY (R X C):

R. _110_

C. _68_

E. _____

Record on Progress Chart on page 297

Exercise II–5

57

1. torrid   parched   horrid   florid   morbid   porridge

2. bad   wad   tadpole   had   gad   inferior

3. cowl   hoof   hook   hood   hoop   howl

4. wind   mind   bind   kind   twist   tinder

5. frugal   nominal   struggle   stubble   economical   frustrate

6. ignore   floor   door   overlook   roar   ogle

7. avert   assert   pervert   convert   prevent   habit

8. nymph   goddess   lymph   symphony   limp   gym

9. prey   pray   victim   fray   day   voyage

10. salve   save   have   soothe   halve   delve

11. carol   barrel   song   oral   laurel   sorrel

12. taint   faint   feint   blemish   rant   bailiff

13. writer   fighter   scribe   girder   lighter   stab

14. bat   rat   mat   fat   sat   stick

15. char   mar   far   car   scorch   share

16. endure   cure   bear   sure   pure   benumb

17. gain   gabardine   gander   gauge   get   gentlefolk

18. gown   frown   down   dress   abound   round

19. map   nap   chart   lap   cap   gap

20. menace   dentist   finesse   apprentice   tenacious   threat

21. parade   pageant   tirade   scourge   braid   chard

22. rash   headlong   rare   flash   crash   hash

23. scour   power   dower   tower   courage   clean

24. strut   nut   glut   stray   brutal   brace

25. undefiled   pure   mild   wild   tile   pun

Time_____Sec.   RATE (from table on page 307):   R. _____

No. Correct:_____   COMPREHENSION (4% for each correct answer):   C. _____
(key on page 317)

II–5   EFFICIENCY (R × C):   E. _____

Record on Progress Chart on page 297

Exercise II-6

1. baker   cook   shaper   shaker   rook   took

2. abode   mode   rode   node   pod   house

3. salmon   fish   lemon   salad   balsam   fallow

4. trough   rough   gutter   sought   soft   golf

5. flare   dare   care   bare   blare   blaze

6. herb   grass   barb   bard   bird   garb

7. grade   fade   raid   cage   level   staid

8. insult   affront   cult   result   stint   basal

9. plait   plate   late   rate   place   braid

10. meant   rent   intended   sent   dead   fed

11. sob   weep   rob   mob   rod   bob

12. thrifty   rift   cliff   whiff   shriek   saving

13. weed   seed   ready   really   plant   udder

14. appeal   seal   prayer   real   apple   peel

15. bust   rust   chest   must   cuss   dust

16. cove   rove   dove   hove   inlet   ion

17. edit   reveal   eddy   merit   rain   revise

18. frown   down   scowl   town   sound   sown

19. affirm   blurt   worm   assert   squirm   skirt

20. luck   due   duck   duct   chance   cluck

21. occidental   accidental   rental   western   wobble   sleep

22. proceed   procure   recess   advance   desist   arrow

23. role   roll   dole   foal   part   pole

24. spell   hell   well   relieve   bell   relish

25. torn   thorn   worn   ripped   born   rope

Time 60 Sec.   RATE (from table on page 307):   R. 150

No. Correct: 20   COMPREHENSION (4% for each correct answer):   C. 80
(key on page 325)

II-6   EFFICIENCY (R × C):   E. _____

Record on Progress Chart on page 297

Exercise II-7

1. bauble   bubble   stubble   trouble   gobble   trifle

2. blur   whir   stir   our   obscure   endure

3. denote   remote   rote   vote   quote   mark

4. haven   port   raven   leaven   sort   sport

5. groom   manservant   room   broom   croon   doom

6. knelt   felt   belt   cent   centaur   bent

7. mice   rodents   rice   lice   trice   ice

8. motor   mortar   tartar   carter   snow   dynamo

9. recall   stall   remember   fall   ball   gall

10. shin   bin   fin   gin   leg   grin

11. sworn   vowed   worn   horn   corn   born

12. vapor   taper   mist   caper   maker   favor

13. allay   alley   alloy   ally   relieve   lay

14. boyish   fish   dish   coy   youthful   toy

15. comply   yield   die   dye   fry   cry

16. pill   fill   ball   pall   rill   fall

17. flank   rank   rancor   thigh   hank   thank

18. habit   bit   rabbit   costume   fit   hit

19. regal   legal   lately   beagle   stately   fate

20. mystic   ritual   mist   stick   physic   enigmatic

21. plod   clog   clod   drudge   pod   fog

22. repentance   pence   penitence   pants   stance   lance

23. sinner   system   sister   criminal   dinner   hysterics

24. temptation   location   generation   seduction   inspiration   nation

25. volcano   canoe   eruption   volt   cameo   canto

Time_____Sec.   **RATE (from table on page 307):**   R. _____

No. Correct:_____   **COMPREHENSION (4% for each correct answer):**   C. _____
(key on page 317)

II-7   **EFFICIENCY (R × C):**   E. _____

Record on Progress Chart on page 297

Exercise II-8

1. shrill   keel   keep   still   <u>frill</u>   (keen)

2. clergy   energy   clerk   allegory   clear   <u>ministers</u>

3. devour   <u>eat</u>   devout   devote   devoid   sour

4. vacant   dummy   cant   <u>empty</u>   rant   pant

5. ham   <u>pork</u>   cam   dam   jam   lamb

6. jingle   tingle   <u>jangle</u>   simple   jungle   single

7. misplace   space   lace   <u>lose</u>   race   trace

8. pepsin   resin   lessen   <u>medicine</u>   lesson   tension

9. regarding   retarding   guarding   lauding   harboring   <u>concerning</u>

10. silverware   fair   fare   sliver   bare   <u>cutlery</u>

11. taxation   ration   relation   <u>levy</u>   sensation   station

12. vile   <u>disgusting</u>   file   tile   pile   guile

13. ammonia   pneumonia   phone   bony   bone   <u>gas</u>

14. broom   loom   <u>brush</u>   doom   boom   tomb

15. conquer   her   stir   <u>vanquish</u>   whir   burr

16. dove   love   (pigeon)   done   rove   move

17. folder   moulder   <u>holder</u>   solder   bolder   boulder

18. hock   dock   <u>lock</u>   rock   (pawn)   sock

19. lesser   <u>smaller</u>   dresser   fester   tester   jester

20. net   bet   <u>met</u>   yet   (trap)   new

21. port   sort   <u>harbor</u>   sport   wart   snort

22. rage   sage   <u>fury</u>   page   cage   beige

23. sly   (furtive)   cry   high   rye   try

24. thicken   thicket   sicken   chicken   <u>coagulate</u>   lichen

25. waste   taste   washer   waist   <u>squander</u>   haste

Time _65_ Sec.

No. Correct: _21_
(key on page 325)

II-8

RATE (from table on page 307):

COMPREHENSION (4% for each correct answer):

EFFICIENCY (R × C):

R. _138_

C. _84_

E. _116_

138
84
552
1048

Record on Progress Chart on page 297

Exercise II-9

1. alligator   agitator   fascinate   crocodile   mediator   cliff

2. brand   stigma   sand   grand   hand   land

3. consecrate   devote   secret   freight   locate   donate

4. wage   stage   wager   salary   dot   aged

5. fondness   soundness   largess   affection   afoot   jolt

6. hoist   foil   ghost   moist   lift   loiter

7. lecture   picture   fracture   conjecture   discourse   decry

8. necessity   perplexity   need   city   complexity   nationality

9. policy   police   rule   docility   folly   mollify

10. risk   danger   frisk   brisk   wrist   disk

11. spacious   vast   gracious   specimen   narcissus   vacillate

12. token   broken   spoken   army   sojourn   sign

13. buzz   fist   his   jazz   hum   hive

14. assume   room   pretend   doom   broom   psyche

15. statute   statue   flute   random   law   stature

16. crook   brook   book   shook   look   hook

17. emit   permit   remit   submit   venal   voice

18. garnish   varnish   vanish   adorn   vanquish   aroma

19. ability   adversity   legality   power   illiterate   pillory

20. make   male   form   drake   slake   fake

21. oral   sorrel   floral   moral   morale   verbal

22. prow   sow   now   how   row   bow

23. rural   pastoral   fuel   full   gruel   purchase

24. squirrel   quarrel   chipmunk   whirl   furl   square

25. tremble   thimble   assemble   shake   bungle   semblance

---

Time_____ Sec.

No. Correct:_____
(key on page 317)

II–9

RATE (from table on page 307):

COMPREHENSION (4% for each correct answer):

EFFICIENCY (R × C):

R. _____

C. _____

E. _____

Record on Progress Chart on page 297

Exercise II-10

1. ashamed   claimed   <u>humiliated</u>   named   tamed   rash

2. cape   shape   <u>headland</u>   grape   tape   hap

3. crow   row   stow   <u>boast</u>   bow   dough

4. empire   spire   inquire   <u>dominion</u>   bier   dire

5. refute   <u>deny</u>   refund   lute   rest   male

6. incapable   traceable   escapade   <u>enable</u>   enchant   incompetent

7. madden   sadden   dampen   gladden   each   <u>enrage</u>

8. stubborn   stung   <u>inflexible</u>   subsequent   escape   ice

9. property   proper   density   prosperity   <u>possessions</u>   prophetic

10. scarf   <u>muffler</u>   scoff   slough   harp   maze

11. straw   draw   thaw   paw   <u>stalks</u>   ball

12. udder   rudder   <u>shudder</u>   utter   buddy   bag

13. zoological   tropical   biological   <u>topic</u>   surgical   book

14. behold   fold   gold   see   sold   ~~bold~~

15. chisel   <u>sizzle</u>   cheat   drizzle   gizzard   look

16. deity   lemon   preen   <u>divinity</u>   screen   problem

17. expedite   <u>hasten</u>   extradition   condition   tradition   hexagon

18. grocer   dealer   poacher   <u>roach</u>   brooch   loafer

19. idea   for   <u>flee</u>   concept   sea   cease

20. mince   since   quince   <u>rinse</u>   hash   hind

21. peal   <u>resound</u>   deal   feel   fealty   real

22. recovery   delivery   <u>covertly</u>   mockery   recalcitrant   restoration

23. semblance   blanch   <u>dance</u>   arrogance   form   female

24. suitor   neuter   looter   cuter   <u>wooer</u>   wry

25. unnecessary   commissary   crazy   <u>student</u>   ugh   useless

---

Time 37 **Sec.**

No. Correct: 16 (key on page 325)

RATE (from table on page 307):

COMPREHENSION (4% for each correct answer):

II-10   **EFFICIENCY (R × C):**

R. 158

C. 64

E. 101

Record on Progress Chart on page 297

Exercise II–11

1. audible   beard   trouble   word   stirrup   heard

2. cattle   tatter   fetter   tattle   bovine   wine

3. dame   woman   wane   same   fame   luminary

4. fashion   style   file   fasten   false   snub

5. glare   flare   gaze   graze   raze   raise

6. inflammation   fervor   information   cleaver   fever   flyer

7. marble   marvel   warble   limestone   tomb   larceny

8. outing   boating   doubting   flouting   excursion   eunuch

9. purify   clear   purchase   hear   testify   rectify

10. seclude   prelude   conclude   isolate   date   fate

11. subterranean   suburb   years   hidden   bidden   terrace

12. ungracious   dude   rude   lavish   hood   food

13. acorn   nut   ache   adorn   hut   torn

14. bin   came   sin   win   box   name

15. clearness   friendliness   closeness   cleverness   limpidness   lesson

16. develop   envelop   mature   gallop   manure   lope

17. famish   furnish   furnace   carve   family   starve

18. halloo   shout   bald   look   small   too

19. jug   tug   rug   pitcher   slug   richer

20. modify   solidify   grange   change   defy   deify

21. perpetuate   perpetrate   endure   penetrate   sure   awake

22. relic   frolic   soon   clip   croon   ruin

23. sham   slam   room   tan   doom   pretense

24. suspect   respect   distrust   must   rust   trust

25. useful   awful   baleful   capsule   doubtful   helpful

Time_____Sec.   **RATE (from table on page 307):**   R. _____

No. Correct:_____   **COMPREHENSION (4% for each correct answer):**   C. _____
(key on page 317)

II–11   **EFFICIENCY (R × C):**   E. _____

Record on Progress Chart on page 297

Exercise II–12

1. abash   sash   flash   crash   ado   embarrass

2. certificate   testimony   alimony   antimony   delicate   triple

3. dawn   faun   fawn   sand   morn   lawn

4. eruption   corruption   temptation   outbreak   snake   rake

5. gall   fall   stall   cemetery   prosperity   temerity

6. inquire   require   ask   task   fire   fin

7. massive   lassie   flighty   tryout   dread   weighty

8. overseas   oversee   mourn   torn   foreign   tree

9. quest   adventure   best   west   test   wrest

10. senior   elder   junior   juniper   fell   enigma

11. sulphur   suffer   element   cement   sultry   couple

12. pity   flighty   conversation   conversion   compassion   city

13. admit   admire   deceive   receive   calendar   purple

14. bled   fed   lead   read   injured   extinguish

15. club   rub   stud   staff   raft   dub

16. dig   rig   fig   delve   shelve   big

17. fawn   yawn   cringe   spawn   singe   ridge

18. hardware   tools   swear   fool   tear   rare

19. kennel   fennel   stutter   mutter   house   flannel

20. moonbeam   seam   ray   day   deem   say

21. phase   aspic   raze   aspect   beige   craze

22. supervisor   sector   reflector   nectar   factor   director

23. shown   threw   through   mew   guest   manifested

24. swollen   pollen   expanded   expend   boll   strand

25. vanquish   conquer   varnish   swish   vanish   query

Time ____ Sec.

No. Correct: ____
(key on page 325)

II–12

RATE (from table on page 307):

COMPREHENSION (4% for each correct answer):

EFFICIENCY (R × C):

R. ____

C. ____

E. ____

Record on Progress Chart on page 297

64

Exercise II-13

1. barefoot   bear   shoeless   root   shoot   care

2. calculate   regulate   coagulate   rate   estimate   nominate

3. defraud   laud   hod   paw   caw   cheat

4. excuse   refuse   refuge   condone   amuse   news

5. gravity   laxity   morality   seriousness   anxiety   casualty

6. intoxicated   liberated   sated   concentrated   waited   drunk

7. mental   rental   dental   gentle   intellectual   lent

8. parcel   marcel   bundle   cell   par   trundle

9. rate   date   hate   gate   estimate   fate

10. sage   wage   rage   age   beige   wise

11. suspicion   uncertainty   position   transition   condition   resolution

12. usher   rush   user   she   escort   bush

13. ahead   dead   front   red   said   bed

14. boost   roost   boot   lift   coot   door

15. commit   comment   entrust   comma   comet   come

16. disobey   refuse   hay   hey   bay   say

17. film   haze   craze   helm   limb   kiln

18. heavily   heave   vile   heat   dully   villa

19. lame   dame   infirm   blame   came   fame

20. municipal   principal   munificent   city   cipher   cider

21. plaintive   plainness   captive   plane   deceptive   melancholy

22. relish   lucky   dish   taste   fish   rely

23. silken   soft   welcome   sill   ken   bill

24. tassel   tuft   rascal   vessel   pass   castle

25. vigor   victor   snicker   liquor   stricter   strength

Time_____Sec.

No. Correct:_____
(key on page 317)

II–13

RATE (from table on page 307):

COMPREHENSION (4% for each correct answer):

EFFICIENCY (R × C):

R. _____

C. _____

E. _____

Record on Progress Chart on page 297

Exercise II–14

1. abundant   bun   <u>plentiful</u>   abuse   abusive   dance

2. bet   met   beta   <u>stake</u>   belt   get

3. coach   coachman   ~~teach~~   broach   roach   loath

4. diligent   <u>industrious</u>   dilute   dilate   dilemma   lie

5. feather   father   farther   gather   weather   <u>plume</u>

6. hark   harp   <u>listen</u>   ark   dark   bark

7. juicy   interest   loosely   ruthless   <u>succulent</u>   ruefully

8. moisten   mosaic   <u>wet</u>   moss   choice   ten

9. persecutor   persevere   perspective   <u>tormentor</u>   persist   person

10. rely   <u>depend</u>   deny   lye   relax   relay

11. situation   <u>site</u>   sit   abbreviation   caption   carnation

12. tenderness   tend   actress   <u>compassion</u>   alertness   aloofness

13. vacillate   late   vacancy   ventilate   violate   oscillate

14. alter   altar   <u>alto</u>   change   halter   falter

15. bride   bridge   ride   pride   <u>wife</u>   side

16. consul   official   <u>consult</u>   council   counsel   con

17. dresser   presser   <u>bureau</u>   dress   lesser   jester

18. foresee   <u>anticipate</u>   fore   see   forearm   forest

19. hopeless   hop   hostess   <u>bottomless</u>   useless   boundless

20. likely   lively   literally   like   lightly   <u>probable</u>

21. nag   fag   bag   keg   <u>torment</u>   gag

22. pouch   couch   pout   pour   <u>bag</u>   vouch

23. resign   design   sign   resin   repine   <u>quit</u>

24. soak   sock   joke   broke   oak   <u>drench</u>

25. threw   drew   flue   <u>flung</u>   shrew   brew

Time _84_ Sec.

No. Correct: _21_
(key on page 325)

II–14

RATE (from table on page 307):   R. _107_

COMPREHENSION (4% for each correct answer):   C. _84_

EFFICIENCY (R × C):   _107_ _84_   E. _90%_

Record on Progress Chart on page 297

Exercise II–15

1. ado   flew   grew   sad   stir   cur

2. bloom   strew   flower   stew   few   flew

3. commonplace   comma   comment   truism   tomato   place

4. dispense   distribute   expanse   expense   tribute   defense

5. financial   romance   pinafore   pecuniary   dance   monkey

6. heavy   levee   weighty   levy   weave   bevy

7. watch   leap   over   observe   patch   wall

8. mound   hill   round   sound   around   hound

9. pillage   oil   pill   village   sill   spoil

10. resist   oppose   desist   sister   fist   pose

11. smear   pulley   fear   beer   rear   sully

12. tacit   silent   facet   tact   tack   sac

13. waterfall   cascade   water   cater   fall   waterfowl

14. anoint   appoint   annoy   ran   rub   sleep

15. bulb   tub   bulk   bull   flower   tuber

16. corrupt   interrupt   truck   rupture   vicious   connect

17. earnest   furnace   ear   serious   sardine   nest

18. freedom   dome   free   kingdom   liberty   leeward

19. hurl   curl   throw   swirl   twirl   turkey

20. lone   bone   solitary   stone   son   condone

21. nursery   hospital   nurse   purse   incubator   ivory

22. pretext   prefix   apology   text   prepaid   pretense

23. rib   bib   crib   fib   tiara   bone

24. sovereign   souvenir   ruler   rein   rain   dominant

25. tact   fact   back   diplomacy   rapt   lack

Time_____Sec.

No. Correct:_____
(key on page 317)

II–15

RATE (from table on page 307):

COMPREHENSION (4% for each correct answer):

EFFICIENCY (R × C):

R. _____

C. _____

E. _____

Record on Progress Chart on page 297

Exercise II–16

1. astray   bay   bayou   day   wrong   wasteful

2. carrier   bearer   terrier   ferry   lexicon   barrier

3. cure   lure   heal   pure   sure   hurdle

4. engineer   guide   sheer   fear   rear   gnaw

5. cloth   there   close   back   crepe   century

6. indignant   filament   angry   pant   rant   andirons

7. malice   spite   talon   louse   shallow   callous

8. orbit   ascribe   fit   hit   path   prayer

9. prudence   prune   wisdom   fence   ascent   wrung

10. safe   secure   waft   missive   saber   salutary

11. stuck   adhered   luck   truck   rude   attune

12. underfoot   undertook   route   below   root   boar

13. absurd   work   foolish   heard   lurid   fabricate

14. beset   debt   let   kept   perplex   session

15. circumference   conference   inference   tense   piratical   perimeter

16. describe   date   rate   fate   relate   rescue

17. earn   burn   ear   learn   garnet   get

18. gulf   rough   chasm   golf   charm   fluff

19. jade   fire   raid   jewel   fade   tadpole

20. mishap   nap   tap   mist   aisle   accident

21. pent   spend   rent   confined   sent   cent

22. refusal   trial   file   denial   filial   defunct

23. server   soothe   lever   weaver   howsoever   tray

24. wise   shrew   show   shrewd   shrank   shred

25. untouched   unhappy   untie   flush   couch   unaffected

Time _46_ Sec.

No. Correct: _15_
(key on page 325)

II–16

RATE (from table on page 307):   R. _____

COMPREHENSION (4% for each correct answer):   C. _____

EFFICIENCY (R × C):   E. _____

Record on Progress Chart on page 297

Exercise II–17

1. affright   terrify   alight   align   alike   taffeta

2. charitable   mesa   variable   benevolent   cant   rant

3. decision   revision   temptation   terror   incision   conclusion

4. evermore   forever   swore   tore   sever   boar

5. lamentable   tableau   table   mournful   men   mama

6. murderer   killer   mud   shudder   death   sturdy

7. retreat   react   readjust   recede   reappear   defeat

8. painful   hurtful   armful   baleful   careful   deceitful

9. railway   rail   railroad   railing   doorway   highway

10. servile   revile   subservient   defile   violent   revelry

11. supplant   haunt   case   race   replace   daunt

12. unusual   hair   fair   rare   snare   air

13. ignorant   ignore   finger   illiterate   rant   significant

14. chopper   hopper   cutter   robber   stopper   copper

15. college   colleague   ledge   league   university   varsity

16. disciple   tipple   ripple   molar   scholar   cider

17. fertile   specific   pacific   tile   ferment   prolific

18. explanation   excavation   relation   donation   sense   constitution

19. irresistible   irresponsible   digest   combustible   powerful   iridescent

20. pastoral   moral   sorrel   floral   choral   rural

21. district   restrict   construct   stricken   disc   region

22. lattice   trellis   lettuce   radish   cabbage   latter

23. believe   deceive   trust   receive   conceive   relieve

24. taffeta   sordid   fete   staff   fact   fabric

25. faraway   sway   distant   stay   tray   quay

Time_____Sec.	RATE (from table on page 307):	R. _____
No. Correct:_____ (key on page 317)	COMPREHENSION (4% for each correct answer):	C. _____
II–17	EFFICIENCY (R × C):	E. _____

Record on Progress Chart on page 297

Exercise II–18

1. ambiguous   antipathy   hurt   obscure   pinch   omelet

2. convene   concave   conceal   assemble   concede   sonorous

3. contemplate   con   consider   conclusive   plate   contempt

4. housework   household   homemaking   horse   homelike   homemade

5. forfeiture   fortune   forefather   feather   penalty   pore

6. nostril   nosegay   trill   fill   nose   trail

7. lettuce   vegetable   terrace   fruit   certify   date

8. neutrality   frugality   lake   rocky   immunity   grey

9. bearable   quarterly   notable   relax   tolerable   tortoise

10. romantic   gigantic   fanciful   frantic   you   save

11. somebody   somber   someday   pomegranate   person   dome

12. respect   depreciate   help   reciprocate   epoch   esteem

13. efficiency   competency   leniency   regent   frog   cedar

14. lookout   flout   watch   doubt   mount   woodland

15. statute   statue   stature   law   match   latch

16. cupboard   closet   headboard   cupola   rubber   clad

17. deceive   receive   beguile   perceive   rod   because

18. eventual   evenly   effectual   fact   fennel   final

19. indictment   foment   indicate   statement   torment   sincerity

20. instructor   factor   adapt   teacher   toy   rector

21. outcast   outbreak   mast   last   duteous   degraded

22. purchaser   pursuer   purser   chase   burden   buyer

23. compound   unite   ponder   pound   around   competition

24. stately   grand   lately   greatly   slightly   quietly

25. disturbance   turbid   turbine   cistern   ran   confusion

---

Time 52 Sec.   **RATE (from table on page 307):**   R. _____

No. Correct: 17   **COMPREHENSION (4% for each correct answer):**   C. _____
(key on page 325)

II–18   **EFFICIENCY (R X C):**   E. _____

Record on Progress Chart on page 297

Exercise II-19

1. angrily   inwardly   silly   indignantly   candidly   fully

2. anxious   noxious   concerned   gracious   rapacious   canyon

3. convince   quince   convert   fence   rinse   onward

4. durable   curate   insure   lasting   fable   lurch

5. hurricane   bean   flurry   cyclone   sour   curriculum

6. however   yet   bower   sour   never   youthful

7. likewise   also   bait   dike   size   bill

8. prejudice   reproduce   bias   fudge   juice   breezy

9. poultry   chickens   sully   paltry   motley   courtly

10. rubbish   publish   pugilist   litter   furious   lubber

11. spotless   seedless   senseless   shameless   stainless   shapeless

12. transfer   convey   defer   confer   refer   gopher

13. banquet   feast   croquet   shut   quit   fang

14. backbone   tone   telephone   phone   sack   spine

15. cataract   contract   waterfall   catarrh   fact   watch

16. ceremonial   testimonial   crane   money   formal   ferment

17. ensnare   ensue   ensure   pare   trap   tart

18. abandon   band   ranch   renounce   don   bank

19. infernal   thermal   hellish   internal   vernal   hermit

20. masonry   fashion   ration   occasion   sash   stonework

21. overlook   book   cook   rover   disregard   dove

22. birthplace   birth   earth   place   dearth   origin

23. satiate   retaliate   prelate   nominate   gather   satisfy

24. discontinue   disc   disk   con   stop   sister

25. philosophical   philanthropy   rhapsody   abdominal   beneficial   rational

---

Time_____Sec.   **RATE (from table on page 307):**   R. _____

No. Correct:_____   **COMPREHENSION (4% for each correct answer):**   C. _____
(key on page 317)

II-19   **EFFICIENCY (R × C):**   E. _____

Record on Progress Chart on page 297

Exercise II-20

1. desirous   rouse   covetous   liars   cypress   iris

2. peasant   rustic   pheasant   resent   sent   scant

3. credulous   duly   louse   credit   greed   naive

4. redbreast   quest   west   wrest   robin   best

5. gabardine   grenadier   sardine   cloth   grandee   cabin

6. impenetrable   abominable   bachelor   inscrutable   baronial   imaginable

7. highness   elevation   fineness   lightness   sickness   weakness

8. thankful   healthful   grateful   uneventful   vengeful   wakeful

9. produce   process   reduce   conduit   manufacture   modulus

10. satisfy   multiply   petrify   deny   gratify   gather

11. confess   dress   fuss   acknowledge   rest   anywhere

12. floor   mooring   base   booing   doing   cornice

13. highway   day   high   say   road   bay

14. calamity   disaster   salad   credulity   forcibly   formality

15. chemistry   chemise   history   science   dentistry   shelves

16. creator   theater   crater   meditate   producer   preacher

17. exchange   range   flange   trade   derange   text

18. gratitude   thankfulness   servitude   multitude   food   trash

19. interview   consultation   made   one   twinkle   toes

20. impartial   imperial   marshal   martial   farthing   fair

21. sportsman   worst   hunter   abortive   dart   horse

22. rebuild   skilled   filled   trilled   meat   mend

23. sadness   gladness   confess   redress   daddy   depression

24. subsist   resist   exist   consist   desist   eulogy

25. everywhere   mountainous   tree   fuss   obey   omnipresent

---

Time_____Sec.   **RATE (from table on page 307):**   R. _____

No. Correct:_____   **COMPREHENSION (4% for each correct answer):**   C. _____
(key on page 325)

II–20   **EFFICIENCY (R × C):**   E. _____

Record on Progress Chart on page 297

SERIES III
Phase Meaning Exercises

Instructions

In these Series III exercises, the emphasis on meaning is extended from words to phrases. They also should help to increase your eye span as you are to try to grasp the meaning of each phrase at a single glance. Do not read them word for word; treat each group of words as a unit of meaning. Each of the phrases is set off by spaces to allow you to concentrate on group meaning with a single eye fixation.

Look at the key phrase, and think about its meaning. Concentrate on the ideas you associate with this phrase. Then glance at the phrases that follow until you find one that means approximately the same as the key phrase. Try to shift rhythmically from each phrase to the next until you find the right one.

Mark this correct answer by underlining or checking it, and go on to the next line. As soon as you have finished the last line, ask for your time and look up your rate in the table on page 309. Use the keys on page 318 or page 326 to check your errors. Compute comprehension and efficiency scores as indicated in the scoring directions, and record your rate and efficiency on the Progress Chart on page 297.

Here again the key words in a phrase are a measure of your vocabulary. Take the key words from any phrases you miss, and list them in your vocabulary list for further study.

These exercises begin on page 75: rate tables are on page 309; progress charts on page 297. Keys are on pages 318 and 326.

Example

17. to acquit	to assemble one part of	to set free	likely to to stop doing
18. about dawn	fun to see break of day	to account for	over and done power to
19. with promptness	without delay larger task	all included	in lieu of too many of
20. mountain top X	pine forest vacation time	highest peak	highly active now ended

Time 70 Sec.   RATE (from table on page 309):   R. 257

No. Correct: 19   COMPREHENSION (5% for each correct answer): (5 × 19)   C. 95

(key on page 318)

III–0   EFFICIENCY (R × C): (257 × .95) = 244.15   E. 244

Suggestions

These exercises should provide you with the greatest challenge and the greatest satisfaction of any of those you have done thus far. Here the game of reading becomes more complex. Rate of eye movement, increased eye span, and mental processing of verbal symbols become interinvolved; and you should begin to see your first real indication of *seeking the ideas behind the words*.

Here you should try to free yourself from the compulsion of word-by-word reading and to see that many words are more meaningful in groups than they are alone. You need to focus on the *phrase* as the unit of meaning and to learn to recognize such blocks of words as meaningful blocks in vocabulary development. As you learn to think in phrases, you will find it much easier to increase your eye span as well.

The first phrase is still the key unit to think

about and to be sure you understand. From it you must organize your ideas and goals so that you know what you are looking for as you move to the answer block of phrases.

One of the major features of this series is the emphasis on increasing your eye span. From beginning to end, the phrases become progressively longer. If you can increase your eye span enough to continue to read all phrases in a single eye fixation, you should achieve real carry-over value to your other reading activities.

You may find that when one phrase is located immediately below another, you can scan them both in one glance, thus increasing your vertical eye span as well as your horizontal eye span.

In the latter part of this series, phrases are arranged in a vertical order. Here the ideas are more important than the specific words; and you should practice vertical movements of your eyes, focusing on the center of the line and trying to expand your eye span enough to get meaning from the whole line at one glance. Such skills are very helpful in newspaper and news magazine reading for new ideas and current information.

Practice with the vertically organized materials shifts your emphasis on key materials from the first to the top position; and you can see how headlines, headings, and lead questions are designed to help focus your thinking on theme ideas in preparation for the materials that follow.

Vertical skimming and scanning techniques become more important as you consider this type of reading. Some individuals begin to develop a vertical eye span that enables them to perceive and transmit to the brain larger units of verbal symbols.

This series of exercises offers you the opportunity to experiment with a variety of adjustments in your eye span. Feel free to try out various ways of looking at these exercises to find ways that are easiest and most effective for you. You may be surprised to find that your brain is much more efficient than you thought in being able to handle larger blocks of verbal symbols.

This series of exercises should also provide a real challenge to your reading and thinking skills. Here you should begin to see the first real evidence of significant increase in rate of reading, but at the same time you should begin to appreciate the depth of meaning behind various word combinations. Quick thinking and sensitivity to a breadth of meaning variations become essential aspects of good reading skills.

Taking time to think about key ideas and to anticipate possible answers will make your reading much more interesting and should enable you to get a great deal more done in less time than before.

Exercise III-1

1. diamond ring   in these days   an average   a precious stone
     short period   is obvious

2. spoken word   to say something   will provide   be used to
     against him   full extent

3. a passageway   little less than   practical way   to all
     an opening for   perhaps this

4. share equally   that reason   divide evenly   almost here
     with those men   have their

5. very joyous   is taken   never again   other hand
     quite happy   may compensate for

6. in the middle   judgment of   such as   about medium
     as assumed by   plan to go

7. a mature person   one fully grown   is merely   benefit all
     away from   to wait long

8. an outrage   another day   plan to go   so you can
     does not require   a violent wrong

9. to precede   college life   to go ahead of   affect all
     to believe   not in here

10. human speech   make adjustment   may record   too loud
     articulate sound   not yet heard

11. to inspect   same always   likely to   view critically
     it is also   tend to do

12. a scamp   a rascal   fine person   looks ahead
     can be expected to   always able to

13. not very full   to ignore   of the group   have said
     decline to state   rather meager

14. to droop over   may sound   to lean down   are near here
     near the top   to be seen by

15. to play   which occur often   are used by   these words
     rates low   to amuse

16. large plant   so that he   might be   a big tree
     green grass   under no conditions

17. nose of a man   for smelling   such terms as   can define as
     you can make   does not imply

18. a meek person   along with her   wanted to go   has some kind
     may be ahead   has mild temper

19. church song   to be given   morning hymn   one can go
     many more that   not wish to

20. act of hunting   free time   never will go   to enjoy life
     lead to   a search for game

Time_____Sec.   **RATE (from table on page 309):**   R. _____

No. Correct:_____   **COMPREHENSION (5% for each correct answer):**   C. _____
(key on page 318)

III–1   **EFFICIENCY (R X C):**   E. _____

Exercise III-2

1. to remember   set it up   to enjoy life   to recognize again
        might lead again   can be

2. pure gold   is equal to   worth more   living alone
        has shown to be   precious metal

3. bright luster   can read by   great care of   to play as
        a high polish   it may happen

4. drain off   to empty out   be considered   perhaps others do
        in this sense   what is this

5. an opinion   the use of   a belief held   state support of
        because of   good life

6. a short novel   to advance   of the new   prose fiction
        to put into   need for more

7. rather narrow   the result of   more than ever   other means than this
        of little breadth   too active

8. a member of   in time of   to expend   the story of
        in every way   to belong to

9. without limits   infinite in size   his limited views   new order of
        most of us   subject to

10. act as host   best way   entertains another   for that
         his school   let that do

11. the ground   surface of earth   can be seen   the four levels
         all above   blue sky

12. to jab   about half of   to poke something   on each day
         to increase some   method of

13. given freedom   to obtain all   as with   made independent of
         as with him   be sure to

14. end hostilities   we profess   it appears   he said
         to make peace   their names

15. omit something   present time   until later   is made
         public life   leave it out

16. a noble person   possessing dignity   the work of   was able to
         was urgently   his own

17. large monster   way of   an enormous animal   its cause
         the facts   was absent

18. hold court   last year   come down from   administer justice
         be said   make wise

19. be inaccurate   should be   it also   lack of
         not correct   without loss of

20. hopeful person   he argued   the needs of   stand upon
         to guide   one who expects

Time _49_ Sec. _19_   RATE (from table on page 309):   R. _368_

No. Correct: _19_   COMPREHENSION (5% for each correct answer): _368_   C. _95_

(key on page 326)

III–2   EFFICIENCY (R × C):   _368_ / _95_   E. _____

Record on Progress Chart on page 297

Exercise III–3

1. sign of force — physical vigor / he grows up — to say so — for those / afraid of war

2. looks flat — can develop / their jobs stop — even surface — very rarely / no one could

3. sign of famine — in the period / they are — fine school — scarcity of food / near to home

4. showing spite — was reached / exhibiting envy — low point of — could be / in an age

5. always near — high rent / rural area — the future — has also been / close at all times

6. to expose — to reveal openly / along the way — to describe as — leave alone / return to

7. is desperate — not knowing / buying in — in great need — look for work / showing off

8. of good humor — design for / at work — can often be — a cheerful person / take more

9. in reality — true to life / method of work — may assume — in each class / of this type

10. a shy fellow — on the surface / in conflict — a new home — to build / a modest person

11. without delay — to forget / less than his — after these — other times / with promptness

12. act of haste — we learn / be a factor in — the sense — quickness of action / four days

13. will float — miles away / a real income — the point — higher rates / lighter than water

14. marked faulty — no ambition / made imperfectly — cited as — has become great / the rest

15. to be exposed — open to view / to increase — due to this — arise from / for the aged

16. ruling over — for reasons / can afford now — act of dominating — coming of age / upper limit

17. being partial — the ideal of / more alike — in which — show preference / as defined by

18. as a result of — in the future / too soon after — to report — believe in / brought about by

19. to startle — as a sign / to frighten suddenly — for many days — to do with / to search for

20. to acquit — to assemble / likely to — to set free — certain cue / one part of it

---

Time _____ Sec. RATE (from table on page 309): R. _____

No. Correct: _____ COMPREHENSION (5% for each correct answer): C. _____
(key on page 318)

III–3 EFFICIENCY (R X C): E. _____

Record on Progress Chart on page 297

Exercise III-4

1. proper place   be sold at   because of   correct position
     one year   an election day

2. tame horse   gentle animal   to do better   this age group
     in a box   a few years

3. a gentle slope   useful to   a sort of   a hot day
     a gradual decline   instead of him

4. to grow small   to control   diminish in size   they give
     led by you   no one can

5. ample food   began in   few if any   a long look
     to do good   abundant harvest

6. to be confused   child's life   to consider   be flustered
     is well to   must not be

7. standing erect   upright position   to walk to   over the top
     first period   has called

8. very durable   they are   the source   a large part
     to be stable   for peace only

9. being drowsy   as well as   rather sleepy   part of this
     term used   said that

10. to be desolate   first day   his life is   sort of damp
     to revert   ruinous condition

11. be delinquent   in spite of   which are   neglect of duty
     strong arm methods   goes on

12. to groan   expressive of pain   a form of   pay for all
     the desire for   any later

13. a fixed limit   the center of   may lead   for less
     are some more   marked boundary

14. cease to exist   two weeks   to annihilate   to a degree
     so often   the behavior pattern

15. present time   number of   at one place   more usual
     this very instant   this is not

16. trudge about   our purpose   by himself   ramble along
     as a whole   is easier to

17. chief concern   most valuable part   to assert   in some
     new plan of action   are able

18. without grace   under the   to serve fish   made upon
     being clumsy   value to us

19. to break down   to secrete   to collapse   most basic part
     on the stage   is obvious

20. make difficult   as fast as   who can be   the content of
     calls for   to complicate

Time 57 Sec.   **RATE (from table on page 309):**   R. 325

No. Correct:_____
(key on page 326)   **COMPREHENSION (5% for each correct answer):**   C. _____

III-4   **EFFICIENCY (R × C):**   E. _____

Record on Progress Chart on page 297

Exercise III–5

1. prompts an action   go beyond it   more to be done   some incentive
in some form   possible to define

2. a forward step   brought to light   seldom mention   the rank order
will be found here   to move ahead

3. on being decisive   pride and joy   in some cases   from the rest
man of decision   give us the word

4. a careless mistake   not using care   when he comes   to leave home
number of men   of this group

5. a catastrophe   can set up   a sudden calamity   to represent all
a passing phase   all afraid to

6. unable to recall   to indicate   the cause of   act of forgetting
it is possible to   of modern life

7. beginning point   real danger here   go to college   among this group
a little older   the threshold

8. of no value   of all sorts   will have less   to earn part
completely worthless   may be presented

9. to understand   gain full meaning   to be desired   an expert in
in social events   for that reason

10. no fixed value   which relates to   no set price   they can help
have been listening   be alert to

11. great enjoyment   show satisfaction   to think so   the time being
to talk about him   to come down

12. to verify the act   comes to mind   confirm the deed   of this nature
an end result   well known

13. to alternate   we talk about   tentative period   to take turns
perhaps in a sense   complex part of

14. rather peculiar   taken for granted   too high   upon the basis
on the party line   something odd

15. most likely   when they agree   at the end of   lags far behind
in all probability   become more fixed

16. making attack   on the offensive   provide for   for some reason
also appear to be   final answer

17. drive with force   on this point   make a thrust   less selective
a better risk   by such action

18. little importance   in this process   often possible   a trivial matter
study made by him   in any aspect

19. being unlimited   almost half of   the greater part   he should help
can best be   have no boundary

20. pattern to go by   need to know   the third session   back them up
serve as a guide   did not know about

Time_____Sec.   **RATE (from table on page 309):**   R. _____

No. Correct:_____
(key on page 318)   **COMPREHENSION (5% for each correct answer):**   C. _____

III–5   **EFFICIENCY (R × C):**   E. _____

Record on Progress Chart on page 297

Exercise III–6

1. rushing for help — be taken as / hurrying for aid — has been paid — tends to change in this area

2. almost as simple — keep in mind / rate as superior — nearly as easy — high level of / legion of others

3. more than enough — the next series on the test — he may not — in their review / more than needed

4. in minute amount — very small quantity / below average — to possess manly — exist among / who rates low

5. either of the two — may accept this / fortunate enough — there are two — one or the other / in a study

6. a colossal mistake — as a starting point / a great error — in the light — later than / as a sort of

7. it became obvious — may be assumed / a state of health — plain to see — in terms of / a clear example

8. not concerned with — the most interested man / not interested in — to predict what — what things / the most effective

9. shameful action — scandalous conduct / in the session — would not accept — less accurate / new to them

10. on the contrary — loss to himself / grain of salt — more and more — just the opposite / try to classify

11. from the origin — as an agency / at the beginning — provides a chance — the influence of / are held to

12. a small fragment — no matter how / to make sure — a surviving part — an excuse for / to feel superior

13. being transparent — whole new area / to be fewer — a small number — they may turn / obviously clear

14. break of day — about dawn / by the same token — it is interesting — the power to / called to account

15. guilty of crime — advantage of / is usually bound — it may appear — he who is a criminal / low nor high

16. to strongly desire — can be aided / craving something — some new ones — may thus help / be more able

17. willing to serve — may be overt / there is trouble — offer your service — may observe / an effort to

18. keeping clear of — described as / what extent — not at exactly — just before the / avoiding something

19. true to history — being historical / do occur together — the progress of — has failed to / does not deny

20. of a lazy nature — who are already / average age of — in summing up — dislike to work / years earlier

Time __ Sec.

No. Correct:_____
(key on page 326)

III–6

RATE (from table on page 309):

COMPREHENSION (5% for each correct answer):

EFFICIENCY (R × C):

R. _____

C. _____

E. _____

Record on Progress Chart on page 297

Exercise III-7

1. place of union — to bring out | a study of | a common junction
   a broad interest | | for college life

2. a parting wish — to bid farewell | within the law | eager to protect
   he can learn | | the advice is

3. an endless time — no matter how | may only be | give everything
   on the side | | eternal existence

4. to set free — for their money | act of liberation | has to talk
   to the contrary | | no one expects

5. being confidential — in the night | little interest | without him
   keeping a secret | | a message from

6. that which ceases — we are here | would not hurt | comes to an end
   just as it was | | in the capacity

7. display of wit — an exhibit of humor | to state this | in any type
   it is difficult | | aid in general

8. appropriately placed — in the office | major cause of | this is done
   what he knew | | in correct position

9. out of reach — not even if | that which is beyond | the form of
   the passing of | | is not clear

10. full of activity — there may be | only a step | has the best
    being very busy | | the same was true

11. hold spellbound — best interest of | all but one | to fascinate
    point of view | | much depends upon

12. an angry dispute — likely a quarrel | sets of forms | were not used
    another type of | | one item of

13. great quantity — who will fail | some phases of | of the function
    considerable amount | | the purpose of

14. without delay — all are omitted | with promptness | all too many
    the larger task | | there is much

15. general routing — to build up | from the office | be extended to
    regular procedure | | first of all

16. threatening aspect — the latter plan | be given first | a severe look
    does not require | | will secure

17. unite in a body — join in a group | a lag from | tend to avoid
    of the present day | | the reason why

18. state of silence — basic to all | does not mean | any other kind
    for other forms | | absence of sound

19. being sincere — may be both | honesty of mind | the fault of
    have claim to it | | learns most from

20. roughly sketched — a correlate of | no small part | some part of
    not completed | | some are operated

Time_____Sec.

No. Correct:_____
(key on page 318)

III-7

RATE (from table on page 309): R. _____

COMPREHENSION (5% for each correct answer): C. _____

EFFICIENCY (R × C): E. _____

Record on Progress Chart on page 297

Exercise III-8

1. promoted in rank — but hardly more / any given day — be wise to — may suggest / rising in power

2. should be granted — working hard / to describe — should be allowed — barely escaped / to leave alone

3. concerning truth — in assuming / according to facts — as late as — as most likely / is far from home

4. to do away with — to be elected / held until notice — allowed to search — to dispose of / died instantly

5. achieve the summit — to reach the peak / to avoid going — must fall back — able to go / not innate

6. produced by means of — all has been / it may be true — trying to climb — always able to / brought about by

7. ready to proceed — is confronted / not the thing — prepared to go on — in this case / tend to do

8. all by oneself — are all obvious / exclusive of others — will refuse to — he is afraid / to participate in

9. lull in activity — they may be / to do something well — how to play — not very busy / as is usual

10. act of slaying — death by violence / is crucial to — if he has — habit of refusing / who reads poorly

11. worthy of respect — what to expect / in some places — it may be — so far as / decent in character

12. without a spot — may differ from / the most part — free from reproach — high level / so much more

13. hold in position — most sinister man / keep from falling — not in accord — has stopped / annoyed to find

14. a loud clamor — may be made to / could be observed — a decided drop — a great outcry / the effect of

15. something vital — very necessary / which was done — in low esteem — the bottom of / the only solace

16. over fatigued — in the future / not so clear — happens often — very fact of / completely exhausted

17. mountain lodge — social dancing / the other end of — place for vacations — counter to / were less active

18. a prompt person — most crucial / one who is punctual — an area in which — in our culture / turn the dial

19. brave person — little relation to / same classroom as — be helpful — a motive for / one who is courageous

20. broken to bits — shattered to pieces / does not support — in all events — show as great / are found to

---

Time 49 Sec.

No. Correct: 18
(key on page 326)

III-8

RATE (from table on page 309):

COMPREHENSION (5% for each correct answer):

EFFICIENCY (R X C):

R. 341

C. 9

E. 347

Record on Progress Chart on page 297

82

Exercise III-9

1. jumble things up   to conclude by saying   pave the way to   to mix confusedly   an opportunity for   invite your attention to

2. mark of distinction   to be outstanding   remains to be done   a major obstacle   some of these issued   need for a system

3. a time of crisis   can be relied upon   awarded to each   free to choose   a decisive moment   cost of providing information

4. an abundant supply   the lack of time   more than is needed   a large section   one school of thought   to synthesize methods

5. contrary to reason   an emergency situation   will profit   the required ability   result of experience   thought to be absurd

6. very appropriate   be allowed to participate   will not remain   especially suitable   in order to learn   in cooperation with

7. the extent of space   capacity of anything   gaining more   an adequate answer   a disturbing failure   covering all phases

8. grasp the meaning of   on a large scale   to approve   able to speak clearly   to comprehend   in relation to the city

9. an acquired habit   secret sign   usual way of doing something   return in the fall   the greater interest   to organize

10. place of residence   to be washed away   which seemed to him   the other   to remove from sight   where one lives

11. lowest in a rank   a word of caution   held responsible   the last in the series   marked by failure   process of defining

12. that which confines   boundary line   no right to expect   in other instances   to gain prestige   for what he plans to do

13. indicative of grief   kinds of pressure   not too subtle   the first activity   a sound like a moan   conferred with the group

14. picture of a landscape   cannot be disrupted   a scenic painting   standard practice   deserves mention   the final word

15. state of privacy   a joint responsibility   a kind of service   usually small   person being referred   not in public nature

16. to make a recess in   will want to know   for his own needs   to set back   a simple question   an explanation

17. living a lonely life   a solitary existence   a small group   a type of program   at a casual level   to destroy the function of

18. furnish with a subsidy   achieve the goal   tend to disappear   to express oneself   provide financial aid   a nursery school

19. neat in appearance   an appropriate suggestion   a tidy person   a separate volume   center of it   examine the situation

20. display of kindness   the rapid growth of   best way out   few specific changes   a sense of balance   an act of good will

---

Time_____Sec.   RATE (from table on page 309):   R. _____

No. Correct:_____
(key on page 318)   COMPREHENSION (5% for each correct answer):   C. _____

III–9   EFFICIENCY (R × C):   E. _____

Record on Progress Chart on page 297

Exercise III-10

1. forced to pay a fine — punishment for an offense / remains to be done / to be commended / level of skill / the basic terms used

2. be granted admittance — avoid the difficulty / used for centuries / no one can doubt / an act of entering / a thing observed

3. a definite difference — really consistent / in only one situation / sort of estimate / method of improving / in complete contrast

4. act of condemning — an economic necessity / not a part of / to pronounce guilty / to be stressed / obtaining accurate data

5. make more difficult — universally accepted / to complicate matters / a radical change / relationship between / one point of view

6. an innocent person — free from blame / to be arranged / one of the essentials / to fill in a gap / very accurately described

7. to hurl into space — of the plan / of special importance / degree of freedom / to throw with violence / some previous prejudice

8. henceforth from now — the same problem / the valid use of / a number of ideas / with the real issue / from this time forward

9. looked upon as an enemy — are less expensive / should be made / a military foe / an estimated budget / type of floor covering

10. cease from being — the important ingredient / to come to an end / the rate of speed / the principal reason / after much searching

11. to shape by cutting — words of wisdom / after much searching / kind of a tree / the art of carving / taking over too much

12. a flat-bottomed boat — the immediate circle / meet the test / a large river barge / to discover when / certain satisfactions

13. an object of dislike — beyond the bounds / to have an aversion to / to get pleasure from / be supported by / motivated by love

14. admittance to a hearing — to be part of an audience / with wear and tear / may be acute / contacts in business / a new example

15. belonging to antiquity — feeling of hostility / a staff member / to help others / anything very old / time before midnight

16. gruff in appearance — a dominant factor / rough in countenance / to stop growing / varying needs of pupils / be initiated at

17. a friendly greeting — an ancient landscape / the new building / father and son / a losing battle / pleasant salutation

18. the angry canine — one mad dog / not to be seen / to go forward / misunderstood husband / a disgusted feline

19. move forward in haste — at one time / likely to wander / to rush someplace / would be favorable / superior to long periods

20. secure from danger — found to promote / particularly effective / to retard forgetting / forced to check / to be in a safe place

---

Time ___ Sec.

No. Correct: ___
(key on page 326)

III–10

RATE (from table on page 309):

COMPREHENSION (5% for each correct answer):

EFFICIENCY (R × C):

R. _____

C. _____

E. _____

Record on Progress Chart on page 297

Exercise III–11

Directions: In the following exercises, the answers appear in a vertical column beneath the key phrase. Read the key phrase, and then let your eyes drop, trying to keep them centered on the line and trying to grasp the meaning of each phrase by a single glance. Place a check mark beside the phrase most nearly the same as the key.

1. a craving for water
   field of endeavor
   not willingly change
   a feeling of thirst
   not to be disturbed
   must guard against

2. rather indefinite
   regarding the other
   to know something
   ability to exist
   not certain to occur
   resolution of conflict

3. execute the commands
   discuss the alternatives
   a source book of
   dispense with it
   dealing with students
   to be obedient

4. something in the future
   that which is to come
   to take the raps
   a sense of resentment
   a complex program
   may come from

5. a boisterous laugh
   result may decrease
   showing hilarity
   excellent argument for
   not easy to accept
   have more control

6. exemption from work
   some simple rules
   from the office
   an acquired holiday
   a direct outgrowth of
   trustees of human values

7. guilty of crime
   cross section of society
   a parallel effort of
   to help answer
   one who is a criminal
   a chain of events

8. to vanish in thin air
   by this time
   born of a need
   too many people
   to be defensive against
   pass quickly from sight

9. fitting and proper
   to be in right accord
   our greatest fault
   apt to respond
   the latter part of
   on the way toward

10. on his own accord
    might be applied to
    of his own free will
    was addressed to
    more obvious signs
    our basic insecurity

11. making a selection
    stating our strengths
    in a rough way
    choosing from several
    reactions of others
    much more to be said

12. causing to assemble
    much to learn
    because of long life
    for what they are
    to come together
    as a young profession

13. plainness in manner
    beneath the surface
    suffer a kind of
    most other fields
    from exterior behavior
    simplicity of style

14. not completed in detail
    roughly sketched
    with whom we deal
    often accused of
    will readily recognize
    may be expressed

15. considerable strength
    from time to time
    state of being strong
    one of the solutions
    a couple of hours
    the human factor

16. only a glimpse
    a big boon for
    no particular merit
    source of irritation
    a short hurried view
    give every indication

17. that which is unique
    become less concerned
    it is essential
    only one of a kind
    jammed with affairs
    to appear at ease

18. different from usual
    everything possible
    of the group
    reason why
    the largest amount of
    changed in appearance

19. cease from motion
    to stand still
    thoughtful interest in
    act of coming to
    in one common connection
    we cannot assume

20. sign of gratitude
    for all that happens
    to be thankful
    never seem to feel
    a very perplexing thing
    the liability of

Time_____Sec. RATE (from table on page 309): R. _____

No. Correct:_____ COMPREHENSION (5% for each correct answer): C. _____
(key on page 318)

III–11 EFFICIENCY (R × C): E. _____

Record on Progress Chart on page 297

Exercise III-12

1. entitled to reverence
   should be an aid
   a key phrase
   visualized form
   distraction to thinking
   consecrated as sacred

2. to commit treason
   level of popularity
   betray a trust
   the same experiment
   to leave school
   be allowed to decide

3. a wrong statement
   it should always be
   in the environment
   much of the work
   not according to facts
   content of a book

4. the lowest point
   bottom of the scale
   respect for
   cannot be helpful
   contribute to misunderstanding
   given careful attention

5. an act of exercising
   newly decorated
   operate effectively
   training for an event
   not a valid one
   economical manner

6. in terms of largeness
   more beautiful than
   form of publicity
   to make contacts
   very good reason
   that which is immense

7. to impart knowledge
   lowered into the sea
   an act of teaching
   simply lay limp
   love the out-of-doors
   did not appear

8. act of justifying
   state of excitement
   await the results
   to get an education
   prove to be right
   the village school

9. set form of procedure
   an orderly arrangement
   in a distant city
   across the fields
   ask his advice
   the day before

10. a division of the year
    a closely knit group
    corn in the fields
    one of the seasons
    a short period
    under no obligation

11. article of furniture
    a table in a room
    time to study
    in order to present
    conscious effort to look
    train of thought

12. state of being near
    recreation is fun
    a sense of humor
    in a close-by vicinity
    give the keynote address
    it is apparent

13. an affirmative reply
    concerning the role
    to change human nature
    prone to limit
    structure of society
    to answer yes

14. be in opposition to
    to enhance the quality
    to be against
    groping for words
    be frightened by
    bit of conversation

15. a gallant person
    assigned to work
    during slack period
    more natural light
    one noble in spirit
    easily identified

16. state of inattention
    lack of attention
    usually enough
    type of position
    something hard to believe
    near the state line

17. the inside of anything
    pleasant experience
    in the home
    that which is interior
    a great honor
    compelled to study

18. keep possession of
    a brave life
    born in slavery
    good deal of expense
    to live in a small town
    retain ownership of

19. to make an offer
    almost immediately
    to present for acceptance
    almost like a dwarf
    a great name
    to show skill

20. hesitant to answer
    not at all pleased
    soon to be at home
    an immediate appeal
    to pause undecidedly
    type of occupation

Time ____ Sec.

No. Correct: ____
(key on page 326)

III-12

RATE (from table on page 309):

COMPREHENSION (5% for each correct answer):

EFFICIENCY (R × C):

R. _____

C. _____

E. _____

Exercise III–13

1.   related to the newspaper

      a thirst for great fame
      a working compromise
      associated with the press
      dependence upon authority
      emphasis upon scholarship

2.   the general run of things

      a withdrawal from life
      a method of study
      the force of the spoken word
      to be determined about
      usual course of events

3.   quality of being sensitive

      wrote for publication
      learned men of the past
      very sensible activity
      capacity of receiving impressions
      the unlimited activity of

4.   a very robust person

      a comparison of translations
      an ideal preparation for
      to be greatly praised
      to study mathematics
      one who displays strength

5.   a person who is altruistic

      cultivation of the body
      the development of good citizens
      one who is not selfish
      a sense of danger
      material to be memorized

6.   a state of bewilderment

      overwhelming amazement
      soon to become a famous man
      as head of the school
      during the hot summer months
      a quality of good speech

7.   characterized by kindness

      a means of eloquence
      simplified method of study
      dynamic and aggressive
      cruel action
      an amiable person

8.   sufficient to satisfy

      the language of instruction
      a leader in public affairs
      service to the state
      an ample amount of anything
      a model of best style

9.   something which is distinct

      excellent skill in logic
      a liberal education
      to cover a large area
      one of the unstable elements
      set apart from others

10.   following a given course

      acquired fame as a teacher
      adhering to a set plan
      a method of discipline
      due to organization of
      close personal relations

11.   throughout the universe

      the aim of the school
      the most striking contrasts
      best for the purpose of
      all over everywhere
      a careful use of words

12.   be concerned with the result

      to make a new demand
      of the many studies made
      to anticipate the outcome
      a variety of accomplishments
      along new lines

(continued on next page)

13.   increasing in difficulty

becoming more complex
an occasional work of charity
to vary widely in capacity
conditions of the time
in their prime condition

17.   an official announcement

the administration of the plan
authorized by proclamation
a consensus of opinion
a successful program
a series of serious talks

14.   to be scattered abroad

to discover the nature of
the scientific method
that which is dispersed
rights of the individual
in the same way as before

18.   to be denied an opportunity

the most unusual feature
the plan in operation
to prove very helpful
to withhold a privilege
out of the picture

15.   looked upon as important

to be equipped with pins
thought to be significant
on the part of others
training in manual skills
to delay the growth of

19.   a violation of the law

on a less extensive scale
an act which is illegal
social opportunity for all
suggested by tradition
forcing a rule upon men

16.   according to the facts

related to the truth
to lack of facilities
no provision is made by
it is encouraging to note
should be considered now

20.   that which might be available

to be potentially obtainable
the proper thing to do
helps to limit cost
to fulfill their purpose
the best chance of success

Time_____Sec.   **RATE (from table on page 309):**   **R.** _____

No. Correct:_____   **COMPREHENSION (5% for each correct answer):**   **C.** _____
(key on page 318)

III–13   **EFFICIENCY (R ✕ C):**   **E.** _____

Record on Progress Chart on page 297

Exercise III-14

 1. **at a marked disadvantage**

possessed with a severe handicap
a tendency to evasion
an opportunity to learn
included in this report
unable to attend now

 2. **process of becoming essential**

does not rank very high
soon to be indispensable
a genius for memorization
an active force
the better choice

 3. **as frequently as needed**

to think through a problem
to gain a great deal from it
as often as necessary
a conflict in the soul
to sacrifice truth

 4. **occurring once each year**

welcoming the newcomer
more than this number
not upon a class basis
an annual event or happening
to be isolated from fear

5. **matter added to a book**

helpful in this regard
be adopted generally
the appendix of a book
less important than the other
of like-minded friends

6. **to apply oneself to a task**

to engage with close attention
to work and play together
necessary for the future
is being done carefully
take the part of

 7. **approximate or nearly exact**

in the attainment of
close to correctness
the sense of belonging to
sharing in a common cause
on the honor system

 8. **to hear and then decide**

a varied social program
the most recurrent problem
brief word of warning
to submit to arbitration
the poorest showing

9. **body of men armed for war**

by those who instruct
securing more cooperation
a military organization
far more recent origin
about every two years

 10. **that which is artless**

validity of the argument
the average length of time
implied or stated power
equip the new engine
something made without skill

 11. **a violent onset or attack**

to assault another person
a qualified worker
more suited to serve
a different view of the matter
open to criticism

 12. **act of taking for granted**

found most effective
the acceptance of an assumption
to use up excess energy
advantage in keeping open
in their own planning

 13. **outrageously cruel or wicked**

resentment of authority
a building program
used for special occasions
occur in another year
quality of being atrocious

 14. **to attempt to do something**

the central part of
a wholesome program
the equalizing of cost
to make trials or experiments
social event of the year

(continued on next page)

15.   activities at an auction

           cutting down the cost
         a drain on the resources
        the most vexing problem
           a series of
   sale of goods to highest bidder

16.   having a genuine origin

    to better existing conditions
     that which is authentic
    on a less extensive scale
    voluntary pay into a fund
       opportunity for all

17.   to clothe with legal power

        definite limitations
      a philosophy of life
    in an assured manner
   to establish by authority
   more difficult to attain

18.   manuscript of an author

     widely adopted means
    may not be included in it
  that written by his own hand
    three times each hour
     to arrange a date

19.   a desire to turn away

feeling of aversion toward something
     fairly well integrated
    the most powerful force
     a successful plan
      noted by many

20.   strong conviction of truth

    an artificial separation
     it is quite obvious
    one can learn to swim
    all learning situations
    a belief of some sort

Exercise III-15

1.   a radiant brightness

considered to be brilliant
in response to the question
a change in personnel
over a period of years
to receive the benefits

2.   to inflict a bruise on

a surface injury to flesh
a little more under control
to be derived therefrom
the extent to which
included in the survey

3.   to confer or bestow upon

the value of democracy
principles of sound health
that which is awarded
in the given order
to decide a given policy

4.   not adapted to its purpose

opposing points of view
belief on any matter
something awkward or unhandy
those elected to office
learn by living

5.   directed or turned backward

rights of others
in a contrary or reverse way
social changes take place
a mode of behavior
must be so guided

6.   a baffling situation

wholesome way of life
adapted to local conditions
a major purpose
a perplexing and frustrating experience
it becomes true

7.   barracks used by the army

to select wise leaders
the amount of power
complete control of
concerns itself with
buildings for lodging soldiers

8.   a tract of barren land

has general oversight
under this type of
may lack knowledge
be present at all times
not capable of producing vegetation

9.   combat between two persons

a possible disadvantage
serve to remind us
a battle between two individuals
important details
eligible to vote

10.   lives by asking alms

be reduced to a state of beggary
in terms of its needs
in an advisory capacity
a well-rounded opinion
must be decided

11.   rhythmical flow of language

a fair representation
rise and fall of the voice
may safely be regarded
a negligible role
in the drama of life

12.   to strike or cross out

on the highest level of thought
cancel out the effects of
a tenth of the total
indicate the bases for
the most emphasis

13.   the seat of government

a fair scholastic record
rely on personal appeal
for the best interest of
the capital city of a state
to compete for office

14.   exercising or taking care

an equal chance to
the great majority of
a position of dominance
a state of being careful
one most capable of working

(continued on next page)

15.   that which effects a result

                can be considered good
                by making such mistakes
                will learn for the better
                one can hardly say
                the cause of an event

16.   a numbering of the people

                certain other problems
        taking a census of the population
                merit specific attention
                its primary purpose
                to hold public office

17.   thoroughly established

        in an unsatisfactory manner
        with serious consequences
        can solve the problem
        to keep a diary about
        that which is indisputable

18.   to be challenged to a duel

          involved in the process
          is to be arranged at once
          a summons to fight
          better than doing nothing
          for the most part

19.   to gather into one body

          suggested by the title
          a valid philosophy
          based on two categories
     to assemble or accumulate together
          may be expressed adequately

20.   a contest between rivals

          to contend in rivalry
          under what conditions
          types of development
    two principal aspects of the job
          can be separated

Exercise III-16

1.   to maintain possession of

   learn to cooperate
   one's own behavior may be good
   product of his experience
   be limited to
   ~~to have and~~ to keep

2.   causing acute suffering

   result in desired learnings
   effort should be made
   never takes place singly
   ~~that which is~~ tormenting
   purposive in nature

3.   without the least delay

   in any given situation
   that which is done instantly
   must be borne in mind
   to win high marks
   means to desired ends

4.   an embarrassing situation

   some sort of an award
   the joy of participating
   oriented at the time
   a chance to appreciate
   a confusing predicament

5.   to beware of something

   be on your guard
   by which it may be achieved
   most vital to everyone
   covered by study last year
   from time to time

6.   that which is deducted

   ~~cuts across all activities~~
   a search for friends
   the part that is taken away
   represented to all
   be well aware of

7.   to wander from direct course

   a brief description of
   the form of inquiry
   to designate all functions
   a degree of guidance
   having gone astray

8.   a main division in a book

   to mold public opinion
   a somewhat greater degree
   to arrange into chapters
   to learn by doing
   keep in touch with

9.   talk in an informal manner

   promote greater interest
   idle chat in a conversation
   a result of many requests
   to grant freedom
   to try to stop it

10.   the chief of the group

    giving some trouble to
    a definite tendency
    to prevent for safety's sake
    the leader of the organization
    in a hurry to go

11.   to make pure and clear

    to clarify the issue or report
    an intelligent outcome
    a radical group
    a difficult time existing
    to make a necessity

12.   the act of classifying

    a chance to learn
    spent to good advantage
    the end of the year
    to group or segregate in classes
    not in itself harmful

13.   a device for measuring time

    instrument such as a clock
    made for the sake of
    to be unbiased and fair
    to keep before them
    a period for study

14.   a systematic body of law

    closely related to
    the one just discussed
    to find some way
    the wrong attitude toward
    any system of rules or principles

(continued on next page)

15. of the farther side of

a distinct advantage
that which is beyond
in the graduate school
problems which arise daily
on various issues today

16. land adjacent to a border

help to the committee
obviously of little value
that which lies next to
duplication of work
very easily accomplished

17. that which is borrowed

at a later period
to receive with intention of returning
a primary advantage
chosen for their ability
only in one sense

18. the lowest part of anything

that which is the bottom
a possible opportunity
to learn democracy
unable to practice
a higher standard of living

19. a device used for stopping

not very probable
among the most important
in a very sincere sense
to apply a brake to
highest total number

20. shortness of duration

to be circulated
combine to control members
characterized by brevity
change from previous form
true in many cases

Time 81 Sec. **RATE (from table on page 309):** R. 375

No. Correct: 17 **COMPREHENSION (5% for each correct answer):** C. 85
(key on page 326)

III–16 **EFFICIENCY (R × C):** E. 318

Record on Progress Chart on page 297

Exercise III-17

1. a king who rules over a kingdom

    an act of binding up wounds
    extending to a great distance
    in the direction of the wind
    a group of related plants
    the monarch of a kingdom

2. situated below the normal level

    all under one household
    to suffer extreme hunger
    that which is relatively low
    having intimate knowledge of
    may not be interfered with

3. to magnify or to exaggerate

    quality of being impure
    not of any one style
    an act of impelling force
    an addition that improves land
    to enlarge either in fact or appearance

4. anything suggestive of a map

    land used for crops
    conducted in a false manner
    a representation of the surface of the earth
    to affect the conscience
    printed for several issues

5. one who voluntarily suffered death

    an approaching obstacle
    with excellent qualities
    along the sandy shore
    being of a very quiet nature
    a martyr for the sake of principle

6. recalling what has been learned

    surrounded by fresh water
    using the faculty of remembering
    in some other place besides this
    an act of the legal officer
    precise indication of results

7. represented on a small scale

    closely resembling someone
    as frequently as needed
    not knowing what to do now
    responding to the loud noise
    reproduced on a miniature level

8. a time unit of one minute

    working in pleasant surroundings
    the sixtieth part of an hour
    commenting on the subject
    tend to produce sleep quickly
    allowed special privileges

9. to be considered as moderate

    marked by serious crimes
    a resting place at night
    short pause in reading prose
    which is within reasonable limits
    a bell-shaped flower

10. that which instills moral lessons

    a joint at this point
    a system of teaching morals
    open hearth of a furnace
    in place of military services
    pertaining to the feudalism

11. to be classified as a moron

    no possible hope for the future
    a moderately feeble-minded person
    showing a liking for all
    a desire to conceal something
    realizing the real danger

12. something difficult to explain

    planned according to specifications
    to go out and search for work
    qualified for some type of work
    a complex situation or mystery
    at a severe disadvantage

13. have but a little margin

    to have very narrow limits
    a method of storing up energy
    including most of the past
    forgiving that which was done
    anticipate an approaching event

14. not engaged on either side

    acquire a sense of belongingness
    part of the life at home
    being in the same situation
    quality or state of being neutral
    involved to such an extent

(continued on next page)

15. to name as a candidate for office

a state of being nominated
usually not returned too soon
serious and of sincere purpose
forced to leave school
to clarify their own thinking

16. that which is counted normal

various phases of the project
go toward their new job
of some value to others
does not deviate from the average
development in growth

17. an obstacle or hindrance to

that which stands in the way
to be of some service
having a large vocabulary
one of the better opportunities
act according to arrangements

18. a type or fashion out-of-date

necessary for successful learning
instead of the other
counted as obsolete in style
being careful in what one does
in the light of changed plans

19. to prove or show to be just

an object of special devotion
decorations for festivals
to vindicate or justify an act
dapper hero of a great drama
a member of an organization

20. a cruel exercise of authority

under the oppression of a tyrant
one who usually does his best
for those who understand
before the opening performance
the one who is never on time

Exercise III-18

1. the act or process of explaining

   a salutation or greeting
   to combine in a group
   a network of pipes
   operated by gravity
   to make plain by means of interpretation

2. having an intimate knowledge of

   state of being unbleached
   a large citrus fruit
   a grainlike particle
   closely acquainted or familiar with
   to act or serve as a governess

3. conventional usage in dress

   for extinguishing a fire
   the gloom or melancholy
   that which is in fashion
   goal made by a drop kick
   to catch a glimpse of

4. that which is frail or flimsy

   any plant of a family
   that which is without strength or solidity
   divided into two equal parts
   often used in police work
   that which gathers

5. something that floats on water

   a kind of a watertight structure
   a tale of adventures
   the center of the earth
   an entire range or series
   a transaction involving risk

6. the terminal part of the leg

   the foot of an animal or a person
   an increase in profits
   to silence by authority
   the functions of a public office
   to hit a foul ball

7. valid or existing at all times

   a large amount of light
   to be eternal or infinite in duration
   to receive and retain
   any of the various weeds
   an opening through anything

8. the event which takes place

   to impose restraint upon
   a score made by playing
   that which happens or occurs
   the person in possession of
   the acts of one who hoards

9. one who acts as a witness

   a place of business
   a tight hold or grasp
   a narrative of events
   a person who gives evidence as to what happened
   a natural elevation of land

10. quality of being excellent

    to receive payment of
    deviating from the common rule
    in some future time or state
    to form or put into a herd
    extremely good of its kind

11. state of going beyond limits

    extent to which sound may be heard
    destitute of courage
    in a state of good health
    operated by the hand
    that which exceeds what is usual

12. suitable to the end in view

    sudden stroke of success
    to hit the right note
    a cart pushed by hand
    personal conduct motivated by expediency
    where prisoners are confined

13. contrary to natural instincts

    state of being important
    intensity of the stimulus
    something considered as abnormal
    careful denoting the action of
    occupy the same position

14. living in a state of disguise

    of the essence of mental concentration
    living under false pretenses
    to follow as a pattern
    quality of being immense
    not separated in time or space

(continued on next page)

15.   following in consecutive order

     sequence with no interval or break
     manage with frugality
     the flower of the plant
     pertaining to water power
     regards for the interests of others

16.   delightful in a high degree

     in the nature of an enchantment
     an uncertain state of mind
     marked by a lack of food
     turn in such a state or position
     to be held as hostage

17.   devoted to a sacred and holy cause

     found on old walls and roofs
     consecrated to a noble purpose
     become the head of a family
     passing through the earth
     the character of a person

18.   the customary thing to do

     the famous place of execution
     considered as promising too much
     a habitual course of action
     belonging to a larger order
     of some remote ancestor

19.   of the nature of an illusion

     a tank holding green liquid
     in order of arrangement
     avoid an embarrassing position
     that which has a deceptive appearance
     an exclamation of surprise

20.   near the beginning of a period

     so that all are included
     arising from bad character
     a restricted portion of space
     plants of related genera
     that which happens early

Exercise III-19

1.   the planet which we inhabit

    the earth upon which we live
    divisible by two or four
    what might not be expected
    in about the same place
    the period from sunset to darkness

2.   the act or process of educating

    the melting or freezing point
    to develop and cultivate the mental processes
    triumph over a discovery
    a motor fuel
    to present on the stage

3.   excessive love and thought of self

    the practice of referring overmuch to oneself
    in commendation of someone
    the science of moral duty
    a river current
    form an opinion of

4.   to feel resentful toward another

    a literary composition
    to be envious of the other person
    one who writes essays
    to gain complete control
    ideally perfect or complete

5.   exactly the same in measure

    a mode of behavior
    the fulfillment of the conditions
    to be equal in quantity or degree
    equivalent to a triangle
    with intent to deceive

6.   belief in what is untrue

    an error in the way a person thinks
    state of being erected
    from some particular date
    an instant of time
    to complete the plan of the work

7.   that which no longer exists

    due to external causes
    that which becomes extinct
    a way of winning the peace
    belongs to the newly formed group
    preceding the owner's name

8.   that which is very convincing

    a case demanding action
    testing all possibilities
    to be supported by evidence based on facts
    for use as evidence
    to reveal by signs

9.   to be in the nature of a formula

    a perceptible effort
    that which is exhaled
    be given off as a vapor
    to have a prescribed or set form
    to release from some liability

10.   to throw into a state of alarm

    terror excited by sudden danger
    serving as a warning
    given in excess of actual loss
    a model or a pattern
    any person earning his living

11.   holding all it can contain

    that which justifies a fault
    to be full or complete in quantity
    permission to practice
    an officer of the state
    extremely good of its kind

12.   the act of gaining something

    a bill of exchange
    to go beyond the limits
    the accumulation or increasing of profits
    a testing of knowledge
    ascertaining the truth of

13.   motion intended to express an idea

    condition of being fit
    a sending forth
    making an excursion
    a gesture used to enforce an opinion
    suitable for the end in view

14.   the act of giving a present

    connected with an institution
    to evaporate moisture from
    sold under eminent domain
    that which is expected
    to give a gift to someone

(continued on next page)

15.   to move gently and smoothly

a laying out of money
a particular study or work
to unfold the meaning of
one who has special knowledge
the act or action of gliding

16.   the mark set to bound a race

that which is exported
by means of a probe
the goal to obtain in winning the race
to search for a discovery
the influences of climate

17.   in the nature of an interview

that which exemplifies
a common expression
usually followed by with
a meeting face to face with a client
a public exhibition or show

18.   act or process of irrigating

indicative of character
expected to do his duty
delusions of greatness
beyond the established limits
to supply water to the land by canals

19.   tract of land surrounded by water

seized to secure payment
to understand the void of space
commence or enter upon
unable to speak intelligibly
that which is regarded as an island

20.   the first month in the year

without a sense of fear
the embodiment of joy
cast light on a surface
January, named after the Latin deity, Janus
being in the first category

Time_____Sec.   **RATE** (from table on page 309):   **R.** _____

No. Correct:_____   **COMPREHENSION** (5% for each correct answer):   **C.** _____
(key on page 318)

III–19   **EFFICIENCY (R X C):**   **E.** _____

Record on Progress Chart on page 297

Exercise III-20

1. to grant or pay a pension to

    an allowance to one retired from service
    various points along the way
    soon after the movie
    seeking a helping hand
    those often in distress

2. an involved state of affairs

    shortly after the rain
    absorbed in international affairs
    believed to be of sound mind
    that which is perplexed
    going inside the house

3. related to the matter in hand

    as far as that goes
    pertinent to the present condition
    in many ways the best
    this is advisable to all
    not interested in stirring up doubt

4. capable of being molded or modeled

    to return to something
    concerned with the truth
    formative in nature as clay or plastic
    should be removed at once
    in detailed reply

5. suitable to the public in general

    quality or state of being popular
    a small decrease in enrollment
    recent influx of workers
    should not be tolerated
    for an hour or more

6. one who carries luggage for hire

    many still stand in line
    a lack of responsible help
    wired for a public address system
    at the same time each day
    the duties of a porter

7. the state of being possible

    to make better personal adjustment
    within the powers of performance
    on the part of the college
    within each building
    one of long standing

8. an act of safety taken beforehand

    a feeling of security
    able to make the grade
    spoken of in various ways
    a precaution taken in advance
    who has learned to help others

9. a question proposed for solution

    the prime purpose of
    in reaching this goal
    a query relative to a problem to be solved
    a set of new conditions
    satisfied with everyone

10. under the protection of providence

    safeguarded by divine care and guidance
    an over-all plan
    seriously looking forward to
    it was evident to everyone
    his greatest error

11. to solve or discover by ingenuity

    a state of being frozen
    combined with another element
    to puzzle out a mystery
    a railroad baggage car
    an inevitable conclusion

12. a measure containing two pints

    expressed in algebraic symbols
    a glimpse of the future
    the first in time or in place
    a measure in music
    a vessel holding one quart

13. to go from place to place

    an inflated ball to be kicked
    to ramble or wander with no set goal
    support for the feet
    to waste precious time
    one in charge of an office

14. the purpose of a reservoir

    one who loads a ship
    prescribed manner of behaving
    a person who seeks a fight
    a place where anything is kept in store
    to make a defense

(continued on next page)

15.   made in the likeness of a robe

to attempt to defeat
the plot of a dramatic poem
action which is extravagant
that which is not expected
a long loose outer garment

16.   a sample portion of the whole

a sudden hostile movement
the pupil of the eye
one expert in penmanship
a part presented for inspection
to form a mental image of

17.   to scatter or distribute widely

the orbit of the eye
to separate in different directions
a very poor person
vessel with a narrow stern
a thing to be regretted

18.   preceding in the order of time

coming first in logical order
a contest for a reward
of standard quality
to translate or paraphrase
prompt in action or thought

19.   not ready or prompt in moving

wreck due to a collision
a thickly populated street
to be slow or tardy in action
water pent up behind a floodgate
part of a railroad

20.   to patrol a given territory

his first voyage to Europe
should arrive any day now
please come whenever possible
he never will do that again
the guard going the rounds

Time ____ Sec.   **RATE (from table on page 309):**   R. ____

No. Correct: ____   **COMPREHENSION (5% for each correct answer):**   C. ____
(key on page 326)

III–20   **EFFICIENCY (R × C):**   E. ____

Record on Progress Chart on page 297

SERIES IV
Sentence Meaning Exercises

Instructions

You should now be ready to combine some skills and to deal with total meaning of sentence units. The Series IV exercises are designed to develop still further your eye span and ability to recognize similar ideas quickly. This ability is of great importance in being able to read for meaning or in reading to find the answer to questions. Quick recognition of basic meaning is essential to developing rapid reading through skimming and scanning techniques.

In these exercises you are given a key statement that expresses a certain idea as the basic part of that sentence. Read this statement carefully, and identify the key words that give meaning to the idea. Then think quickly and carefully about its meaning. Ten statements follow this key statement. With each of these ten, you are to scan quickly, looking for key words and ideas. Then decide whether the basic idea is quite similar to that of the key sentence or whether it is basically different. If the idea is the same, place the letter *S* in the space after the number. If the idea is different, place the letter *D* after the number of the sentence. As soon as you have completed the last sentence, call for your time, and look up your rate in the table on page 311. Then correct your answers by using the keys on pages 321 or 329, and compute comprehension and efficiency as indicated. Then record rate and efficiency on the Progress Chart.

These exercises begin on page 105; rate tables are on page 311; progress charts are on page 297. Keys are on pages 321 and 329.

Example

It is difficult for a woman to be a great mother unless her children have serious problems and need her help.

7. Unless problems occur in the family, a mother has little chance to demonstrate her true value.   7. S
8. Few women have problem children.   8. D
9. A woman may never have an opportunity to show her real greatness   X   9. D
10. It is easier for a mother to gain recognition and appreciation in times of stress.   10. S

Time 54 Sec.   RATE (from table on page 311):   R. 200

No. Correct: 9   COMPREHENSION (10% for each correct answer): (10 × 9):   C. 90
(key on page 321)

IV–0   EFFICIENCY (R × C): (200 × .90) = 180.00   E. 180

Suggestions

With this series, we move to the recognition of meaning in still larger blocks. This series is designed to help you become sensitive to clues and new content. Think first about the key sentence. Be sure you understand and relate it to your previous knowledge and experience with this topic. Then you can begin to sort out ideas relating to it.

With the large bulk of mass mailing, extensive reading assignments, and the maze of periodical literature, you must be discriminating in what you read. There is no need to read variations of the same basic idea over and over again, unless, of course, you are doing extensive research on that topic. In that case, a good reader will be screening carefully for new ideas or different interpretations. In either case, assessing *what* you know first will speed the process of identifying new material.

Reading materials for new ideas or new perspectives can be done fairly rapidly if you already have an understanding of your own starting point. Skimming techniques can be used to help you pick up new concepts quickly and to decide which materials deserve more careful attention for more detailed information to extend your knowledge and understanding of the topic.

This series provides good practice in the basic steps of good study practice. First emphasize the careful thought about the key ideas to be studied—relating them to personal orientation and previous experience.

This group of exercises should provide good vocabulary experience, good exercise in a variety of sentence structures, and good application of concentrative skills and should incorporate into your reading rate a high degree of perception and comprehension in grasping ideas.

Application of this type of reading to research papers or general reading can produce some real time saving and some much deeper understandings. By setting up a theme idea that you want to support or to challenge, you can provide a focus and a purpose for related reading. This then enables you to do much more effective scanning and skimming to select materials appropriate for more detailed study.

Reading in this sense is much more than looking at words in a passing parade across a page.

Reading is thinking, comparing, setting goals, questioning, and weighing the relative values of new ideas as they are found. Reading rate and efficiency in this type of reading involve much more than the traditional word-by-word measurement of progress on a printed page.

Perhaps this type of reading is best characterized by the advice:

Think first . . . then read . . . then react!

Exercise IV-1

Some statistics, startling as they may sound, are not unusual.

1. Startling statistics are not always as unusual as one might think.   1. ____
2. Unusual statistics are usually startling to the reader.   2. ____
3. Some compiled data may sound arresting and yet, in reality, be rather commonplace.   3. ____
4. Statistics are unusual to a person engaged in research.   4. ____
5. Students interested in studying many of the college subjects will find a course in statistics mandatory.   5. ____
6. The statistics that we have here may sound startling, but they are really quite usual.   6. ____
7. Unusual facts are more interesting than common ones.   7. ____
8. A table of statistics is very useful in many fields of study.   8. ____
9. Startling facts make startling statistics as a rule.   9. ____
10. Statistics are not unusual just because they attract considerable attention.   10. ____

Time____Sec.	RATE (from table on page 311):	R. ____
No. Correct:____ (key on page 321)	COMPREHENSION (10% for each correct answer):	C. ____
IV–1	EFFICIENCY (R × C):	E. ____

Record on Progress Chart on page 297

Exercise IV-2

There are no special tricks for concentrating, and they are unnecessary.

1. One of the first things that a college student must learn is the knack necessary for concentrating.   1. ____
2. Concentration is an art that college students will find very necessary in their studying.
3. Special tricks for concentrating are not especially needed.   3. ____
4. Concentration, although difficult, does not require the use of particular tricks.
5. Necessary tricks for concentration are special ones and not easily learned.   5. ____
6. It is necessary to learn to concentrate quickly.
7. There are tricks necessary in learning to concentrate well.
8. There are tricks to all trades.
9. Special tricks are not necessary in developing an ability to concentrate.
10. Concentration is a result of a series of special studies by a student.

Time 23 Sec.	RATE (from table on page 311):	R. 288
No. Correct: 3 (key on page 329)	COMPREHENSION (10% for each correct answer):	C. ____
IV–2	EFFICIENCY (R × C):	E. ____

Record on Progress Chart on page 297

105

Exercise IV-3

Spaced reviewing develops better understanding of material.

1. Spaced reviewing is another name for rote reviewing.   1. _____

2. The best way to understand a lesson is to read it and reread it frequently.   2. _____

3. Review is necessary in order to pass the course.   3. _____

4. Reviewing once each week or at regulars intervals is a good way to improve one's
   comprehension of a subject.   4. _____

5. Reviewing at intervals brings about better understanding.   5. _____

6. Teachers use rote learning as a principal method to help students understand material.   6. _____

7. Better understanding is developed by frequent reviewing at regular intervals.   7. _____

8. The time of the reviewing of material is an important factor.   8. _____

9. To better understand material, one should read it carefully at least twice.   9. _____

10. Better understanding is a goal of all good teachers.   10. _____

Time_____Sec.   RATE (from table on page 311):   R. _____

No. Correct:_____   COMPREHENSION (10% for each correct answer):   C. _____
(key on page 321)

IV-3   EFFICIENCY (R × C):   E. _____

Record on Progress Chart on page 297

Exercise IV-4

Power equipment is not essential to productive activity on a farm.

1. Modern farming methods require mechanization on the farm.

2. A farm may be able to produce quite well without power machines.

3. Productive activity on farms can be accomplished without the use of tractors or similar
   equipment.

4. Power equipment is not essential for production on a farm.

5. Horses were once used for farming purposes, but since the widespread use of electricity
   they have become obsolete.

6. Marginal farms are those that have no power equipment.

7. Some farms may become productive without the use of power equipment.

8. Most farms in the United States are not really self-sustaining.

9. The high cost of modern farming machinery has kept many farmers from developing
   their farms into productive units.

10. Good lighting is not necessary on a farm.

Time 30 Sec.   RATE (from table on page 311):   R. _____

No. Correct:_____   COMPREHENSION (10% for each correct answer):   C. _____
(key on page 329)

IV-4   EFFICIENCY (R × C):   E. _____

Record on Progress Chart on page 297

Exercise IV-5

Geographical factors have something to do with the mode of living.

1. The way we live depends on where we live.   1. ____
2. There is no connection between geography and living habits.   2. ____
3. Man's living is modified by physiographic influences.   3. ____
4. The geography of a country will tell a great deal about the people residing in that country.   4. ____
5. Climatic influences are quite apparent in weather maps.   5. ____
6. Geographical environment may affect society indirectly by changing the human physique.   6. ____
7. Geographical environment is one of the factors in determining one's standard of living.   7. ____
8. Religious faith is a result of geographical location.   8. ____
9. Human behavior varies according to the weather.   9. ____
10. The cultural developments that affect one's way of living are often determined by the
    topographical conditions in any given locality.   10. ____

Time____Sec.   RATE (from table on page 311):   R. _____

No. Correct:_____   COMPREHENSION (10% for each correct answer):   C. _____
(key on page 321)

IV-5   EFFICIENCY (R × C):   E. _____

Record on Progress Chart on page 297

Exercise IV-6

Contrary to popular opinion, forgetting is not simply a weathering away of once known impressions.

1. Forgetting is a loss of memory.   1. ____
2. Many people seem to have the mistaken idea that forgetting is merely a gradual loss of
   impressions once held.   2. ✓
3. The process of remembering is complicated.   3. ✓
4. Forgetting is not as simple a process as many people think.   4. ✓
5. Popular opinion is often the incorrect opinion.   5. ✓
6. Psychology is a subject in which one studies many things.   6. ✓
7. Impressions which are gained during life make up what we call memory.   7. ✓
8. Popular opinion on a subject shapes our opinions on that same subject.   8. ✓
9. Impressions of a thing are the same as opinions about that same thing.   9. ____
10. Forgetting consists of more than just losing impressions once held.   10. ✓

Time _39_ Sec.   RATE (from table on page 311):   R. _180_

No. Correct: _4_   COMPREHENSION (10% for each correct answer):   C. _____
(key on page 329)

IV-6   EFFICIENCY (R × C):   E. _____

Record on Progress Chart on page 297

Exercise IV-7

The process of change is one in which the invention comes before we anticipate its social effects.

1. The social effects of the inventions that occur are relatively unimportant. 1. ____
2. Instead of creating stability, inventions force us to unanticipated adjustments to the effects they create in our society. 2. ____
3. Technological developments always precede the social process of adjustment which they cause. 3. ____
4. A moratorium should be declared on invention and scientific discovery until the social institutions of man catch up. 4. ____
5. The inventions already in existence have exerted little influence on our social order. 5. ____
6. We seldom know what social effect will take place due to an invention. 6. ____
7. Before this process of change can be controlled, it must first be anticipated. 7. ____
8. Social effects are generally not only not anticipated; they are not recognized. 8. ____
9. The problem of the control of social change resolves itself largely into the problem of the control of the effects of the environment. 9. ____
10. Inventions come before the social effects which they inevitably cause. 10. ____

Time____Sec.   RATE (from table on page 311):   R. _____

No. Correct:____
(key on page 321)   COMPREHENSION (10% for each correct answer):   C. _____

IV-7   EFFICIENCY (R × C):   E. _____

Record on Progress Chart on page 297

Exercise IV-8

Biological man is fortunately very adaptable, more so than most other animals.

1. Man is capable of making physiological adjustments to environment more readily than most animals. 1. ✓
2. Biological man's adaptability is not infinite. 2. ____
3. Famine is one of the adjustments that man finds very difficult to meet. 3. ____
4. For thousands of years man was adjusted to an environment which called for muscular activity in the open air. 4. ✓
5. Cities are a radically different type of environment from the country. 5. ____
6. Few animals could become adjusted to a variety of living conditions as easily as man. 6. ____
7. Adjustment between man and his culture always will exist as a very serious problem. 7. ____
8. Laborers are able to become better adjusted to factory machines than animals such as the saber-tooth tiger were able to adjust to changing conditions. 8. ✓
9. Down through the ages it has been seen that the human animal is the most adaptable of the animal kingdom. 9. ____
10. It is fortunate that all animals have learned to adapt themselves quickly. 10. ____

Time 54 Sec.   RATE (from table on page 311):   R. 175

No. Correct: 7
(key on page 329)   COMPREHENSION (10% for each correct answer):   C. 2.5

IV-8   EFFICIENCY (R × C):   E. _____

Record on Progress Chart on page 297

Exercise IV–9

Man's inherited nature changes exceedingly slowly via the germ plasm, whereas culture changes more rapidly.

1. Heredity plays a big part in shaping our nature, but environment plays an equally important part.   1. _____

2. Our culture changes radically and rapidly, whereas the genes mutate slowly in individual reproduction.   2. _____

3. Innate personal changes do not come about rapidly, whereas cultural changes may take very little time.   3. _____

4. Social and cultural changes come about more quickly than do changes in human beings.   4. _____

5. We find that man's nature is inherited from both parents and is modified by his culture.   5. _____

6. Man is a creature of habit and, therefore, affects society's actions.   6. _____

7. Studies show that man can change his inherited personality but very little solely by his own efforts.   7. _____

8. A cause of social disorganization is the lack of adaptation of man's inherited nature to the environment of group and culture.   8. _____

9. The changes in man's nature are difficult to understand.   9. _____

10. Changes via the germ plasm are difficult to understand and explain.   10. _____

Time_____Sec.	RATE (from table on page 311):	R. _____
No. Correct:_____ (key on page 321)	COMPREHENSION (10% for each correct answer):	C. _____
IV–9	EFFICIENCY (R × C):	E. _____

Record on Progress Chart on page 297

Exercise IV–10

Careful selection in the breeding of dairy stock will pay dividends in increased milk production.

1. The mating of good bulls and good cows will result in more milk from their offspring.   1. _____

2. Farmers should be more careful in selecting their dairy breeding stock if they wish higher milk records.   2. _____

3. It is necessary to have good dairy livestock for breeding if one expects a good milk production record.   3. _____

4. Dairy farmers find it financially advantageous to invest in high quality stock for breeding purposes.   4. _____

5. Increased milk production is the aim of every dairy owner.   5. _____

6. Adequate food is required for all breeds of dairy stock.   6. _____

7. Certain types of cattle are better for dairy stock than other breeds.   7. _____

8. Breeding of dairy stock must be done carefully to increase milk production.   8. _____

9. It is no wonder that many farmers have low milk production from their dairy stock because the quality is so poor.   9. _____

10. Careful selection in breeding of all livestock will pay dividends in increased production.   10. _____

Time_____Sec.	RATE (from table on page 311):	R. _____
No. Correct:_____ (key on page 329)	COMPREHENSION (10% for each correct answer):	C. _____
IV–10	EFFICIENCY (R × C):	E. _____

Record on Progress Chart on page 297

Exercise IV-11

Although imbeciles learn to talk, there is great lack of ideas among them.

1. Imbeciles can be taught to talk, but we find that they have relatively few ideas.   1. ____

2. All that a true imbecile can learn to do is to talk and not to think.   2. ____

3. Although talking, imbeciles have few ideas.   3. ____

4. Most people think that because imbeciles learn to talk, it is a sign that they can have a great many ideas.   4. ____

5. Ideas are relatively foreign to imbeciles, but speech is not.   5. ____

6. The study of imbeciles is to be found in abnormal psychology.   6. ____

7. Although imbeciles learn to talk, there is great variety of ideas among them.   7. ____

8. It is little use to teach imbeciles to talk because after they learn the language, they find it difficult to express ideas.   8. ____

9. The lack of ideas is one mark of an imbecile although he may have a working knowledge of the language.   9. ____

10. Imbeciles may learn to use the language, but find few ideas to express.   10. ____

Time____Sec.	RATE (from table on page 311):	R. ____
No. Correct:____ (key on page 321)	COMPREHENSION (10% for each correct answer):	C. ____
IV–11	EFFICIENCY (R × C):	E. ____

Record on Progress Chart on page 297

Exercise IV-12

The blueprints for the new schoolhouse are deficient in that they fail to provide for adequate fire protection.

1. The new school building is a firetrap.   1. ____

2. Blueprints for buildings are difficult to read without training.   2. ____

3. In making the school plans, provision of minimum safety facilities to be used in case of fire apparently was overlooked.   3. ____

4. Adequate fire protection has not been provided for in the plans for the new school.   4. ____

5. The architect did not provide adequate fire safety plans for the schoolhouse.   5. ____

6. The blueprints for the new schoolhouse are inadequate in at least one aspect.   6. ____

7. In general, good blueprints for buildings provide adequate fire protection for all occupants.   7. ____

8. The blueprints as drawn by the architect for the new school building are not adequate in that they fail to provide for protection from fire in some cases.   8. ____

9. The city law states that all schools must be fireproof and entirely safe.   9. ____

10. Adequate fire protection for the blueprints of the new schoolhouse has been neglected.   10. ____

Time____Sec.	RATE (from table on page 311):	R. ____
No. Correct:____ (key on page 329)	COMPREHENSION (10% for each correct answer):	C. ____
IV–12	EFFICIENCY (R × C):	E. ____

Record on Progress Chart on page 297

Exercise IV–13

The assets of the business have increased threefold within the last decade.

1. Business has been unusually good in the last three years.   1. _____

2. By studying records of the business we find that its assets have grown three times greater in the last ten years.   2. _____

3. Successful businesses must have assets greater than their liabilities.   3. _____

4. In a boom, business does well whereas in a depression, business does poorly.   4. _____

5. Increases in assets over a span of years are indications that the business is prospering.   5. _____

6. During the last decade the business has increased its assets 300 per cent.   6. _____

7. The increase in the assets of a business is a good indication of how well the business is doing.   7. _____

8. Careful records must be kept for a business so that the owner can tell how much his assets have increased.   8. _____

9. A threefold increase of assets of the business is shown in the last ten years.   9. _____

10. The balance sheet for the business shows that the assets have tripled within ten years.   10. _____

Time_____Sec.   RATE (from table on page 311):   R. _____

No. Correct:_____   COMPREHENSION (10% for each correct answer):   C. _____
(key on page 321)

IV–13   EFFICIENCY (R × C):   E. _____

Record on Progress Chart on page 297

Exercise IV–14

Horseback riding is beneficial to the physique in general, but may have detrimental effects on the leg bones.

1. When we ride horseback, the horse buffets the rider violently.   1. _____

2. A number of horses make up a herd.   2. _____

3. Horseback riding is good for one in spite of the fact that one's legs may be adversely affected.   3. _____

4. We receive some benefits from horseback riding, but may become bowlegged.   4. _____

5. Riding horseback is healthful exercise, but has a tendency to cause curvature of the legs.   5. _____

6. Dancing requires a certain amount of work plus natural talent in timing and balance.   6. _____

7. Horseback riding is good exercise, but it may develop undesirable changes in the lower appendages.   7. _____

8. "A donkey can walk between his legs without its ears being touched" is frequently said of the people who ride horseback a great deal.   8. _____

9. When one approaches the horse, the rider is expecting to indulge in an enjoyable exercise.   9. _____

10. Riding generally is unhealthy from the standpoint of general physical condition.   10. _____

Time_____Sec.   RATE (from table on page 311):   R. _____

No. Correct:_____   COMPREHENSION (10% for each correct answer):   C. _____
(key on page 329)

IV–14   EFFICIENCY (R × C):   E. _____

Record on Progress Chart on page 297

Exercise IV–15

History has shown that it is difficult for a president to be a great man unless some crisis occurs in his administration.

1. Presidents usually do not secure lasting prominence unless there has been a serious crisis during their administrations.   1. ____
2. Social and economic control is generally exercised by or through the president in time of crisis. 2. ____
3. The history of many a country shows a period of particularly great prestige which is usually associated with the administration of an outstanding president.   3. ____
4. We tend to overestimate the originality, initiative, and even the ability of the president in times of stress.   4. ____
5. Presidents of the United States have often taken credit for prosperity when it was due to favorable rainfall or to the discovery of gold mines.   5. ____
6. It is natural that presidents are blamed for business depressions which they play little part in making.   6. ____
7. Unless a crisis occurs during his administration, a president seems to have little chance of becoming famous.   7. ____
8. The difficulty of becoming president prevents many great men from securing the office.   8. ____
9. A man may become president who is not destined for greatness during his term.   9. ____
10. It is easier for the man in office to be a great president in time of crisis.   10. ____

Time____Sec.	RATE (from table on page 311):	R. ____
No. Correct:____ (key on page 321)	COMPREHENSION (10% for each correct answer):	C. ____
IV–15	EFFICIENCY (R × C):	E. ____

Record on Progress Chart on page 297

Exercise IV–16

It has been pointed out that it is sometimes necessary to adjust yourself to those who fail to adjust to you.

1. People often find it necessary to make adjustments in their lives in order to satisfy other peoples' idiosyncrasies.   1. ____
2. It is sometimes necessary to force all others to adjust to one's desires for certain periods of time.   2. ____
3. We have learned in various life situations that sometimes we must follow other people's ways since they can't seem to follow our ways.   3. ____
4. International tension could be lowered if each nation could learn to adjust itself to other nations.   4. ____
5. Adjustment is a constant problem to the spider monkey.   5. ____
6. Imitation is one way of adjusting one's life to that of others with whom one wishes to live happily.   6. ____
7. Other people in order to get along well with a certain individual may have to learn to adjust to him.   7. ____
8. It has been pointed out that there are always two sides to every problem which must be considered.   8. ____
9. Instead of going our own way when someone does not agree with us, it may be necessary to learn to make adjustments to his wishes.   9. ____
10. It has been pointed out that people like to have their own way.   10. ____

Time____Sec.	RATE (from table on page 311):	R. ____
No. Correct:____ (key on page 329)	COMPREHENSION (10% for each correct answer):	C. ____
IV–16	EFFICIENCY (R × C):	E. ____

Record on Progress Chart on page 297

Exercise IV-17

Surveying the site for the new highway was very difficult because of the rugged terrain.

1. The presence of surface irregularities made mapping out the new highway very difficult.   1. _____
2. Surveying for the new highway took almost three months due to the moisture in the soil.   2. _____
3. George Washington when a young man went on a surveying party for the site of the
   new Cumberland Road over difficult and rugged terrain.   3. _____
4. The new highway would have been relocated to go through a certain section of the country
   if the terrain had been smoother.   4. _____
5. Many severe eroded gulleys and prominent outcroppings of rock provided extreme
   obstacles in the preliminary work on the new highway.   5. _____
6. The final location of the new highway is always of vital interest to the people through
   whose land it might go.   6. _____
7. The rugged terrain made difficulties in surveying the site for the new highway.   7. _____
8. Engineers had great difficulty in surveying the land for the new highway because of the
   very rugged terrain over which they worked.   8. _____
9. Surveying is not a difficult thing to do if the land is smooth and the landowners are
   cooperative.   9. _____
10. Broken and irregular topography caused the engineers a great deal of trouble in
    surveying for the new highway.   10. _____

Time_____Sec.   RATE (from table on page 311):   R. _____

No. Correct:_____   COMPREHENSION (10% for each correct answer):   C. _____
(key on page 321)

IV–17   EFFICIENCY (R × C):   E. _____

Record on Progress Chart on page 297

Exercise IV-18

The home economics courses taught in our high schools can be of great use to the boys and girls who take them.

1. Boys and girls who take courses in home economics probably will find them useful.   1. _S_
2. The home economics courses taught in high schools are too impractical to be of real use.   2. _D_
3. The boys and girls who take home economics in high school learn many things that will be
   of value to them.   3. _S_
4. The equipment found in the high school for the home economics course is so different
   from what the students have at home that they gain no real value from using it.   4. _D_
5. One of the most difficult courses offered in high school is economics.   5. _D_
6. Since most girls marry, home economics should be taken by them.   6. _D_
7. Students in high school will find that home economics can be a very useful subject.   7. _D_
8. Throughout the years of high school life the students should take those subjects which
   will be of the most use to them after they graduate.   8. _S_
9. The boys and girls will find that the things they learn in home economics can aid them
   greatly.   9. _S_
10. Home economics as taught in present day schools is of little practical value to boys.   10. _D_

Time 28 Sec.   RATE (from table on page 311):   R. _____

No. Correct:_____   COMPREHENSION (10% for each correct answer):   C. _____
(key on page 329)

IV–18   EFFICIENCY (R × C):   E. _____

Record on Progress Chart on page 297

Exercise IV–19

One of the student's problems is recognizing what should be known and then fixing it in memory so that it will be there when wanted.

1. One student problem is knowing what facts are important and then being able to remember them.   1. _____
2. The success of an individual depends on how well he adjusts to the new school environment.   2. _____
3. Rote learning is highly desirable for students so that they may have the facts needed always in mind.   3. _____
4. Learning the important things is a problem and remembering them in order to use them is a part of that problem.   4. _____
5. A good way to study is to read the lesson at least twice, and then listen closely to the instructor in class.   5. _____
6. Recognizing key ideas and establishing systems for retaining them are two important problems in learning how to study.   6. _____
7. Many students find that one difficulty in studying is their inability to recognize what is important and to apply effective techniques for remembering ideas.   7. _____
8. Students find that it is important to analyze the salient facts and keep them in mind for later use.   8. _____
9. Universities are good places to learn what is important.   9. _____
10. The solving of problems is the best way to learn important facts.   10. _____

Time_____Sec.	RATE (from table on page 311):	R. _____
No. Correct:_____ (key on page 321)	COMPREHENSION (10% for each correct answer):	C. _____
IV–19	EFFICIENCY (R × C):	E. _____

Record on Progress Chart on page 297

Exercise IV–20

To look upon the faces of high school seniors, one would never guess that at least one out of twenty eventually will be found in a hospital for the insane.

1. The chances of a child being placed in a mental hospital sometime during his life are about 1 in 20.   1. I
2. Insanity is just another form of illness, no more reprehensible than physical disease.   2. E
3. High school students are very inclined to become mentally ill.   3. I
4. Sentiment seems to prevail that insanity is increasing in our society.   4. I
5. Every individual who shares group life with others develops a personality.   5. E
6. By looking at the faces of the high school seniors one can tell that at least one belongs in a hospital.   6. I
7. Hospital space should be enlarged to meet the heavy demands now being made on it.   7. I
8. The tragic fact that five out of a hundred of the high school seniors will eventually find their way to a mental hospital is hard to realize.   8. I
9. The high school seniors should face the fact that of their group half of them will become mentally ill.   9. I
10. One can't tell by looking at high school seniors that a certain ratio of them will enter a hospital for the mentally disturbed.   10. I

Time 23 Sec.	RATE (from table on page 311):	R. _____
No. Correct:_____ (key on page 329)	COMPREHENSION (10% for each correct answer):	C. _____
IV–20	EFFICIENCY (R × C):	E. _____

Record on Progress Chart on page 297

SERIES V
Idea Reading Exercises

Instructions

Series V should help you to develop the upper potential of your reading rate.

These exercises are designed to help you to read for ideas in short selections of material. These articles are all standardized at 900 words in length and should be read as rapidly as possible—preferably in one minute or less. In reading, you should try to grasp the main ideas, the recurrent theme, and the purpose for which the author seems to have written the article. Remember that headings frequently provide clues to this.

At the beginning of each article you will find the length of the article and the readability scores as computed by the Flesch Formula (12). The higher this score is, the easier the material is to read. General levels of readability are as follows:

READABILITY SCORE	GRADE LEVEL OF READING DIFFICULTY
0-30	College Graduates
30-40	College Juniors and Seniors
40-50	College Freshmen and Sophomores
50-60	High School Students
60-70	Junior High Students

Exercises are arranged so that each successive exercise will be a little more difficult than the one preceding it. Therefore, you will be striving to increase both your reading speed and your reading level. Spaced at intervals down the center of the page are numbers indicating the number of words read to that point. As the instructor calls time intervals, you can glance quickly at these numbers and note your approximate speed.

Read each article as rapidly as possible, and ask for your time when you have finished. This time will be given in seconds, and you then can find your rate of reading by using the table on page 313, which will give you your *rate of reading in words per minute*.

Then answer the two questions that deal with the main ideas of the article. You should have no difficulty in answering these correctly. In the multiple choice (MC) questions, select the answer that seems most appropriate, and place a check on the line before that answer. On the true-false (T–F) questions, circle either the *T* or the *F* to indicate your understanding of the accuracy of the statement. If you answer both of the questions correctly according to the key, your comprehension will be 100 percent, and your *efficiency* score will be the same as your rate. Missing one question cuts your efficiency to one half of your rate; so you should concentrate on the main ideas you read.

When you have computed your efficiency, turn to page 299, and record this score on your progress chart. If you have missed a question, you should record both rate and efficiency to show the comparison. Keys are on pages 321 and 329.

Suggestions

This series provides experience in the type of high-speed reading or skimming that is most frequently used in our daily lives when we want a preliminary processing of masses of reading material for later use or immediate disposal. Personal mail, business correspondence, professional journals, news magazines, and other current newspapers or news digests can be processed in this fashion.

The general purpose of this series is to help you get a quick identification of general content, general ideas, and author viewpoints and to use this quick review as a basis for your own selective judgment as to subsequent use of the materials. Often reading for further detail is unnecessary or inappropriate.

Effective use of idea reading involves use of headings and context clues in searching out key ideas. Posing questions from titles or headings helps to provide goals for reading.

Thinking first about the topic and what you already know about it will provide a mental setting in which you can best evaluate the general content that follows.

In this workbook, this series is provided as an opportunity for you to free yourself from the compulsion for detailed comprehension. Comprehension scores are relatively unimportant here, and you should not be disturbed if you occasionally miss both questions. You should push yourself to improve reading rate as much as possible in this series. Try to eliminate all backtracking. Experiment with new and expanded ideas of eye span. Consider the bad habits discussed in "How Do We Read?" on page 9, and concentrate on trying to overcome them as you practice on these exercises.

Let yourself go: See how fast you can breeze through these exercises without any concern for retaining content for any future use. You may be pleasantly surprised at how much you do remember even then. In the process, you may discover flexibility of eye usage that you had not recognized or used before.

Exercise V–1

Curse of the Pharaohs

DONNA MARTINEZ

(from an original article of the Uniwyo Reading Research Center)

WAIT FOR SIGNAL TO BEGIN READING

The curse on Carnarvon

The sun outside beat down heavily on the sand and the rugged stone sides of the ancient pyramid. Inside it was dry and stuffy. Every move of the crew working deep in the interior seemed to stir up more clouds of arid dust.

For three months Lord Carnarvon and his crew had been working through underground passages and anterooms of the tomb of King Tutankhamen. Each night the tunnels mysteriously seemed to fill with hoards of bats which had to be cleared out each morning before the work could be started. Impatient to locate the main chamber of the tomb, they had ↩100 cursed the bats and the time they lost each day in clearing them out.

But on this particular day, February 17, 1923, the excitement was extremely high. Lord Carnarvon was sure that the new entrance they had discovered that morning was different from any other. As they worked through it and on into a larger chamber, he knew that, at last, they had reached the king's tomb. After years of eager anticipation, he finally had found one of the great prizes for which the Egyptologists had been searching for years.

But even as Lord Carnarvon flashed his feeble 200↩ light around the walls of this newly discovered chamber, he began to feel uneasy and found breathing more difficult. He decided to close up the room for the day and climb back to daylight.

The pain continued, however, and soon he was suffering acutely from breathlessness, headache, lassitude and swelling around some of his glands. He decided to return to Cairo to the Continental Hotel, where he had rooms. He did not respond to any medical aid, however, and soon developed a serious case of bilateral pneumonia. A few weeks later, on April 6, he died. All the natives who had been on 300↩ his work crew were sure that he was a victim of the ancient "Curse of the Pharaohs."

The conditions of his death certainly suggested the supernatural. According to some reports, all of the lights in the Continental Hotel blacked out completely at the moment of his death, then came back on momentarily, only to go out abruptly shortly thereafter.

Although no medical cause of the illness that led to his death ever was established, some journalists conjectured that he must have been bitten by a mosquito that caused blood poisoning which in turn 400→ weakened him too much to fight off the pneumonia. But the local residents remembered the centuries-old legend of the "Curse of the Pharaohs."

Mace and Benedite follow

In the succeeding months, Arthur Mace, assistant director of the New York Department of Egyptian Antiquities, came to Egypt and visited the Tomb of Tutankhamen. Shortly thereafter he died very suddenly of unexplained causes. George Benedite, an Egyptologist from the staff of the Louvre in Paris also visited the famous tomb. He, too, died mysteriously soon after that visit. These deaths reinforced the superstition and led many others to 500→ believe that there was some substance to the mystical "Curse of the Pharaohs."

Rice dust

Some specialists in tropical medicine have suggested that any one of a large number of selective diseases may have affected all three of these men and caused their deaths. They noted evidence in other cases of death from inhalation of rice dust. One of them reported a case of a fungus carried in rice dust in Sri Lanka which had affected only fifty people in a large community. Since it seems to act in a selective fashion, this same fungus might be an 600→ explanation of the deaths associated with the Egyptian tomb.

Blame the bats!

Now, more than fifty years after Lord Carnarvon fell victim to the "Curse of the Pharaohs," a Dublin medical specialist thinks he has found the answer to the King Tut mystery.

Dr. George Dean, Director of the Medico-Social Research Board in Dublin, Ireland, is convinced that the men all died from an infection from some fungus dust which they inhaled. He is sure that dust from bat droppings could cause this kind of infection. He had been involved in research in Rhodesia, where he had interviewed and examined many government officials and research specialists who had explored some remote caves in the Urungwe [700] district where the bat droppings were sometimes as deep as six feet. These men had contracted a fungus histoplasma from the dried bat dung dust.

So he believes that infection was introduced to the tomb by the bats which came in after the tomb was opened for exploration. He conceded that there is no way of ever knowing this with any degree of certainty. He does feel, however, that all three men did walk through underground corridors which were deeply crusted with large quantities of dried bat droppings. Were the bats, then, the instruments of [800] the "Curse of the Pharaohs"?

Experts disagree

Many Egyptologists find Dr. Dean's theory hard to accept. They point out examples of other anthropologists who have been exposed to similar circumstances and who have lived to a ripe old age. They argue that there could be many types of selective fungi which could have been involved.

Dr. Dean defends his position, however. He argues that it is soundly based on evidence from his research in Rhodesia. But many people do not believe his theory. The legendary "Curse of the Pharaohs" [900] will continue to persist for many more years.

———STOP———ASK FOR YOUR TIME———
Record time immediately and answer
the questions on content.

Time 22 Sec.	RATE (from table on page 313):	R. 454
No. Correct:_____ (key on page 321)	COMPREHENSION (50% for each correct answer):	C. 50%
V–1	EFFICIENCY (R X C):	E. 12 27

Record on Progress Chart on page 299

ANSWER THESE QUESTIONS IMMEDIATELY

1. (T-F) The "Curse of the Pharaohs" has finally been explained in a way that is generally accepted as a reasonable explanation.

2. (MC) Dr. Dean believed the cause of death was a fungus histoplasma developed from the inhalation of:
_____(1) the damp stale air in the central tomb room.
_____(2) the dust from the deposits of dry bat dung.
_____(3) the dust from ancient rice left in the tomb.
_____(4) the dust from the walls of the tomb.

LENGTH: 900 WORDS

READABILITY SCORE: 57

Exercise V–2

World between the Tides

JOAN E. RAHN

(from *National Wildlife* magazine, October–November 1966)

WAIT FOR SIGNAL TO BEGIN READING

The sea has a split personality

At high tide it can be a powerful and often cruel giant that crashes on the rocks and beats to death the very life it holds.

At low tide it can be a meek and gentle soul, showing the tenderness of a mother caring for the creatures who depend on her for their existence.

As she withdraws from her assault at high tide, she exposes a world teeming with life in the sands and rocks of the beach.

It is this world that is studied at the Oregon Institute of Marine Biology, one of several marine 100 biology stations along the western coast of the United States. The station is a small one, and the neighboring fishing village of Charleston is but a tiny dot on a map of Oregon, but the abundance of plant and animal life in the intertidal zones of the area make it a marine biologist's paradise.

At high tide these rocky shores seem inhospitable and unlikely habitats for plants, for the algae at high tide are covered by water and only bare rocks are seen emerging from the ocean—rock that frequently may be inaccessible to humans. Furthermore, when the waves are high and violent, it seems 200 impossible that anything—plant or animal—could maintain a hold under the unmerciful pounding that may continue for hours.

Creatures between the tides

But when the tide is low a whole new world is revealed. Here the rocks are as luxuriant with vegetation as those a few feet above were barren, and the dividing line may be quite sharp. The slimy surface of the algae that covers the rocks in such profusion can make footing treacherous, and a newcomer is hard put to keep from slipping and catching a foot among the rocks. The bases of these algae 300 are a broadened holdfast, and secrete a cementing substance which glues the plant firmly to the rock. The attachment is so secure that none but the most violent action can separate a healthy alga from its footing as anyone who has tried to do so will testify. Indeed, it is sometimes easier to tear the stalk of the plant than to make a clean break between the holdfast and the rock. At low tide, deprived of the buoyancy of water, the algae lie draped over the rocks, for they have no sturdy supporting fibers as 400 land plants do.

Most of the intertidal plants large enough to see with the naked eye are brown and red algae. Green algae are fewer in number, and only a few diatoms are large enough to be seen with the unaided eye. All algae, of course, contain the green pigment, chlorophyll, but the browns and reds receive their common names from the colors of the other pigments that they contain—fucoxanthin in the brown, phycoerythrin in the red, and phycocyanin in blue. Because of the varying proportions of these 500 pigments, brown algae may appear to be any shade from brown to olive to almost green. The red algae are red to brown in color—frequently a rusty red— but sometimes are even blue-green. The algae plants have no flowers—in fact, marine plants seldom flower —only the eelgrasses with their long thin leaves, grow and flower in salt water.

Strange animals

Marine animals, like mussels, which are frequently covered with barnacles, are welcomed by the less-than-surefooted human intruders, for their rough surfaces are a relief to have underfoot after walking on the slippery algae. (The barnacles are not quite so welcome, though, if you fall and cut yourself on them.)

600 Starfish, sea urchins, and anemones are some of the animals more obvious to the first glance. Many starfish have five or six arms, but larger ones have a multiple of these numbers—the big Pycnopodia has about 20! The beautiful purple of the sea urchins will never be forgotten by anyone who has seen them in their rocky niches. Anemones exposed by the receding tide retract their tentacles and are exceedingly unattractive, but those that are covered by the water remaining in a tidepool expand the tentacles with which they trap food, and then resemble a many-petalled flower.

700 The nudibranches, or sea slugs, range in color from a drab tan to the orange and iridescent blue trimmings of Hermissenda. The bryozoans could easily be mistaken for plants; indeed their name means "moss animals."

Inspection of the intertidal zones

The biologist who would search out these treasures on a summer day must be prepared to brave the cold early morning hours. The summer tides which are the lowest, and therefore the best for collecting, occur on the Oregon coast about dawn, but meeting the tide often requires arising before the sun. Cold water welling up from the ocean bottom keeps the air cold and if there is a fog, as there so 800 often is, heavy clothing is in order.

Despite the fog, the low temperatures, and the care required in scrambling over the rocks, a visit to the intertidal zone is exciting, and well worth the effort. It can be fully enjoyed only through personal experience; for the breeze coming off the ocean, the sound of pounding waves with their fascinating beauty, and that pleasantly tired feeling that follows physical effort in the fresh air are all part of the story, and these can never be completely captured 900 in words and pictures.

——STOP——ASK FOR YOUR TIME——

Record time immediately and answer
the questions on content.

Time ___ Sec.	RATE (from table on page 313):	R. 3000
No. Correct:___ (key on page 329)	COMPREHENSION (50% for each correct answer):	C. 100
V–2	EFFICIENCY (R × C):	E. 3000

Record on Progress Chart on page 299

ANSWER THESE QUESTIONS IMMEDIATELY

1. (T F) The sea has consistent and dependable moods with little difference shown in the changes of the tide.
2. (MC) At low tide, when deprived of water, the algae will:
    ___(1) lie draped limply over the rocks.
    ___(2) create a rough surface for walking on the beach.
    ___(3) flower into small green and brown blossoms.
    ___(4) be fed upon by the sea urchins and anemones.

Exercise V–3

Man and the Synthetic Age

CLIFF BOSLEY

(from *Wyoming Wildlife*, December 1965)

WAIT FOR SIGNAL TO BEGIN READING

The atomic and synthetic age

On August 6, 1945, a bomb fell on Hiroshima, Japan and with that single event the world entered the Atomic Age. The dropping of the atomic bomb on that Japanese city has, perhaps, influenced the human race more significantly than any event since the advent of iron. Certainly, it has been the most spectacular. About the same time the Atomic Age was loudly ushered in, the world's chemists created synthetics. So man also entered the Age of Synthetics, a period less spectacular, but no less important, than the Atomic Age.

Synthetics have had a profound effect on the 100 life of every American although we generally seem unaware of the fact they exist. We read with awe of cyclotrons, megatons, and fallout, but the words nylon, rayon, detergent, DDT, and plastic have become part of everyday conversation. We speak these words with a somewhat blasé attitude simply because they represent tangible articles which are available to everyone.

Synthetics are things we use everyday and things that are within the financial means of everyone. They appear, as if by magic, on the shelves of our local stores. Unlike the atomic bomb, which we like to think was forced on us, we have whole- 200 heartedly accepted synthetic products with little thought of the impact they have had, or will have, on us in the future.

A definition of synthetics

The word synthetic, which is applied to this age, is appropriate since the world of synthetics is the world of the artificial: Artificial in the sense that no synthetic material exists in, or is produced by, nature. They are the result of man manipulating the structures of natural compounds to form completely new substances which, not having been produced by nature, frequently do not willingly respond to the laws of nature. 300

Since nature cannot readily break down these "foreign" materials and put the components to work for her benefit, she either tolerates or rejects them. This is good when the durability of some articles manufactured from the "tolerated" materials, such as plastic, is considered. But man has also used the compounds which nature "rejects" such as insecticides and herbicides, in an attempt to control nature itself and has succeeded in one segment but not without creating secondary or undesirable effects of man's war against nature which has become cause for great concern to many conservation agencies.

Synthetics as a destructor

400

In some cases, the use of various synthetic compounds caused a considerable loss of wildlife, much of it needless.

A rancher, in one case, used a combination of benzidine hexachloride and lindane to spray his cattle. Following spraying operations he washed his spray apparatus in a nearby stream. That one careless act caused complete destruction of all fish food organisms in about nine miles of stream, destruction of all fish (the stream received about 1,500 catchable rainbow trout every year), and removal of that portion of stream from fisherman use until the feed 500 reestablished itself about a year and a half later.

Investigation of a declining fish population in another stream revealed that the area had been sprayed the past four years to control mosquitoes. The decline in the fisheries coincided with the years DDT had been used to affect mosquito control. Although the fish population has not been eliminated in this case, the fish food supply has been seriously depleted. Fish remaining in the stream are carrying sub-lethal doses of DDT in their tissues and continued spraying will result in their death as the dose increases.

Some segments of our society, mainly those 600 who produce and apply these compounds, argue that losses such as the ones mentioned are insignificant when compared to the gains. Unfortunately, however, the side effects may go even further than game and fish losses. As mentioned before, synthetic products are not products of nature and do not have to obey its laws. Man is a product of nature and must obey its laws whether he wants to or not. Therefore, compounds such as DDT, endrin, aldrin, dieldrin and heptachlor that are known to build in the tissues of fish and animals will also build in man's tissues. Each 700 time a man consumes a piece of flesh from an animal

121

or fish containing an insecticide, the amount of chemical in that flesh is transferred and stored in his tissues, AND THEN MAN TOO HAS HIS LETHAL LEVEL OF THESE HARMFUL SYNTHETIC COMPOUNDS.

Here's an old tale that man might heed in his use of dangerous synthetic compounds. There was once a wise man who discovered he could create living beings out of sand. The creatures could be made to do whatever the wise man demanded and as a result he accomplished great things. There was one drawback, however, of the creatures that the man created. They kept growing and as they grew <u>800</u> larger, they became exceedingly dangerous to the man and his neighbors. The man controlled them by writing the letters D-E-A-D on their foreheads before they became too large to handle and with the writing of those letters, the creatures then crumbled to dust. One day, the man let one of his sand creatures grow larger than usual. When he attempted to write D-E-A-D on its forehead, the creature killed him.

Would it not be ironic if man, in his great desire to control nature, became a victim of the <u>900</u>→ "sand man" he has created?

——STOP——ASK FOR YOUR TIME——

Record time immediately and answer
the questions on content.

Time____Sec.	RATE (from table on page 313):	R. _____
No. Correct:_____ (key on page 321)	COMPREHENSION (50% for each correct answer):	C. _____
V–3	EFFICIENCY (R × C):	E. _____

Record on Progress Chart on page 299

ANSWER THESE QUESTIONS IMMEDIATELY

1. (T–F) It is because men misuse certain synthetic compounds that we are threatened with results more devastating than the powerful atomic bomb.
2. (MC) The use of compounds such as insecticides and herbicides have resulted in:
    _____(1) the much needed preservation of wildlife.
    _____(2) extensive support and praise by conservation officials.
    _____(3) only minimal losses as compared to the more significant gains to society.
    _____(4) creating undesirable side effects in man's battle to control nature.

Exercise V-4

Guidelines to Efficiency

(from *The Royal Bank of Canada Monthly Letter*, January 1974)

WAIT FOR SIGNAL TO BEGIN READING

A modern necessity

In a simpler world the pioneer could follow the lead of his instinct in tackling jobs, but in the complex life of today we need consciously to apply efficiency even in making a plan for doing the chores.

Efficiency gets things done in the smoothest way, with least wear and tear, and with the smallest expenditure of energy. This involves a certain amount of thinking. One must observe, apply knowledge and experience to the circumstances, and decide what to do and how to do it. An efficient person will use facts and skill: he needs also good judgment. 100

To the gifted craftsman, whatever his occupation, his work has dignity. There is a simple but pleasurable grace in the pursuit of everyday jobs as if they were the liberal arts.

Precision is vital in many manufactured articles, but the degree varies according to the requirements of the product. While a tolerance of an eighth of an inch may be allowable in fitting a wheel to a wheelbarrow, it would be grossly inefficient in an electronic device where tolerances are measured in thousandths of an inch.

The ingredients

Some ingredients of efficiency are: knowledge, time, energy and material. One of the most important 200 of these is time. Procrastination is the great enemy of efficient time use. Putting off necessary tasks causes additional labor, and reduces the time available for the development of new ideas.

The person who is striving for efficiency needs a good head of steam. No machine that is a hundred percent efficient has ever been invented, but engineers keep working on the problem of increasing the percentage of energy the machine uses effectively.

Here is an example from track sport, given to us by Walter B. Pitkin in "More Power to You." To some persons the act of running may seem to be a 300 simple activity: you merely move your legs faster than in walking. But one who races knows better. The old style called upon a runner to fling his advancing foot as far forward as possible. It came to earth somewhat in front of the runner's body, acting as a momentary brake on the body's forward motion. Then runners learned to keep the body ahead of the advancing foot. This eliminates the waste of energy in lifting the runner over his advanced foot.

Economy of energy is illustrated in the kitchen, 400 where compact grouping of sink, stove, refrigerator, cupboards and counters reduces the amount of walking needed in preparing a meal, and in the workshop, where planned arrangement of tools reduces the waste of time and energy used in searching for them.

To continue to work in an efficient manner requires the worker to keep informed of what is happening in his profession or trade. An effective person does not allow changing circumstances to escape his notice, but makes an adjustment of thought and action to cope with the altered situations.

Facing difficulties

The person who works efficiently is in good 500 position to face difficulties with assurance. He has, in fact, an inclination to look for and to like difficult tasks, because it is in doing them that he shows his worth.

When difficulties thicken upon him, the efficient person has the tendency to persevere. He recognizes the problems and anxieties that may arise in a task, but does not dwell upon them. He knows that he is displaying the highest quality of efficiency when he tackles a job that is extremely tough and does it so that the result approaches perfection.

To such a person a check to progress is temporary. The measure of his efficiency is what he suc- 600 ceeds in doing in spite of unfavorable circumstances rather than because of favorable circumstances. Great works of scholarship, of creative skill, and of technical complexity have been carried to conclusion under disadvantageous conditions.

The person who persists in trying, using the best means he knows of, is likely to attain efficiency even if he has but ordinary intellectual gifts. He is wiser and more competent today than he was yesterday, because he is constantly learning.

To the efficient person a mistake is part of his 700 learning process. He isn't always on top of the world: even great musicians and painters have their comparatively uninspired periods.

Every person who contributes anything significant to life is wrong some of the time. That is why pencils have erasers, but the eraser should not wear out before the lead.

Be confident

Having developed your plans with the greatest possible efficiency, whether they are plans for business expansion or solving a household problem, move with confidence. Knowledge that you have prepared efficiently raises your morale, and your cheerful, confident and zealous manner will inspire others with a sense of purpose, enthusiasm, and a feeling for success.

What then is our aim? To direct our expendi- $\underset{\leftarrow}{800}$ ture of energy and time toward a purpose with the best principles to guide us. We will use patience and enthusiasm, tact and vigor, a single mind to the job in hand. We will have planned imaginatively, used careful co-ordination of resources, and acted with determination.

This may appear to be a large order, and in truth it is, but it is the only known way to move from mediocrity to excellence. Being efficient means the difference between wavering performance and fixed indubitable achievement. A person's efficiency $\underset{\rightarrow}{900}$ is the secret of his value to the world.

————STOP————ASK FOR YOUR TIME————

Record time immediately and answer the questions on content.

Time _49_ Sec.	RATE (from table on page 313):	R. _1102_
No. Correct:_____ (key on page 329)	COMPREHENSION (50% for each correct answer):	C. _100_
V–4	EFFICIENCY (R × C):	E. _____

Record on Progress Chart on page 299

ANSWER THESE QUESTIONS IMMEDIATELY

1. ((T)-F) Efficient people always seek better ways of doing things.
2. (MC) The definition of efficiency most acceptable to this writer is:
    _____(1) thinking and thoughtful planning.
    _X_ (2) good use of knowledge, time, energy, and material.
    _____(3) precision and economy of material usage.
    _____(4) always putting your best foot forward.

Exercise V-5

Freedom Demands Self-discipline

ADMIRAL ARLEIGH BURKE

(from *Scouting* magazine, February 1966)

WAIT FOR SIGNAL TO BEGIN READING

Standards deteriorating

A breakdown in morality is the major threat facing the United States and mankind—the acceptance of lower standards in our personal life, in our organizations.

When we think of Scouting and Scouts, we think of character, integrity, honesty, hard work, individual initiative, teamwork, respect for people, love of country. These high standards are what you leaders teach, what you live by.

The Scouts of today will be able to tackle the problems of tomorrow because they will have character—and a set of principles to live by. They will have these necessary characteristics because you will instill these elements in the boys. If you fail or if not 100 ← enough boys become Scouts or if for any other reason not enough young men of our country have character and integrity, then they will be inadequate to solve the problems they will face.

We live in an affluent country in an era with more creature comforts than men have ever had, but we also live in an era when personal responsibility does not seem to be fostered in youngsters as it was in the past. We as a people seem to prefer to be liked more than we prefer to be respected. Although 200 ← competition is still an American trait, more of us are trying to get guaranteed security without doing the hard work or taking the risk that competition requires.

These are the reasons your tasks as leaders of boys are difficult and also the reasons your duties of teaching personal responsibility, self-reliance, trustworthiness, individual initiative, willingness to compete and do one's best are more important now than ever.

A necessary characteristic

Of all the qualities inherent in a respected person or a respected nation, the one dominant characteristic is self-discipline. The challenge we face today is a conflict between two types of discipline: 300 ← The self-discipline that free men and free nations choose to govern their lives and ensure their progress, versus the alternative, a ruthless, godless form of discipline imposed by external pressures, the discipline of force, of terror and intimidation—the discipline used by the Nazis and now the Communists.

Without discipline, any organization, any society crumbles and disintegrates. When a nation does not have the stamina and the will to discipline itself, it falters and decays; and eventually external discipline is forced upon it.

Most important, those who view discipline as 400 → an irksome imposition do not realize that our democratic system is based on it. They do not understand that a free government depends absolutely on disciplined individuals who freely adhere to a set of rules prescribing the relationships within their own society. Yet, in recent soft, self-indulgent, complacent years, many observers have warned of a trend away from the fundamental, intangible virtues of self-discipline and individual responsibility.

You see this trend reflected in increased juvenile delinquency, organized crime, deceit and deception in various segments of our society.

But what is far worse, there seems to be little 500 → sense of shock any more. People just don't seem to care, for they don't want to be bothered. They just want to be left alone in their own little worlds.

Far too many Americans are too preoccupied with creature comforts to be disturbed by evidences of corruption and dishonesty. As our comforts increase, as our unprecedented wealth grows, there are even those who seek to avoid the discipline that gave us our wealth; the discipline of hard work— "an honest day's effort for an honest dollar."

Confronting ourselves

Let us face this problem squarely. A nation can slip slowly, bit by bit, until one day it reaches 600 → the point where the effort to recover, the plain honest hard work required, is too much, is too difficult for its weakened will and diminished strength. That's when an old law of nature takes over. The strong survive, and the weak fall by the wayside.

Now a very limited amount of discipline can be achieved by compulsion, by making laws and punishing people if they break them. Whenever there is a lack of discipline, lack of responsibility, you will hear people say, "There oughta be a law." We already have laws that affect our actions in almost every field of endeavor. But laws alone cannot pro- $\overset{700}{\leftarrow}$ vide the discipline required by a free society. If we as a nation and as individuals fail to meet our responsibilities, no laws can do it for us.

This personal acceptance of responsibility for our way of life must come from within, from the willingness of every citizen to work for his nation as well as for himself. This, of course, demands the only really effective form of discipline—self-discipline.

Our world of choice is confronted by a world of coercion. We must choose by our actions whether we will remain free.

Our country was founded by men who knew $\overset{800}{\leftarrow}$ the importance of principles. We are fortunate to

have had staunch men who put their principles ahead of their interests, their business, their personal ease and comfort. Their principles were the driving force behind their actions.

These men didn't merely pay lip service to their ethics. These men didn't carve a great nation out of the wilderness by slogans and catchwords. They lived and died by their principles. Character, integrity, high standards, principles, are what you stand for— what you inspire in Scouts, what you teach. May $\overset{900}{\rightarrow}$ God bless you as you get on with it.

——STOP——ASK FOR YOUR TIME——

Record time immediately and answer
the questions on content.

Time____Sec.	RATE (from table on page 313):	R. ____
No. Correct:____ (key on page 321)	COMPREHENSION (50% for each correct answer):	C. ____
V–5	EFFICIENCY (R × C):	E. ____

Record on Progress Chart on page 299

ANSWER THESE QUESTIONS IMMEDIATELY

1. (T–F) The major threat facing our nation and mankind is the decrease in the exercise of self-discipline by responsible citizens.
2. (MC) According to this author, any society or organization will crumble and disintegrate because of:
   ____(1) ineffective rules and laws to live by.
   ____(2) individual needs being ignored in the armament race.
   ____(3) lack of stamina and will to discipline oneself.
   ____(4) society's inability to cope with juvenile delinquency.

Exercise V–6

Safer Ways to Drive at Night

THE CHANGING TIMES STAFF

(from *Changing Times*, the Kiplinger magazine, March 1967)

WAIT FOR SIGNAL TO BEGIN READING

The mid-teen girl got a good grade in driver education, had no trouble passing the state driver's license test and enjoys driving in the daytime, but at night, she's terrified.

The older man, proud of his 50-year driving record, has several close calls at night and wisely decides to do his future motoring in daylight only.

The healthy, 40-year-old executive with a quarter of a million accident-free miles behind him begins to find himself tense in evening rush-hour traffic and exhausted when he reaches home.

The housewife who drives half a dozen errands a day through all kinds of traffic asks her husband to ←100 take over to deliver a few Girl Scouts to an evening meeting.

These drivers operate under widely varying conditions; yet, the same problem worries them all— the difficulty and danger of nighttime driving.

Night driving hazardous

Well they might worry, for in 1965, the latest year for which figures are available, 25,800 traffic fatalities occurred at night. Barely more than half of our annual death toll, true, but remember that most driving is done during daylight. The death rate for night driving is more than *two and a half times greater* than the daylight death rate. 200 ←

What makes night driving so difficult? Reduced vision due to insufficient light is only one of the problems; for most of us, there are other notable nighttime impediments to good driving. They may arise from the car you drive, the road you ride on, or your own physical condition, and frequently, mishaps involve all three.

The car you drive

Your windshield has been pock-marked by flying gravel, spattered with muddy or salted water, speckled with rain, dust or bugs, or smeared with a greasy wiping rag. Your night vision is impaired. Glare from street lights, electric signs, and oncoming headlights is an irritating product of a dirty wind- →300 shield, but the broken-up picture you see is a worse enemy. Filmed-over eyeglasses can sabotage you too; keep them polished.

A car with a dirty windshield will have headlights that are even dirtier. A spattery roadcoating on them robs you of road illumination you need and dims the marking of your car for oncoming traffic. Also, headlights must be aimed right—if too high, they blind oncoming drivers; if too low, they fail to pick out dangers in time for you to evade them.

At night, worn wipers can dangerously alter 400→ your view with streaks of water and dirt. The blades wear gradually; yours may be worse than you realize. Check the blades and if they're streaky, replace them now. Don't wait for a rainy night to get the message the hard way.

Sixteen one-hundredths of 1% of odorless, invisible carbon monoxide in the air you breathe can kill you in an hour and even tinier amounts can seriously affect your night vision before you realize you're being poisoned. Your car's exhaust system can be leaky without being noisy, so the only safe course is to check the muffler and pipes twice a year, 500→ oftener on older cars.

The roads you travel

Bumper-to-bumper driving in rush-hour traffic may not be as necessary as you think. If you experiment with leaving work 15 minutes earlier or later than usual, you may find traffic that's easier to live with. If a schedule change isn't practical, try lesser-known routes or a nearby new freeway. In many metropolitan areas it's possible to go a mile or two out of your way and still get home 15 minutes earlier—and on less gasoline—in traffic that is less dense.

When you have a choice of several routes for 600→ getting to a night meeting or party, choose the way that has good lighting, a minimum of intersections, little or no construction in progress, few schools or stadiums to attract crowds. Avoid large shopping centers and areas with drive-ins that teenagers frequent. Familiarize yourself with the special perils of roads you must travel at night—the spots that get slick in a new rain, ditches easily disguised by a little drifted snow, places where spasmodic splotches of bright neon confuse you, the fast-breaking curves and bridges at the bottoms of hills, chuckholes, dips, loose gravel, soft shoulders, places where rain water $\overset{700}{\leftarrow}$ collects.

You the driver

About a third of our auto accidents occur during the first four hours of dusk and darkness, the National Safety Council says. Peak traffic is one reason why this is the most dangerous driving period. Another is that drivers may be below par physically and mentally at this time of day.

You know how it is—a tough day at the office and you're fatigued, nervous, perhaps a bit short-tempered. Hundreds of others sharing the streets with you are in the same condition, which is hardly a situation conducive to safety.

Fatigue reduces your visual acuity. Your re- $\overset{800}{\leftarrow}$ flexes slow as you tire and even your muscle coordi-

nation may be temporarily impaired; consequently, at these high speeds or in heavy traffic, these deficiencies can allow you to make a serious mistake. Also the fatigued worker who has smoked heavily and who stops for a quick one before starting the drive home is truly operating on only partial vision, especially if a few whiffs of carbon monoxide are added to the mix.

Finally, watch ahead for advance warning and information signs; then you'll avoid snap decisions that may force you into sudden, perhaps tragic, $\overset{900}{\rightarrow}$ maneuvers in the dark hours.

——STOP——ASK FOR YOUR TIME——

Record time immediately and answer the questions on content.

Time 47 Sec.	RATE (from table on page 313):	R. 449
No. Correct:_____ (key on page 329)	COMPREHENSION (50% for each correct answer):	C. _____
V–6	EFFICIENCY (R × C):	E. _____

Record on Progress Chart on page 299

ANSWER THESE QUESTIONS IMMEDIATELY

1. (T-F) For most of us there are problems other than reduced vision that impede good nighttime driving.
2. (MC) About a third of our auto accidents occur during:
    ____(1) the first four hours of dusk and darkness.
    ____(2) periods of fatigue and nervousness.
    ____(3) the rush hour and bumper-to-bumper traffic.
    ____(4) the "cocktail" hour.

Answered Befor Reading 100%

Exercise V-7

French at the Fork

(from *Friends*, February 1974)

WAIT FOR SIGNAL TO BEGIN READING

French and Indian War

In the 1750s, only two decades before our revolutionary movement was to begin its ferment, America was humming with activity as its inhabitants worked to develop its rich potential. The Colonial States along our eastern shore were still unquestioningly loyal to Great Britain and its king, although the forces looking westward for the development of the wilderness—particularly in Pennsylvania and Ohio, at that time—were already restless.

The French, allied with several Indian tribes, had established a number of strongholds and interfered with British Colonials' access to the profitable fur trade in the Mississippi and Great Lakes regions. 100 This set the scene for the last and most important conflict over French and British possessions in America—the French and Indian War.

Conflict area

One conflict area was in western Pennsylvania where the French built a chain of forts along the Allegheny River. In 1753, young Colonel George Washington was sent by the State of Virginia to urge them to withdraw from what was claimed to be British Colonial territory. The next year, Washington led a small force against them and was repulsed. Then, British General Braddock led a much larger force to dislodge the French. He met with a catas- 200 trophic defeat.

Finally, in May of 1758, General John Forbes, in service of his majesty the King of England, was commissioned to gather forces in Philadelphia to march against one of the important French strongholds. It was Fort Duquesne, located at the fork that formed the Ohio River.

The French had held the fork unchallenged since Braddock's ill-fated campaign in 1755. It was a location that would not be ignored, however, for it was a key to the western region.

Colonel Henry Bouquet, a Swiss mercenary soldier and second in command to Forbes, was charged with recruiting a regiment of citizens from 300 Pennsylvania, Virginia, and Maryland. The regiment was called the 60th Regiment of Foot or Loyal Americans.

Colonel Bouquet encountered inevitable delays in recruiting, training, and equipping the men, but finally the regiment was as ready as it could be and Forbes set out.

The result was a grueling march for Forbes' men. The regiment and all of its equipment had to be transported over a rugged mountain wilderness that had not been penetrated by anything more complex than a scout on horseback. Forbes' men had to carry artillery, foodstuffs, weapons, ammunition, clothing, 400 medical supplies, and personal furnishings for 8,000 soldiers and their officers. He had to cut his own road through hostile territory, secure his flanks, and hopefully arrive unannounced at the doorstep of the French fort.

The next 30 miles were all over mountain terrain and must have tried the regiment's perseverance. The last of the big hills that Forbes had to negotiate probably was Laurel Mountain. Forbes' goal lay only three miles farther west. It was a site where his scouts determined that he could build Fort Ligonier, the last major camp of his regiment and the base for 500 his assault against the French Fort Duquesne.

Grant's Hill

A young officer named John Grant, one of the early arrivals at Fort Ligonier, persuaded Bouquet to let him take the Royal Highlanders under his command and reconnoiter the terrain between Ligonier and the fork. It is doubtful that Bouquet understood his real intent.

Grant proceeded to the fork and initiated his own mini-campaign for the glory of the king, or perhaps just for the glory of John Grant. Placing forces in ambush position, he sent a small vanguard to sortie in view of the French. His aim was to lure the defenders into pursuit of his men and then to 600 lead the French into the ambush he had set. The place where his men lay hiding is today known as Grant's Hill.

However, Grant grossly underestimated the strength of the garrison and his troops were overwhelmed by the combined French and Indian force. In the best tradition of frontier warfare, the winners of the battle mutilated their victims, lopped off their heads, and placed them on pikes as a warning to any other intruders who might wish to challenge the occupants of Fort Duquesne. Grant had betrayed the position of the British.

May had faded into October and with the ap-⟵700 proach of cold weather, Forbes, Bouquet, and their advisors tentatively decided to abort the campaign and prepare to spend the winter right there. However, gleaning information from captured French, Forbes became convinced that his target was still vulnerable.

Plans were amended and a three-pronged attack force moved against Duquesne. The armies were camped only a few miles from the fork, anticipating battle the next day, when an explosion of considerable magnitude was heard.

The building of Fort Pitt

On investigation, Forbes found Fort Duquesne ablaze. The magazine had exploded and the last of ⟵800

the French defenders were soon seen retreating down the Ohio River. The site had been burned and abandoned and was occupied by the British on Thanksgiving Day 1758. Subsequently, Bouquet himself supervised the construction of Fort Pitt on the site of the destroyed Fort Duquesne. One of his blockhouses stands today in restoration in Pittsburgh's Point State Park.

Fort Pitt's location at the fork of the Ohio River made it an important stopover for river traffic en route to the interior, and the plentiful supply of water made it inevitable that the city of Pittsburgh ⟶900 should develop on the site.

——STOP——ASK FOR YOUR TIME——

Record time immediately and answer the questions on content.

Time_____Sec.	RATE (from table on page 313):	R. _____
No. Correct:_____ (key on page 321)	COMPREHENSION (50% for each correct answer):	C. _____
V–7	EFFICIENCY (R × C):	E. _____

Record on Progress Chart on page 299

ANSWER THESE QUESTIONS IMMEDIATELY

1. (T–F) Fort Pitt was constructed on a site of old Fort Ligonier.
2. (MC) The fort is located on the _____ River:
   _____(1) Ohio.
   _____(2) Allegheny.
   _____(3) Mississippi.
   _____(4) Pennsylvania.

Exercise V–8

What Price Recreation?

ERNEST SWIFT

(from *Wyoming Wildlife*, December 1965)

WAIT FOR SIGNAL TO BEGIN READING

No new problem

To millions of people recreation signifies some form of sport or relaxation, to other millions it has become a commercialized means of livelihood, and more recently to science, the recreationist has become an organism for study. The recreationist's habits, desires and range of habitat now are being observed with the same interest as a new and multiplying amoeba.

Federal and state resource agencies—with increasing concern and sometimes dismay—have long watched this multiplication without too much outside attention until the past few years. They struggled alone with the problem because the recreationist is not a new phenomenon to them. 100

Those in research are taking off on different tangents with a variety of conclusions. Some feel that the recreationist has such a mass impact that what he wants he should have, regardless of consequences, while others are alarmed at the lacking basic interest in esthetics which is manifest by the now thundering herd.

In attempting an objective look it must be realized, distasteful as it is, that our personal likes and dislikes are not the same. We defend our own preferences and are astonished with the peculiar attitudes of others. For example, camping is no longer a primitive form of recreation or an escape 200 from civilization. Research has proven that a majority of campers encumber gadgets—often from lack of experience or because of fast-talking salesmen and that many wish to squat in the midst of a hundred other campers, wheel to wheel and tent peg to tent peg.

The most cherished spot for rare wildflowers, including several varieties of orchids and trilliums, was turned into a campsite. There are no longer any flowers and, if there were, I doubt if the invaders would be able to identify them. Another spot could have been chosen, but the demands of campers were 300 paramount to the preservation of some delicate and rare species of flora.

Modern camping

Studies have shown that many campers want the complete city image at their camp site—people, electric lights, noise and bridge game; and that picnickers appear to be as gregarious. They stay close to the parking lots and herd together. Why continue to claim that people have a deep affinity with the elements of the earth when it is not so?

Many camp and park custodians are now advocating a period of "summer fallowing" for camp and 400 picnic grounds, so that the dusty, beaten-up vegetation can regenerate. In many areas, rare or old-growth trees are dying because of too much trampling, like an overgrazed woodlot with cattle.

Research has also discovered that a substantial number of wilderness campers can stand only a few days of isolation. Even visitors to the Minnesota Boundary Waters Canoe Country stay at motels and satisfy their gospel of purism by a brief day or so of paddling near the perimeter, or not even that because they insist on an outboard motor. It is being proven more and more that where the esthetic urge interferes 500 with comforts, it is easy to satisfy.

The urgency to save wild rivers is now being touted and acclaimed as one of the last sports of the dyed-in-the-wool outdoorsman. Yet I find in the Great Lakes states that the most avid of wild river enthusiasts would rather remain in the amateur class than rise to the craftsmanship that canoeing deserves. True craftsmanship with a canoe dictates poling upstream as well as paddling down, and a good boat handler does not paddle wildly through shallow rocky stretches; he snubs his craft downstream a little 600 at a time with a pole. I have yet to see a modern wild river enthusiast who could buck upstream rapids with a pole.

Because they refuse the challenge of becoming master craftsmen, there must be ingress roads to take out their plunder, and so they become traitors to their wilderness idealism.

What people want

It is logical to ask then, are these people willing to place all resources in jeopardy by demanding conveniences regardless of the drain or abuse on resources? I feel that they are willing to do so. They are either ignorant or will not conform to the limits 700 which can be placed on resources without damaging them. Their recreational attitudes reflect their attitudes toward the use of all resources.

Much is written today about men's desire to commune with nature, to be alone, to enjoy the solitude; and if given a chance, to revel in the primitive esthetics of nature. This is wishful thinking and being proven so as recreational pressures increase. People apparently are looking for a change from the humdrum of daily living, but they are not looking for nature in the raw or even in a parboiled version.

Has security in all forms become such a national fetish that it now reflects in the various $\overset{800}{\leftarrow}$ forms and attitudes of recreation? Are we shying away from risk, challenges, self-reliance and the

ability to walk alone? I think we are, and let it be remembered that the strength of a nation is only as great as the strength of each individual citizen. Recreation is showing a trend in national character for better or for worse. What people want is not so important in the long run as why they want it, especially when it points to the destruction they are $\overset{900}{\rightarrow}$ willing to inflict to obtain their ease and security.

——STOP——ASK FOR YOUR TIME——

Record time immediately and answer
the questions on content.

Time ___ Sec	RATE (from table on page 313):	R. _2,700_
No. Correct: _2_ (key on page 329)	COMPREHENSION (50% for each correct answer):	C. _100_
V–8	EFFICIENCY (R × C):	E. _2,700_

Record on Progress Chart on page 299

ANSWER THESE QUESTIONS IMMEDIATELY

1. (T - F) The author feels that security and comfort have become such a natural fetish that it now reflects in the attitudes of recreation.
2. (MC) Recent studies indicate that most campers prefer:
    _____(1) isolation on their camping jaunts.
    _____(2) the wilderness areas where they must fend for themselves.
    _____(3) to revel in the primitive esthetics of nature.
    __X__(4) conveniences and society while camping.

Exercise V–9

New Life in the Old Quarter

DENNIS J. CIPNIC

(from *Adventure Road* magazine, Winter 1966–1967)

WAIT FOR SIGNAL TO BEGIN READING

The Quarter—a true renaissance

The Quarter, as it is locally known, is in the midst of a true renaissance—a sweeping awakening of all its faculties. The overhaul started with the establishment of the Vieux Carre Commission to enforce laws designed to preserve the historical color and charm of the 80 square blocks of the Quarter. Every building must look old, even if it's brand new and property owners cannot so much as change the color of paint on their shutters without the commission's approval. The laws forbid demolition by neglect and encourage restoration of old properties.

At the same time, a new residential atmosphere 100 came over the Vieux Carre. Artists, writers, scholars, architects, sculptors, all began moving in, which made it an "in" place, so they were soon followed by up and coming young-in-mind people from the business world and the professions. This started a trend toward restoring the Quarter's residential ascendancy which has now reached proportions of a land boom. Over half the buildings in the Vieux Carre are either restored, being restored, or in the planning stages. Property values have quadrupled in five years and hundreds of new air-conditioned apartments have been created inside 150-year-old town houses, which 200 on the outside, still look exactly as they once were.

These new inhabitants turned out to be "with-it" purchasers. Whereas, up until about two years ago, when the new influx reached appreciable proportions, the Quarter was hard put to support its traditional praline shops and antique stores. Now there has suddenly sprouted along the main thorough-fares of Bourbon, Royal, St. Peter and St. Ann Streets a new world of art galleries, boutiques, Mod clothiers, cafes, and import decorator shops. Antiques, wrought iron, hand-made candles, Hong Kong tailoring, paper flowers, painting of every description, the latest fashions from London—you name it, and you can 300 find it.

A new turn

New Orleans has always been a night town; the Quarter doesn't wake up till noon, and doesn't shut down again until 4 A.M. or so. The street life starts with a stroll around the art displays in Jackson Square and Pirate's Alley during the afternoon, some galleries and stores are open until midnight, dinner is best taken after eight, and the wail of the blues starts promptly at eight-thirty at Preservation Hall.

Preservation is the ground floor of a Quarter home on St. Peter Street which features bare benches, 400 old soda shop chairs, peeling walls, a church pew in the foyer, and some of the purest jazz extant. Several years ago it didn't exist; the Negro musicians who invented jazz as a musical form were still alive, many of them living a forgotten existence in Quarter tenements. Al and Sandra Jaffe, two young Philadelphians who came to New Orleans with the "New Wave" inhabitants, decided something needed to be done about this lamentable situation.

They opened the Hall, which features nothing but live music and soft drinks, brought the musicians 500 out of limbo, and started the re-birth of traditional jazz. Preservation is packed every night, at a dollar per customer. You can stay as long as you like for your dollar; the bands use no sheet music, so they never play the same number the same way twice in a row. The Hall has led to several imitations, one of them, Dixieland Hall, around the corner on Bourbon Street, being quite good in its own right.

Jazz in New Orleans

Jazz belongs to New Orleans. Basin Street, Rampart Street, Bourbon Street, Storeyville, Louis Armstrong, Jelly Roll Morton, they all blend together 600 to make quite a concoction. And with the new life which has come to the Quarter, New Orleans has inherited two new ingredients as well: Pete Fountain and Al Hirt. Both bearded, both native sons, both very popular international stars, they both have nightclubs on Bourbon Street where before stood only clipjoints.

Museums too have had a renaissance; a fine wax museum, in the true tradition of the famous Madame Tussaud's, is now open on Conti Street. There are several excellent period homes open as museums—one, a three story apartment in the oldest high rise condominium in the New World, the 700 Pontalba on Jackson Square, is exactly as it was in 1850. A fascinating colonial pharmacy is also in the

133

Quarter, as is the Mother Cabrini Doll Museum and several other special collections.

In many ways, New Orleans is a living museum as rows of antique shops on Royal Street have more treasures, free for the browsing, than many a fee-charging museum elsewhere. Raymond Weill's Stamp Shop, also on Royal, is world famed as headquarters of the finest rare stamps in existence, and some of his wares are always on display in the windows or inside the showcases. Within three blocks are at least $\overset{800}{\leftarrow}$ a dozen art galleries displaying works of every conceivable style, and one of them, also on Royal Street, features a rather interesting collection of archaeological antiquities from the middle Americas.

At night, along Bourbon Street, the barkers at clubs open the doors to give strollers a peek at the show which is just starting.

If you'd passed the buildings in New Orleans several years ago, you'd never have guessed that one of the most important acts in American history was consummated there: The Louisiana Purchase. Today these buildings stand, restored, bringing America's past to life, and symbolizing the new life in the Old $\overset{900}{\rightarrow}$ Quarter.

——STOP——ASK FOR YOUR TIME——

Record time immediately and answer
the questions on content.

Time____Sec.	RATE (from table on page 313):	R. _____
No. Correct:_____ (key on page 321)	COMPREHENSION (50% for each correct answer):	C. _____
V–9	EFFICIENCY (R × C):	E. _____

Record on Progress Chart on page 299

ANSWER THESE QUESTIONS IMMEDIATELY

1. (T–F) The New Orleans French Quarter, in the midst of a first-class facelifting, has attempted to restore the exteriors of old historical edifices with air-conditioned interiors for comfortable living.
2. (MC) "Preservation Hall" has been instrumental in bringing back the nearly forgotten:
   ____(1) lifelike wax museums.
   ____(2) the praline shops.
   ____(3) traditional jazz music.
   ____(4) art galleries featuring paintings of Old New Orleans.

Exercise V–10

Something about Loyalty

(from *The Royal Bank of Canada Monthly Letter*, February 1974)

WAIT FOR SIGNAL TO BEGIN READING

Patriotism

What is patriotism? A nineteenth-century orator described it in this way: "This almost universal instinct for which more men have given their lives than for any other cause, and which counts more martyrs than even religion itself. It has produced great and splendid deeds of heroic bravery and of unselfish devotion; inspired art and stimulated literature and furthered science; fostered liberty and advanced civilization."

The word "patriot" comes from the French, where it was used as early as the fifteenth century in the sense of "citizen." By-and-by it came to imply a *good* citizen and a lover of his country. Patriotism 100 is a belief in and a desire for the national good, a lively sense of collective responsibility.

Patriotism is nothing to be ashamed of. It is founded on valid principles and supported by great virtues. It stands for the good objectives of one's country and inspires the individual to sacrifice his selfish interests when the broader interests of his fellow citizens make it desirable. He knows that his own welfare is best served by that which he knows to be most advantageous for the others.

Patriotism exists in normal times as well as in times of crisis. It does not need a hate object like an 200 enemy to keep it alive. Those who are truly patriotic do not lapse into disinterest between wars, but are diligent in carrying out their peace-time duties and responsibilities.

Some, of course, exalt what they think of as being patriotism and enshrine it as an absolute and unconditional virtue to which even their conscience must bow. Such a spirit stirs up national vanity and people who have it will seek to enhance the greatness of their country at the expense of ill to its neighbours.

What is chauvinism?

"Chauvinism," a word coming into general use 300 in the language used by organizations promoting new ideas, means zealous and belligerent national spirit. It was named after N. Chauvin, a soldier in Napoleon's army noted for his loud-mouthed patriotism. It is patriotic feeling isolated from other moral values. It starts with the firm belief that your country is superior to all other countries because you were born in it, and it tends toward the making of blind zealots.

Far above this in virtue and value is true patriotism, which is a sense of public duty. We give 400 proof of patriotism when we take our full share of public service and responsibility within our communities. Ralph Waldo Emerson wrote in his *Journals:* "I have generally found the gravest and most useful citizens are not the easiest provoked to swell the noise, though they may be punctual at the polls."

The government's duty

The men and women in many countries and over many centuries have drafted charters setting forth what they believe governments should be and should do. The nearer governments come to meeting these requirements, the more loyal support they receive from citizens. Loyalty is given to a political 500 system because people have hope and confidence that their aspirations can be met within that system.

A government may derive its *power* from words printed in statute books, but its *principles* come from much farther back. The *Bible* and Greek and Latin classics constitute the bed-rock of the civilization in which democratic governments exist. Some of the watchwords of the ethical environment are truth, liberty, justice, humaneness, religious freedom, and respect for the worth and dignity of the individual. The state that has these virtues as its guide is the state to which intelligent citizens can give unstinted loyalty.

Patriotism sets standards

600 We demand of the government to which we are loyal that it maintain certain standards. We ask that it shall be inflexibly open and truthful. We require that it manage the life of the country so as to secure the greatest happiness of the greatest number of its citizens, and an adequate minimum standard of living for all.

Rebecca West, author of many books of criticism and biography as well as novels, wrote: "A nation that deserves loyalty is one where all talents are generously recognized, all forgivable oddities forgiven, all viciousness quietly frustrated, and those who lack talent honoured for equivalent contributions of graciousness."   700←

Governments must deal with a great complexity of affairs, and must be entrusted with great powers. They need to hold the imagination of the people, to show a sense of national purpose, to give everyone something tangible to be loyal to. Most people have a need to be needed. If individuals feel "lost" or not part of the picture they will be driven to shoddy substitutes to bolster their ego.

People's desires are not wholly materialistic. Governments have made available much that contributes to improved living conditions: health services, pensions, minimum wages, short working hours.

Having reached this plateau, far above the level 800←

of fifty years ago, people have new desires. They value material security, but they have developed psychological needs: recognition and respect as individuals and appreciation for their contribution to the well-being of the country. They are looking to government to answer their earnest wish for the opportunity to do something, to join in something, that will fill their lives interestingly.

Sometimes the spirit of loyalty suffers by the emphasis placed upon "rights." There are natural rights and civil rights. Every person has the right to 900→ exist, and to live his life in the best way he can.

——STOP——ASK FOR YOUR TIME——

Record time immediately and answer
the questions on content.

Time ___ Sec.	RATE (from table on page 313):	R. ___
No. Correct: ___ (key on page 329)	COMPREHENSION (50% for each correct answer):	C. ___
V–10	EFFICIENCY (R × C):	E. ___

Record on Progress Chart on page 299

ANSWER THESE QUESTIONS IMMEDIATELY

1. (T–F) The article states that patriotism exists only in times of crisis.
2. (MC) Chauvinism was named after:
   _____(1) a French government agent.
   _____(2) a French word for citizen.
   __X__(3) a soldier in Napoleon's army.
   _____(4) a woman civil rights leader.

LENGTH: 900 WORDS

READABILITY SCORE: 47

Exercise V–11

Island in the Sun

FURMAN BISHER

(from *Adventure Road magazine*, Winter 1966–1967)

WAIT FOR SIGNAL TO BEGIN READING

A new island resort

Every red-blooded, fun-loving American has the built-in desire to live like a millionaire. There is a place on the coast of Georgia where it can be done for a price that any average citizen can afford.

Jekyll Island is located in the South Atlantic eight miles southeast of the seaport town of Brunswick and six miles off U.S. 17, one of the eastern seaboard's major north-south motoring arteries.

Once it sat there abandoned, neglected, the scene of dilapidation. But today it is a glittering star in a coastal chain known as the "Golden Isles," including the socially exclusive Sea Island, St. Simon's Island, Sapelo Island, Cumberland Island and many others with fewer inhabitants and lesser personality.

On the west side of the island stand the remains of one of the most unusual colonies of the world, relic of a former grandeur that America will never know again. In the age of the rise of the American tycoon, a club of millionaires came to Jekyll to create a retreat where they could be alone with their kind and enjoy relief from the north during the blast of winter. It was called the Jekyll Club.

Its membership included an astoundingly impressive collection of names from among the country's financial pioneers, John D. Rockefeller, J. Pierpont Morgan, Joseph Pulitzer, Cyrus McCormick, Vincent Astor, and a lineup that at one time was said to have represented one-sixth of the nation's wealth.

The millionaires village consisted of what residents referred to as "cottages," but what were mansions by any other standards. The center of the settlement was the Jekyll Club itself, a rambling gingerbread, mansard-roofed building which serves as a hotel today. Here the members gathered for dining and entertainment. In the privacy of this island village, they lived and enjoyed their flings without intrusion by the unwashed masses. It was said that in the years of its existence, from 1886 until 1942, no unwanted foot touched the island.

With all this wealth gathered in one location and World War II coming close enough that a German submarine torpedoed a tanker in St. Simon's Sound, the Federal government ordered the island evacuated in April 1942, while the "season" was in full swing.

From private to public

The Jekyll Club was never reactivated. Time had passed it by after the peace. The younger set turned to the swifter life and so the island village gathered moss and mildew, and the cottages, with furnishings just as they had been left, waited for an age and a society that never returned.

Presently, the island is under the administration of state-constituted Jekyll Island Authority and the direction of its executive secretary, A. J. Hartley, who runs it like a small kingdom.

Until 1960 on Jekyll, there was no place to sleep at night. Executive secretary Hartley went out and interested motel entrepreneurs in building on the island. Today there are six luxury motels strung along the Jekyll beach: the Wanderer, Jekyll Estates, Seafarer, Corsair, Buccaneer and Stuckey's Carriage Inn. Rates run from $11 per day in the November-January season to $22 in the summer months when Southerners flock to the beach. Suites, with kitchenettes, are available at $14 during November-January and $21–$36 during the peak season. Excellent restaurants, offering a broad variety of seashore delicacies, are located in each motel.

The Rockefeller "cottage," known as "Indian Mound" because of the nearby presence of an Indian mound, and the least pretentious of the millionaires' quarters, has been converted into a museum. The public can tour the old residence for 35 cents and view room after room full of relics of the financial barons' days on the island, from Robert Lorillard's "Red Bug Scooter" to the Rockefeller's walk-in safe, where it is said that he kept his pocket change.

The Jekyll Authority has in the works now, however, a project to make more of this rare legacy. This winter, restoration of the entire millionaires' village will begin. It is Hartley's plan to reproduce every residence and every facility as it was in the halcyon days. Only Faith Chapel, their quaint little place of worship, will be left in its present state.

Jekyll Island—rich in history

Historically, Jekyll Island has had its day, but $\underset{\leftarrow}{700}$ much of it has been kept under a blanket. Adventure, war, slavery and men looking for a place to live their private existence have all left their footprints there. Guale Indians originally lived on the island. Later, about 1556, the Spanish established a fort there, but gave way to the British in 1642, when General James Oglethorpe defeated their army in the Battle of Bloody Marsh.

Oglethorpe used the island as his outpost when he settled Georgia with a band of Britishers in 1732. Until then, its name was Ospo, so called by the Indians. Oglethorpe changed the name to Jekyll in $\underset{\leftarrow}{800}$ honor of Sir Thomas Jekyll, who helped sponsor his expedition.

In the 1790's, a French family named duBignon settled on Jekyll and lived there until one of the descendants sold out to the millionaires in 1886.

It was the millionaires' village then that made the rest of Jekyll's history, until the State of Georgia turned it into a resort island for vacationers.

Although it's still off the beaten path, Jekyll Island is growing into a winter playland, where families can bask in the sun, yet satisfy their curiosity $\underset{\rightarrow}{900}$ for the unusual.

———STOP——ASK FOR YOUR TIME———

Record time immediately and answer
the questions on content.

Time_____Sec.	RATE (from table on page 313):	R. _____
No. Correct:_____ (key on page 321)	COMPREHENSION (50% for each correct answer):	C. _____
V–11	EFFICIENCY (R X C):	E. _____

Record on Progress Chart on page 299

ANSWER THESE QUESTIONS IMMEDIATELY

1. (T–F) Jekyll Island is located in the South Atlantic on the coast of Florida.
2. (MC) The Jekyll Island Authority, administrator of the island, plans as a future project the:
   _____(1) restoration of the entire millionaires' village.
   _____(2) expansion of the docking facilities and charter services.
   _____(3) construction of a new and luxuriant 18-hole golf course.
   _____(4) remodeling of the old Jekyll Club for public accommodation.

Exercise V-12

The Rockies' Riotous Ski Festivals

DON CANNALTE

(from United Airlines' *Mainliner* magazine, January 1967)

WAIT FOR SIGNAL TO BEGIN READING

Ever since the slumbering mining town of Aspen, Colorado awoke twenty years ago from a deep sleep, and went about the business of becoming America's most glamorous ski resort, its citizens have been toasting nature's blessings and their own ingenuity.

Every winter ski-hungry vacationers converge on the town, laying claim to most or all of more than 6,000 beds, cutting through powder snow and traffic down superb mountains, and generally adding to the crush of *après-ski* goers.

Aspenites respond to this fun-loving immigration with a twinkle in their business eye, and a bit of hi-jinks themselves. At no time does this happy ¹⁰⁰ wonderful town unveil its personality more than during Winterskol—Toast to Winter.

Winter carnivals are a good-times addition to any ski vacation for young or old, the family or the unattached, and there are many worth attending.

A welcome to ski-enthusiasts

The Colorado community of Breckenridge every February declares itself a "free sovereign and independent state" for one three-day weekend and holds its colorful Ullr Dag festival. Ullr, the mythical Nordic God of mountain sports and skiing, reigns over the festivities, which include races, parades, and the right to celebrate independence. A visa (costing 25 cents) is required to enter the Kingdom of ²⁰⁰ Breckenridge.

Carnival-goers at Jackson Hole, Wyoming, must hug the sidewalks during the All-American Cutter Races, in which chariot-like cutters drawn by two-horse teams, race through the streets of Jackson. Winter sports connoisseurs also will be treated to Ski-Doo races and snowplaning on Jackson Lake.

At Leadville, Colorado, snowshoe baseball sets the tone for the town's annual frolic-filled Winter Carnival weekend. The feature at nearby Steamboat Springs (Ski Town, U.S.A.) is ski-joring, as men on skis rope themselves to horses which charge along the street toward the finish line.

A winter Mardi Gras

Perhaps none is more colorful and vibrant than Aspen's Winterskol, held in mid-January. Winterskol was born as an idea to stimulate community interest among the townspeople. The first Winterskol wasn't too elaborate, although Lana Turner showed up. There was a parade with most of the local residents participating, and few people watching, some ski races and a Winterskol Ball, held in a drafty cold hall with a roof that leaked.

There was a hockey game, although no rink, ski-joring down Main Street, and two of the saloons challenged each other to team racing with trays of beer. Lack of funds may have limited the activities but lively imaginations carried the day. One restaurant was decorated with underwear hung on a clothesline and strung above the bar.

Still, the festival was considered a success and was held again the next year, and Miss Turner liked the idea enough to return for the second year to stay a week.

The spirit, informality and many of the events of that first Winterskol have prevailed over the years (ski-joring was replaced by dog-joring in later years due to lack of open space), and this year's annual fun-filled carnival was no exception.

From a roaring Christmas tree bonfire, cheered by the blaze, everyone then gathered at the foot of Little Nell to watch 70 skiers weave a graceful abstract down Aspen Mountain. A hockey match and skating exhibitions at the Ice Palace completed the evening's scheduled events before everyone adjourned for socializing at his favorite *après-ski* warming hut.

There are bigger parades, but few are more colorful than the one concocted by Aspenites for Winterskol. Handsome, suntanned instructors from Aspen and Vail ski schools provided an impressive complement to the unfolding foolishness. A daring young acrobat did somersaults on a moving trampoline while wearing skis. A local haberdasher knitted the longest stocking cap (129 feet) on record and paraded it with the help of a dozen youngsters trailing behind. The festival theme "there is No Aspen" (the subject of an advertising campaign by rival

Steamboat Springs), allowed imaginations to dress up the float entries with a variety of merriment.

Fun for everyone

The fun carried into the afternoon with ski races by teams representing the various lodges and restaurants, dog-joring at the park and something called broomball at the Ice Palace. The social highlight of the festival, of course, was the Winterskol costume ball, featuring no less than 15 entertainment groups 700 and fireside dancing at the Four Seasons.

Action resumed the next morning on Aspen Mountain with the traditional and hilarious Saloon Slalom, entered by employees and proprietors of local bistros, races for the children (urged on by over-exuberant parents, the youngsters slalom down Little Nell, pausing to wolf down a piece of pie before crossing the finish line), and a sky diving–ski meet.

In the latter event, the contestants parachute to the top of the slope, don skis and schuss down the hill. The sky divers take the air drop in stride: the 800 fun begins if and when they get their skis on for most have never been on the boards before. Husky dog-sled races along a 10-mile course fill out a busy day's activities.

Winterskol, like other winter carnivals, never really ends. It signals a season-long of pleasure for ski-addicts and general winter vacationers alike. It's a great way to take the pale out of winter and put a little "spring" in your life.

Winterskol in Aspen is a long and frolicsome holiday which involves every winter sports enthusiast —spectator and participant alike, and we're confident these ski festivities will continue having an enthusi- 900 astic response.

——STOP——ASK FOR YOUR TIME——

Record the time immediately and answer the questions on content.

Time ____ Sec.   RATE (from table on page 313):   R. 6,750

No. Correct ____   COMPREHENSION (50% for each correct answer):   C. ____
(key on page 329)

V–12   EFFICIENCY (R × C):   E. 6,750

Record on Progress Chart on page 299

ANSWER THESE QUESTIONS IMMEDIATELY

1. (T–F) Aspen's Winterskol celebration is focused entirely on ski contests.
2. (MC) Winterskol originally started as an idea to involve:
   ____(1) the townspeople.
   ____(2) the ski enthusiasts.
   ____(3) the university ski teams.
   ____(4) the tourists.

Exercise V–13

Think and Live

GREGORY RAY

(from *Wyoming Wildlife* magazine, July 1974)

WAIT FOR SIGNAL TO BEGIN READING

Safe boating is no accident

More than 1,700 men, women, and children throughout the United States will have a quiet summer this year. They won't be spending lazy afternoons fishing and basking in the sun while being gently rocked to sleep in their boats. Gone are their days of water skiing and swimming; for these are the 1,700 people that met a grim death in boating accidents last year.

It is hardly shocking to find that the number of casualties is roughly proportional to the number of boaters. But surprisingly few of all watercraft accidents are caused from collisions; rather they are individual upsets most often a result of an overloaded boat combined with inclement weather.

Weather conditions are a major factor. Thunderstorms can engulf boats miles from the dock before the occupants hardly even notice a cloud in the sky. Such storms are common during summer and approach suddenly, bringing violent winds and often torrential downpours.

On these vast expanses of water, a boat can suddenly disappear from sight leaving little trace of a tragic accident. Often it takes weeks to recover the bodies of boating victims. Strong underwater currents, craggy ledges, weeds and tremendous water depths often made search operations either difficult or nearly impossible.

Keep your cool

Capsizing a boat, particularly when a person is far from shore, can be not only a chilling experience, but also a terrifying one. This writer observed a group of Girl Scouts last summer purposely capsizing their canoes so they would know what to do if they overturned accidentally. While most of the girls remained relatively calm, some of the scouts panicked even though all the girls were carefully supervised and help was nearby. In addition, the young canoeists were wearing approved life jackets and the exercise was conducted on a small, shallow lake within 50 ft. of shore.

But despite this, several of the girls were panic-stricken. As in so many incidents of this type, if a person maintains composure there is often a good chance of making it to shore safely. Unless a boat is completely submerged, it usually is advisable to hang onto the hull, since even capsized boats will usually have some buoyancy. In addition, if any portion of the hull is still showing, it will be easier to spot than a single person in the water—hence a good reason to stay with the boat.

Wear a preserver

Leaving a boat and heading for shore is often a deadly mistake without a life preserver. Land is almost always farther away than it appears and in the cold water so common for the large reservoirs, even excellent swimmers find it difficult treading water for several hundred yards. A number of reputedly good swimmers have died during the last five years attempting to make it from their boats to shore. Some of these people collapsed from fatigue, while others became entangled in weeds and were unable to free themselves.

In looking over the grim tales of boat-related drownings for the last several years, it appears many of the deaths could have been prevented had the boat occupants been wearing life preservers; yet last summer, 34 people were arrested for using their boats with either too few life preservers or no life preserver at all. The law requires one "personal flotation device" to be within ready access of every person on board a boat.

If tradition is any fortune teller, there will be more boat-related deaths during the July 4 week than any other time of year. This is why the National Safe Boating Council annually designates this period as National Safe Boating Week in hopes of focusing attention on safety.

Follow these easy rules

Though safe boating is largely common sense, unusual conditions prevailing on certain waters make it extremely important to pay particular attention to "basic" rules. Here are some that are continually violated and consequently result in a number of deaths each year: (1) Check the capacity plate on your boat. If it says the boat can carry six people, figure on four. Rough weather can easily swamp a boat filled to capacity; (2) Head for shore immediately when dark clouds start gathering. Don't wait until it starts raining and blowing—it's too late then; $\overset{700}{\leftarrow}$ (3) If caught in a storm, immediately have everyone in the boat don a life preserver; (4) Carry plenty of extra gas. A boat that is left powerless in a storm can easily be capsized or washed onto rocks; (5) Be exceptionally careful when boating in the late fall and early spring. The cold weather during this time of year makes death from exposure a real threat, since even in 40 degree water a person may succumb in as little as half-an-hour; (6) Make sure every child on board is wearing a life jacket at all times. There are $\overset{800}{\leftarrow}$ several sizes available, so make sure the one your child is wearing fits properly.

Though this is by no means a complete list of boating tips, nearly all the boating deaths over the years could have been avoided had one or more of these simple rules been followed. More information can be obtained from the U.S. Coast Guard Auxiliary as well as the American Red Cross. These agencies both conduct courses not only to improve boating safety, but also boating skills as well.

Remember the slogan "Safe boating is no $\overset{900}{\rightarrow}$ accident."

——STOP——ASK FOR YOUR TIME——

Record time immediately and answer
the questions on content.

Time_____Sec.	RATE (from table on page 313):	R. _____
No. Correct:_____ (key on page 321)	COMPREHENSION (50% for each correct answer):	C. _____
V–13	EFFICIENCY (R × C):	E. _____

Record on Progress Chart on page 299

ANSWER THESE QUESTIONS IMMEDIATELY

1. (T–F) Most watercraft accidents occur individually as a result of excessive speed and inclement weather.
2. (MC) All of the following were given as good safety rules for boating except:

_____(1) head for shore if it starts to rain.

_____(2) never stay with a capsized boat.

_____(3) always keep a life preserver within easy reach.

_____(4) always carry extra gas.

Exercise V–14

The Guns That Went West

DICK KIRKPATRICK

(from *National Wildlife*, October–November 1966 edition)

WAIT FOR SIGNAL TO BEGIN READING

A tradition of fine firearms

Through the middle of the Nineteenth Century, the first few cautious Americans began to penetrate the vast unknown wilderness west of the Missouri and Mississippi Rivers, pushing our young nation's territories toward the Pacific. Some, like Lewis and Clark who blazed the trail to the Northwest in 1804, went in large, well-organized groups. Others went into the vast unknown alone or in small groups—all of them necessarily living off the land, taking its fruits and its hazards as they found them.

One thing they all had in common: They carried the finest firearms they could find and afford, for the raw West was unforgiving of anything but the best in men or weapons. Hostile Indians, fearless grizzlies, stampeding bison, and a thousand lesser hazards demanded instant and accurate shooting, while months and years away from civilization demanded faultless dependability.

The men whose guns failed them were seldom seen again; the ones who came back told stories, not only of the unbelievable wonders they had seen, but also of the faithful firearms that saw them through their adventures. The builders of these successful guns prospered, and founded an industry as well as a tradition that survives to this day—a tradition of fine firearms in the hands of self-reliant men who built a nation. Even today, millions of westerners and other Americans still use sporting firearms for hunting and target shooting.

The development of American firearms parallels the "winning of the west" so closely that it is difficult for historians to decide which sparked the other. Indeed, the two complemented each other through their history.

Types of weapons used by pioneering Americans

The first party west, Lewis and Clark, carried Model 1803 flintlock rifles made at the Harpers Ferry Arsenal. They served adequately, certainly being superior to the military smooth-bore muskets of the period, and set a pattern for the next few years' military expeditions.

The Mountain Men needed absolute reliability, superior accuracy, and were willing to pay for the best. Many of the best of them—Jedediah Smith, Jim Bridger, Kit Carson, Jim Clymen, the Ashley-Henry expeditions, and the Fremont expeditions, bought sturdy .50 caliber percussion rifles from Jake and Sam Hawken of St. Louis, then the fitting-out and jumping-off place for hunters, trappers, and explorers. That they lived to become celebrated scouts and guides is a tribute to the reliability of the Hawken rifles.

Following the Mountain Men's trails—indeed, using them often as guides—came the military expeditions under Pike, Kearney, Cooke, and others, and the first wagon trains of pioneers. Like the military, the pioneers took the advice of the experienced hunters and trappers, and invested in good rifles.

Along with his rifle, the well-armed early westerner often carried a handgun. Most popular through the early years were the heavy but powerful percussion muzzle loaders, called "horse pistols" from the practice of holstering them on the saddle. Most prized among them was the .54 caliber dragoon model.

In the later 1840's, percussion six-shooters came onto the market, and were greeted with enthusiasm by the firepower-hungry pioneers and soldiers. The huge early Colt dragoon models quickly developed into lighter, more efficient handguns, the most popular being the .36 caliber 1851 Navy Colt. Only the later Peacemaker has been so immortalized in literature of the West.

Another handgun which enjoyed great popularity down through the middle century, though perhaps not with such legendary characters as Kit Carson and John Fremont, were the small percussion pocket pistols made by Henry Derringer and others.

Major trends in firearm development

The demand for more firepower produced developments in shoulder arms at the same pace, and the first major breakthrough was the breech-loading rifle—first developed as a carbine because of its convenience to a mounted rifleman. As cavalry and mounted infantry were sent west to fight the Indians

143

and protect the settlers, they took with them the faster-firing breech loaders. The Hall, Sharps', Remington and Springfield carbines became the standard long guns and stories of their effectiveness helped advertise them across the West.

Military and civilian demand from the West had brought steady improvement in American firearms, but the War between the States brought almost feverish development of more efficient, faster-firing 700 ↰ guns of all kinds.

In 1866, the first breech-loading rifles with metallic cartridges reached the West, and spelled doom for the Indians. In their first full battle use, 27 Remington rollingblock rifles in the hands of experienced drovers turned away repeated charges of 3,000 Sioux. The favorite tactic of the Plains Indians, the massed charge, became obsolete and the end was soon in sight for the "wild" west.

One of the most widely used, but least glorified, of frontier guns was the double-barreled shotgun.

Many makes saw action; so many that no brand 800 ↰ stands out among the others.

After the turn of the century, the Westerner left his rifle in its scabbard or over his mantel, and if he went armed at all, it was with a smaller pocket or belt pistol. The rugged big guns of the west disappeared into attics and scrap heaps, to remain until the post-World-War-II renaissance of interest in the frontier and its accoutrements put them in collectors' cases, often at prices that would have shocked their original purchasers.

And the principles that grew up with them—that of the armed American defending himself, his 900 ↰ loved ones, and his property—live on today.

——STOP——ASK FOR YOUR TIME——

Record the time immediately and answer questions on content.

Time____Sec.	RATE (from table on page 313):	R. 3,000
No. Correct:_____ (key on page 329)	COMPREHENSION (50% for each correct answer):	C. 100
V–14	EFFICIENCY (R × C):	E. 3,000

Record on Progress Chart on page 299

ANSWER THESE QUESTIONS IMMEDIATELY

1. (T F) The Mountain Men demanded absolute reliability and superior accuracy from their weapons.
2. (MC) At the turn of the century, the heavy rifle was laid aside or discarded because:
   _____(1) the collectors were accumulating them for their showcases.
   _____(2) the terrific firepower of the rifle was not in demand by the average citizen.
   _____(3) the individual no longer needed to defend his life and property in contemporary America.
   __X__(4) the smaller lighter pistol was preferred in place of the larger gun.

Exercise V–16

Faculty Travel Abroad

WILLIAM McCORMACK

(from *School and Society* magazine, April 1972)

WAIT FOR SIGNAL TO BEGIN READING

Reliable data needed

A colleague once stated that a good college or university was one in which ten percent of the faculty were in the air at any one time. The remark was made in jest, but it did touch on some interesting issues: How extensive is faculty travel abroad? Where do professors travel, how long do they stay, and who pays the bills?

Apparently, there are no reliable data on this subject. While the Institute of International Education publishes an annual survey on the movement of scholars, the figures for some institutions, such as the University of California at Berkeley, seem un-⤶100 usually low. For 1968, for example, only 74 of the Berkeley faculty were reported to have traveled overseas. This seems more like a fair estimate for one college, such as engineering, rather than for the campus as a whole. It is not too difficult to speculate as to the reason for this questionable finding. At Berkeley—and probably at most institutions—no one has been assigned the responsibility, and no resources have been allocated, to provide the Institute with truly reliable data.

To shed light on this and other issues, the writer recently conducted a survey of the travel ⤶200 activities of the Berkeley faculty. This inquiry was part of a larger study of the international activities of the University of California's nine-campus system. A questionnaire sent to 1,725 members of the Academic Senate yielded a return of 1,184 (69 percent).

Berkeley faculty is well traveled

The survey revealed that the Berkeley faculty is well traveled indeed. Some 80 percent traveled abroad during 1965–1969. Of this group, 20 percent went abroad two or more times. The frequency of travel is roughly the same for various departmental groups. Some distinctions are evident when the data are analyzed by rank. Of the full professors, 85 ⤶300 percent traveled abroad, as compared to 78 percent of the associate professors and 64 percent of the assistant professors. On the average, 20 percent of the faculty traveled abroad each year. Areas most frequently visited were: Europe (including the U.S.S.R.), 51.6 percent; Latin America, 14.3 percent; Canada, 10.1 percent; Far East, 7.8 percent; Southeast and South Asia, 4.8 percent; Middle East, 3.2 percent; Africa, 2.5 percent; "other," 3 percent; and a combination of two or more areas, 1.6 percent.

Most of the trips (85 percent) were for six ⤶400 months or less. Of these, 45.7 percent were for less than four weeks, 23 percent for four to eight weeks, and 15.3 percent for three to six months. Longer sojourns of six to twelve months were reported by 11.2 percent of the faculty. Leaves of one or two years were taken by only 3.9 percent.

Reasons faculty traveled abroad

The purposes for which the faculty traveled abroad are also of interest. The reasons given—with multiple responses permitted—were: research, 42 percent; conference, 33 percent; general-cultural, 18 percent; personal and recreational, 14 percent; teaching, 12 percent; and administrative, 5 percent. One interesting datum which is probably involved with ⤶500 the travel issue was 70 percent of the faculty reported that some of their work has been published abroad.

Who supports this travel? In 57 percent of the cases, the funds come from a single source. Nearly one-third of the time (32 percent), that source is personal savings. Federal and university funds account for 23 percent of support; foreign governments, 17.8 percent; private foundations, 15.3 percent; and international agencies, 5 percent.

No clear pattern emerges in terms of which departments or which faculty groups received the most support, except in a few instances. Federal sup-⤶600 port for the travel of Berkeley scientists, for example, exceeded support for faculty in the arts and humanities by a ratio of five-to-one. However, this Federal support was offset by the university, which underwrote 13 percent of the travel cost for faculty in the arts and humanities, while paying only seven percent of the travel costs of its scientists. Perhaps of greater significance is the extent to which faculty have to fall back on personal funds for professional travel. Relying upon personal funds, the figures are: social sciences, 8.3 percent; physical read life sciences, 9.6 percent; engineering, 11.5 percent; humanities, 13.3

147

percent; and arts, 17 percent. While the data show 700 sources of support, the identification of the underlying reasons for this variance was beyond the scope of the survey. The entrepreneurial capacity of artists who perform or sell their work and the consultative demands made on the engineering faculty could be reasons that a greater number of respondents from these fields cited personal sources of support.

Travel was beneficial

Did travel enhance the faculty member's professional competence as a researcher or teacher? Not surprisingly, the replies were almost unanimously affirmative.

While it would be inappropriate to assume that the survey shows that travel enhances professional competence, at least the data point in that direction. 800

Clearly, one of the most prestigious faculty groups in the U.S. engages in extensive foreign travel. The highest achievers within that group travel the most frequently.

These results should be seen merely as exploratory. It would be useful to trace the careers of junior faculty to determine whether there appears to be any relationship between travel and subsequent professional success. These and other questions regarding the influence of travel should be explored in the future if we are to understand the new international dimension of higher education made possible by the 900 revolution in air transportation.

——STOP——ASK FOR YOUR TIME——

Record time immediately and answer
the questions on content.

Time _8_ Sec.	RATE (from table on page 313):	R. 6750
No. Correct: 100 (key on page 329)	COMPREHENSION (50% for each correct answer):	C. 100
V–16	EFFICIENCY (R × C):	E. 6750

Record on Progress Chart on page 299

ANSWER THESE QUESTIONS IMMEDIATELY

1. (T–F) The survey revealed that more than half of the Berkeley faculty travel was financed by state or federal funds.
2. (MC) The largest portion of faculty travel abroad was for the purpose of:
    ___(1) general-cultural improvement.
    ___(2) personal and recreational values.
    ___(3) teaching abroad.
    _X_(4) research.

Exercise V-17

John Muir

RUSSELL McKEE

(from *Colorado Outdoors* magazine, November–December 1966 edition)

WAIT FOR SIGNAL TO BEGIN READING

John Muir's early youth

Some say John Muir was the father of our national park system while others say he was America's first great conservationist. Still others bill him as founder, custodian and majordomo of the whole wilderness concept in American thinking. John Muir himself claimed he was, by profession, a tramp.

Who was this bearded, ascetic little man who lived most of his life alone in the wilderness, existing on tea and dry bread, that he could meet with presidents, and fire the imagination of a whole nation with his zeal for the delights of natural beauty?

Muir was born in Scotland in 1838, and emi-100 grated with his family to Kingston, Wisconsin, in 1849. There the Muir family hacked out a quarter-section homestead farm and young John got his first taste of American wilderness. He educated himself at night after working 16 hours in the fields, and at age 22 left home for study at the University of Wisconsin. He had a genius for mechanical inventions and contrived a working clock (though he had never seen the inside of one) and various other gadgets. After graduation from Wisconsin he was well on his way to a fortune in various manufacturing ventures, 200 when an accident blinded him for several weeks. During this time of worried convalescence, he determined to quit the cities and spend the rest of his life among the wild things he loved.

A cross-country walk

Accordingly, when he recovered, he walked cross-country from Kentucky to the Gulf Coast, went on to Cuba, and after various other rambles took passage from New York to San Francisco. Soon he found the luxuriant Central Valley and the high Sierras of California, always walking and living for the most part on a Spartan supply of tea and dry bread.

He rambled up and down the Sierras and other 300 parts of the West, carefully recording all he saw, and gradually began to write and lecture about the natural beauties he found in these mountain areas. One of the periodicals that printed his articles was the "Century Magazine," and in 1889, the editor, Robert Underwood Johnson, traveled to California for a camping trip with Muir. Together, they saw the growing destruction of those forest areas by lumber, mining, and sheep grazing interests. Johnson suggested that Muir stump for establishment of what would be 400 called Yosemite National Park, a public area protected from exploitation. In the excited talk that followed, Muir saw that his life work could be the awakening of America to the preservation of its natural beauties. Johnson published Muir's articles on Yosemite and a bill was introduced into Congress immediately, but it failed to pass that year. However, the bill was entered again the following year, and on October 1, 1890, Yosemite National Park came into existence.

Muir stumped for more such areas and in 1892 helped found and was named president of the Sierra Club, still a powerful conservation organization. Through this club, he rallied new support for public 500 lands, and by 1893, the Federal government had set aside 13 million acres in western parks and forests. However, destruction on these lands continued despite Federal laws, and in 1896, Muir served as guide and adviser to a forestry commission of six men, who toured the West viewing the remaining natural areas and the devastation being wrecked on others. The commission reported to President Cleveland in 1897, who promptly created 13 new forest reservations in eight western states, urged repeal and modification of fraudulent timber and mining laws, called for scientific management of forests to maintain a permanent timber supply, and created two new na-600 tional parks—Grand Canyon and Mount Rainier. A total of 21 million acres was involved.

Roosevelt aids in the battle for conservation

By then the lumber, mining and stock grazing interests were thoroughly aroused, and through their lobbies were able to overturn in Congress much of this, but still the fight went on, and when Theodore Roosevelt entered the White House, public sentiment was swinging steadily in favor of more conservation. Roosevelt did much to stimulate the work that Muir had started, and even traveled west to camp with

Muir soon after taking office. The two men, virtually alone during this historic four-day outing, tramped $\overset{700}{\leftarrow}$ over part of Yosemite and talked about the tremendous problem of land preservation during this great period of national expansion. The effect this camping trip had on development of the national parks and forests now available in this country can hardly be estimated, but it is perhaps enough to note that 43 million acres of land were in national forest when Roosevelt became President; that another 151 million acres were added during his two terms of office; and that the number of national parks was doubled.

John Muir died in 1914, but in his honor a $\overset{800}{\leftarrow}$ lake, a Sequoia grove, a glacier, a mountain peak and a butterfly have been named. Trails, passes, peaks of land and promontories also bear his name. His stern Scottish father had taught him that all vanities and touches of pride were bad seeds to chew and John Muir would perhaps be embarrassed by the esteem in which his name is now held. Yet for all his modesty, John Muir was himself an able conservationist who shook a nation from its lethargy, and who preserved our country's natural gifts. We $\overset{900}{\rightarrow}$ can claim ourselves fortunate for his existence.

——STOP——ASK FOR YOUR TIME——

Record time immediately and answer
questions on content.

Time_____Sec.	RATE (from table on page 313):	R. _____
No. Correct:_____ (key on page 321)	COMPREHENSION (50% for each correct answer):	C. _____
V–17	EFFICIENCY (R × C):	E. _____

Record on Progress Chart on page 299

ANSWER THESE QUESTIONS IMMEDIATELY

1. (T–F) John Muir was a revered conservationist who stimulated American thinking about wilderness concepts.
2. (MC) One of Muir's staunchest supporters, Theodore Roosevelt, aided land preservation efforts by:
    _____(1) signing the bill which established Yosemite National Park.
    _____(2) creating 13 new forest reservations in eight western states.
    _____(3) doubling the number of national parks.
    _____(4) urging the repeal and modification of fraudulent timber laws.

Exercise V-18

Log Exports

HON. DON YOUNG

(from the *Congressional Record*, April 2, 1973)

WAIT FOR SIGNAL TO BEGIN READING

Operations at full capacity

Today, ninety-five percent of Alaska's sawmills are operating at one hundred percent capacity on two shifts per day. Three shifts per day operations are not presently possible, due to the time required to perform daily maintenance, and with the mills operating year around, shutdowns are limited to those caused by breakdown.

At present, twelve to fourteen different Japanese trading companies are in vigorous competition for the production of these mills. By way of comparison, in 1967 there was only one such trading company in the Alaska market, none of the mills operated the year around, and none of them were on 100 double shift operations.

Existing export regulations critical to growth

Forest Service regulations controlling the extent of primary manufacture in Alaska necessary before export to Japan would be permitted, have been critically important to the development of Alaska's export market in Japan. Recognizing that Alaska's own domestic demand would not support a viable sawmill industry in Alaska within the regrowth cycle of Alaska's existing forests, and that Alaska sawmills had little chance of ever placing their production into the domestic United States market at a profit, they did, and still do, permit the export from Alaska of 200 lumber up to a nominal eight inches in thickness. This limitation was determined over the years to be the stage of primary manufacture which would give Alaska the optimum benefits of primary manufacture, while at the same time giving them a market for their product.

Effect of Jones Act

A repeal of the Jones Act would enable the Alaska lumber to be marketed into the domestic United States at a profit, due to the supposed reduction in shipping rates which would follow if we were permitted to use foreign bottoms to move our product; this is simply not so for several reasons. 300

Alaska lumber is being lifted by Japanese ships with capacities in excess of eight million board feet.

This lumber is loaded at rates in excess of one million board feet per day; the ships are highly sophisticated, and represent a huge investment made over the past ten years by the Japanese, specifically designed for the Alaska lumber trade. There are no other ships available to Alaska to move Alaska lumber at the volume and the loading rates required. If our export to Japan is cut off, the Japanese obviously 400 will not allow us to use these ships to move our products into the United States domestic market. During the time required for other foreign or domestic shipping to develop the necessary shipping capacity for Alaska's use, the Alaska timber industry would have gone out of business.

Second, the cost of producing lumber in Alaska is so much higher over the cost of production in the Northwest, that there is simply no way meaningful competition in the United States domestic market for Alaska lumber could be achieved. Labor costs in logging camps and sawmills range twenty-five to thirty-five percent higher in Alaska over Northwest 500 costs. Gross logging costs exceed Northwest costs by thirty-five to forty percent. Local purchase costs are twenty-five percent higher than the Northwest. When these higher costs are considered with the fact that the Alaska timber produces a much higher percentage of low grade lumber than does the Northwest timber, it becomes obvious that the Alaska product cannot be marketed at a profit in the domestic United States market, regardless of a lowering of shipping rates.

Four and one-half inch limit will not create more jobs

Assuming that the Japanese market would accept Alaska's lumber production in sizes not exceeding four and one-half inches in thickness, no real 600 benefit to the Alaska economy would be achieved. Four and one-half inch lumber can be produced with the same equipment as is presently being utilized for six and eight-inch lumber without any significant increase in employment. Production costs would increase, because the rate of production would necessarily fall in accommodation to sawing the lumber down to the smaller dimension. At the same time, although some of Alaska's lumber does in fact bring a fair return from the Japanese market in four-inch-thick sizes, most of Alaska's lumber would suffer a reduction in market value if sold in thicknesses below $\xleftarrow{700}$ the present six and eight inches being used. Here, again, we come back to the problem of the high percentage of defect in Alaska timber. Reducing the thickness limitations to four and one-half inches would force Alaska mills to cut the defect out thus increasing the resulting waste. Leaving the defect in, however, permits the Japanese to cut the defect out in a manner which gives them much more than wood chip recovery from the defect at higher values than wood chip recovery. In other words, Alaska sawmills can sell an eight-inch-thick piece of lumber to the Japanese at a higher price than could be obtained $\xleftarrow{800}$

for two four-inch pieces. The four-inch lumber presently being sold by Alaska industry to Japan is primarily obtained from trees which, due to their small size, cannot produce a merchantable product in excess of four inches in thickness. As the tree size increases, the tree can accommodate the production of six and eight-inch-thick lumber with a higher return to the Alaska timber industry and Alaska economy than would be recovered if the industry were forced to reduce all of their production to the $\xrightarrow{900}$ four and one-half inch limits.

——STOP——ASK FOR YOUR TIME——

Record time immediately and answer
the questions on content.

Time____Sec.	RATE (from table on page 313):	R. _7,710_
No. Correct: _1_ (key on page 329)	COMPREHENSION (50% for each correct answer):	C. _50_
V–18	EFFICIENCY (R × C):	E. _3,850_

Record on Progress Chart on page 299

ANSWER THESE QUESTIONS IMMEDIATELY

1. (T–F) cost of producing lumber in Alaska is less than the cost of production in the Northwest.
2. (MC) he major threat from the proposed repeal of the Jones Act would be:
   ____(1) increasing costs of shipping to the West Coast markets.
   _2_(2) reducing the Japanese market for timber.
   ____(3) reducing the shipping facilities now in use.
   ____(4) reducing the amount of timber available for harvest.

Exercise V–19

Sludge Slough

R. C. BURKHOLDER

(from *Wyoming Wildlife*, November 1973)

WAIT FOR SIGNAL TO BEGIN READING

Henry David Thoreau had his Walden Pond, John Muir had his High Sierras, Bob Marshall had his Wilderness Area, and I have Sludge Slough!

Sludge Slough is an environmental phenomenon —as world-famous for the study of *hydro*-ecological life cycles as McGruder's Gully is for the study of *terra*-ecological life cycles.

What makes Sludge Slough so captivatingly interesting, at least to the limonogol . . . limnygo . . . limnomol . . . fresh water expert, is the fact that the life cycle of Sludge Slough is much easier to research and study than the more complex life cycles found in other lesser-known bodies of water such as Lake Erie, the Salton Sea, and the Panama Canal. 100← In addition, each link in the food chain found in Sludge Slough is a rare, threatened, endangered, and/or picked-upon species.

Inasmuch as you are now goose-pimply with academic interest, let me briefly describe, in scientific detail, the hydro-ecological life cycle of Sludge Slough.

To begin with, all life cycles can be depicted as a closed circle, and the cycle of Sludge Slough has no beginning and no end, so let's start between the beginning and the end with the sludge of Sludge Slough.

A. Sludge

Sludge Slough is surrounded by, underlain with, 200← and wallows in the ickiest, gooiest, and muckiest sludge. There are two primary sources of this sludge: (1) deceased organic debris of every imaginable kind, and (2) decomposed aluminum foil, snuff cans, beer bottles, old tires, and cardboard cartons.

At this point in the cycle, the sludge don't do nothin'; it just lays there—dead, lifeless phhht!— and smells a lot, but then, comes the spring and summer thunderstorms with the dark, billowing clouds scurrying across Sludge Slough. Thunder rumbles overhead and lightning flashes into the muck making complex electro-chemical reaction which takes place and, lo, we have life in Sludge Slough! 300← Honest . . . plain, ordinary, run-of-the-mill sludge is now . . . *bio-sludge!*

B. Bio-Sludge

Bio-sludge consists of many, many billions and trillions of microscopic one-celled ugly little animals, plants, and combinations thereof which swim, crawl, slither, float, wiggle, hop, and squirm all over the place. This bio-sludge performs three bio-socio-ecoenvironmental functions: (1) it eats common sludge, (2) it chases other bio-sludge back and forth through the slough, and (3) it serves as the one and only food source for the *sludge guppy*.

C. Sludge Guppy

Sludge Guppies are tiny fish ranging in size 400→ from 0.00085 mm to 0.00635 in. in length which feed exclusively on bio-sludge when they are not cannibalizing each other. Since the sludge guppy population is all-male in character, reproduction takes place through a process known as photosexo-frustration. Every evening individual sludge guppies turn green and go all to pieces, a reproductive technique which assures a goodly supply of sludge guppies for the *slough sludgeminnow*.

D. Slough Sludgeminnow

The slough sludgeminnow can be readily identified by:

1. an invisible lateral line encircling the body from tail to anal fin,
2. dorsal fins located on the ventral side of the body,
500→ 3. one large greenish-blue eye and one small yellowish-red eye, and
4. the fact that there are no other minnows in Sludge Slough.

Unlike other minnows found in Sludge Slough, the slough sludgeminnow does not form harems in the late summer, mate in the fall, and spawn in the spring. Slough sludgeminnows spawn first, then mate, forming up into large schools which are fed upon by the voracious *sludge sloughfish*.

E. Sludge Sloughfish

The sludge sloughfish, although it ranges from 8″ to 45 pounds in size, is inedible, unpalatable, and as a sporting gamefish, the sludge sloughfish provides less thrills and excitement than an empty bottle of $\underleftarrow{600}$ Geritol on the end of a line. One avid sludge slough-fish fisherman stated on our official Sludge Slough Recreation User Questionnaire and Interview Form 146-c (6/73):

> Reeling in one of them there fish is like dragging a pair of shorts across the slough but it sure beats watching the chrome rust on my pickup every weekend!

The last link in the Sludge Slough life cycle/food chain—the *sludge sloughfish fisherman*.

F. Sludge Sloughfish Fisherman

The sludge sloughfish fisherman plays a very important role in the hydro-ecological life cycle of Sludge Slough, specifically, if the sludge sloughfish fisherman did not routinely provide source material $\underleftarrow{700}$ for sludge; i.e., trash and garbage such as aluminum foil, snuff cans, beer bottles, old tires and cardboard cartons; there would be no sludge and no Sludge Slough.

Recommendations

Naturally, we have developed some suggestions and recommendations for the administration (tech-nical interference with) and management (scientific manipulation of) the hydro-ecological life cycle of Sludge Slough.

1. To assure an adequate supply of bio-sludge, we suggest that the U.S. Weather Bureau—in coop-eration with the Environmental Protection Agency and General Services Administration—plan, pro-gram, and schedule lightning strikes into Sludge Slough on a year-round basis.

$\underset{\rightarrow}{800}$ 2. Assuming the recommendation above is initiated, we should have no difficulty in maintaining an acceptable population level of sludge guppies, slough sludgeminnows, and sludge sloughfish in their natural and pristine habitat.

3. However, consideration should be given to stocking Sludge Slough with barracuda, piranha, and shark just to see what happens to the natural and pristine habitat mentioned in item No. 2 above.

4. On second thought, forget it . . . we just received word that someone bought Sludge Slough and is planning to drain it, level it, and build a combination Museum of Natural History and Insti-$\underset{\rightarrow}{900}$ tute for Ecological Studies on it!

——STOP——ASK FOR YOUR TIME——

Record time immediately and answer
the questions on content.

Time_____Sec.	RATE (from table on page 313):	R. _____
No. Correct:_____ (key on page 321)	COMPREHENSION (50% for each correct answer):	C. _____
V–19	EFFICIENCY (R × C):	E. _____

Record on Progress Chart on page 299

ANSWER THESE QUESTIONS IMMEDIATELY

1. (T–F) The author recommended further funding for ecological research on the Sludge Slough.
2. (MC) This analysis of the hydro-ecological life cycle of Sludge Slough is:
   _____(1) an analytical analysis.
   _____(2) an ecological experiment.
   _____(3) a hydrological history.
   _____(4) a fictional fantasy.

Exercise V–20

Report to the President

(Modified from an actual report made by an anonymous Counseling Center Director)

WAIT FOR SIGNAL TO BEGIN READING

History

Guidance services at Coronado State College have been evident for some time. A Guidance Office, which has now been disbanded, offered academic, educational and testing functions for the students.

However, a Counseling Center was established in the summer of 1971 under the initiative of the Vice-President for Academic Affairs, Dr. Gordon C. Seward. A counselor was hired in the spring of 1971 and during the summer of 1971 did some initial counseling and research. A staff member of the Psychology Department had been performing psychological counseling functions on the campus for seven years. He continued counseling and was released by $\underset{\leftarrow}{100}$ the Psychology Department one-quarter time as a professional member of the Counseling Center staff.

New director

Dr. Mortimer A. Trag was appointed Director in August of 1971 and facilities were provided in various locations on campus for the Center staff. Furthermore, Dr. Trag was asked to supervise the Special Services program under the directorship of Mr. Roy Sanchez. Limited funds were available from the regular college budget for the establishment of the Counseling Center. Therefore, affiliation with the Special Services program seemed administratively purposeful, since Special Services was committed under its program contract to provide regular counseling services to the specially selected students in $\underset{\leftarrow}{200}$ that program.

Special Services primarily was concerned with educational, tutorial and academic problems. At the time the program was started the only professional psychological counselors available were in the Counseling Center and with various faculty on campus who had professional counseling skills.

The Counseling Center was hindered in development by (1) poor facilities; (2) lack of acceptance by administration, faculty and staff; (3) confusion with Special Services program; (4) confusion of goals and objectives with the old Guidance Office; and (5) lack of recognition and cooperation from other counselors that psychological counseling is a main func- $\underset{\leftarrow}{300}$ tion of a College Counseling Center.

As the summer ended, it seemed an almost insurmountable task to overcome all the obstacles. The Administration had taken steps for improvement before the Director came on campus, however, and the problem of adequate facilities was soon solved, as Dr. Seward had workmen completing a well-designed Counseling Center in Herring Hall. Both Counseling Center staff and Special Services staff moved into the newly renovated facilities in the basement of Herring Hall in December, 1971.

During these early months of the summer and fall terms, much time and energy were expended in $\underset{\rightarrow}{400}$ ordering supplies and materials, office furniture and equipment, and becoming familiar with local business office procedures in Coronodo.

In addition, mastering the system of budgeting, requisitions and purchasing with the business office was demanding, time-consuming and often confusing.

Goals, guidelines and philosophy of the Counseling Center had to be established, as well as policies regarding the relationship of Special Services to the Counseling Center. Job descriptions and professional responsibilities of counselors and counseling psychologists had to be developed in relation to the overall problems of students at Coronado State College.

Reorganizing the staff

Of even greater importance was the task of $\underset{\rightarrow}{500}$ hiring and mobilizing a new and inexperienced professional and clerical staff as a unified team, to effect systematized procedures, and to implement, at a high level of professional standards, the psychological counseling and related services that had not heretofore, to such an extent, been provided by the college. In this respect, emphasis was placed on coordinating the Special Services program into the comprehensive aspect of the Counseling Services program. Furthermore, as students came to the Center looking for help, it became evident that personal, emotional and psychological services were lacking at Coronado $\underset{\rightarrow}{600}$ State College—and an emphasis needed to be placed in this area. We had the professional staff to do this; therefore, psychological or therapeutic counseling became an important aspect to the goals and functions of the Counseling Center.

Thus, program development and role definition were the essential tasks that needed to be carried out by the Director and his staff. A brief mimeographed handbook was prepared by the Director and staff. It includes: (1) General Philosophical Base for Operation; (2) Objectives of the Counseling Center; (3) Specific Objectives; (4) Functions and Intake Procedures. These are referred to later on in the report.

Briefly, then, the primary emphasis and philosophical thinking were to develop services for help-$\xrightarrow{700}$ ing students adjust in all aspects of their educational, vocational, personal, and social adjustment.

Another early objective was that of publicizing and explaining the nature of the services and how best the Center staff could collaborate with faculty, administration, staff, and management in furthering the students' total educational development. Therefore, articles announcing the appointment of a counseling psychologist and a Director occurred early in the student and local newspapers; memos and mimeographed materials were circulated to faculty and staff; a brochure was developed and distributed to major offices, classrooms, and dormitories on $\xrightarrow{800}$ campus. The brochures were mailed to every faculty member and staff member on campus. Additional brochures were placed in showcase areas in the administration building, the Offices for Academic and Student Affairs, the Graduate School offices, the Library, and the Student Union. Continued effort was made to inform students and faculty about the professional counselors available, where they were located and how to arrange for appointments. Signs were placed on the outside of the Counseling Center complex. Despite this concentrated effort, some students and faculty members still are not aware that a Counseling Center exists on the campus with two $\xrightarrow{900}$ full-time counselors.

——STOP——ASK FOR YOUR TIME——

Record time immediately and answer
the questions on content.

Time ___ Sec.	RATE (from table on page 313):	R. ___
No. Correct: ___ (key on page 329)	COMPREHENSION (50% for each correct answer):	C. ___
V–20	EFFICIENCY (R × C):	E. ___

Record on Progress Chart on page 299

ANSWER THESE QUESTIONS IMMEDIATELY

1. (T–F) The report is a quantitive review of the work of staff members of a Counseling Center.
2. (MC) The primary activities of the Counseling Center stressed in this report for the year were:
    ___ (1) business management and administration.
    ___ (2) program development and role definition.
    ___ (3) public relations with students and alumni.
    ___ (4) meeting heavy demands from students for psychological counseling.

SERIES VI
Exploratory Reading Exercises

Instructions

The Series VI exercises are designed to develop your ability to read continuously one long article and then to recite on the material at the end. This type of reading will be contrasted with that of the exercise in Series VII, where you read in smaller units and do a spaced recitation. Many students argue that they do not have time for the SQ4R method of study or for self-recitation. A comparison of your efficiency scores between these two types of exercises is one of the best objective answers to your own possible hesitancy to try these study techniques.

As in Series V exercises, you will find the length and the readability scores at the top of each article and you will find the numbers in the center margin that will help you to estimate your speed. Articles become progressively more difficult as you proceed through the series, and here again you are working toward increasing reading speed and reading level. In this case, however, you have more material and more ideas to retain, and you will be tested more thoroughly on the material read.

When given the signal to begin an article, you should read as rapidly as possible, concentrating on main ideas and watching for any clues to those ideas. When you finish reading, ask for your time immediately, and compute your rate in the same manner as in Series V by using the table on page 315.

Then go on to the ten questions on the material, and answer them as accurately as possible. Answer the (MC) and the (T–F) questions as instructed before. In the Completion questions (C), you are to fill in the word or words that will best complete the meaning of the sentence. After these are scored according to the keys on pages 322 and 330, you compute your comprehension by multiplying your number of correct answers by ten. You may then compute your *efficiency* by multiplying the *rate* by the *comprehension* and record the efficiency score on the Progress Chart on page 299.

Suggestions

These are referred to as Exploratory Reading Exercises because they are designed to help polish tools of reading for new ideas, greater detail, or further understanding of materials with which you are already familiar. These may be materials already sorted by the Idea Reading approach and identified for a little more thorough reading. Materials identified by this type of reading for specific study purposes or for significant long-range use normally will be marked and set aside for study reading or critical reading.

Normally, this reading procedure will not result in long-range retention of details unless the content is closely related to personal needs and unless reading is reinforced by additional study skills focused on long-term comprehension.

For general reading about new ideas or new interests, this type of reading utilizes high-speed reading skills tempered with selective judgment of materials appropriate for more careful study.

Your rate on these materials will depend on much more than the arrangement on paper, the content, or the instructor's motivation. You will determine your rate and efficiency by your personal motivation and attitude. What you already know about the topic, how you feel about the topic, and what previous associations you may have with the topic or the author will have a strong effect on your reading activity.

In this longer reading material, one criterion is especially important, however, and that is your ability to concentrate for an extended period of time without interruption. This will require effort on your part. You will have to avoid the tendencies to daydream, to let your attention be distracted by nearby audio or visual factors of passing interest. Perhaps you should review again the materials on pages 19–24 of this book regarding concentration and basic study skills. Content of these articles will cover a fairly wide range of material, some of which may be of immediate interest to you and some of which may not. For the purpose of these exercises, you should try to develop an inquiring mind and try to seek new ideas. You can apply a fairly rapid reading rate to such materials. You may be surprised to find out how much content you can pick up even at relatively high-speed reading.

Thinking about the title, checking out your own knowledge of the topic, and posing questions to which you want to find answers will provide a mental setting in which you should achieve effective concentration and maximum reading efficiency.

Exercise VI-1

Noisy Chorus of the Sea

WILLIAM N. TAVOLGA

(from *Natural History*, April 1967)

WAIT FOR SIGNAL TO BEGIN READING

Some fishes gnash their teeth, others sound like foghorns—the porpoise whistles and squeals—crustaceans add to the clamor by clicking and rasping. Through use of the spectrograph, we now know more about the sounds of alarm, feeding, mating, and reconnaissance.

In recent years most people have come to realize that the sea is not the "silent world" of Jacques Cousteau's well-known book on undersea adventure. In reality, the oceans are at least as noisy as, *and often noisier than,* our average terrestrial environment. One of the reasons for this, as we shall see later, is the varied and large amount of sound ⤶100 contributed by water currents and marine animals. Another lies in the very nature of the medium, for water is a far better conductor of sound than air because it is about a thousand times denser; also it is virtually incompressible under normal circumstances. Consequently, more energy is required to start the movement of sound through water, but once started, this acoustic energy will be transmitted farther and much faster. The velocity of sound in air is about 330 meters per second (1,080 feet per second); in water it is almost 1,500 meters per second (4,920 ⤶200 feet), and these figures are significantly affected by changes in temperature and pressure. In the oceans, since salt water is denser than fresh, the velocity may go as high as 5,050 feet per second—almost five times greater than in air.

The transmission of sound through sea water is further enhanced because much of the sound is conserved by reflection. It is reflected from the surface of the water (up to 99.9 percent of the energy is reflected back); from the sea floor; and from the interfaces formed by layers of water that are at different temperatures.

One other fact must be considered for we are ⤷300 not aquatic beings. Even with Scuba gear we cannot match our air-adapted ears to underwater sounds, and it is difficult for us to conceive what the marine environment sounds like. We must, therefore, use artificial hearing aids, as it were, to translate for us.

Measuring the sound

In addition to the frequency of a sound, commonly called its pitch, we must know something of its intensity, or volume. This we express in units called decibels (abbreviated to dB). Decibels are actually logarithmic values, and it just happens that our sensory processes, including hearing, follow some ⤷400 approximation of a logarithmic law. Our perception is such that when one sound seems twice as loud as another, the actual difference may be very large or very small, depending on the absolute intensity of the two sounds. One decibel is close to the minimum difference that we can detect in the intensity of two sounds, but a one-decibel difference in a very soft tone is an extremely small difference in pressure, while at a loud tone it may be ten or a hundred times greater. A decibel, therefore, is a relative measure and is always given in reference to some preselected ⤷500 zero point.

If we measure the sound pressure in the sea, including noise produced by wave motion, by vertical and horizontal currents, by water friction against the sea floor, by the noise of boats and ships, and superimposed on all that, the noises of marine animals, the average level of ambient sea noise becomes about 10 or 15 decibels *above* the one-microbar reference level. This is comparable to a busy office with typewriters clattering, papers rustling, people walking and talking, telephones ringing, and the din of outdoor traffic.

The marine animals commonly recognized as ⤷600 sound-producers can be broadly divided into three groups. (1) The invertebrates include crustaceans (crab, shrimp, lobsters) as principal sonic forms; also some mollusks and a few other forms. (2) The vertebrate class of fishes includes many sonic species among the 20,000-odd known forms; perhaps a majority of these are at least potential sound-producers. (3) Virtually all known species of marine mammals are sound-producers, principally the cetaceans (whales, dolphins, porpoises).

The noisy crustaceans

Most crustaceans can produce various clicking or rasping sounds with their claws, mandibles, and other parts of their shell-encrusted bodies. The sounds often accompany normal locomotion; how- ⤷700 ever there are many species that produce sounds at other times by specialized structures.

We can only guess at the functions of the crustacean sounds. Some may be related to territorial defense; others may serve as cues in reproductive behavior; in many cases they may be merely incidental to feeding. There has been virtually no experimental work in this area of invertebrate behavior, and the field is wide open for research.

Sounds from fishes

Marine fishes produce three general types of sounds: stridulations (rubbing or rasping), swim-bladder vibrations, and hydrodynamic disturbances.

The stridulations roughly compare to the sound of crickets rubbing their wings together. Such movement of one rough surface against another gives a $\overset{800}{\leftarrow}$ rasping noise, a series of short broad-band pulses. Many species of fish produce them when they gnash their teeth or rub patches of denticles in the pharynx. Usually the sounds come during feeding; other times during fright or serious difficulty, as when the fish is captured. There is some evidence that such seemingly incidental sounds are actually a primitive form of communication. For instance, a fish hearing these "feeding sounds" can associate them with the presence of food and respond accordingly.

The most efficient and highly evolved sonic mechanism in fishes is the swim-bladder. Originally, $\overset{900}{\leftarrow}$ this thin-walled, air-containing sac probably served to control the buoyancy of the fish. It now has several other functions. In many species it is equipped with a set of specialized muscles capable of vibrating at surprisingly high rates (up to at least 300 contractions per second in some species). For this drumming sound the entire swim-bladder with its enclosed air serves as an underwater loudspeaker of considerable efficiency. Prominent producers of such sound are members of the drumfish family (family Sciaenidae), including croakers, sea trout, and sea drum.

The biological significance of many of these sounds remains obscure. In a few cases, as with $\overset{1000}{\leftarrow}$ toadfish and drumfish, the drumming is clearly related to spawning behavior and comes only from males. In others, as with groupers and squirrelfish, the explanation is territorial behavior—a resident animal sounds off when approached by an intruder, but there are also puzzling areas. Alarm and fright

often evoke sounds; just as often, they halt the sonic activity.

The marine mammals

In contrast to fishes, cetaceans are warm-blooded, air-breathing mammals, and include a variety of forms, commonly called whales, dolphins, and porpoises. These produce sounds that fall into $\overset{1100}{\rightarrow}$ two general categories: (1) short, broad-band sound pulses, or clicks, and (2) sustained whistles, squeals, and other cries.

As far as is known, all the species of toothed whales produce the short, pulselike clicks. The clicks come from a specialized vibrating organ found within the complex of air chambers leading to the blowhole. It has been shown that these clicks are primarily intended to locate objects by means of the returning echoes. This highly efficient and accurate sonar system rivals that of bats. Echoes from the clicks give the marine animal much information about its en- $\overset{1200}{\rightarrow}$ vironment, especially the location and type of food that it is hunting.

It is not really surprising that marine animals in general show so many adaptations that utilize the acoustic channel for various behavior patterns. The surprising aspect is that only recently have biologists come to appreciate this fact.

With underwater vision often masked by turbidity, with the chemical senses hampered by disturbing currents and slow diffusion rates, sound is therefore the most efficient long-range mechanism for supplying marine animals with necessary information about each other and the rest of their environment.

Meanwhile, technological advances over the past twenty years have given scientists an acoustic $\overset{1300}{\rightarrow}$ window into the ocean, and marine biology now can enlarge our meager knowledge of the behavior and distribution of marine life. This knowledge is essential and basic to all oceanographic studies, which are growing in importance as it becomes evident that future generations of man will depend increasingly $\overset{1350}{\rightarrow}$ on the seas for their food resources.

——STOP——ASK FOR YOUR TIME——

Record time immediately and answer
the questions on content.

Time 26 Sec. RATE (from table on page 315):

No. Correct:_____ COMPREHENSION (10% for each correct answer):
(key on page 322)

VI–1 EFFICIENCY (R × C):

R. 3116

3116
6

C. _____

E. _____

18696

Record on Progress Chart on page 299

ANSWER THESE QUESTIONS IMMEDIATELY

1. (T–F) In reality the oceans are often noisier than our average terrestrial environment.

2. (T–F) Air is a better conductor of sound than water.

3. (T–F) More energy is required to start the movement of sound through water than through air.

4. (C) Measuring the intensity and volume of sound is expressed in units called ___ Hma (decibles) ___.

5. (MC) Marine animals commonly recognized as sound producers are the marine mammals, the invertebrates including crustaceans, and the:

____(1) vertebrate of class of fishes.

____(2) mollusk and shell fish.

__X__(3) drumfish family.

6. (T–F) Movement of one rough surface against another, as when fish gnash their teeth, is called a hydro-dynamic disturbance.

7. (C) The most efficient sonic mechanism in fishes is the ___ tail / swim bladder ___

8. (T–F) Scientists have discovered a specific biological significance in many of these fish sounds.

9. (T–F) An acoustical window to the sea becomes more important as it becomes evident that future generations of man will become increasingly dependent upon the sea for food resources.

10. (MC) Echoes from the "clicks" give the marine animal much information about:

____(1) density of the water.

__X__(2) its environment.

____(3) location of nearby boats.

____(4) changes in current.

Exercise VI–2

Letter to a Dead Teacher

BEL KAUFMAN

(from *Today's Education*, March–April 1975)

WAIT FOR SIGNAL TO BEGIN READING

Dear Mr. Stock:

You probably wouldn't remember me, even if you were alive. I sat in the third row back in your English 512 class in South Side High School in Newark, New Jersey. You gave me an *A* minus for being unprepared.

You had asked us to write a composition in class about one of Hardy's heroines (Was it Tess?), but I had neglected to read the book assigned. Caught off guard, writing frantically against the clock, I described a young woman, the room she sat in, the beam of light from the high window, her hands 100 in her lap, her thoughts in her head. I anticipated failure, disgrace, worst of all—your disappointment. Instead, you gave me a minus for being unprepared and an *A* for something uniquely mine. Your scrawled comment in red ink on my paper read, "This isn't Hardy's character, but you've made yours very real."

Startled into gratitude, I became aware of my own possibilities. You *recognized* me.

I needed recognition, I was a shy, uneasy girl, too foreign, too intense. The English language, newly learned, lay clumsy on my tongue. Long sausage curls coiled down my shoulder blades—this, in the age of the shingle bob and the spit curl. Instead of 200 the scarlet Cupid's bow mouth, I was allowed but a pale touch of Tangee lipstick. How I longed for spikedheels and gunmetal silk stockings. How I yearned for plucked eyebrows, flapping galoshes, a slicker with boys' initials painted on it, the boys themselves!

From the time I arrived in this country at 12 until skipping had brought me to the approximate age suitable for high school, I had been the oldest in the class, the last to be called, the least to be noticed. I was monitor of nothing.

I don't think you knew what you did for me, 300 Mr. Stock. We teachers seldom know whom we influence or how or even why. It was not my defects you emphasized, but my worth. For the first time I realized that what I had made up inside my mind could be real to someone else. Great teaching has to do with that first time, that gasp of discovery: "Eureka!" "Oh, I get it! I see!"—a new planet in the sky or letters of the alphabet that suddenly form a word.

Other teachers dealt differently with us. One 400 would silently, lips pursed, enter a meticulous zero into an ominous black notebook. Another, down the corridor from you, would review publicly and with exquisite sarcasm all our past misdeeds, of which the current one was the ultimate transgression.

Actually, I recall very few of my teachers. In Latin, the teacher made us sit quietly, hands on desk, eyes front. This was called "maintaining discipline." In history, our teacher perched on the windowsill, dangled his legs, and wooed us with false camaraderie.

You assumed one simple fact: If the lesson was interesting, we would be attentive. We were more 500 than attentive. We hated to see the period end, for you knew when to ask the provocative, unexpected "Why?" which tumbled upside down our whole cluttered cart of preconceptions and set us thinking long after the dismissal bell. You did not try to charm or to beguile us. You never pretended to be a pal. You were a *teacher*. Your dignity was unassailable. Because you respected yourself and us, we were able to respect ourselves.

Another time you called my handwriting distinctive. Did you say *distinctive* or *distinguished*? I no longer remember. What matters is how much 600 that meant to me. In my skipping of grades, I had skipped right over the Palmer Method of ovals and strokes; consequently, my handwriting was different. But *distinctive*—imagine that!

Somehow, you made everyone feel special. Once you quoted from Shakespeare: . . . who can say more than this rich praise—that you alone are you?" I knew you meant me. And so did each of the 34 others in the room.

When one of us returned after an absence, you would say, "We missed you." When one was unprepared, you would shake your head: "Too bad; we were hoping to know what *you* think." When one 700 came late, you assumed there was good reason for it that need not be asked. You treated us as adults, your equals, and so—in your class—we were. "Don't be captious," you would say, taking it for granted that we either knew the word or would look it up in one of several dictionaries you always left scattered around the room. We looked it up. Because you knew we were fine people, punctual attenders, conscientious homework doers, honorable test takers, devoted scholars, and responsible citizens, we were. For you, we were! You were sincere, before the word 800 became suspect; tolerant, before the word became loaded. Kids know what is phony. Children and lovers always know. It was unthinkable to offer you anything shoddy or second-rate. I see only now that your demands on us were enormous.

I don't remember clearly what you looked like; you were short, I think, and roundish, but I recall the sound of laughter in the room. You were never one to buy a cheap laugh at the expense of someone else or to stoop to a gag, but—quick to see absurdity —you shared it with us.

And you shared with us your loves. "Listen to 900 this!" you would say, eagerly opening a book, unashamed to be moved by a poem, unafraid to use words like "magnificent."

Those were the days of the after-school clubs (We called it "enrichment"), school spirit, Field Day, and the senior yearbook with its photos of (except for one black girl) white, middle-class, alphabetized children with neatly brushed hair, over inscriptions such as: *Reading Maketh a Full Man* and *Future Plans: College and Professional School.*

Those were the days when teachers, especially to my European eyes, were creatures set apart. I recall my shock when I noticed one morning that my algebra teacher had a run in her stocking like 1000 any ordinary person. Those were the days of obedience as absolute as the silence, when a demerit for conduct could destroy us, when chewing gum in class was a serious infraction, when "Sez you!" to a teacher was unheard of insolence.

Those were the days of our innocence, and I recall them with nostalgia, especially now, especially as a teacher.

I wonder how you would fare in today's urban public high school, where teachers have become The *Enemy* and students—mostly angry Blacks and frustrated Puerto Ricans trained in failure from the 1100 day they were born—wage daily war against us. Are teachers like you really dead? I try to imagine you in a school I know, one of the worst in New York, where frightened teachers look the other way and helpless administrators send forth streams of directives advising them to lock their doors, hide their window poles, and hold on to their pocketbooks, because there are cops in the lobby, pot on the stairs, muggings in the halls, assaults in the lavatory, robbery at knife point, vandalism, arson, and worse.

You would have a rough time of it today, Mr. 1200 Stock, but I think you would be unafraid. You would not look the other way or talk only from the mouth out. You would treat each child as a human person. And you would still expect students to do their best —not Hardy's or anyone else's but their own—whatever that best might be.

Teachers like you are not dead as long as there are children who can one day say, "I had a teacher once. . . ." Perhaps at this very moment, someone, someplace, is saying this about one of us. That is our immortality.

 1300 Dear Mr. Stock, I wanted to show you by recalling the past, how different schools are today, but I see this has turned out to be a love letter to you. Well, there are times when a love letter needs to be written, even if it is never mailed.

Your Unforgetting Forever Pupil,

Bel Kaufman

 1350

——STOP——ASK FOR YOUR TIME——

Record time immediately and answer
the questions on content.

Time___Sec.	RATE (from table on page 315):	R._____
No. Correct:___ (key on page 330)	COMPREHENSION (10% for each correct answer):	C._____
VI–2	EFFICIENCY (R × C):	E._____

Record on Progress Chart on page 299

ANSWER THESE QUESTIONS IMMEDIATELY

1. (T–F) The writer of this letter remembers the teacher giving her an *A* minus for being unprepared.

2. (MC) She was impressed that the teacher:

   _____(1) complimented her.

   _____(2) recognized her.

   __X__(3) scolded her.

   _____(4) promoted her.

3. (T–F) The writer remembers clearly all of the teachers she ever had.

4. (T–F) She resented the fact that Mr. Stock made such enormous demands on students in his classes.

5. (MC) Mr. Stock always impressed the writer most as being a:

   _____(1) friend.

   _____(2) charming person.

   _____(3) teacher.

   __X__(4) disciplinarian.

6. (C) He once called her handwriting _terrible_.

7. (C) She praised him because he seemed to make everyone in his class feel _needed_.

8. (T–F) With her European background, the writer always viewed teachers as something special and extraordinary.

9. (T–F) The writer feels that Mr. Stock would have a very rough time in New York schools today.

10. (T–F) The writer concludes that teachers like Mr. Stock are really dead and gone in today's school system.

Exercise VI-3

How to Become a Millionaire

ARNOLD TOLAR

(from *Moderator*, December 1966)

WAIT FOR SIGNAL TO BEGIN READING

At 38, John Diebold, the Automation man, is a millionaire. "Half the stuff in the *Wall Street Journal* isn't so," says John Diebold, the man who should know.

You get the feeling John knows which half.

There he is, the founder of automation in the entrepreneur outfit with the Snoopy face. Fantastic— the combination is shattering: there's the guy who wrote the book, *Automation* (1952), invented the word we have nightmares about, and he's this shy, yet almost impulsive, ex-merchant marine who might look good in a huge pinafore, but there he is hung out in his double-breasted Saville Row duds and he's 100 telling you how to become a millionaire.

It goes like this: You're a student, and in order to get started, you first should have a good liberal arts background, including a healthy injection of math. Instead of bothering with undergrad business courses, start sizing yourself up in terms of the crucial question: Am I a businessman or a managerial prospect? Try running your own campus enterprise and then try managing a going concern. Which do you like to do more?

Your big decision

Once you've answered that crucial question, you are ready to go management or go business. 200

If you go management, you will probably head for business or public administration graduate school where the training is not utterly essential. Diebold admits he scarcely knows how many degrees his men have, and notices only when he's sending out a recommendation letter for someone. Besides, business schools aren't exactly in bed with the computer age. "Business schools still teach you how to make decisions on too little information."

If you go business, you will probably go one of three routes: 1) start as an assistant to a top executive; 2) start with a small company, rise rapidly, and leapfrog to a top position with a large 300 concern; 3) start your own company. As you may have guessed, "business" means the hard-nosed entrepreneurial way. Don't go near it, says Diebold, if you don't like the heat in the kitchen or on the production line.

The vast majority of students, Diebold predicts, will go the managerial route when faced with the business vs. management choice. "The great development in the country is the professional manager." The professional manager is not driven by the profit motive, as is the businessman; feeling equally at home 400 in a profit or nonprofit institution. To illustrate that, the professional manager and the businessman are "worlds apart," Diebold tells this story about one great international management association, meeting in New York: only one of twelve businessmen he talked to in the city while the meeting was in session knew about it.

Be aggressive

You've chosen your route to take and now in choosing your company, don't look for starting salary: it's an illusion, especially given inflation. Says Diebold, "I took the lowest starting salary of all my Harvard Business School classmates—$300 a month" plus a future: The boss looked him over 500 closely. Diebold got a launching pad, and took off, later absorbing the boss's firm into the Diebold Group.

Also, be aggressive in looking over companies, visit brokerage houses and get their readings. Be tough with recruiters. Read a lot, especially biographies of contemporary businessmen and don't overlook sick companies. A bad balance sheet can indicate an opportunity. If you catch those companies at the right moment, you could help turn the tide and end up riding the crest. The good balance sheet is fine for finding "nice, secure jobs."

The main thing is not the job but the man. A 600 young man should spend most of his time understanding his options. "A job is mostly a man understanding himself." That's where the new technology comes in: Unless a young man is used to thinking like that, he's not going to be ready to make his way in the new management environment.

The main thing is to stay on top of the relevant information, and to use it properly. That's what automation is all about, says Mr. Automation.

Staying on top means, first, reading everything you can get your hands on. Diebold reads the *New*

York Times thoroughly, usually one other city newspaper, two news magazines, all the general business ⁷⁰⁰← magazines, including the *Economist* and *The Wall Street Journal* which are clipped for him. He even considers women's magazines important; you never know when you'll spot something relevant.

Once you get moving, though, the press isn't enough, for usually, if you read about a development in the press, it's too late, really. You've got to develop your own intelligence network so you find out ahead of time and can check for the real meaning of events. Was that promotion really a promotion? Did an announcement of success really signify failure? A young man must have the desire to get ⁸⁰⁰← behind the news, for if he doesn't, says Diebold, he's lost.

The language of the computer man sounds familiar when labeled intelligence network. The young executive with the desire to know what's really true is the one who's going to make the most of the new technology. Soon the machinery will enable the executive to know anything he wants—instantly, the premium then, being on asking the right questions. Since you can't just learn answers anymore, like absorbing the front page of the *Times,* you've got to learn how to ask questions which is what you do when you put together an intelligence network. ⁹⁰⁰←

By and large, management today is not asking the right questions; by getting the hang of it, you'll get a head start. Diebold has loads of fun with this in his speeches and articles such as the *Harvard Business Review* article, where Diebold lashes at conventional managers for "overemphasis on hardware and underemphasis on the design of comprehensive systems." More fundamentally, he writes, the contemporary corporate structure has gotten in the way of the cross-departmental responsibilities and vision needed by the modern executive who asks the right questions. "Executives are doing little ¹⁰⁰⁰← more with ADP than adding speed and economy to tasks performed with earlier equipment." Diebold's favorite weapon is the word "change." "Technology means to business not only a change in how you do things but a change in what you do—a change in goals as well as in the route you take to reach goals."

So if you want to be an executive of the future, and make your million, you've got to ask fundamental questions about organizational goals. You must be a broadly educated man, free of overspecial- ¹¹⁰⁰→ ization, and continually learning. You must have an intimate knowledge of what people want, for "it is the human desires that shape the opportunities which spawn enterprise." This is crucial because automation means social change more than it means new machines.

Computers are remaking the business environment by removing the constraints on business structure, and making decentralization, for example, unnecessary. The future executive will be able to talk to a computer, literally, and it will feed back information on the total enterprise. Market intelligence, control information, strategy decisions already made, and feedback for change will all be made available instantly. A nearby infinite number of options will ¹²⁰⁰→ be at your fingertips.

John Diebold, practicing what he preaches, is constantly asking new questions, seeking out new sources of information, and when you ask him what it's all about he probably will say, "I'm interested in the development of fluid computers which work either with liquid, or air, and animal languages." If that stumps you, don't stop him, or he'll be off on something else.

If you want to bat in Diebold's league you'd better get moving. The new technology creates a vacuum, and it's guys like Diebold who jump in there with solutions. There's a Charles Addams cartoon ¹³⁰⁰→ on his office wall which goes like this: As two caterpillars are looking up at a butterfly, one says to the other, "You'll never catch me up in one of those things."

You can either get caught up in it, or like mil- ¹³⁵⁰→ lionaire John Diebold, you can go out after it.

——STOP——ASK FOR YOUR TIME——

Record time immediately and answer
the questions on content.

Time _73_ Sec.

No. Correct: _____
(key on page 322)

VI–3

RATE (from table on page 315):

COMPREHENSION (10% for each correct answer):

EFFICIENCY (R × C):

R. _1100_

C. _70_

E. _770_

$\frac{110}{7}$

770

Record on Progress Chart on page 299

ANSWER THESE QUESTIONS IMMEDIATELY

1. (C) John Diebold is known as the _Money_ _____ Man.

2. (T–F) He recommends that young men try out small business ventures of their own on the college campus.

3. (C) The first step in becoming a millionaire is to get a good liberal arts background, including a healthy injection of _business_ _____.

4. (T–F) Diebold feels that undergraduate business courses are unessential.

5. (T–F) Mr. Diebold makes a point of knowing what college degrees his men have.

6. (T–F) Diebold predicted that most students go the business route when confronted with the business vs. the management choice.

7. (MC) In order to "stay on top," you must first:

_____(1) have a sound background in undergraduate business courses.

_____(2) read everything you can get your hands on.

_____(3) have essential training in public administration school.

_____(4) learn how to make quick decisions on a minimum of information.

8. (T–F) Diebold claims that management today is not asking the right questions.

9. (T–F) Having answers to all the questions asked by associates is considered one of the greatest attributes of success in management.

10. (MC) If you want to be an executive of the future, you must:

_____(1) develop a high degree of specialization.

_____(2) exercise great caution in data interpretation.

_____(3) ask questions about organizational goals and processes.

_____(4) memorize complex computer language.

Exercise VI-4

Anger

(from News Release of the American Medical Association, December 1966)

WAIT FOR SIGNAL TO BEGIN READING

Anger has been defined as a sudden violent displeasure, often accompanied by a compelling impulse to make some efforts to retaliate. Getting angry or mad, as we sometimes say, is rather a common occurrence with normal individuals. And after a sudden or violent show of deep wrath, perhaps we have tried to rationalize and ask ourselves what it was in our normal mental make-ups that could trigger such a quick change from mental tranquillity to seething anger and indignation. Why did we shout, swear, say harsh things or get involved in actions that we later deeply regretted? Why were we not able to control our emotions better? Is it helpful 100 or harmful to us physically, to get mad occasionally and to pop off, blow our stacks, vent our spleens so as to get the anger out of our systems? Do you feel that you get angry or irritated more often or more easily than your associates?

In universities and research foundations throughout the country, scientists have been making some interesting studies, tests and discoveries about anger in humans as well as in animals. Perhaps some of their findings may provide answers to a few of the questions you've pondered concerning anger and 200 what it may reveal with regard to your own personality.

If you seldom get angry, does that mean that you have a better-balanced personality than one who does? No, it is perfectly normal for a person to feel anger, resentment or indignation when faced with irritating or provoking situations. In psychiatric studies conducted at Columbia University, hundreds of people were given personality tests, and then purposely subjected to maddening situations of every variety. In virtually every case, well-balanced individuals had a stronger and more pronounced anger reaction than unbalanced or abnormal persons. And other psychiatric studies showed that one of the out- 300 standing symptoms of mental unbalance is emotional apathy and lack of concern or feeling. So, if you frequently get burned up or mad when people or circumstances rub you the wrong way, don't fret too much about it—psychologically it's a perfectly normal reaction.

Gripes and pet peeves

What about people who have a multitude of gripes and pet peeves, and are constantly being irritated by little things? Scientists have found that the more small pet peeves a person has—the more minor things he finds irritating—the more likely he 400 is to be neurotic. Any normal person will likely suddenly exhibit anger when someone deliberately steps on his toes, yet he isn't likely to be hypersensitive and doesn't have a long list of little gripes. Incidentally, Rockefeller Foundation studies show that neurotic people easily become irritated when they are kidded even lightly, while well-balanced individuals tend to take it in their stride and perhaps appreciate the attention shown them.

Anger studies conducted at Columbia University and Oregon State College show that the average man gets angry and really loses his temper on an average of about six times a week, whereas 500 the average woman gets angry enough to blow her top an average of only three times a week or only half as often as men. The study also showed that women got mad most frequently at other people (real or fancied slights, and assorted personal grievances). Men's tempers were more likely to flare up at inanimate objects (such as a flat tire, a missed train, a faulty razor, etc.).

People in some walks of life tend to have shorter tempers than others. Perhaps the most authoritative and widescale study of this matter has been conducted by the late Hulsey Cason, a psy- 600 chologist who surveyed the anger reactions of thousands of persons from all walks of life. He found men and women engaged in professional callings (doctors, lawyers, etc.) tended to be slowest to anger. Farmers and those engaged in related agricultural occupations, ranked next. Businessmen and skilled workers averaged more frequent anger flare-ups and office workers and laborers lost their tempers more often.

Little things make us angry

Studies show that the power of so-called little things to provoke hostility and resentment—to exasperate a man to the point where he gets hot under the collar—cannot be overestimated. This is due to the fact that (1) they occur most frequently, 700 (2) they don't seem little at the time, and (3) like the mosquito, they possess an ability to irritate that is far out of proportion to their size.

Can you usually tell by looking at a person whether he is angry or not? Studies conducted by psychologists at the University of Pennsylvania showed that—contrary to popular belief—anger is one of the hardest emotions to discern purely from facial expression. When pictures of extremely angry individuals were shown to hundreds of college students (including those majoring in psychology) only two percent were able to correctly identify the emo- 800 tion. Indeed, expressions of angry people were most typically misjudged as "bewildered," "pleased," "amazed," or "puzzled."

Barnard College studies show that there are three times a day when people are quickest to anger —during the half-hour period preceding breakfast, lunch, and dinner. The investigators found that almost half of the temper outbursts of the subjects studied occurred during those times. The moral is— don't bring up a controversial subject on an empty stomach because people are most irritable when they're hungry.

Do most people "feel better" after an anger experience and after they had calmed down? In the 900 Barnard College study, only 15 percent of the subjects reported that they actually felt better after an anger experience while two-thirds said it left them feeling irritable and fatigued.

Just what determines the after-effect of getting angry? Studies at the Institute of Psychoanalysis, Chicago, show that it depends largely on whether you give expression to your anger, or whether it is repressed. Tests show that when anger is continually bottled up and consistently denied means of expression it builds up severe tensions which can do actual physical harm.

What should you do when you get angry?

Providing for safe and sane means of express- 1000 ing it, working it off, or getting it out of your system, calls for discretion. If you go around punching people in the nose who make you angry, you'll soon end up in trouble. If you blow your top whenever the boss or an associate says something that burns you up, you'll likely soon be out of a job and minus friends. And social relations will suffer if you are not mature enough to control your actions and too frequently allow yourself the luxury of telling off the offending person.

1100 If you desire to be known as a person with emotional maturity, then determine to be alert and on your guard so as to make a special effort to control your anger the next time you see that you are getting upset. Don't be afraid to laugh at yourself and try to put the incident that stirred your ire into its proper perspective.

Also, you can learn to talk to your friends about the anger-provoking incident once you have cooled down a bit, with the idea of getting the incident completely off your chest. It may surprise you 1200 to know that talking rationally with another is an effective escape valve for most resentments; besides, it provides a healthy release of anger-inspiring tensions.

And still another safe and sane means of letting off steam is work and exercise. Maybe a brisk walk, a short run or any reasonable exertion for that matter. The idea is to provide an outlet and to work off your resentments and get them out of your system before they have a chance to fester and build up harmful tension.

Try not to let trifles trip you

Take a positive approach to your angry out- 1300 bursts if they are excessive. Think about your own failures, weaknesses and mistakes before you become too inconsiderate of others.

Remember that things said and done in times of sudden anger have cost much in time, tears, and health.

The following old aphorism has much truth: "The things that burn you up can also burn you 1350 out."

——STOP——ASK FOR YOUR TIME——

Record time immediately and answer the questions on content.

Time _50_ Sec.

RATE (from table on page 315):

No. Correct:_____
(key on page 330)

COMPREHENSION (10% for each correct answer):

VI–4

EFFICIENCY (R × C):

Record on Progress Chart on page 299

ANSWER THESE QUESTIONS IMMEDIATELY

1. (C) _Fight_ has been defined as a violent displeasure.

2. (T-F) It is not really normal for a person to feel anger when confronted with provoking situations.

3. (C) The hypersensitive person with a multitude of gripes is likely to be _Fired / Nuerotic_.

4. (T-F) An outstanding symptom of mental unbalance is emotional apathy.

5. (MC) Recent anger studies indicate that the average man gets angry about:

_____(1) six times a month.

__X__(2) six times a week.

_____(3) once a day.

_____(4) once every other day.

6. (T-F) Women usually get angry more often than men.

7. (T-F) It's easy to tell, by looking at a person's facial expression, whether or not he is angry.

8. (MC) People are most susceptible to anger when they are:

_____(1) hungry.

_____(2) teased and taunted.

_____(3) depressed.

_____(4) fatigued.

9. (T-F) Most people do not feel any better after an angry outburst.

10. (T-F) Work and exercise are effective ways of letting off steam.

Exercise VI–5

Mother Nature's Boiler

(from *Friends magazine*, February 1974)

WAIT FOR SIGNAL TO BEGIN READING

Are we sitting on the solution to the energy crisis? Not coal, oil, or gas, but the barely tapped sources of geothermal power?

This is not speculative. In seven countries, including our own, power is being produced in this fashion. Millions, watching the hourly eruptions of Old Faithful in Yellowstone National Park, have gotten a suggestion of the potential. But Old Faithful, glorious as she is, is a pigmy when measured against other geysers that have been harnessed.

Amazing source of power

Steam—dry steam, it is so superheated—is generated when moisture from the earth's surface seeps down to the molten core miles below. The enormous pressure thus created must find an outlet (which must be upward), and it does, whether it be in our many hot springs or in the geysers of Yellowstone or those in Sonoma County in California.

In Sonoma County, the practicality of harnessing this power has been proven. But here there was an abundance of evidence, in the form of geysers, that the core of the earth was an unstoppable percolator. Elsewhere, exploratory drillings will be needed to determine if the solid rock layer can be tapped. The idea is to inject moisture into the earth deep enough to be turned into steam. The heat to do this exists in the magma, or liquid ball of fire at the center of the earth.

The system employed in California is to preserve the natural geyser by tapping into its main channel beneath the surface. There are eight such wells now, furnishing steam to drive turbines that generate more than 300,000 kilowatts. After use, the steam is cooled into water and returned to the earth, ultimately to be converted back into steam for more power.

Fragments of earth

The steam leaves the wellheads at a temperature of about 350°F, but it is not pure steam. On its way, it has picked up fragments of earth. These are removed by whirlers to prevent damage to the turbines. The steam then is fed into the turbines.

Only tests will tell if such steam punctures can be made near such spas as those at Saratoga Springs, N.Y., Mt. Clemens, Mich., and the hot springs in Arkansas, West Virginia, Florida, and other states. One thing is certain: the center of the earth is a gigantic boiler, ready to make steam when man can find a way to feed water to it.

Quite unnoticed by many, a kind of geothermal race among nations is on to find less costly ways of stoking the boiler with moisture. Near Mexicali, Mexico, a research and development program wound up last year with the completion of its first geothermal plant, rated at 75,000 kilowatts.

Geologists believe that the magma has a temperature of 3,000°F. It must be kept in mind, however, that the molten core of the earth also is a ball, and this source of potential energy is available in equal amounts to every nation on earth. It took hundreds of millions of years for the surface to cool to an average depth of 20 miles; so the supply of geothermal energy can be described as being beyond the foresight of man, if not endless.

Only a waterfall, producing hydroelectric power, can generate energy more cheaply. But Mother Nature's boiler is constant, whereas rainfall can limit the productivity of a waterfall.

Noise level

The Geysers, as the group of vents about 90 miles northwest of San Francisco is known, commit one affront to ecology—noise. As the vents are approached, they take on the pitched roar of hundreds of screeching 747s shattering the sky.

Closer to the power plants and well vents scattered over the steep slopes of an extinct volcano, the steam shrieks from the earth with enough decibels to compel one to wear special earmuffs, to escape risk of being deafened.

The man who discovered The Geysers, explorer-scientist William Bell Elliott, thought he had come to the gates of hell. That was in 1847.

It was not until 1922 that the first attempt to harness the steam was made. Drillers were successful in tapping the source, but the project had to be abandoned because the dirt and rocks in the steam made it a literal piece of sandpaper. It corroded everything it touched.

Use of stainless steel alloys

Scientists knew the potential, but they were helpless. Whistling Annie, one of the larger wells at the Geysers, raged uncontrolled as it spilled off 10 times the energy of Old Faithful.

Magma Power Company and Thermal Power Company, working jointly and joined later by Earth Energy, a subsidiary of Union Oil Company, had another go at it in 1956. By that time, they had stainless steel alloys—corrosion-resistant—on their side, and the economic feasibility of extracting preheated energy from the bowels of the earth was established. 800 ←

The development goes on, headed toward an expected maximum of about one million kilowatts' capacity in the Big Sulphur Creek in Sonoma County.

Besides the United States and Mexico, the other nations in the geothermal rush are Italy, New Zealand, Iceland, the Soviet Union, and Japan. But this is a market no one can corner. To each its own. Simply find where moisture is reaching the stratum overlying the magma, and the kilowatts will catapult.

The first uses of steam

The geothermal field is one in which the U.S. cannot claim a "first." That must go to Italy and the 900 town of Larderello, about 40 miles outside Florence.

The first written record of this steam field dates from the Romans of 21 centuries ago. The belching fumarole in Larderello inspired Dante to write his "Inferno." With another quill, Elliott might have been able to write similarly of Sonoma County in 1847.

For nearly 70 years, production of electric power generated by the magma-heated steam has been in progress. Near Larderello, Italy, however, the layer of magma is only two miles or so deep. Wells driven to 3,000 feet come close enough for industrial purposes. 1000 ←

Italian geologists have estimated, on the basis of present energy, withdrawal from the geothermal areas attainable at that level can be sustained for more than 11,000 years.

Iceland, in 1925, began the use of geothermal steam in homes, and New Zealand has used such steam to generate electricity since the early '50s. The

Mexican development, constructed by Toshiba Electric Company of Japan, has been estimated to be drawing less than one percent of its potential. Other taps are in the making.

Russian geologists have discovered a great hot-water basin, larger than the Mediterranean Sea, lying 1100 → beneath Siberia, as unlikely a spot for geothermal heat as one might imagine. The initial output is going into health spas, more experimental drilling, and heating for nearby towns.

Exploratory drilling has been been commenced also in Cameroon, Taiwan, the Dominican Republic, Ethiopia, Israel, Kenya, Nicaragua, Saint Lucia, Turkey, Czechoslovakia, Burundi, Chile, Costa Rica, El Salvador, Guatemala, Jordan, Morocco, Tunisia, Hungary, and the Philippines.

Until the actuality of the energy crisis was made clear in the U.S., development of geothermal power limped along at a dawdling rate, but now it is full speed ahead.

In the Salton Sea area of southern California 1200 → alone, covering only 12,000 acres, it has been calculated that 100 wells could be driven to produce more than a million kilowatts, or more than that of a baker's dozen of Coulee Dams. This evidence that geothermal power is adaptable to man's needs has been seen in this California area.

And there are fringe benefits. The minerals belched in the raw steam, for example, can be made into a brine that can be processed and sold by chemical companies.

After desalination, which occurs naturally when steam reverts to water, the fluid would be useful to 1300 → irrigate arid lands as it settles back to the magma stratum from which it came.

Where will it all end?

Just because man has never drilled 20 miles into the mantle of the earth doesn't say that he couldn't if he had to.

And it would be a good bet.

When Mother Nature turns the boiler on, some- 1350 → thing's cooking.

——STOP——ASK FOR YOUR TIME——

Record time immediately and answer
the questions on content.

Time_____Sec.	RATE (from table on page 315):	R. _____
No. Correct:_____ (key on page 322)	COMPREHENSION (10% for each correct answer):	C. _____
VI–5	EFFICIENCY (R × C):	E. _____

Record on Progress Chart on page 299

ANSWER THESE QUESTIONS IMMEDIATELY

1. (T–F) Fragments of earth in the steam have delayed the development of methods to harness the thermal power.

2. (C) The liquid ball of fire at the core of the earth is called the _____.

3. (MC) Geologists believe that the earth's core has a temperature of:

____(1) 2,000°F.

____(2) 3,000°F.

____(3) 4,000°F.

____(4) 5,000°F.

4. (T–F) Geothermal power can generate energy more cheaply than waterfalls.

5. (T–F) William Bell Elliott discovered The Geysers near San Francisco in 1847.

6. (T–F) Any country with financial backing can control the market for geothermal energy.

7. (T–F) The U.S. was first in the world to harness the geothermal fields.

8. (C) One of the earliest countries to use geothermal steam in homes in 1925 was _____.

9. (MC) In Siberia, geologists have discovered a great hot-water basin larger than the:

____(1) Mediterranean Sea.

____(2) Dead Sea.

____(3) Salton Sea.

____(4) Adriatic Sea.

10. (T–F) The molten core of the earth is only about 20 miles below the surface in most parts of the world.

Exercise VI-6

Emotions within the Family

(from pamphlet of the Metropolitan Life Insurance Company, 1967)

WAIT FOR SIGNAL TO BEGIN READING

When we show our children our love and give them our sympathetic understanding, we help to give them a large measure of protection against many of the disturbing conditions so common among adults today. Children need to grow in an environment that provides not only physical nourishment but emotional support as well.

Love and closeness which a child experiences within the family are positive forces that help him to grow strong and self-confident. Faith in his parents, and in the security of his home, helps him to have faith in himself. When parents are reasonably well-adjusted and get along together, they are better able 100 to be sensitive to their children's needs. As they learn to deal maturely with their own problems, parents become freer to give their children emotional support. Of course, "maturing," a process that goes on all through our lives, frequently involves a good measure of self-discipline and self-control. It comes not only with experience but with our sincere efforts to understand ourselves and those around us and to use this understanding to make our lives and our relationships more satisfying.

Family living, of course, is never all sweetness and light, for it is subject to subtle pressures—job and money worries, illnesses, large and small emergencies. 200 And, try as we may, we sometimes cannot help taking out our tensions on the people nearest and dearest to us. Yet, most of us know that it is very disturbing to children when parents quarrel and argue in front of them. Although it would be unrealistic to expect that an argument would never occur in front of the children, it is wise to avoid airing grievances this way. Constantly quarreling before the children is not only very upsetting to them, but makes them unwilling participants in a conflict over which they have no 300 control.

Even the happiest married couple may sometimes give vent to anger and irritation, all a part of living, in the presence of the children. However, constructive efforts on the part of parents to cooperate and resolve their difficulties outweigh these occasional upsets. It is only when quarrels and bickering permeate the atmosphere that children are harmed. Continual conflicts within the family can threaten a child's security, make him fearful, and undermine his chances of developing healthy attitudes. A child's fears and insecurities may show up in so-called problem behavior—nail biting, bed wetting, 400 bad dreams, wakefulness, fear of the dark, perhaps even trouble with school work. Family tensions are certainly not the only source of nervous reactions among children, but they obviously have an influence.

While no parent and no family is perfect, it is worth every effort to make family life as peaceful and cooperative as possible. Problems have a way of shrinking, or even being prevented, when we take the time really to listen to and enjoy our children. Moments for relaxed, light-hearted companionship and sharing of interests may actually have to be squeezed into our busy days and weeks but the time 500 can and should be found, even if it's just a pleasant hour around the family dinner or breakfast table.

Lessons for us all

It is not wise—it's definitely unhealthy—to keep emotional tensions bottled up. Instead we should look for the most reasonable way to work them out. For some of us, just talking over our problems fully and freely with a sympathetic friend or adviser helps to clear the air. It can often help to relieve any feelings of guilt we have about our own disagreeable thoughts and feelings when we discover similar ones in others. This is one of the values of group discussion 600 and study groups—especially among parents. These sessions give people a chance to exchange ideas and viewpoints which can lead to keener insights and better understandings.

It is important to learn how to handle our emotional tensions—to know and to accept our physical and emotional limitations. All this is easier said than done, but understanding is the first step. As we reach a better understanding of the common emotional stresses and are able to recognize them instead of trying to ignore them, we shall begin to see a reduction in those illnesses that strike out at 700 us through our own inner conflicts.

We can all, in our own way, practice an important bit of preventive medicine by applying this knowledge to our children. Childhood is not the happy, carefree time of life we may like to imagine it on looking back. Most of us have forgotten or repressed many of our childhood tragedies because they were too painful for us to remember, but we can help our children by learning to become more sensitive to their needs and to see, insofar as it is possible, that they are free from excessive worry and tension. 800 ←

It is not emotions that are at fault when we refer to emotional problems. After all, an emotion, whether pleasant or unpleasant, is simply a person's response to his understanding and judgment of a fact or a situation as he sees it. It is not our job to help our children hide their feelings; it is our job to help them to express and use their emotions constructively.

When we're upset or angry, we can try to blow off steam or work off our feelings with physical exercise. Pitching into some activity, like working in the garden; taking a long walk; playing a game of 900 ← tennis or going in for some other sport not only helps to relieve anger but makes it easier to face and handle irritating problems more calmly. (Besides, getting some regular exercise is a great way to keep yourself in good physical condition.)

It helps to get it off your chest sometimes by confiding worries to a sympathetic friend. When what appears to be a serious problem starts to get you down, it's wise to discuss it with your family physician, or your clergyman, or with an understanding member of your own family. Often another person 1000 can help you to see your problem in a new light. This may be the first step toward a constructive solution. If your problems seem to be getting out of hand, your own doctor may want to recommend a specialist, or refer you to a guidance clinic or a family service agency.

Many of us get upset about circumstances which are beyond our control. Sometimes we even try to make people over to suit our own ideals and then feel frustrated or let down when we find that this 1100 → cannot be done. We can look for the best in others while realizing that nobody is faultless.

When you feel that you are going around in circles with a problem or a worry, try to divert yourself. As simple a thing as going to the movies, reading a story, or visiting a friend can help you out of a rut. And there's no harm in running away from a painful situation long enough to catch your breath and regain the composure you need to come back and face the problem. When possible and practical, a change of scene can give you a new perspective. 1200 → There are times when we all need to "escape"— even if it's just a letup from routine. Certainly everyone needs and should have a few hours to call his own, away from immediate cares and worries. For some of us this might well mean a few moments just to be alone.

If you should need medication, your physician may prescribe medicine which temporarily helps you to relax without affecting your mental agility. But avoid self-medication. There are different types of sedatives and tranquilizers available for various purposes. Only a doctor can usually know and prescribe the amount and type that's right for the individual person.

1300 → A person's physical condition affects his outlook on life. There are no simple solutions to the problems of life which cause undue stress and tension, but if you keep yourself physically fit, you will have more zest for living and be able to take stress 1350 → and handle everyday tensions more easily.

——STOP——ASK FOR YOUR TIME——

Record time immediately and answer the questions on content.

Time 20 Sec. RATE (from table on page 315): R: 405

No. Correct:_____ COMPREHENSION (10% for each correct answer): C. 80%
(key on page 330)

VI–6 EFFICIENCY (R × C): E. 324 0 0

Record on Progress Chart on page 299

ANSWER THESE QUESTIONS IMMEDIATELY

1. (T–F) "Maturing" is a process that goes on all through our lives.

2. (C) Constant ___fighting___ between the parents is very upsetting to the children.

3. (MC) The first step in learning to handle our emotional tensions is that of:

   X_(1) understanding.

   _____(2) consultation with an expert.

   _____(3) saying the opposite of what we feel.

   _____(4) learning to keep them under control.

4. (T–F) It is probably wiser to keep our emotional tensions to ourselves and not share them with others.

5. (T–F) Childhood was a happy, carefree time of life for most of us.

6. (T–F) Emotions are usually at fault when we refer to emotional problems. *ideas / emotions*

7. (C) Our job is to help our children express their ___ideas / emotions___ constructively.

8. (T–F) When we're angry, a good means of outlet is physical exercise.

9. (MC) When we are confronted with a painful situation or problem, usually the best solution is to:

   X_(1) consult an expert.

   _____(2) escape—try to divert yourself.

   _____(3) take tranquilizers.

   _____(4) become involved in happy family relationships.

10. (T–F) A person's physical condition affects his outlook on life.

Exercise VI-7

Edison and Electricity

(from pamphlet of the same name)

WAIT FOR SIGNAL TO BEGIN READING

New Year's Eve in Menlo Park

It was New Year's Eve, 1879. A strange air of expectancy and excitement gripped the New Jersey village of Menlo Park. Nearly 3,000 persons restlessly milled about the streets, and crowded close to the piazza of Mr. Edison's laboratory. Some had driven as far as 20 miles in carriages and wagons, but most had come by special trains run by the Pennsylvania Railroad for the occasion. They were there to witness the first public demonstration of Edison's wonderful new light.

As the early winter twilight deepened into darkness, the murmur of the throng was hushed in antici- 100 pation. Inside the laboratory, a deft stroke of a finger made 60 lamps, placed on poles up and down the snow-covered street, spring to light among the bare branches of the trees. A ripple of involuntary applause ran through the audience. One old farmer was heard to remark, "We-ell sir, it's a pretty fair sight, but danged if I kin see how ye git the red-hot hairpin in the bottle!"

In the days and weeks that followed, Menlo Park became a kind of Mecca for the intelligently interested and the merely curious. Farm folk and city folk, scientists and businessmen, came nightly in 200 ever increasing numbers to see the "Edison lights."

An indifferent public

But widespread public acceptance of incandescent illumination was extremely slow—or so it seemed to the Edison group. For some time Menlo Park was the only place in the world where a complete incandescent system was on display. Relatively few, therefore, were able to see it in operation. Even the most glowing newspaper description could not arouse a general public interest in the new lighting.

Then too, there was opposition from gas and arc-light companies. As it became apparent that the new lamp threatened to displace the older illuminants 300 this opposition increased. On at least two occasions attempts were made to discredit the new system while it was being demonstrated before municipal officials. A member of one such visiting party managed to short-circuit a part of the system at Menlo by means of a piece of wire running up a sleeve, over his shoulder, and down the other sleeve. Special watchers, appointed by Edison, caught the erstwhile saboteur in the act. When the fact leaked out that the man had an interest in a gas company, public senti- 400 ment in favor of the electric light was greatly enhanced.

Among the city officials who made the pilgrimage to Menlo Park was a delegation representing New York's Board of Aldermen. The outcome of their visit was an agreement by which Edison was to install a trial lighting system in an area on lower Manhattan—an area soon to become famous as Edison's "First District." The Edison Illuminating Company of New York was formed to do this job. The Wizard was now committed to making an historic step; his dream of "great cities alight from central stations" was coming ever closer to reality.

The task begins

500 Putting the project on a profitable commercial footing proved to be a Herculean task—a far greater undertaking than the impatient New Yorkers realized. Plans for the installation were complete in essential detail, but devices had to be invented, developed, and built as the need for them arose. Necessity was the mother of these inventions—and Edison was the father.

Of necessity, Edison became a manufacturer. "There was nothing we could buy," he related, "or that anyone could make for us." So new companies were formed by Edison men to supply the new devices.

Since the Illuminating Company was reluctant 600 to manufacture them, Edison formed a lamp company and began producing lamps in one of his old Menlo Park buildings. Although the first lamps cost about $1.25 to make, Edison offered to supply all the lamps required by the Illuminating Company at 40¢ *apiece!* He was sure that he could produce them at a profit by effecting economies in production methods and by mass production.

The lamp factory was moved to larger quarters in Harrison, New Jersey, in 1880, when about 30,000 lamps were produced, at a cost of nearly $1.10 each. As production rose in the next few years, costs went 700 down. "The fourth year, I got the cost down to 37¢," related the inventor, "and with a 3¢ profit per lamp, made up in one year all the money I'd lost previously. I finally got it down to 22¢, sold them for 40¢, and they were made by the millions. Whereupon the Illuminating Company thought it a very lucrative business and bought us out," he recalled.

Jumbo and the Mary Ann

One of Edison's greatest triumphs in dealing with electrification of the First District was his development of a suitable generator. The project required electric current in undreamed of quantities. 800 ← Existing generators were far too small and inefficient.

The Wizard began by studying the design of dynamos then in use. Then he proceeded to fashion one unlike any of the others. It had two huge parallel magnets which made it resemble the Roman numeral II, and earned it the nickname *Long-Waisted Mary Ann*. Though the design violated accepted principles, it worked. What's more, it was nearly 90 percent efficient.

The famous Jumbo dynamo was developed and exhibited at the Paris Electrical Exposition in 1881. The bipolar Mary Ann design was coupled with a huge 150-horsepower steam engine. Where previous 900 ← generators had been driven by complicated belting and shafting, the Jumbo's engine was linked directly to the dynamo. Its size alone caused people to gape. It weighed 27 tons and was capable of lighting 1,200 incandescent lamps.

No one knew what to expect when the Jumbo was first tested one winter's night at Menlo Park. Heretofore the speed of stationary engines was rarely more than 60 revolutions per minute, but this machine was designed to turn up 700 rpm, and at a much higher steam pressure than most engines.

The shop in which the machine was set up 1000 ← stood on top of a shale hill. Edison amusingly recalled that at 300 revolutions "the whole hill shook under her," and at 700 rpm "you should have seen her run! Why, every time the connecting rod went up, she tried to lift the whole hill with her!"

After this harrowing experience, the Jumbos were not run at more than 250 rpm, which was really all that Edison had wanted anyway.

"65" becomes a Mecca

Early in 1881, the Edison Electric Light Company leased an ornate brownstone mansion at 65 Fifth Avenue, New York, for an office. The house 1100 → was an ideal place for showing off the lights in everyday operation, and also provided a headquarters from which Edison could closely supervise the many activities connected with the First District lighting installation.

For the next four years, "65" was a beehive of activity, day and night. Every day after dark, thousands of visitors came to see, to ask questions, and to marvel.

As they had at Menlo, Edison and his men worked with utter disregard of time. But all who worked at "65" remarked about the wonderful spirit of comradeship which existed there. They were all pioneers together, working for a common cause, all 1200 → enthusiastic believers in the electric light. Edison himself was never closer to his men than during this period of their work together.

The year 1881 was one of tremendous strain and back-breaking toil for Edison. The host of new and important business interests had to be tended, and the First District installation demanded much of his time. Somehow he managed to keep up his research, taking out about 89 patents that year. In addition, he built experimentally the world's first fullsize electric railway at Menlo.

Success

By the end of the following year, the First 1300 → District had become a profitable success. Edison had achieved his goal. He had subdivided electric current when others said it couldn't be done. He had invented a practical incandescent lamp where hundreds had failed and had made an efficient dynamo. He had planned, built and operated a complete electrical 1350 → system powered from a central station.

——STOP——ASK FOR YOUR TIME——

Record time immediately and answer
the questions on content.

Time_____Sec.	RATE (from table on page 315):	R. _____
No. Correct:_____ (key on page 322)	COMPREHENSION (10% for each correct answer):	C. _____
VI–7	EFFICIENCY (R × C):	E. _____

Record on Progress Chart on page 299

ANSWER THESE QUESTIONS IMMEDIATELY

1. (C) The occasion of all the excitement on New Year's Eve, 1879, at Menlo Park was the first public demonstration of Edison's new _____.

2. (T–F) The public accepted this new method of illumination very rapidly.

3. (C) Attempts to sabotage some of Edison's demonstrations were made by representatives of the _____ companies.

4. (T–F) The first installation of electric lights made necessary the invention of many additional control devices.

5. (T–F) Edison manufactured his first lamps at a great financial loss.

6. (MC) Edison did not develop a profit margin on the sale of his lamps until:

_____(1) the second year of manufacture.

_____(2) the fourth year of manufacture.

_____(3) the sixth year of manufacture.

_____(4) the tenth year of manufacture.

7. (MC) The Jumbo dynamo was designed to operate at how many revolutions per minute?

_____(1) 60

_____(2) 350

_____(3) 700

_____(4) 1,000

8. (T–F) The mansion at 65 Fifth Avenue was purchased as a home for Mr. Edison and his family.

9. (T–F) Edison was a rather autocratic supervisor and never got to know any of his men very well.

10. (T–F) By the end of 1882, Edison had achieved his goal of subdividing electric current.

LENGTH: 1350 WORDS

READABILITY SCORE: 51

Exercise VI–8

Crusader in the Pine Barrens

GLEN EVANS

(from *Dynamic Maturity*, November 1974)

WAIT FOR SIGNAL TO BEGIN READING

Elizabeth Woodford at age 59 has absolutely no problem in finding valuable and satisfying ways to use her time and talents. Quite the contrary. She calls herself "a sort of mishmash of a person—part naturalist, part botanist, part conservationist." She could add that she also is a top-notch nature photographer, a teacher, a writer, a rescuer of wild birds and animals, and a compelling lecturer. In addition to all this, she's a wife, mother, and grandmother.

The focal point for all of Elizabeth Woodford's activities and goals is her "home country," New Jersey's Pine Barrens, a wildland of swamps, lakes, and 100 pine woods that still cover around 1.3 million acres (more than 2,000 square miles)—a strange and peacefully quiet place to find in an industrial state. The term "barrens" is misleading, coming from the fact that the loose sandy soil isn't suited to conventional crop farming. But nature finds the Barrens ideal for many other things. This is an amazing land of pyxie moss, pitch pines, wild orchids, cranberries, sundews, bog asphodel, and at least 400 other varieties of plants. It is a region of more than 150 species of wildlife: Birds, deer, muskrats, raccoons, harmless snakes, frogs, rabbits, foxes, flying squirrels, and 200 even an occasional beaver lodge.

Living with nature

She and her husband Jim, a vocational agriculture instructor, are working to keep at least part of the Barrens that way—undeveloped and natural, preserving the unique and ecologically important character of this land. The Woodfords are part of that environment. They live in an unpretentious house beside Cedar Run Lake, near Medford Township, and use their 130 acres as a wildlife refuge and outdoor classroom to teach classes in Environmental Nature. Scattered around the grounds are the pens of an animal "orphanage" where orphaned and injured birds and animals are cared for until they can 300 be returned to their wild habitat. "We're careful not to make pets of them," says Mrs. Woodford. "They have to learn to take care of themselves, not depend on us, if they are to survive in the world."

"It's a wonderful place to live," Elizabeth Woodford told me when I interviewed her at her home. "But there's so much to do and to be done." As we talked, she sat bottle-feeding two tiny 8-day-old raccoons whose mother had been killed by a car. 400 Later she showed me her menagerie, which included as a permanent resident a large red-tailed hawk which can never fly again because one wing was shot away by a hunter's bullets. As "temporaries" there were a family of small-fry possums, a treeful of young raccoons, and a baby gray squirrel. These are only a few of the orphaned and wounded skunks, owls, fawns, foxes, and others that have received another chance at life in the Barrens through the ministrations of the Woodfords.

"But there's so much to be done," Elizabeth Woodford repeats. She was thinking of the inward 500 push of development. The Pine Barrens lie in south central New Jersey just a few miles east of one of America's major thoroughfares—the Jersey Turnpike—35 miles from the Philadelphia-Camden complex and only slightly more than 100 miles from New York.

The threats to the Pine Barrens come from many directions. As one of the largest tracts of "open," relatively unsettled areas in the industrial northeast, aviation planners see the Barrens as an ideal location for a gigantic jet airport. One such project, a supersonic jetport, was defeated by the active opposition of conservationists some years ago, but other proposals for air bases, and industrial 600 complexes keep popping up. The rivers and lakes among the piney woods, as well as the expanses of land, are attracting the attention of developers who have bought up large tracts to be bulldozed and shaped into "new towns."

As environmentalists see it, such large-scale "development" could bring ecological disaster to this unique wilderness. They point out that the natural balance of sandy soil, water, vegetation, and wildlife in the area is a very delicate one. Stripping away the pine woods, for example, could set in motion destructive forces, such as erosion, that would quickly 700 degrade the character of the land, lakes, and rivers, and would mean the doom of much of the wildlife which now thrives in the Barrens.

Getting the message across

A sturdy, brown-haired woman of extraordinary zeal, Elizabeth Woodford says, "It's through our various activities—all of them—that Jim and I hope to get the Barrens' story across."

These activities are numerous, indeed. For some time the Woodfords have been active in the movement, presently being conducted by the Jersey Shore Audubon Society, to set aside a major portion of the forest land as the Pine Barrens National Monument and Reserve. This plan would embrace the heart of the forest, nearly 550 square miles. 800⟵

Mrs. Woodford believes that if enough people could *see* what the Barrens are really like, and the kind of wildlife they support, they would understand why this unique area is worth saving. Toward this purpose she has become a skilled photographer and has taken thousands of beautiful color slides of the plant and animal life and the scenery of her beloved Barrens.

"In the beginning I pestered several camera shop owners for information," she says, "but mostly I learned by trial and error." She now expertly uses a fine Swiss camera and has an assortment of special 900⟵ lenses and lighting equipment. But far more important than the camera is the "eye" she has developed for spotting natural subjects, be it a bird, flower, or scene, and the skill to dramatize it on film. Most of her photos are taken on hikes around the Barrens, and she points out that her subjects always are photographed in their natural setting, "as they are," a process that sometimes requires infinite patience to wait for just the right moment to snap the shutter.

These photographs—thousands of them—have become part of a series of 12 illustrated lectures 1000⟵ that Mrs. Woodford has presented to conventions, schools, clubs, and study groups.

As if all this wasn't enough to keep her busy, Mrs. Woodford writes a weekly column, "Wild and Free," in the Burlington County *Times,* teaches an evening adult education class on the Pine Barrens at two separate county high schools, and conducts field trips and tours for groups at the Cedar Run Wildlife Sanctuary.

Then there are the many conservation and natural science groups in which she is active—among them the Medford, N.J., Conservation Commission, the Burlington County Natural Sciences Club, Phila- 1100→ delphia's Botanical Club, the New Jersey Audubon Society, and the Federation of Conservationists.

Elizabeth Woodford's crusade is no recent development. Even as a girl she carried home wounded wild animals and birds, and the natural sciences were her favorite subjects in school; she graduated from the Barnes Horticultural School in Merion, Pa. "I spent most of my spare time outdoors, in the company of my creature friends," she says. For almost 30 years now she has been spreading the message about the uniqueness and ecological importance of the Pine Barrens in every way that she can.

1200→ As I was leaving the Pine Barrens, I thought about the chances of saving this land of pitch pine, sand, and tea-colored cedar water—of mysterious swamps and green shadows, curly fern grass and bright-colored tree frogs. I thought about what Elizabeth Woodford had told me about the delicate fabric of this land in which the strands of plant and animal life are interwoven and interdependent and can so easily be disrupted and destroyed by works of man. There's no doubt that the Pine Barrens are in jeopardy—just as are so many parts of our beautiful country. But I'm cheered by the fact that, like Eliza- 1300→ beth Woodford, there are people who have no intention of abandoning their crusades. "There's simply too much important work remaining to be done," she says. "I plan to keep at it for many more years. We have the Pine Barrens today. But we want to 1350→ save them for those who follow us tomorrow."

——STOP——ASK FOR YOUR TIME——

Record time immediately and answer
the questions on content.

Time 27 Sec.

No. Correct:_____
(key on page 330)

VI–8

RATE (from table on page 315):

COMPREHENSION (10% for each correct answer):

EFFICIENCY (R × C):

R. 3000

C. 60%

E. 1800

Record on Progress Chart on page 299

ANSWER THESE QUESTIONS IMMEDIATELY

1. (T–F) Elizabeth Woodford claims that she hasn't enough to do.

2. (T–F) The Woodfords keep many small animals around their home as pets.

3. (T–F) The Pine Barrens are located within fifty miles of a large city.

4. (C) The conservationists organized a few years ago to defeat a proposal to build a large _Jet-Port Park_.

5. (T–F) Mrs. Woodford uses many special lenses and lighting equipment for her nature photography.

6. (C) She believes the best way to convince people of the values of the Barrens is by showing them through _pictures_.

7. (C) Which of the following was not mentioned among Mrs. Woodford's activities?

_____(1) Illustrated lectures series.

_____(2) Weekly newspaper column.

__X__(3) T.V. series on wildlife.

_____(4) High school field trips.

8. (T–F) The author really was convinced that the Pine Barrens were in jeopardy.

9. (T–F) The Woodfords are not in favor of setting aside 550 square miles of their land as a Pine Barrens National Monument.

10. (MC) Mrs. Woodford has been an active ecologist for about _30_ years.

_____(1) 50

__X__(2) 30

_____(3) 10

_____(4) 5

Exercise VI-9

Three Black Executives

DONNA MARTINEZ

(from an original article of the Uniwyo Reading Research Center)

WAIT FOR SIGNAL TO BEGIN READING

Man's drive to improve himself financially is not new in our current society. It has been a motivating factor for many men of many colors for many years. Following are brief accounts of three black men who were recognized by the *New York Times* for such achievements.

LeRoy Callender, engineer

At 42, LeRoy Callender was a professional engineer, licensed in thirteen states. He showed great pride in the record of his company for the past six years. With federally subsidized housing projects, public schools, and multi-service centers he has been responsible for projects totaling over $350 million. And at the normal consultant fee of about one half 100 of one percent of that total, he has established himself fairly well as a successful consulting structural engineer. He was particularly proud of some recent contract work for IBM and of the very strong endorsements he had received from that company.

He admits that he is considered brash and cocky, and that he is often labeled a "black militant." He feels that these characteristics gave him the drive to move up from the streets of Harlem, where he was raised by his mother. He did all kinds of work on the way up—newsboy, bootblack, dishwasher, 200 and sales clerk.

The real turning point in his career was when he passed the tough entrance exams for admission to Brooklyn Technical High School, from which he later graduated first in his class in Architecture. He later completed his engineering education at City College, working his way through as he gained experience in some engineering firms in New York.

In 1968 he made the big decision, resigned from a position as project Engineer with Severud Associates, where he had been employed for ten years, and set up his own company in the corner of a friend's office on Park Avenue. His timing was 300 good, and, although the pay was often slow, there were many opportunities on new housing projects and he got out and hustled for all the work he could get.

Two years later he moved to a 3,000-square-foot office location on the third floor at 401 E. 37th Street and invested $35,000 in revamping the space to an ultramodern office area developed from his own plans. He shows pride in his firm's capability with a staff of eleven draftsmen and engineers, two secretaries, and a computer terminal.

400 City College has recognized LeRoy Callender with an award as an outstanding graduate. He was also a member of the board of the College Alumni Association, and has served the College as an Adjunct Professor of Engineering.

Although divorced from his wife several years ago, he shared his family life with his college-age son, who has established Law as his professional goal. For years they were active in the Police Athletic League in Harlem, where LeRoy felt that he served as a father image for many boys from broken homes.

James Llewellyn, retailer

The pride of ownership was quite obvious as 500 James Llewellyn walked around the spacious aisles of the East Harlem supermarket in a fine modern building at 1718 Madison Avenue. This was only one of the fourteen stores in his food chain which showed gross sales of over $26 million in 1973. At 47, James Llewellyn was the president of the company and owned sixty percent of the stock.

His parents migrated to New York from Jamaica in the West Indies, and settled in White Plains where his father ran a restaurant and a couple of apartment buildings. Through helping his father and running paper routes, James got an early start 600 in business.

At 16, he graduated from White Plains High School and enlisted in the army where he had the opportunity to study Engineering at Rutgers. With income from a small liquor store in Harlem and his GI benefits, he worked his way through City College and through the Columbia Graduate School of Business. He then went on for two years in an honors program at New York Law School and passed the state bar examinations in 1960. With several of his classmates, he set up a commercial law firm which provided a basis for his activities for the next several 700 years.

During his association in the law firm, he tried out one job after another on the city payroll. Finally he achieved the position of supervising the federal programs designed to help put blacks into business. He felt that each change was an opportunity to make more money and a step up the ladder of political power and prestige. Finally, however, he had had enough of the political arena and was glad to take an opportunity to go into business for himself.

Through one of his legal clients, he learned that the Fedco Food Chain was for sale. All he needed ⁸⁰⁰← was someone to loan him $2.25 million so he could close the deal. This search for funding was frustrating and discouraging, but finally a friend helped him to get a loan from Prudential Life Insurance Company, and he was into the retail business.

His family welfare was the driving motivation for his business zeal. His wife and two daughters shared a cooperative apartment in Riverdale and a summer home on Martha's Vineyard.

He has been active in many other affairs. He was Board Chairman of Harlem's Freedom National Bank, on the Board of the New York State Food Merchants Association, and a long term leader in ⁹⁰⁰← "100 Black Men," an influential civic group of black professionals.

Frederick Wilkinson, p.r. man

At 53, Fred Wilkinson was busy making a transition to public service work because he wanted to deal with a larger consumer group in a more direct way. In his first four months on his new job with the Metropolitan Transit Authority, he had been out in the field almost daily. The $50,000 per-year position as First Executive Officer for Passenger Services and Public Information had involved him in many challenging experiences and in many opportunities for direct and concrete action. ¹⁰⁰⁰←

Fred Wilkinson was never particularly concerned with segregation or skin color. He had grown up with two sisters in a home in Washington, D.C. He had always felt secure in the social circles of the Howard University campus. His father had a Law degree from Howard, but spent most of his professional life as a registrar at the University. Fred was a graduate of the well-known Dunbar High School and of Howard University.

He met his wife at Howard, where she was securing a master's degree in psychology while he was achieving his magna-cum-laude A.B. in business administration.

¹¹⁰⁰→ He used his army experience to enhance his training in business law and accounting, and then used his GI Bill to finance his graduate work at Harvard's Graduate School of Business.

Macy's selected him for an executive training program when he left Harvard, and thus began a 26-year career with that company, moving from a position as a junior assistant buyer to the position of vice-president and manager of the Jamaica branch —the position he left to join the Metropolitan Transport Authority.

As a self-described storekeeper, he had supervised a staff of over 300 employees and an annual ¹²⁰⁰→ sales volume of over $10 million. The new TA challenge led him to resign rather than wait out a few more years till he would have qualified for extensive retirement benefits.

His wife, Jeane, was thoroughly supportive of his change and gets actively involved with some of his plans for posters and slogans. Their two daughters are both actively involved in careers in international affairs.

Fred says that he feels an obligation to help fellow blacks. He has been treasurer of the National Urban League, and very involved with the Black Executive Exchange Program. He has been a Board ¹³⁰⁰→ Member of Harlem's Freedom National Bank.

For 25 years, Fred has taught a teen-age Sunday School class at the Forest Avenue Congregational Church. He says that he tried to teach that the essence of religion is the application of the four-letter word *love* in all of one's relationships with his fellow ¹³⁵⁰→ man.

——STOP——ASK FOR YOUR TIME——

Record time immediately and answer
the questions on content.

Time_____Sec.	RATE (from table on page 315):	R. _____
No. Correct:_____ (key on page 322)	COMPREHENSION (10% for each correct answer):	C. _____
VI–9	EFFICIENCY (R × C):	E. _____

Record on Progress Chart on page 299

ANSWER THESE QUESTIONS IMMEDIATELY

1. (T–F) The three black executives had all been featured in *Time Magazine*.

2. (C) The one executive who did not spend his childhood in New York was _____.

3. (MC) LeRoy Callender made most of his money from:

   _____(1) state and federal government contracts.

   _____(2) housing projects and public school buildings.

   _____(3) bridge and highway construction.

   _____(4) slum clearance salvage projects.

4. (T–F) LeRoy Callender spent many years in service to boys in Police Athletic Clubs.

5. (T–F) James Llewellyn spent many years as a city employee.

6. (T–F) James Llewellyn is the sole owner of the Fedco Food Chain.

7. (C) The only one of the three executives who had a law degree was _____.

8. (T–F) All three executives have had successful marriages and have wives who support them in their current executive positions.

9. (MC) Fred Wilkinson has his graduate degree in Business from:

   _____(1) Howard University.

   _____(2) New York University.

   _____(3) City College.

   _____(4) Harvard University.

10. (T–F) Religion and Christian love have been powerful influences on Fred Wilkinson's professional and private life.

Exercise VI–10

Concepts of Communication

(from *Guidebook for Prospective Teachers*, Ohio State University Press, 1948, Chapter IX)

WAIT FOR SIGNAL TO BEGIN READING

Communication

You can get a hint concerning the higher purposes of communication by looking at the word itself. Communication is much more closely related to the word community than it is to any of the instruments of communication which man has created, such as language, radio, and pictorial or dramatic art. This point suggests that you will miss the deeper meaning of communication if you allow yourself to think only of the machinery of communication. You might get a further hint if you really examine the meaning of the word *community*.

What is a community?

You probably think of houses and streets full 100 of people at first, but as you think of modern means of transportation you remember that many teachers teach in consolidated schools and have to think of their community in a broader sense. We have come to think of community boundaries more in terms of "time of travel" than in terms of linear distance. Modern research in aeronautics makes it possible to travel to any part of the world within a few days' time. The major cities of the world are connected by many air lines that make them only a few hours' flying time apart. Whether we wish it or not, we find 200 ourselves drawn into a world community.

Breadth of community

Our means of communication today enable us to hear people in distant lands as they speak, and our recent progress in television, such as Telstar, enables us to see events in other parts of the world as they happen. All this makes us realize that linear boundaries no longer define a community. We need to look for a better definition. To have a community there must be something in common. Above all there must be some common values and some common 300 ways of living. One has a true community only to the degree that men enjoy common understandings and work together for common ends. A world community can be achieved only as men of different races and nationalities come to some common understandings, recognize some common problems, and

work together for some common ends. The physical community must be supplemented by a community of mind and spirit. An insane asylum cannot become a community without becoming sane, for by community one always means a community of mind. One must have mind or spirit to build common understandings with others. Unless one can communicate 400 his meaningful experiences to others, he cannot enter a community of understanding with them.

Purpose of communication

The primary purpose of all communication, then, is to build increasingly more community of mind in the world. All the machinery of communication whose creation has been sponsored by a democratic state comes into its own, only when it is consciously employed to this end, namely, the end of building community of mind. It is in this enterprise that you must learn to take your central satisfactions. It is this purpose which must determine the quality of your enjoyment. Perhaps it is desirable to 500 take a more deliberate look at what all of this means.

All communication, if it is really communication, brings about some community of mind. Even when a man swears at you or threatens you, he establishes a temporary community of mind. You share the thought that he has expressed and you have had a momentary meeting of minds. But such a getting together is very much like a meeting of the match and powder keg. Communication moves between two extremes. Sometimes it is used primarily to inflate the ego, and the speaker indulges himself 600 with the momentary sympathies of his audience; but unless all that is said has been designed to benefit the hearers as well as the speaker, the delightful meeting will result in a delayed explosion. Language, therefore, when used in the wrong spirit, brings community of mind into being for a moment in such a way as to make subsequent understanding almost impossible.

Severing communication channels

Of course civilized people do not, as a rule, swear at one another. They have more refined and more subtle ways of cutting people down to such a size that they can more conveniently see over their heads. Probably some of the members of this class $\overset{700}{\leftarrow}$ have such smooth techniques along this line that they can combine a word, an inflection, and a look so artfully that no one but the person for whom the remark is intended will object, but that one person may want to die or commit murder. It is psychologically necessary for some people who become the victims of certain attitudes to go around setting themselves up by cutting other people down. Even the best persons are a little guilty of this kind of behavior at times. The extent to which a person allows himself to indulge in this pastime determines in large $\overset{800}{\leftarrow}$ measure the extent to which he can communicate with others. He soon finds that the doors at every entrance are being quietly shut in his face, and that day by day he is standing more and more alone. An invisible wall builds itself around such a person. The lines of communication leading into and from the world in which he lives mysteriously disintegrate. No loud talk, no cursing of his luck or of others, and no grant of power can enable him to penetrate this spiritually suffocating barrier to communication which he has brought into being by his attitude. $\overset{900}{\leftarrow}$

What, then, is this quality which communication must have in order that it may serve the larger purposes of deepening sympathies and broadening understandings? Perhaps the problem can best be approached by recalling that every man is different from every other man. Since each person differs from everyone else, if people associate it is as inevitable as night following day that they will differ with one another. However inevitable this situation may be, it is true that when people differ they often make that fact cause for offense. When people "beg to differ $\overset{1000}{\leftarrow}$ with you" in a cocky or belittling way, you are almost sure to take offense. Some take offense when differences are expressed respectfully or even with humility.

Odd, is it not, that one should feel called upon to apologize for the fact that he is different from one, that he differs with another. If persons take offense, even polite offense, because one grew up with red hair, another with black skin, one as a Republican,

and another as a Democrat, they are taking offense at differences rather than taking a sympathetic interest in differences with others. They are making it $\overset{1100}{\rightarrow}$ difficult to communicate with one another.

Scientific attitudes

A look at the method and spirit of science also gives a feeling for the spirit of communication which builds community of mind. Regardless of race, creed, language, or nationality, the true scientist is interested in, sympathetic to, and open-minded about, the sincere and honest opinions of any other scientist whose thinking comes within his field of work. Differences of opinion are exchanged, cross-fertilization takes place, and new ideas spring up where only old ones grew before. They build an even broader community of mind, and science grows apace. Tolerance and $\overset{1200}{\rightarrow}$ open-mindedness prevail in order that conflicting opinions can be exchanged and men may grow in wisdom.

The spirit, therefore, of your personal and private conversations as well as of your public or professional exchange of ideas may or may not be marked by democratic qualities. If, as a consequence of attempts at communication, more community of mind, more common understandings, have been brought into being, then may you be assured that human communication is serving a purpose which justifies the invention of ingenious devices for extending the blessings of communication among men.

Communication—a two-way road

$\overset{1300}{\rightarrow}$ As time passes you must rate yourself in two different roles. As the actor playing the active role of communicating, how well can you call this spirit of ethical community into being? As audience, how well can you foster this spirit in the way you partici- $\overset{1350}{\rightarrow}$ pate in any enterprise of which you may be a part?

——STOP——ASK FOR YOUR TIME——

Record time immediately and answer
the questions on content.

Time____Sec.	RATE (from table on page 315):	R. _____
No. Correct:_____ (key on page 330)	COMPREHENSION (10% for each correct answer):	C. _____
VI–10	EFFICIENCY (R × C):	E. _____

Record on Progress Chart on page 299

ANSWER THESE QUESTIONS IMMEDIATELY

1. (T–F) The primary purpose of communication is economic.

2. (C) These authors believe that basic to understanding communication is the understanding of the word
_____truth_____.

3. (T–F) They state that community boundary lines today are thought of in terms of traveling time.

4. (T–F) The idea is presented that a community implies common standards of speech, religion, money, and politics.

5. (C) Basic to any community in the true sense, these authors believe there must exist a community of
_____.

6. (MC) These authors believe that civilized people put other people "in their place" by:

_____(1) tactful choice of words and speech inflection.

_____(2) swearing at them.

_____(3) exerting political pressure.

_____(4) use of police force.

7. (T–F) True communication necessitates a sympathetic interest in individual differences.

8. (MC) The characteristic of the scientific attitude which makes better communication possible is:

_____(1) the limited range of interest.

_____(2) the absorption in pure science.

___X__(3) the mind open to new ideas.

_____(4) the technical level of vocabulary.

9. (T–F) Ideas do not always accompany the words that express them.

10. (T–F) The spirit essential to communication is the conviction that you have a good idea to which you must convert others.

Exercise VI–11

The Old Mint

(from government document "The Old Mint")

WAIT FOR SIGNAL TO BEGIN READING

There's Gold! In California

When the rare yellow metal was found at Coloma (Sutter's Mill) by James W. Marshall in 1848 the cry of discovery ricocheted around the world.

The temptation of untold riches to be found in the land could not be denied. The California gold rush was on.

Prospectors swarmed into the territory and, by 1850, the gold mined in the hills had grown from a trickle to a deluge. The heavy outpour swamped the refining and coining facilities of the distant Philadelphia Mint. To continue to expose the precious cargo to the hazards of the time-consuming journey 100 intensified the dangers to the ponderous load.

The coinage situation in the West was in a chaotic state. Many different kinds circulated— French Louis-d'ors, Dutch guilders, Indian rupees, Mexican reals, English shillings, and our own American pieces. Even so, there was a scarcity and gold dust, while acceptable, was not a convenient medium of exchange. To remedy the difficulty, private mints sprang up which converted gold into coins—but this was not a solution.

In a four year period, 1848 to 1852, California had turned from a collection of sleepy Spanish villages into a restless, prospering territory that led to 200 statehood in 1850. The population had increased from 15,000 to about 250,000 and the mines had produced $200,000,000 worth of gold.

Then, concurring in a recommendation from President Millard Fillmore that a branch Mint be established in California, Congress acted on July 3, 1852, and authorized the construction of a United States Mint at San Francisco.

A small building, just 60 feet square, was erected on Commercial Street and the Mint started receiving deposits on April 3, 1854.

Obstacles connected with the supply of materials retarded and diminished the coinage operations during that year. However, $4,084,207, all in gold pieces, was coined between April and December, 1854, and gradually the coins there replaced the miscellaneous assortment in circulation.

Within ten years, it was apparent that the little Mint was sorely inadequate to meet the expanding coinage demands of the region. Again, a Mint with ample capacity to provide for the great mineral districts of the West was proposed. Not until 1872–1873, was the building completed and the work of fitting up the necessary machinery.

The new Mint at 5th and Mission was occupied in the summer of 1874, and was one of the best 400 appointed Mints in the world. It was first considered unnecessarily large but the Director stated, ". . . in fitting it up with a refining and coining capacity equal to the present demand it has been found necessary to occupy the entire building.

"The San Francisco Call," in its November 1, 1874, issue, described the Mint as a noble, substantial structure and reported: "The fire department will have little trouble quenching any conflagration that may arise within its walls, and unless an earthquake gives it a subterranean quietus, it bids fair to stand up for centuries."

The Mint was destined to live up to this early 500 assessment of its sturdy construction. The first critical test of survival was the holocaust that was the San Francisco earthquake and fire of April 18, 1906.

The disaster devastated the City of San Francisco. The city's water pipes broke under the onslaught of the violent quakes and fires raged unchecked throughout the area.

Just three weeks before the calamity, the Mint had completed a private water supply system of hydrants and hoses on each floor. Two wells located in the inner court supplied sufficient water for Mint employees and U.S. soldiers to fight a seven hour 600 battle against the towering flames that licked at the iron shuttered windows.

The intense heat melted the glass in the windows and flying embers ignited a dozen small fires on the roof and in the courtyard where lumber and timber were stacked.

Fifty employees of the Mint whose own homes were in the path of the fire made it to work that day. Family worries competed with their devotion to the mint. Duty won out. They remained to man the water hose. The Mint and its contents were saved. The destruction of the city gas works, however, 700 forced a halt to the melting, annealing and assaying operations fueled by gas.

Left standing virtually alone amid the rubble of the disaster with $200,000,000 in gold in its vaults, the Mint was the only financial institution in the city able to open its doors for business.

The subtreasury had been destroyed, bank buildings lay in ruins; the banking system ground to a dead stop.

An orderly flow of money in and out of the city was vital to its survival and to the well-being of the people. Only the Mint was in a position to begin accepting and administering the relief funds that poured in and, until the banks could once again 800← operate, the Mint handled all remittances to and from the city and disbursements within the city as well.

San Francisco didn't take long to restore and revitalize itself and the Mint was there as the city grew and prospered anew.

The commercial demands of the nation also increased and further expansion of minting facilities was necessary. In the summer of 1937 San Francisco personnel made another move; this time into an imposing marble edifice some distance from the principal business center where the old building is located.

Known as the San Francisco Assay Office, today it manufactures one-cent pieces for general 900← circulation bearing the famous "S" mintmark. It also produces the proof and uncirculated coin sets for sale to the public. In 1971, it added the 40% silver proof and uncirculated specimens of the Eisenhower dollar coin to its special coin programs.

After minting operations were transferred from Mission Street to the new location at 155 Hermann Street, the Old Mint was occupied by other government agencies until 1968.

Then the Old Mint was finally vacated and declared surplus to government needs. Empty and swiftly deteriorating, the unsightly building became the center of swirling controversy between agitators 1000← for its demolition to make way for a high rise and instigators for its preservation and restoration as an architectural, cultural, and historical landmark.

In the spring of 1972, President Nixon intervened to save the old building from its uncertain fate. He announced the transfer of the building from the General Services Administration to the Department of the Treasury's Bureau of the Mint for restoration and continued use by the government and the enjoyment of the public.

In a sudden burst of activity, workmen began arriving at the old, deserted building to accomplish 1100→ the restoration. A short year later, in April 1973, the Mint's Special Coins and Medals and Computer employees were able to move their mushrooming operations into the commodious rooms in the rear of the building, newly renovated and equipped to speed the processing of millions of mail orders received yearly from the public for the special coins and medals produced by the Mint.

The move back to the Old Mint adds another historical highlight to the continuing story of the building's existence. It is the first public building to open in compliance with Public Law 92–362, pro- 1200→ viding for the adaptive use of surplus historic structures.

Preservation for its own sake is rarely enough. Unless historic buildings can also be made to serve a useful purpose, the danger is always present they will be destroyed as obsolete and a part of our nation's past will be lost forever.

The interior of the Old Mint has been completely rehabilitated to lead this double life and the exterior restoration is expected to be completed soon.

In the meantime, the museum rooms authentically restored to their original 1874 appearance are open to the public. And exhibits of historical and educational significance will continue to be developed. 1300→ Now teeming with new and useful life, the beauty of its past preserved, the welcome mat is out once again. The old building that has survived time, earthquake, fire and abandonment, and that has played such a crucial role in the growth of Cali- 1350→ fornia and the West has re-opened for visitors.

——STOP——ASK FOR YOUR TIME——

Record time immediately and answer
the questions on content.

Time_____Sec.

No. Correct:_____
(key on page 322)

VI–11

RATE (from table on page 315):   R. _____

COMPREHENSION (10% for each correct answer):   C. _____

EFFICIENCY (R × C):   E. _____

Record on Progress Chart on page 299

ANSWER THESE QUESTIONS IMMEDIATELY

1. (C) The early day gold mined in California was sent to the U.S. at _____.

2. (T–F) Gold dust was the only acceptable medium of exchange in California until the new mint issued coins in 1854.

3. (MC) The new and enlarged building, which is now called the Old Mint, was first occupied in:

_____(1) 1854.

_____(2) 1864.

_____(3) 1874.

_____(4) 1906.

4. (T–F) The San Francisco earthquake and fire devastated the mint building.

5. (T–F) Immediately after the fire, the public banking system in San Francisco ceased to function.

6. (T–F) In 1968 the Old Mint was officially vacated and declared surplus property.

7. (MC) Since 1937 the basic product of the Mint has been coined in the:

_____(1) Mission Street Federal Building.

_____(2) G.S.A. Headquarters Building.

_____(3) San Francisco Post Office Annex.

_____(4) San Francisco Assay Office.

8. (T–F) Restoration of the Old Mint building was not begun until 1975.

9. (C) Several rooms have been restored to their original appearance and will serve as a _____.

10. (T–F) Mail orders for special coins and medals produced by the Mint are now being handled in the restored building.

Exercise VI–12

Communication and Propaganda

(from *Guidebook for Prospective Teachers*, Ohio State University Press, 1948, Chapter IX)

WAIT FOR SIGNAL TO BEGIN READING

Communicating with others

Can you imagine yourself living under conditions such that it would be impossible to communicate with other people? You could not get in touch with anyone by using the telephone, telegraph, or letter; you could not turn on a radio and hear other people; you could not attend a motion picture or look at a television screen; you could not get in touch with anyone by writing, talking, painting, reading, or playing any musical instrument. Without some means of communication you would be living in complete isolation. You would be unable to transmit your ideas to other people and unable to receive any 100 ideas from anyone else.

Methods of evaluating communications

In this modern world we are constantly subjected to a barrage of information and misinformation, persuasion, deception, and variations of opinion. In our democracy we prize freedom of speech and freedom of the press. This means that we place on the individual a tremendous responsibility for evaluating the ideas which are relayed to him through the radio, press, movies, newspapers, magazines, and personal contacts. Americans are readers of many kinds of material.

As a citizen you have a responsibility for deciding what to believe and what not to believe; 200 what to read and what not to read; what sources are representing special interests and what sources are striving to be fair. This is a process of evaluation which you will have to continue for life. Teachers have a very important task of helping young people to develop some standards for evaluating the material which they receive from the various media of communication.

One of the purposes of education is to develop individuals who will maintain suspended judgments until all available evidence is collected, act intelligently in terms of available information, and evaluate their activity in terms of other evidence that becomes 300 available. Schools should help to give students a range of knowledge that will enlarge the outlook of their minds. But schools must recognize that there are groups which do not wish to encourage the development of that kind of a thinking citizen. Many groups use methods of mass communication to get individuals to make conclusions on partial, cross-sectional, or distorted information. They are desirous of leading people into attitudes which will make them jump to conclusions without paying much attention to available evidence. These attempts to lead people to emotional thinking are usually called 400 *propaganda*. This threat to clear thinking is used on a large scale in the world today. It may not always be "anti-something," but it may be used to lead you to the support of some cause by painting a rosy picture of all the nice aspects of it. A thinking person should beware of communication channels that appeal to his emotions and that encourage him to act quickly without giving careful consideration to the matter at hand. Propaganda can often be detected by some general techniques which are commonly used to mislead your thinking.

500 *Name calling*—Bad names are given to those the propagandist would have us condemn; good names to those he would have us favor. Examples are "progressive teacher," "Communist," "bureaucrat," "Conservative," "Jew," "Fraternity Man," "Socialist," "regular fellow," etc.

Glittering generalities—We are told that "the American system is threatened" and are lured with such attractive phrases as "social justice," "the more abundant life," "economic freedom," "the welfare of the common man," etc. These vague terms may have different meanings to everyone, and we frequently put our own meanings into the mouth of the speaker rather than try to decide what he really 600 means by seeing how his actions define his terms.

Flag waving—The propagandist associates his cause with the American flag, the Christian religion, or with some person of great prestige. He attempts to make you feel that loyalty to your God and your country dictates that you agree with him.

Slogans—The propagandist finds some catchy phrase which may stick in one's mind. Then he tries to get it generally accepted without an analysis of its meaning. Examples are "democratic way of life," "it's Luckies 2 to 1," "The skin you love to touch," "For men of distinction," "good to the last drop," 700 etc. Applying the question, *why, what,* or *how* to some of these slogans may help you see how superficial many of them are.

Repetition and fabrication—The propagandist loves to take an incident and magnify its importance. He is similar to the old gossip who likes to make the story just a little better before she passes it on. By repeating it over and over he attempts to make you accept its validity. You may protect yourself from this to some extent by trying to get at the source of some of your information which you question.

Bandwagon technique—You are led to believe 800← you should do something because "everybody's doing it," "it's smart to be seen at the Cliff Cafe," etc. Campaign managers and advertisers know the human tendency to follow the crowd and will invariably predict victory for their candidate or widespread use of their product. Here again you need to question, "Who is everybody?" "Why is it smart?"

Suppression and distortion of facts—Many of the socioeconomic cartoons lead to considerable distortion of the facts. Many of our labor journal cartoonists would have everyone believe that employers and capitalists are all bloated bigots with tall silk hats. Each political party has cartoonists who try to 900← make the other party look ridiculous. Pictures showing only a limited view of a situation are often used to distort reality. The things that are omitted in a news report may be just the things that you need to know to reach a wise decision. By withholding the whole truth from you, you may be led to reach a decision which the propagandist favors.

Ambush and showmanship—Wealthy interests and pressure groups sometimes use the ambush method of winning public opinion. They may use pressures to get their employees or their debtors to promote their ideas. They may organize "front" 1000← organizations which take on an attractive name and carry on the publicity. They may give large sums to philanthropic institutions and then make the institution fight their battles. Oratory many times appeals to the emotions and does not present any facts. In case of doubt, you might try to discover who is financing the group of speaker in question.

These and many other methods may be used to lure the gullible thinker into false and sometimes dangerous conclusions. The tenseness of our international situation and the war of ideologies now 1100→ going on make it important for you to consider carefully the ideas to which you are exposed.

One of the most important factors influencing the communication of ideas is the reader's understanding. Dr. Edgar Dale, has suggested several questions which might be asked in an effort to evaluate your own ability as a reader. Although these questions apply to reading of newspapers primarily, you can frame some parallel questions to apply to magazines, radio programs, movies, speakers, etc.

1. Am I familiar with a number of newspapers, not only the good ones but the poor ones as well?
1200→ 2. Do I plan my reading in terms of (a) time spent, (b) material read, and (c) the order and speed in which the material is read?
3. Have I examined all parts of the material to find out what's in it?
4. Can I find desired information quickly by using the index, summary, etc.?
5. Am I familiar with the way a typical news story is constructed?
6. Do I get the most out of the big news stories by following them day by day as they develop?
7. Am I able to read, understand, and criticize the editorials in daily newspapers?
1300→ 8. Do I have an efficient speed and comprehension in reading?
9. Am I familiar with some important factors which influence the nature and accuracy of news: (a) the reader, (b) ownership of the paper, (c) political affiliations, (d) the reporter, (e) the editor, (f) the make-up editor, (g) space restrictions, 1350→ and (h) advertising?

——STOP——ASK FOR YOUR TIME——

Record time immediately and answer the questions on content.

Time _____ Sec.   RATE (from table on page 315):   R.

No. Correct: _____   COMPREHENSION (10% for each correct answer):   C. 40
(key on page 330)

VI–12   EFFICIENCY (R × C):   E.

Record on Progress Chart on page 299

ANSWER THESE QUESTIONS IMMEDIATELY

1. (C) In a democracy the evaluation of ideas presented to the public is the responsibility of the _____ ___media___.

2. (T–F) Teachers should evaluate all materials presented to students to protect them from misunderstanding the ideas.

3. (T–F) Some people do not believe that students should be taught to analyze and evaluate the material they read.

4. (C) Attempts to lead people to emotional thinking are called _____.

5. (MC) The technique which appeals to one's own definition of terms such as "economic freedom" and "American way of life" is called the technique of:

_____(1) repetition.

_____(2) suppression of facts.

_____(3) flag waving.

_____(4) glittering generalities.

6. (T–F) The author suggests that you apply the questions *why, what,* and *how* to any slogan approach.

7. (T–F) The "bandwagon" technique is described as that which uses a popular "name band" to gain attention.

8. (T–F) Socioeconomic cartoons usually present an accurate view of a situation.

9. (T–F) The "ambush" technique implies the use of some "front" organization to expound the ideas.

10. (MC) According to the author, one of the most important factors influencing the written communication of ideas is:

_____(1) the reader's understanding.

_____(2) the political affiliation of the writer.

_____(3) the size and style of type used by the publisher.

_____(4) the newspaper that carries the story.

Exercise VI-13

Stress — and Your Health

(from pamphlet of the Metropolitan Life Insurance Company, 1967)

WAIT FOR SIGNAL TO BEGIN READING

What is stress?

Stress is commonly defined as intense exertion —strain and effort—the wear and tear of life. A mother in childbirth and her baby being born, a child on that first day of school—or a student facing an important examination—is sure to experience some stress.

The athlete striving to win a race—the circus performer walking a tightrope—the artist trying to produce his best work—all are under stress. A working man with a sick wife, trying to double as father and mother to his family, is under considerable stress as well as the mother who works to support her 100 children and comes home to a housewife's job at night is also under stress.

A businessman who worries continually about office problems while he's at home, or about home problems while he's at the office, is under stress.

There are varying degrees and different forms of stress—mental, emotional, physical—all having some impact—sometimes good, sometimes harmful —upon health. Stress can often be the spice of life or, depending upon circumstances and a person's capacities and reactions, it may have damaging side effects which may lead to disease, cause us to age prematurely, or sometimes even shorten life. 200

A key to health

Through all normal living and our daily activities, our body cells are continuously being worn out and replaced with new ones. In a medical sense, stress has been defined as the rate of all wear and tear caused by life. All emotions—love as well as hate, for example, and also physical exertion—swimming, golf, or just a brisk walk—involve stress. This type of stress is good for us because the thing that's important is not the stress itself but its effects.

Whether or not the strain caused by our experiences can make our bodies become susceptible 300 to diseases—or perhaps even to accidents—depends to a great extent on our adaptability to these experiences.

Authorities believe that by understanding our individual reactions—and having some knowledge of our limitations—we can help to prevent excessive stress.

Hormones— the body's chemical messengers

The "attack" on the body which can cause stress might be invasion by disease or it might be an injury, or even an emotional crisis. If the trouble is a burned finger, the sudden injury sets off an "alarm reaction" within the body. First the nervous system 400 sends out an SOS and among the physical forces alerted are the body's "chemical messengers"—the hormones—which are quickly sent into action. The tiny pituitary gland, located under the brain, dispatches a special hormone—a substance called ACTH. This pituitary hormone signals the adrenal glands, situated just above the kidneys which, in turn, send out other hormones (corticosteroids) thus putting the body in a state of preparedness to handle the emergency. In response to the "alarm signals," special hormones rush to the injured area where they steady the work of the healing processes, helping 500 to speed up or slow down activity as needed. The pituitary and adrenal glands balance the body's chemistry by helping to coordinate and regulate the functions of other organs in the body. With their help, disease can be resisted or an injury healed without overly disturbing the working order of the rest of the system.

Strong emotions, too, such as fear cause bodily changes because emotions, in general, are meant to make us act. When fear occurs, nerve impulses and hormones (adrenalin) speed through the system causing the heart to beat rapidly. Blood vessels of the stomach and intestines contract, shunting the 600 blood to muscles for quick action; breathing speeds up, and other changes occur which help to pitch us to a point where we can meet an emergency or go through a difficult situation.

Because we can't and wouldn't want to live like vegetables—without feeling or responsiveness—normal emotional stress is useful in many ways.

In contrast to healthy stress, however, intense and persistent anger, fear, frustration or worry, which we may bottle up inside ourselves, can threaten health.

Mind + body = psychosomatic

One of the advances of modern medicine is the increasing recognition of the importance of emotions in influencing body health. This view recognizes that mind and body work together as one (not as separate units), with the body reacting upon the mind, and the mind upon the body.

The knowledge that illnesses must be considered and treated in relation to the whole person forms the basis for psychosomatic medicine (psyche, mind + soma, body). Much has been written about this concept, but much has been misunderstood; so let's examine a few popular misconceptions.

After listening sympathetically to a neighbor's detailed account of her latest symptoms, a Mrs. R. said: "Just you forget about it, my dear; it's probably only psychosomatic—you know—when you imagine you're sick."

Mrs. R. meant to reassure her neighbor, but she fell into the all-too-common error of thinking that psychosomatic illnesses are not real ones. People feel pain just as intensely whether the cause is physical or emotional, and failure to seek professional advice at the first warning sign of trouble can and often does lead only to more serious difficulty later on.

When Mr. J. was told that his wife's illness was emotional in origin, he said to himself, "Well, that's a relief, anyhow. If it's only psychosomatic, it can't do her any real harm."

Like Mr. J., many people have the mistaken idea that a psychosomatic illness is one that is purely imaginary, that if the patient would only forget about his ailment, it would quietly and quickly disappear.

Many people think that since psychosomatic has something to do with the mind or the emotions, such illnesses cannot cause any physical damage. In order to see why these notions are untrue, let us look first at some of the common effects of emotions on the body—not in illness, but in everyday situations.

Physicians base their knowledge—that emotions play an important part in many types of physical illness—on facts with which we are all familiar. All of us have experienced some of the effects of emotions on bodily functions. Most of us can recall blushing when embarrassed or having a tight feeling in the chest or a weight in the pit of the stomach before an examination or having our heart pound and our hands perspire when excited or afraid. These are normal reactions of the body to specific situations, and are beyond the control of our will power; they generally disappear quickly once the cause is removed.

Knowing how these normal emotions influence body functions, we are better able to understand how strong and persistent emotional conflicts may, over a period of time, disturb the working of body organs, such as the heart or the stomach. It is believed that in some cases they can eventually result in actual change in the organ itself.

Prolonged emotional tensions are thought to play a prominent role in certain kinds of heart and circulatory disorders, especially high blood pressure; digestive ailments, such as peptic ulcer and colitis; headache and joint and muscular pains; skin disorders; and some allergies.

What's to be done?

First, and always in discovering the causes of illnesses in which there are emotional factors, a complete physical checkup must be made. It is most important for the patient to have confidence in his doctor so that he will feel free to express troublesome thoughts without fear of being ridiculed or belittled. The physician needs to know about the life of his patient and his responses to various situations. With this knowledge, he can help him to become aware of how fears and worries may have caused or contributed to the illness.

Because of knowledge about the emotional factors involved in many types of illness, there is less reason than ever for neglecting to consult a physician at the first warning sign of trouble. Many ailments of a psychosomatic nature can now be treated with greater hope of success than ever before, if brought to the early attention of the family physician.

——STOP——ASK FOR YOUR TIME——

Record time immediately and answer
the questions on content.

Time_____Sec.	RATE (from table on page 315):	R. _____
No. Correct:_____ (key on page 322)	COMPREHENSION (10% for each correct answer):	C. _____
VI–13	EFFICIENCY (R × C):	E. _____

Record on Progress Chart on page 299

ANSWER THESE QUESTIONS IMMEDIATELY

1. (T–F) Stress is usually thought of as intense exertion—strain and effort—the wear and tear of life.

2. (C) The different forms of stress are mental, emotional, and _____.

3. (MC) Whether or not the strain caused by our experiences can make our bodies susceptible to diseases depends chiefly upon:

_____(1) bodily resistance to invading viruses.

_____(2) ability to handle daily living without stress.

_____(3) adaptability to these experiences.

_____(4) symptoms of heart palpitation and severe headache.

4. (T–F) The hormone dispatched by the pituitary gland is a substance called ACTH.

5. (T–F) Fortunately for us, strong emotions cannot precipitate bodily changes.

6. (T–F) The mind and the body function as separate units in maintaining bodily health.

7. (T–F) Because a psychosomatic illness is purely imaginary, if the patient would forget his ailment, it would go away.

8. (T–F) Normal reactions of the body to specific situations are beyond the control of our will power.

9. (MC) To discover the cause of an illness *the first thing* to do is to:

_____(1) have a session with your psychologist.

_____(2) investigate past life experiences.

_____(3) resolve any internal conflicts.

_____(4) have a complete physical checkup.

10. (C) Many ailments of a _____ nature can now be treated with greater chances of success than previously thought.

Exercise VI-14

Student Travel: The High-Risk Route

WILLIAM A. SIEVERT

(from *Chronicle of Higher Education*, November 11, 1974)

WAIT FOR SIGNAL TO BEGIN READING

News items

"A Boston University student is seen hitchhiking near the campus. A few days later her body is found in a field in New Hampshire."

"Near Ypsilanti, three Eastern Michigan University students are slain by a fourth student who had offered each of them a ride. Two University of Michigan students and two nonstudents are also murdered before a 20-year-old killer is apprehended."

"In Santa Cruz, Cal., four female student hitchhikers—two from the University of California at Santa Cruz and two from Cabrillo Junior College—are raped and murdered by a former mental patient."

Thumbing

The uplifted thumb has become almost as big ¹⁰⁰ an institution on American college campuses as blue jeans.

Unfortunately, as the popularity of hitchhiking has increased among students, so have the risks. So much so, in fact, that many campus security forces and student groups alike have been developing new strategies to deal with the dangers of thumbing.

For the most part, student organizations are lobbying for safety controls on hitchhiking while campus police and security forces are waging informational campaigns to convince students not to hitchhike at all.

"Hitchhiking is certainly one of the greatest concerns of college security officers, a concern based ²⁰⁰ on the high incidence of crime reported," according to John W. Powell, executive secretary of the International Association of College and University Security Officers.

Mr. Powell says that the number of hitchhiking-related rapes, robberies, injuries—and occasional deaths—has continued to rise, despite the efforts of campus authorities to warn students. "The current emphasis of campus security people everywhere is on educating students to the dangers," he says.

Education is really about all campus police can do. Donald Ryan, security officer at Boston University, says, "There's not much we can do. You can't ³⁰⁰ enforce laws against hitchhiking any more than you can against jaywalking."

Adds Melvin Fuller of the Eastern Michigan University security force. "A person hitchhiking is usually standing on city streets, not on campus where we have our authority."

Nonetheless, Mr. Fuller says that "whenever our officers go to the dorm for talks, the dangers of hitchhiking are brought up."

At the University of California at Santa Cruz, security chief John C. Barber admits, "We realize it is futile to say, 'Don't hitchhike,' in an area like ours where everything is casual and friendly. We still urge students not to hitchhike, but we say—if you do, ⁴⁰⁰ at least follow a few tips."

Four hitchhiking students were among those killed in a highly publicized series of nine murders in the Santa Cruz area in 1972 and '73. Edward Kemper, 28, who picked up the students in a car with a university parking sticker (his mother worked on the campus), later was convicted of the slayings.

"Not a Victim"

Since then, says Mr. Barber, the university has been showing a film made at the Santa Barbara campus and passing out a companion brochure called "Not a Victim" to offer students specific precautions they can take:

—Ride with a friend.
⁵⁰⁰ —Look into the back seat before entering a car.
—Check out the driver's appearance and clothing.
—Make mental notes of the car's description and license number.

In addition, Mr. Barber urges students to make sure the car has an inside door handle on the passenger's side; Kemper's did not.

Boston University's Mr. Ryan says he reminds students that it is not only the hitchhiker who is in danger by accepting a ride from a stranger. "It works both ways," he says. "The driver can find himself in trouble, too."

"Anyone can resemble a student, carry books ⁶⁰⁰ under his arms; a driver feels sorry for him, gives him a ride, and gets robbed. It happens all the time."

In 1967, during the period when three students

—all thought to be hitchhikers—were murdered in separate incidents by a fourth student, Eastern Michigan's security force began taking out advertisements in the student newspaper urging people not to thumb rides.

"Every time we have a problem, we advertise again. We have to keep harping on it," Mr. Fuller says. "But people are quick to forget."

At least some students are not forgetting and are launching programs they hope will protect hitchers around their campuses.   700
←

Two of the more advanced of these programs are located in Colorado university towns—Fort Collins and Greeley.

With the approval of the city council of Fort Collins, students at Colorado State University are operating the "Community Carpool" project. This year-old program licenses both drivers and hitchhikers.

Hitchhikers register with the carpool committee for 25 cents, providing identification and their home addresses. Upon registering, the hitchhikers are issued official, brightly colored hitching cards.

"The hitchhiker holds up the card instead of his thumb and shows it to the driver before entering a car," explains Steve Smith of the Colorado Student 800
Lobby and the Colorado State student association.←

Similarly, drivers who register with the committee are issued windshield stickers that are easily visible from the curb.

The Fort Collins streets department has cooperated with the program by erecting more than 40 signs designating certain corners as "safe turn-out" points.

The turn-out points provide students with convenient locations for seeking rides and offer drivers safe areas to pick up passengers without blocking traffic.

Last spring, students at the University of Northern Colorado at Greeley started a similar program.

Clarifying a "confusing" law

Mr. Smith says that the Colorado Student Lobby will be seeking legislation this winter to ex- 900
pand the two programs statewide. The lobby also is ←
working toward companion legislation that would legalize hitchhiking throughout the state—or at least clarify what the lobby considers to be the "confusing" law currently on the books.

The California state legislature this year turned down an even tougher proposal to license hitchhikers. Under the California plan, introduced by Assemblyman John F. Dunlap with the support of some student groups no person would be issued a permit if he had criminal action pending against him, if he was on parole or probation, or even if he 1000
had an outstanding traffic violation.←

The California Student Lobby had not yet decided whether to support the highly restrictive bill when it was killed. The lobby expects one or more similar, but perhaps milder, bills to be introduced next year.

From Brandeis to San Francisco State University, more colleges are establishing designated hitchhiking stands on their campuses or at the edges. Many institutions first set up such stands in campus parking lots during last winter's energy crisis, when car-pools and group travel were being encouraged.

The stands allow hitchhikers to seek rides in
1100→ groups and seem to provide more protection because they are located on college property rather than on public streets.

"Share-a-ride" stops

California State College at Hayward, for instance, has "Share-a-Ride" stops at its campus entrances to encourage students to give one another lifts up and down the large hill on which the classroom buildings are located.

The University of California at Santa Cruz operates a free bus and tram service from its classroom complexes to the campus gate a mile and a half away. In the evenings, the trams are used for a "Dial-a-Ride" service. Students call the service, and
1200→ a university-sponsored tram or bus picks them up and takes them wherever they want to go around the five-square-mile wooded campus.

Similarly, telephone "ride-wanted" switchboards are rapidly replacing bulletin-board listings as a means of coordinating long-distance travel.

Campus discussions

At Ohio State University, student groups—particularly those in dormitories—have sponsored seminars featuring both campus and city police discussing the problems associated with hitchhiking.

On several occasions, policewomen have visited the Ohio State campus to lecture to women's groups. At Santa Cruz, a special program provides instructions for women on how to protect themselves.

Other campuses concentrate on radio and news-
1300→ paper advertising or posters to remind students of the dangers of thumbing.

One of the more visual posters has been created by Syracuse University's "Eyes and Ears" student marshal program.

The poster depicts a pretty country meadow with a human body lying in it. A white sheet covers
1350→ the body—except for one huge extended thumb.

——STOP——ASK FOR YOUR TIME——

Record time immediately on next page
and answer the questions on content.

Time___37___Sec.

No. Correct:_____
(key on page 330)

VI–14

RATE (from table on page 315):

COMPREHENSION (10% for each correct answer):

EFFICIENCY (R × C):

R. 230

C. 90

E. 70

Record on Progress Chart on page 299

ANSWER THESE QUESTIONS IMMEDIATELY

1. (T–F) Campus police at many colleges are urging students to refrain from hitchhiking.

2. (MC) The major effort of campus police to reduce the crime associated with hitchhiking is to:

_____(1) patrol the areas where students often thumb rides.

_____(2) post warnings against picking up hitchhikers.

__X__(3) provide educational programs about dangers of hitchhiking.

_____(4) penalize all students who are caught hitchhiking on campus.

3. (MC) "Not a Victim" is:

_____(1) a film used in college classes on safety.

_____(2) a T.V. documentary on dangers of hitchhiking.

_____(3) a book about a happy hitchhiker who got in with the wrong crowd.

__X__(4) a brochure about precautions to keep hitchhikers out of trouble.

4. (T–F) Edward Kemper was the victim of an escaped mental patient who picked him up.

5. (C) Two of the most advanced programs for protection of student hitchhikers are in college in the state of ___Colorado___.

6. (T–F) The "Community Carpool" program licenses both drivers and hitchhikers.

7. (C) In the Fort Collins area, the local street department posts signs designating certain areas as safe ___hitchhiking___ points.

8. (T–F) At the time this article was written, the California legislature had recently passed a tough law to require registration of all hitchhikers.

9. (T–F) In some places "ride-wanted" switchboards are replacing bulletin-board listings in promoting contacts between drivers and students.

10. (T–F) This writer seems to feel that the potential dangers of hitchhiking have been greatly overpublicized.

LENGTH: 1350 WORDS

READABILITY SCORE: 43

Exercise VI–15

Bridge over Time

GREGORY RAY

(from *Wyoming Wildlife*, July 1974)

WAIT FOR SIGNAL TO BEGIN READING

To many travelers, Wyoming looks like nothing more than an arid plateau; yet with every passing car, countless natural wonders are overlooked. Many of these are only a few miles from the major interstate highways and most are marked by a small highway sign.

Such is the case of a modest announcement on the north side of the road near the westbound lane of Interstate Highway 25. Without fanfare it says merely, "natural bridge."

Following the arrow on the off-ramp sign takes motorists four-and-three-quarter miles south on a small road marked "Converse County 13." It's a pleasant drive through the country. Birds fluttering 100 effortlessly through the air and the gentle aroma of summer make it an exceptionally enjoyable side trip from the four-lane asphalt interstate.

Nearing the mountains, the road winds slowly through rolling hills and then veers to the left through a gate and down into a canyon.

Crossing a creek, there is still no sign of a natural bridge; however, a tremendous abandoned building towers above the trees and stands as a silent eulogy of an early-day attempt to build an electrical generation station on the stream to run water pumps for irrigating the land above the canyon. 200

Beyond this concrete and steel mastodon is a grassy area spotted with picnic tables and outdoor fireplaces. Here, sheltered by a large, red sandstone amphitheater, the creek flows sleepily through this quiet valley and under Ayers Natural Bridge.

It's not a huge natural bridge and perhaps is more impressive for its pastoral beauty than its sheer size, though it spans 90 feet at the base and leaves a gapping 20-foot-high archway that is penetrated by the rich, blue sky.

The unusual rock of this area reveals in layers the geological history of these formations. The bridge was formed through the eons of time after the land 300 rose above the vast seas that once covered Wyoming. In terms of geologic time, this natural wonder is relatively new—probably created some 50–100,000 years ago, though an exact determination of this has not been made.

The bridge itself is part of the Casper Sandstone Formation laid down during the Pennsylvanian age more than 280 million years ago. The rock was pierced by the slow sculpturing of La Prele Creek after a narrow neck of sandstone was isolated by the meandering stream. Time eventually eroded this 400 middle-paleozoic rock to what it is today.

The forces of wind and rain also smoothed the rock amphitheater walls that gently caress the small secluded valley that contains the Ayers Natural Bridge Park.

Land donated

Though now a small and well-maintained park of approximately 15 acres, this scenic area was privately owned until 1920, when, partly due to local interest in the bridge, Andrew Clement Ayers, then owner of the land, donated the site as a Converse County free park.

So keen was local interest in the natural bridge and other natural features of the area that residents 500 of the town of Douglas donated their labor to help build an access road to the site.

Nestled among the abundant shade trees and lush grass are picnic and camping facilities—35 cookout grills, four large sheltered picnic tables, 30 fireplaces, and 40 open-air picnic tables as well as a small camping area.

Despite a lack of national publicity or, for that matter, any highway advertising, there are a surprising number of people visiting the park each year. It is estimated somewhere between 25,000 and 30,000 people view the bridge annually. In addition to this, the registration book at the park entrance 600 literally shows entries of visitors from all over the world.

Because of this annual influx of tourists, the park was doubled in size about six years ago. Popularity of the park varies according to the season, however. Springtime traditionally brings the fewest numbers of people to view the stone attraction, while July is one of the most popular times for this side excursion.

Over the years the park has become a favorite spot for hunters during the fall months. The campground facilities can accommodate 20–30 groups, though due to its popularity, there is a three-day camping limit in the park.

Officially the area opens April 1 and closes ⁷⁰⁰← November 1, but weather and water conditions can affect this. During the spring when heavy runoff occurs, there occasionally is danger of flooding, since La Prele Reservoir is located only about a mile-and-a-half up the canyon. If this happens, the park is closed briefly until the possibility of stream overflow has passed.

In early spring and late fall when the weather is highly unpredictable, an occasional snow storm will necessitate either a late opening or an early closing of the park, though during many years the area has been kept open year round.

Best time to visit

It would be difficult to judge the most spec- ⁸⁰⁰← tacular time of year to visit this site. The saturated green of spring and early summer make this area extremely scenic. Spring is also the time of year that La Prele Creek is liveliest. Awakening from the long winter, both the aquatic wildlife and the water itself seem eager for summer to make an official appearance. As if emphasizing this, a local resident pulled a 5-pound rainbow trout from the creek this spring.

In the fall, the turning leaves of this small deciduous-covered valley make it spectacular. The frenzied activities of summer diminish to a sleepy ⁹⁰⁰← pace. The stream flows casually through the bridge and the lazy days of summer gradually relinquish to the cool breezes of approaching winter.

Throughout the year, however, the unique features of the park make it a delightful side trip. In addition to the bridge itself, and the large, red sandstone formation surrounding the area, there is also a mica-speckled crystal cave in the park that is open to the public. Although this cavern is relatively small compared with others in the United States, it adds an additional dimension to this geologically fascinating area.

As if this weren't enough to entice even the ¹⁰⁰⁰← most skeptical sightseer or amateur geologist to the area, colorful lichen formations are found dotting the rocks atop the sandstone bluffs surrounding the park, giving one the impression such colorful green,

yellow, and orange accents were left behind after a careless artist dripped the hues from his pallet.

The climb up to the top of the amphitheater is steep and there is no trail. However, from the edge of this sandstone cliff there is a magnificent view of the natural bridge and the park as well as the sur- ¹¹⁰⁰→ rounding sagebrush landscape. From here the park stands out as an oasis in an otherwise subdued horizon.

The graceful elbows in the stream, framed delicately by the natural bridge archway, disappear quietly into infinity, while the steep canyon walls focus attention on the valley floor where a small walkway crosses the creek leading visitors over to the far side of the sandy riverbank.

Sources of water

There is approximately a mile of stream that wanders through the park. Beyond this, on both the upstream and downstream ends, is private land. La Prele Creek is not the only source of water for the ¹²⁰⁰→ area, however; several natural springs, in addition to two wells, give park visitors an opportunity to savor the natural underground liquid that has over the years been a selling point for several prominent brewers of hops and barley.

Despite the conveniences of the park, there are no concession stands to mar the natural beauty of the area. An attempt to maintain the scenic wonders of Ayers Natural Bridge in pristine condition is performed by a caretaker now residing at the park year round. Though park officials have had little trouble with vandalism, they wish to preserve this sandstone monument to perpetuity.

¹³⁰⁰→ This unique rock edifice was formed by an ancient sculptor over millions of years ago. While it has little of the fame of such huge national parks as Yellowstone and Yosemite, it contains a variety of scenic wonders not found elsewhere and is well worth a five-mile side trip from the interstate high- ¹³⁵⁰→ way.

——STOP——ASK FOR YOUR TIME——

Record time immediately and answer
the questions on content.

Time_____Sec.	RATE (from table on page 315):	R. _____
No. Correct:_____ (key on page 322)	COMPREHENSION (10% for each correct answer):	C. _____
VI–15	EFFICIENCY (R × C):	E. _____

Record on Progress Chart on page 299

ANSWER THESE QUESTIONS IMMEDIATELY

1. (T–F) In the park is an early-day attempt to build an electrical generation station.

2. (MC) The Ayers Natural Bridge Park is impressive for its:

   _____(1) sheer size.

   _____(2) historical past.

   _____(3) tremendous towers.

   _____(4) pastoral beauty.

3. (C) The bridge is part of the Casper _____ formation.

4. (T–F) Douglas Creek sculptured the red sandstone rock bridge.

5. (T–F) The maintained park is approximately 15 acres.

6. (T–F) Camping facilities are not available in the park.

7. (MC) The most popular visitor time for this stone attraction is:

   _____(1) July.

   _____(2) September.

   _____(3) November.

   _____(4) January.

8. (T–F) The opening and closing dates, weather permitting, are April 1 to November 1.

9. (C) In addition to the stream and two wells, there are several natural _____ in the park.

10. (T–F) There is one concession store in the park.

Exercise VI-16

People's Art

ROBERT SOMMER

(from *Natural History*, February 1971)

WAIT FOR SIGNAL TO BEGIN READING

The design of the man-made environment can be so tight and confining that it leaves no room for expressions of individual identity. But sooner or later, like grass growing through cement, these marks of individuals or groups break through the totally designed environment. One manifestation of individual expression is people's art—the beautification or improvement of public spaces without the official approval of the public authorities. Examples include vacant lots converted into playgrounds by neighborhood residents, construction-site fences that have become graffiti galleries, people's gardens and people's trees, junk sculpture along the roadway, and driftwood sculpture along the shoreline. The scale ←100 ranges from a couplet on a toilet wall to a six-story mural on Boston's South Side.

Anonymous artists

The hallmarks of people's art are anonymity, fluidity, and neighborhood identification. Often the identity of the artist is unknown and becomes a matter of local folklore. On the driftwood sculpture of the Emeryville, California, mudflats, I have never seen a person title his work or place his name alongside it. The materials used in the Emeryville sculpture (discarded tires, plastic bottles, driftwood) and the anonymity of the artists indicate respect for the dismal setting—the stillness and ugliness of the east-←200 ern shoreline of San Francisco Bay, raped by industry and freeways alike.

These productions have a fluid quality lacking in formally designed works of art. The people's parks that have sprung up in various cities are constantly changing. The heterogeneous layout of people's parks invites the visitor to add his own flower patch or bench or sculpture. When someone writes a poem and publishes it in a magazine, it stands as a completed work of art. But when a man writes a poem on a construction fence, he expects others to add to it.

Utilization of existing landscapes

Not as arbitrary as formal art, street art usually ←300 incorporates existing features of the landscape. The still-operating People's Park Annex in Berkeley,

California, used litter from the area—discarded car seats for benches and old tires as swing seats. The formal work of art, generally the product of an artist's studio, tends to ignore existing features of the surroundings. For example, a mural in the Sacramento State College cafeteria has an Aztec theme. It is painted around a wall thermostat, which simply remains suspended between two natives. A folk artist would undoubtedly have incorporated the ther-400→ mostat into the mural, making it a woman's breast or a piece of fruit in a basket.

The most creative graffiti build upon existing features of the landscape. Along the cement embankment of the Los Angeles River, hinges of storm drain outlet covers form the ears in a series of cat faces. On several occasions the city fathers have painted over the faces, but each time, the many-lived cats came back.

Artist's intent

These direct expressions of the need for beauty and personalization raise the question of whether it is possible to distinguish between people's art and vandalism. Is it possible to differentiate between someone decorating a dead tree stump in a slum 500→ neighborhood and a young boy carving "C.K. loves Z.B." on a tree in a state park? Although both acts represent the utilization of public space for private expression and communication with others, the intent of the two people is different. One would hope, although there is no guarantee, that the tree painter desired to brighten the cityscape and counteract the drabness of his surroundings. The tree carver violates the anonymity of the true street artist, and his message although accessible to any finder, was probably directed specifically to his girl friend. The 600→ intention of the artist to beautify the landscape is probably the major way of differentiating people's art from vandalism or environmental desecration.

A jury distinguishes between murder and manslaughter on the basis of the defendant's motives. I am not completely satisfied with something as subjective as the artist's intentions as the sole test of people's art, but it is probably the best criterion that we have. The boy who sprays a peace sign on the school wall or chalks the name of his gang on a building is trying to express himself, to communicate something to others, but he is not specifically intent on beautifying or improving the environment. 700 ←

Because these artistic incursions of public space are illegal, they usually are performed at odd hours by an underground group or a single individual. The secrecy involved in such activities necessarily means imperfect democratic decision making. It is not possible to poll all the occupants of the housing project about the sort of playground or mural they want if there is a risk that the authorities will squash the venture before it begins.

Public officials in several cities have taken a cue from street artists and obtained civic support for street decorations and public gardens. David Brom- 800 ← berg, a 36-year-old urban planner in New York City, persuaded landlords to let artists paint murals on building facades at nine locations. Several months ago the Museum of Modern Art held an exhibit of color slides of the murals. The same practice has been followed in Boston, where the city has supplied both paint and encouragement to brighten otherwise drab surroundings. The result has been more than twenty large murals, most in predominantly black neighborhoods, with themes emphasizing black identity and aspirations.

Environment participation

People's art raises important issues about the degree of user participation necessary for an accept- 900 ← able quality of life. According to psychiatrist Matt DuMont, "The extent to which a person can influence his environment will determine his ability to perceive himself as a separate human being." An account of the first People's Park in Berkeley stated that its importance for the young people lay not simply in its status as a park or its location but in its being an outgrowth of their own labor and decision making. To be fully human, one must create as well as choose, make things beautiful as well as admire beauty.

Some architects go so far as to select their 1000 ← client's dishes, silverware, and ashtrays; and interior designers would prescribe desk size, chair style, and the model of desk calendar. The solution is not to eliminate planning but rather to plan for freedom. However comprehensive a design plan is, it should leave opportunity for the individual to exercise options in creating environments that suit his unique needs. Designs must allow for elbow room and foot room, for people to be creative forces in their environment, rather than be components of a design scheme. Good planning permits—in fact, encourages —this freedom.

Overall plan

1100 → In the best cases personalization enhances an overall plan. In the dormitories at the University of California, Davis, students are given paint and brushes at the beginning of the year and are allowed to decorate their own rooms and to work cooperatively on the halls and corridors. A similar procedure could be applied on a larger scale to a city neighborhood. Here an elected body of local residents might be given authority over the esthetics of the visual environment, including sign ordinances, the color and style of light fixtures, hydrants, and billboards. There seems little reason why all lamp-posts must be dark 1200 → green, or gray, particularly if the neighborhood residents prefer warm colors. In San Francisco, unemployed youths constructed a minipark and meditation center in a Japanese style, complete with rock garden and Japanese bridge.

I was delighted to find that the neighborhood park on Olvera Street, an historic Mexican-American neighborhood in Los Angeles, contained the same style of tree sculpture that I had seen outside Mexico City. Why must trees and bushes in neighborhood parks be maintained according to downtown standards of neatness and symmetry?

Most American cities could benefit from Amsterdam's experience with its allotment of people's gardens along the railroad tracks and canal banks. 1300 → Contrast these flower-rimmed plots with the litter-strewn sewers along the railroad tracks into New York City, and one realizes quickly that letting people use public land has to be preferable. If allowed to unfold, people's art lets bloom the creativity and artistic expression crushed by the totally designed 1350 → environment.

——STOP——ASK FOR YOUR TIME——

Record time immediately and answer
the questions on content.

Time____Sec.

No. Correct:_____
(key on page 330)

VI–16

RATE (from table on page 315):

COMPREHENSION (10% for each correct answer):

EFFICIENCY (R × C):

R. ____

C. ____

E. _____

Record on Progress Chart on page 299

ANSWER THESE QUESTIONS IMMEDIATELY

1. (T–F) People's art is that spontaneous art which is supported by and often suggested by public authorities.

2. (T–F) Rarely is the identity of the creators of people's art known.

3. (MC) People's parks are characterized by:

_____(1) formality.

_____(2) change.

_____(3) beautiful landscaping.

_____(4) great size.

4. (T–F) Observers are expected to add their own touch to people's art.

5. (MC) One of the differences between people's art and formal art is that:

_____(1) formal art is more creative.

_____(2) people's art is not legitimate art.

_____(3) people's art is always outdoors.

_____(4) formal art tends to ignore existing surroundings.

6. (C) The primary way of distinguishing between people's art and vandalism seems to rest on the _____

of the artist.

7. (T–F) People's art must often be accomplished in secrecy because of its illegal nature.

8. (C) In order to perceive oneself as a separate human being, one must be allowed to influence his _____.

9. (T–F) The author clearly advocates the elimination of all architectural and artistic planning.

10. (T–F) Tasteful planning cannot incorporate personalization effectively.

221

Exercise VI–17

Wooded Wonderland

ROGER HART

(from *Natural History*, November 1973)

WAIT FOR SIGNAL TO BEGIN READING

Exploring with Peter

I'd spent an hour searching for Peter because I wanted him to take me to his favorite places. Finally he came whipping along the road on his bike. He took me to his favorite spot and showed me the remains of a model landscape, all but destroyed by yesterday's rain, which his sister and he had built out of shale and twigs.

Chattering away, he hurried me along to his fishing place, convincing me it was *the* fishing place and that no one else knew about it.

Days like this with eight-year-old Peter were part of two years of field investigation into the ex-100 ploration and experience of the landscape by children as they develop from birth to eleven years of age. Ironically, more is known about the relationship of baboons to their habitat than of the activities of children to their outdoor environment. It was important that I spend an extended period of time with a group of children living in a small, distinct environmental unit, so that I could monitor their movements and behavior and obtain reliable data. I selected Wilmington, Vermont, for the study because it not only met these specifications but also incorporated many 200 characteristics of an urban environment.

Children need to explore

For their social and emotional development children need a physical environment that they can comprehend and within which they feel competent and secure. They also have an urge to explore the landscape; this is related to their need to experience the diversity and extent of the components of their environment and to see these as part of a whole.

The need to feel effective as an agent of change is another strong factor in the healthy development of a child. Compared to the complex and ever chang- ing world of people, the natural environment remains 300 relatively stable. A child can immediately see the transformations that he has effected. I have observed that children from about the age of three freely and frequently modify the environment if there are suit- able areas available.

Children will not manipulate or modify an overtly cared for and guarded landscape. Manicured lawns, miniature trimmed trees, and the absence of dirt piles, surface water, and large trees all convey a strong message to a child—"do not touch." This is the situation in most new suburban housing tracts. In this respect the children of impoverished inner-city 400 areas have a richer environment in abandoned lots containing piles of dirt, scrap wood, and other ma- terials suitable for modifying the physical landscape, although such areas lack the special qualities—trees, water, varied topography—that natural elements possess.

The range a child is allowed to travel without accompaniment is limited by parents for a variety of reasons: inferior ability to deal with traffic and the desire to avoid unfavorable social influences are among the most common. Also, because children have to squeeze much of their play into short periods of time defined by institutional and family schedules, 500 they must play within their neighborhood. In this defined space, a child must find a landscape suffi- ciently rich to satisfy the desire for free exploration, discovery, collection, and creation.

Children's needs for a variety of experiences are usually thought of as being provided for by such institutions as playgrounds, organized sports, schools, camps, and clubs. Such solutions, however, lead to more compartmentalization, segregation, and spe- cialization of children. Their desires for play are not sufficiently regular or planned to enable them to prestructure all activities with their friends. Many of a child's most exciting games or projects happen by chance.

Social development may be fostered if children 600 have free access to areas where they can meet casually and engage spontaneously in cooperative activities such as building complex stream systems in the sand.

Children also need places where they can be alone; I have watched children many times playing alone in the dirt or by a small pool of water. Free- dom from interruption and interference by adults is important; time to reflect on experience and develop a personal ordering of his world is essential to a child. By experiencing and re-creating the world in this way, a child can develop the individuality that 700 is needed for healthy relations with others.

223

Importance of a physical environment

The physical environment also plays an important role in supporting a child's emotional security and developing a sense of personal identity. Children who encounter frequent changes of residence or who live in neighborhoods that suffer from heavy wrecking and building activity will find it difficult to construct a stable image of the environment. Continuity of experience is most important. I have observed, for example, that a child can develop such a strong attachment to a tree that its removal, if necessary, must be carried out with care and understanding. It is an indication of the need to give order to the world that a child's most frequently observed creative activity out of doors involves the building of 800 miniature landscapes—cities, houses, garages, and airports.

Using the natural environment

The natural environment offers a wealth of play potential for young children, with trees and small patches of water the most valued elements. One tree can engage a child for days at a time or, periodically, over a span of years. Manufacturers of playground equipment have found it impossible to recreate such richness. The children of Wilmington demonstrated to me that there are countless routes up "a good 900 climbing tree"; many notches, cracks, or rough spots can be used, depending upon the child's desire for challenge at any time. Any kind of bush or tree allows children to exercise great creativity in the construction of houses, forts, tents, and imaginative laboratories. A mature tree is excellent, of course, for hanging a rope swing and has the added attraction of a host of insects.

Children do not need large wooded areas; in fact, many play only on the fringes of woods. But the pressures of land use and an unwillingness to recognize the importance of natural elements have 1000 1350 made them scarce in most urban areas. Natural elements are systematically removed from suburban areas and urban playgrounds in the name of esthetics, durability, and safety.

Adventure playgrounds

One solution to the lack of suitable natural areas for city children are "adventure playgrounds," in which they are given the opportunity and the materials to dig tunnels, plant gardens, and build places by themselves. These playgrounds try to create in microcosm the qualities of a town most valued by children, with trees, varied topography, earth, and building materials as essential elements. Adventure playgrounds were introduced in Denmark during 1100 World War II and caught on in England during the 1950s, but the concept has been slow to take hold in the United States. A major criticism by adults is that these areas are ugly, but the inclusion of trees could do much to alleviate this problem. It is doubtful, however, that such playgrounds could be created in sufficient numbers to be freely accessible to younger school-age children for they require the expense of a permanent and competent supervisor. Small natural areas, or "minicommons," spaced every few blocks and unsupervised except for the care of 1200 trees, could provide a supplement to larger, more widely spaced adventure playgrounds.

One hundred and forty years ago Friedrich Froebel, the German educational philosopher, introduced the concept of kindergarten into education. His ideas anticipated later findings in stating that a child is by nature a doer, and therefore learning is secondary to activity, out of which it grows. Froebel also emphasized the importance of experiencing the harmony of the natural world in the development of the child. Many kindergartens and schools still lack these qualities, but the city designer also has a responsibility in this matter. For the richer and fuller 1300 development of metropolitan children, more minicommon lands, featuring an abundance of trees, water, and soil, should be made as accessible as the wooded adventureland available to children in Wilmington, Vermont. Children do not need to be taught how to explore and learn; they will do so naturally given an environment that will allow it to happen.

——STOP——ASK FOR YOUR TIME——

Record time immediately and answer
the questions on content.

Time_____Sec.	RATE (from table on page 315):	R. _____
No. Correct:_____ (key on page 322)	COMPREHENSION (10% for each correct answer):	C. _____
VI–17	EFFICIENCY (R × C):	E. _____

Record on Progress Chart on page 299

ANSWER THESE QUESTIONS IMMEDIATELY

1. (T–F) The author studied children from birth to eleven years old.

2. (MC) The children studied in this article lived in:

_____(1) Atlanta, Georgia.

_____(2) Wilmington, Vermont.

_____(3) Spokane, Washington.

_____(4) San Jose, California.

3. (T–F) Children usually will not manipulate an overtly cared for and guarded landscape.

4. (C) A child needs to feel that he can modify his _____.

5. (MC) According to this writer, the range a child is allowed to travel is limited for all of the following reasons *except:*

_____(1) Children have an inferior ability to deal with traffic.

_____(2) Parents desire their children to avoid unfavorable social influences.

_____(3) Police do not understand a child's need to play freely.

_____(4) Children must squeeze much of their play into short periods as defined by schedules of home and school.

6. (T–F) Children's needs are adequately met by playgrounds, sports, camps, and clubs.

7. (T–F) Children need some places where they can be alone.

8. (T–F) A child's most frequently observed creative activity out-of-doors involves the cutting down of trees.

9. (T–F) Children need to be taught how to explore and learn in a natural environment.

10. (C) Friedrich Froebel, the German educational philosopher who introduced the concept of the kindergarten, believed that learning was secondary to _____.

Exercise VI-18

A Student Manifesto

PENNFIELD JENSEN

(from *Natural History*, April 1970)

WAIT FOR SIGNAL TO BEGIN READING

The phenomenon of student activism is as much a barometer of global crises as it is a manifestation of personal frustration and organized disruption. The celebrated generation gap is little more than the naturally holistic consciousness of young people facing a way of life that is not only ugly, irrelevant, and neurotic but that threatens to destroy us all. The natural environment, on the other hand, presents to the sensually connected but culturally shocked young person the clear light of moral value and societal obligation. Earth: Love it or leave it.

The impatience demonstrated with the establishment is the best part of today's activism. The 100 worst part is seldom seen for what it really is: a despairing apathy that stultifies all endeavor. The activist is basically a constructivist, a creative and productive person, dedicated to "making it better," while, at the same time, demonstrating that the culture, the economics, and the politics of the United States are hopelessly antediluvian. The healthy concerns of today are directed toward the environment and reach beyond all national boundaries. For nationalism itself is a disease of the mind that settles over a country, smothering its intelligence under a blanket of rot thicker than the smog we breathe. 200 When a young man's life becomes shattered by the blind trauma of a useless war or by the faceless sadism behind an official load of buckshot, one hears windows begin to break the world over. These are dead-ends. Ultimately, activism wants a big answer to a big question. We don't want merely to survive; we want to live. There is only one place to live and that is on this planet and we must live here together.

While individuals of stature and wisdom are arguing for an international ecological congress to establish laws for international use of the earth's 300 resources, the ecological crisis has already precipitated student activism into one of the world's most potentially constructive forces. The activists do not struggle against educational systems because education is despised but because education is needed. The naivete, enthusiasm, and idealism of young people is not a thing to be scorned; it is rather to be celebrated as the raw material of constructive growth.

The ecological perspective shows all of life connected into dynamic processes with ineluctable consequences should those processes be changed.

The ecological sentence for mankind is: "Get with it or die."

What has been

400 In the meantime society is asking its young people to be satisfied with what they have, believe in the American Dream, and accept the heritage of genocide and pollution with pride, patriotism, and purpose. In short, we are asked to volunteer our suicides, and to do so quietly without disturbing the peace of our retiring benefactors, the over-40 generation.

We do not look upon industries, churches, developers, businessmen, and politicians as being necessarily bad; we simply see them as our executioners. I am not going to befriend my executioner. I am not going to dedicate my talent and intelli- 500 gence to his irresponsibility. I am going to dedicate myself to the only element that predicates our survival and the survival of our children: the stable ecology of this planet.

As a species we continue to commute, pollute, and salute in righteous arrogance the despoiled flag of our environment. The irony, and I hope it never becomes the tragic kind, is that never before has mankind had the tools for self-perception and global understanding available today. This statement does not, however, place the argument in the hands of the technocrats of the space-race, the bomb-now-and- 600 study-later school of scientific panaceas, for this is surely a pitiful travesty on the true role of science in the play called "Mankind." Rather, science has given us an understanding of the evolutionary play in the ecological theater and has awakened us to a true and challenging comprehension of man and of man's place on this planet. The future, in spite of its grim protent, is the greatest hope and the greatest challenge any life form has ever had. Let it be clear, though, that the great blight of human overpopulation is the problem of success, and let us further 700 beware lest our epitaph read: *Here lies a species that failed only because it succeeded too well.*

Realistic inner yearnings

The misapprehension of the motives and intentions of today's young activists comes from a larger misapprehension of the age in which we live. The inner yearnings of nearly all young people are for a simple and enriching life. Coupled with the problem of global survival is the much more personal crisis of emotional survival. The cities stink. The rivers are polluted. There is no way to make an honest buck. The goal of most young people is self-realization, riddance from neuroses, anxieties, and guilt. In short, people are seeking and expressing their freedom. It 800 is the crowning achievement of democratic culture; it is for the most part a tremendously healthy thing. The unhealthy things are catchwords in this era: alienated, freaked-out, hung-up, and others, and take their significance with respect to whichever side of the "gap" you happen to be on.

The second part of this urge to emotional wholeness and survival takes the form of a large-scale exodus from the cities to the country, but this cannot last either: there simply isn't enough country. The consequences of this step-by-step introduction to the spiritual, emotional, and physical nourishment 900 of the undeveloped, ecologically whole countryside will be an ever greater demand for access to our natural areas, for more natural areas, and for the information, sustenance, and peace they provide. The ecological perspective provides a picture of life that focuses on a miracle of creation and evolution that is wonderful, brutal, and inspiring.

Positive goals

The constructive nature of student involvement with the issues stemming from environmental awareness is emphasized in the demands of the following manifesto composed by the youth delegates to a recent conference.

On a national scale, we urge:

—The mobilization of the national effort to 1000 attain stability of numbers, and equilibrium between man and nature, *by a specified date,* with the attainment of this goal to be the guide for local and national policy in the intervening years;

—The immediate assumption of a massive, federally financed study to determine the optimum carrying capacity of our country, on the community, city, county, state, and national levels, with this carrying capacity to be predicated on the quality of life, the impact upon world resources, and the tolerance of natural systems;

—The adoption of new measures of national well-being, incorporating indices other than the rate 1100 of growth of the gross national product, the consumption of energy resources, and international credit ratings;

—The immediate rejection of international economic competition as valid grounds for the creation of national policy.

On an international scale, we endorse:

—The proposal that the leaders of all nations through the United Nations General Assembly declare that a state of environmental emergency exists on the planet earth;

1200 —The creation of colleges of human ecology and survival sciences in the member nations of the United Nations;

—The creation of national, regional, and global plans for the determination of optimum population levels and distribution patterns;

—The creation of national, regional, and world-wide commissions on environmental deterioration and rehabilitation;

—The proposal that the United Nations General Assembly adopt a covenant of ecological rights similar to the U.N. covenant of human rights.

Within the changing fabric of activism itself, there is a great role yet to be played by the conservationists. It is to these people that the maturing young are going to look for help, education, and leadership. It is truly to "the men of the earth," to the men of global understanding and international commitment, that the reins of world leadership will 1300 be handed. This is the one area where the cooperation of all sides can be gained and the only area where the power structure can communicate and join forces with today's enthusiastic young activists.

This "Student Manifesto on the Environment" is a warning to all preservation-conscious people 1350 . . . but more than that, it is a supplication.

——STOP——ASK FOR YOUR TIME——

Record time immediately and answer
the questions on content.

Time ___7___ Sec.

RATE (from table on page 315):

R. ___11___

No. Correct: _____
(key on page 330)

COMPREHENSION (10% for each correct answer):

C. ___60___

VI–18

EFFICIENCY (R × C):

E. _____

Record on Progress Chart on page 299

ANSWER THESE QUESTIONS IMMEDIATELY

1. (C) According to the author, the worst part of today's activism is despairing ___violence___ .

2. (T–F) According to the author, the activists struggle against the education system because education is disguised as promoting ecological destruction.

3. (T–F) According to the author, a healthy nationalism is needed to save our national resources.

4. (MC) According to the author, young people look at industries, churches, developers, businessmen, and politicians as:

    _____(1) bad people and organizations.

    _____(2) benefactors of the present young generation.

    __X__(3) executioners of this and coming young generations.

    _____(4) misguided, but basically good-hearted and well-meaning organizations and people.

5. (T–F) According to the author, mankind has better tools for self-perception and global understanding today than ever before.

6. (T–F) According to the author, the inner yearnings of young people involve an opportunity to destroy authority figures in order to replace them with better.

7. (C) The _____ perspective provides a picture of life that focuses on a miracle of creation and evolution.

8. (T–F) The Student Manifesto includes suggestions for both national and international change.

9. (MC) The Student Manifesto recommends adoption of new measures of national well being based on:

    _____(1) growth of gross national product.

    _____(2) consumption of energy resources.

    _____(3) international credit ratings.

    __✓__(4) none of the above.

10. (T–F) The author maintains that there is still a great role to be played by conservationists in the activist movement.

LENGTH: 1350 WORDS

READABILITY SCORE: 33

Exercise VI–19

Recycling

(from a pamphlet supplied by the American Forest Institute)

WAIT FOR SIGNAL TO BEGIN READING

What is solid waste?

Solid waste is sometimes called "the third pollution"; along with air and water problems, it's high on our nation's list of environmental concerns. Solid waste is the trash and garbage and all the solid materials—from broken-down cars to candy wrappers—that people discard every year.

How big a problem is solid waste?

It's a big problem, but no one knows for sure exactly how big. Agricultural and animal wastes probably account for the largest tonnage: some 2.3 *billion* tons per year, according to an estimate in a 1970 report by the President's Council on Environ-¹⁰⁰ mental Quality (CEQ). These wastes cause very sizable disposal problems, particularly when they're from concentrated operations. Mining and mineral processing produce a second kind of waste; according to the CEQ, they add another 1.7 billion tons a year. Then there are the manufacturing wastes—110 million tons a year according to the CEQ report. Much of the waste from manufacturing operations is recovered and reused in some way, because it is profitable and relatively easy to do so. Finally, there is the solid waste generated by the nation's municipalities. Collected municipal wastes were listed at about 190 million tons per year in the 1970 CEQ ²⁰⁰ report. Even though a recent study indicates the total may be less than that (between 110 million and 120 million tons per year), the municipal problem is the most complex and troublesome of all solid waste problems.

What makes the municipal solid waste problem so different—and so difficult?

At the heart of the problem is people who are crowded together in cities, and generate an incredible array of wastes. Efficient collection and disposal depend on cooperation of hundreds of thousands, sometimes millions, of citizens. Even with citizen cooperation, waste collectors still have to extend ³⁰⁰ their efforts into every corner of the city. The manpower and equipment requirements to do this gobble up huge portions of municipal budgets, and the waste itself, when disposed of, gobbles up land. Many cities are running out of places to dispose of the waste they collect; so they just dump their waste in open areas or bury it in landfills. In some cases, the waste is first burned in open dumps or incinerators to reduce the volume; in any case, available disposal sites are becoming scarcer and scarcer with each new load.

What kind of costs are involved in municipal solid waste collection and disposal?

The total cost is estimated at $5 *billion* a year —with about 80 percent going towards collection; almost all of *that* for manpower. Some 340,000 Americans are employed as collectors and sanitation truck drivers.

How much paper is there in solid waste?

Of 67 million tons of paper and paperboard used by Americans in 1973, about 14 million tons were eventually recycled back into new products. Another 10 million tons of paper went into permanent uses—in files, books, building materials, etc. Four million tons were handled by municipal sewage systems and private septic tanks, by home incineration, and by disposal in rural areas or were exported. Thus 39 million tons were left to become part of the nation's solid waste stream.

Is the paper industry really recycling 14 million tons of paper a year?

Yes, in 1973, waste paper provided 22 percent of all the fiber used in making new paper and paperboard. Besides recycling waste paper, the industry also used other waste materials in its manufacturing process.

What are some of the other waste fibers the industry uses besides those from recycled paper?

Twenty-seven percent of the fiber used in paper ⁶⁰⁰ ← manufacture comes from the wood residues of various other forest industries, such as lumber and plywood, and another two percent comes from rags and other miscellaneous agricultural waste. All together —including both recycled paper and wood residues— over *half* the fiber used in papermaking in the United States is reclaimed from waste material. The paper industry thus kept a total of 32 million tons of waste from the nation's overall solid waste stream in 1973.

Do you call it "recycling" when the industry uses wastes such as lumber and plywood residues?

No, recycling paper means using waste paper ⁷⁰⁰ ← to make new paper. The general term "reclaiming" covers the use of *all* kinds of wastes, *including* recycled wastes. According to the definition of the National Center for Resource Recovery, reclaiming is "the restoration to usefulness or productivity of materials found in the waste stream. The reclaimed materials may be used for purposes which are different from their original usage."

Haven't residues from lumber and plywood operations always been used in the making of paper?

Can reclaiming those wastes really be called a contribution to the reduction of the nation's solid waste problem? Forest industry residues have *not* ⁸⁰⁰ ← always been used in the making of paper, and their use now serves to reduce not only solid wastes, but air pollution as well. Until a few years ago, virtually all lumber and plywood waste was buried or disposed of in smoky "tepee" burners, and industry had to develop new systems and new technology to use the waste. Today, great progress is being made in applying those new developments, for instance, only six percent of sawmill residues in the State of Oregon was reclaimed in 1953. By 1967, the figure had risen to 60 percent—and it is still growing today. ⁹⁰⁰ ←

Is not the municipal solid waste problem the one that needs the most attention?

Every step taken to reduce solid wastes is important, but municipal waste is clearly the fastest growing problem area. The paper industry already takes considerable quantities of recyclable wastes from our cities. Every large city has many waste paper dealers; the New York "Yellow Pages" telephone directory lists 90 in that city alone. The paper

industry works actively to develop new waste paper supplies from municipalities, and it's working hard to improve its ability to use such wastes.

There must be increased efforts—involving co- ¹⁰⁰⁰ → operation among industry, the public, and government—to assure development and acceptance of new waste collection systems, new recycling techniques, and new uses for waste materials. In experimental facilities, ways to separate reusable glass and metals from mixed wastes have already been demonstrated. One such facility—in Franklin, Ohio—also separates waste paper fibers, but at this point the material is only being used in the manufacture of building products, such as roofing felt. There have been experiments to try to utilize these waste fibers from mixed municipal wastes in the making of other paper products. The results, though—technically and eco- ¹¹⁰⁰ → nomically—have been inferior to those achieved by using fiber obtained from waste papers that, before collection, were separated and bundled by the people disposing of them.

What is the paper industry doing to boost recycling within our cities and towns?

Paper companies, often working together through the American Paper Institute, encouraged local governments and civic and charitable groups to carry out efficient newspaper collection programs. One such program—set up and conducted with the industry's help—began five years ago in one section of Madison, Wisconsin, and has since been expanded to include the entire city. Newspapers are tied and ¹²⁰⁰ → bundled in the home, and the municipal sanitation department picks them up at the regular collection times. The newspapers are kept apart from the other trash and stored on a special rack built on the department's compactor trucks. The city of Madison has a steady market for the newspapers it collects; in 1973 it netted $25,415 on the sale of 3,000 tons of waste newspapers. Besides, the city saved $15,000 in disposal costs—as well as valuable space in its municipal landfill.

Nationwide, 22 percent of all newspapers are recycled; however, if city governments, civic groups, ¹³⁰⁰ → charitable organizations, and the paper industry work more closely together, more can be done.

The industry advises supermarkets and other commercial and industrial establishments on the baling, storage, and sale of used corrugated shipping containers. Today, about 30 percent of all corrugated material is collected, returned, repulped, and made ¹³⁵⁰ → into new products.

——STOP——ASK FOR YOUR TIME——

Record time immediately and answer
the questions on content.

Time_____Sec.	RATE (from table on page 315):	R. _____
No. Correct:_____ (key on page 322)	COMPREHENSION (10% for each correct answer):	C. _____
VI–19	EFFICIENCY (R × C):	E. _____

Record on Progress Chart on page 299

ANSWER THESE QUESTIONS IMMEDIATELY

1. (T–F) Trash and garbage are *not* solid waste.

2. (MC) The largest waste tonnage is made up of:

    _____(1) agricultural and animal wastes.

    _____(2) manufacturing wastes.

    _____(3) mining and mineral processing byproducts.

    _____(4) municipal solid wastes.

3. (T–F) Many cities are running out of places to dispose of the waste they collect.

4. (MC) The largest part of the total cost of $5 billion in municipal solid waste disposal is for:

    _____(1) manpower.

    _____(2) purchasing incinerators.

    _____(3) collecting equipment.

    _____(4) purchasing disposal sites.

5. (T–F) In 1973, Americans used 67 million tons of paper and paperboard according to this writer.

6. (C) In 1973 _____ million tons of paper were recycled back into new products.

7. (T–F) Rags and agricultural wastes are *not* a source for recycled paper.

8. (T–F) A few years ago, lumber and plywood were stored in "tepees," and the forest industry reduced waste in this way.

9. (C) _____ wastes are the fastest growing waste problems.

10. (T–F) About 30 percent of the corrugated material is now being returned, repulped, and made into new products.

Exercise VI-20

The Future of the Oceans

HON. LEE METCALF

(from the *Congressional Record*, December 18, 1974)

WAIT FOR SIGNAL TO BEGIN READING

Ocean policy project

In this time of acute awareness of this country's stake in the debate over the future of the oceans, many institutions have become increasingly involved with the law of the sea-related issues. One of the best-known policy research organizations in this field is the Ocean Policy Project of the School of Advanced International Studies, the Johns Hopkins University. Under the leadership of Dean Robert Osgood and Dr. Ann Hollick, the project has provided considerable evidence during its relatively short lifespan of its competence to deal with these affairs.

The Ocean Policy Project recently sponsored a 100 minilaw of the sea conference at Airlie House on the subject "Conflict and Order in Ocean Relations," at which some of the best-informed people in this field got together to evaluate the success of the Third U.N. Law of the Sea Conference, which met last summer in Caracas and to explore what possibilities lie ahead. The conference lasted 3 days and was attended by 150 participants from more than 20 countries, including such distinguished guests as two of my colleagues in the Senate, Senators PELL and HOLLINGS, the Ambassadors of Iceland, Trinidad, and Tobago, the Canadian Ambassador to Austria 200 as well as our own Ambassador Stevenson, the Deputy Special Assistant John Norton Moore, and many other knowledgeable academicians, diplomats, government officials, students, and others interested in the subject.

While no clear consensus emerged from the conference, it served to aid the participants in focusing on the most important issues before the Third U.N. LOS Conference and evaluating its success to date. The general attitude of the speakers was rather pessimistic as far as an overall negotiated package settlement is concerned, although a few felt there was still hope for such a solution. Others expressed the belief that the LOS Conference might produce a 300 series of limited treaties similar to the 1958 Law of the Sea Conference.

It is not my intention to summarize what was said at the conference. Instead I will briefly mention some of the highlights of a very successful proceeding while, of necessity, having to leave out some very interesting ideas mentioned by other speakers.

Authority on sea issues

Ambassador Arvid Pardo, by many considered the foremost authority on law of the sea issues, was not at all optimistic in his assessment of the Caracas session. He concluded that the mandate of the conference would not be achieved. Contending that no attempt was made in Caracas to draft a law of the sea suited to contemporary circumstances, Pardo claimed a large part of the work at the conference would be rendered totally irrelevant by the excessive claims likely to be accommodated in the conference outcome. Discussion on rights of transit through straits was rather pointless since the type of baseline system likely to be adopted will turn most of these international straits into internal waters where rights of transit are more restrictive.

Pardo expressed the belief, however, that some 500 kind of treaty would be adopted, but not in the form of a comprehensive agreement, since most nations are concerned with achieving immediate and rather simple objectives. The resulting treaty would provide exclusively for the protection in ocean space of the interests of major groups of nations, especially coastal nations and more particularly oceanic nations, whether developed or developing.

These interests will center around international recognition of extensive coastal nation jurisdiction in the seas, recognition of the right of coastal countries to exercise comprehensive powers within national jurisdictional areas, and the maintenance of normally unhampered commercial navigation.

600 Pardo drew five basic and somewhat sobering conclusions about the future treaty based on the work of the LOS Conference thus far: First, the treaty will multiply, not hamper conflicts between States; second, it will increase rather than decrease inequities between nations; third, the division of ocean space among the oceanic countries will be an inevitable—though perhaps delayed—consequence of the future treaty; fourth, the future treaty will hamper, not improve the possibilities of effective international cooperation in the oceans; and fifth, it will worsen, not improve, the prospects for continuation of essential transnational activities such as scientific research and navigation, or rational exploitation of

ocean resources and of the preservation of the ma- $\xleftarrow{700}$ rine environment.

Ambassador John Stevenson, the Special Representative of the President to the Law of the Sea Conference and Chairman of the U.S. delegation, was markedly more optimistic than most of the other participants with regard to the achievement of a timely and generally acceptable treaty. Ambassador Stevenson, who as all of you know has testified before a number of Senate committees, based his views on the progress—limited though it was—that was made at Caracas. There was a wide consensus and rapid adoption of rules of procedure and organization, and Ambassador Stevenson argued that $\xleftarrow{800}$ indications of progress on the substantive issues also warrant optimism.

Basic parameters

Over 100 nations expressed support for a 12-mile territorial sea and a 200-mile economic zone as the basic parameters of a generally acceptable solution to the question of limits of jurisdiction, provided other issues were comprehensively dealt with. Stevenson also argued that the nature of the general debate at Caracas was both constructive and moderate, despite earlier fears that it might prove otherwise. While agreeing that the Caracas session did not move beyond the preparatory, exploratory stage to actual adoption of treaty texts, Ambassador Steven- $\xleftarrow{900}$ son felt that the U.N. timetable of achieving a treaty in 1975 could still be met.

Professor Gary Knight of Louisiana State University argued that it is now time to start exploring the alternatives to a comprehensive negotiated treaty to provide for the possibility of a failure of the LOS Conference.

Knight suggests that history shows lawlessness need not prevail in the oceans in the absence of a treaty. The customary lawmaking mechanism could serve to reduce conflict potential and bring order to ocean affairs over a period of time. If, through well-considered unilateral actions, customary law proc- $\xleftarrow{1000}$ $\xrightarrow{1350}$ esses can be allowed to develop, the oceans will not be left without a legal regime. Knight further argues that the United States could take the lead in developing the international law of the seas through the customary international law process, as the actions

of this Government, through legislation and executive actions affecting the oceans, will be keenly observed by members of the international community.

Wise legislation needed

The United States, through its legislative process, must write its legislation wisely so that if it were adopted by other nations in identical or similar $\xrightarrow{1100}$ form, the new concordant practice of states would form an acceptable international legal framework for the use of ocean space and the exploitation of ocean resources. By structuring domestic legislation to minimize conflict and constituting a desirable pattern for worldwide action, the adverse effects of a failure of the LOS Conference could be ameliorated.

Roger Hansen of the Overseas Development Council discussed the issue of the "north-south split" in the law of the sea debate, analyzing the structure of relationships and the transnational forces for change within the international system.

Joseph Nye of Harvard University discussed the oceans rulemaking in a world politics context. In $\xrightarrow{1200}$ his interesting paper, Dr. Nye considers the oceans as an issue system and distinguishes major period in terms of the predominant regimes.

Economist Richard Cooper of Yale University made in his presentation a compelling case for the rational management of the ocean resources in the interest of fully utilizing benefits from the oceans to the world as a whole and proposed some principles for making the most efficient use of these resources.

Three speakers addressed themselves to regional approaches in the law of the sea. Michael $\xrightarrow{1300}$ Hardy, legal adviser to the European Communities, discussed the law of the sea from the standpoint of the European community. Francisco Orrego Vicuna, director of studies, Institute of International Studies of the University of Chile, discussed the Latin American approach to LOS and Francis Njenga, counselor to the Permanent Mission of Kenya to the U.N., addressed himself to the issue from the African point of view.

——STOP——ASK FOR YOUR TIME——

Record time immediately and answer
the questions on content.

Time____Sec.

No. Correct:_____
(key on page 330)

VI–20

RATE (from table on page 315):

COMPREHENSION (10% for each correct answer):

EFFICIENCY (R × C):

R._____

C._____

E._____

Record on Progress Chart on page 299

ANSWER THESE QUESTIONS IMMEDIATELY

1. (MC) The abbreviation *LOS* in the Third U.N. LOS Conference stands for:

___X_(1) Law of the Sea.

_____(2) Law of the States.

_____(3) Lawlessness of Ocean and Seas.

_____(4) Legislature of the Seas.

2. (T–F) Several participants felt this LOS Conference would produce limited results similar to those of the 1958 Conference.

3. (T–F) Ambassador Arvid Pardo is considered an authority on law of sea issues.

4. (T–F) Arvid Pardo felt that the treaty would decrease the conflicts between states.

5. (T–F) Arvid Pardo felt that the treaty would improve transnational activities for scientific research and navigation.

6. (C) The nations expressed support for a twelve-mile territorial sea and a 200-mile _economic_ zone.

7. (T–F) Gary Knight felt that lawlessness on the oceans would *not* prevail because of the absence of a treaty.

8. (T–F) Gary Knight argued that Australia should take the lead in developing the international law of the seas through the customary international law process because it was completely surrounded by oceans.

9. (C) Roger Hansen of the Overseas Development Counsel discussed the issue of "N–S split" in the law of the sea debate.

10. (MC) The position of Ambassador Stevenson was described as:

_____(1) more pessimistic than that of most speakers.

_____(2) deeply concerned about U.S. sea power.

___X_(3) fearful of the loss of American prestige in future conferences.

_____(4) more optimistic than that of Ambassador Pardo.

SERIES VII
Study Reading Exercises

Instructions

You know very well that some of your reading requires concentrated attention to details with emphasis on long-term retention for examinations or other later application.

These study exercises provide practice in a self-recitation type of reading. They are designed to help you understand some of the principles of self-recitation and spaced review. In a limited sense they provide a practical illustration of the fact that it is easier to remember soon after reading than it is after an interval of time occupied by other reading or other activities. In actual practice, however, you will need to make up your own questions for the periods of self-recitation.

Here the stress is still on increasing the reading speed and the reading level, but involved also is a stress on a study technique that will help improve long-range retention of material read. Here you expose yourself to ideas not only by reading about them, but by pausing frequently to think about them and to apply them to practical questions on the material. You should find that this technique helps to break the monotony of reading and to enable you to read with less tension and less fatigue because you bring into use more than one type of study approach.

These exercises are matched with those in Series VI for length, difficulty, and type of questions asked. Comparisons of your reading rate and reading efficiency scores on these drills with the comparable exercises in Series VI will give you some measure of your progress in mastering this technique of self-recitation as you read.

General directions on these exercises are the same as for those in Series VI except that you do not call for your time until you have finished the tenth question in the exercise. You then compute your *rate, comprehension, and efficiency* as before, using the keys on pages 322 and 330. Then record your scores on the progress charts for study reading on page 299.

Suggestions

Although standardized exercises measuring efficiency in higher level study skills have not yet been devised, this series of exercises on a study type of reading provides a unique type of reading activity designed to combine some of the best features of developmental reading skills and higher level study skills. Your use of them will expose you to a practical application of some of the study skills that were discussed in detail on pages 19 to 24 of this book. Perhaps a rereading of that material would help you to develop a better understanding of what is attempted here.

This system of reading provides an automatic break every few hundred words, so that you may stop and think about the material read and answer questions about it. This break gives your eyes a chance to rest and to come back to more effective reading on the next unit. The alternating pattern of thinking, reading, thinking, writing, thinking, reading, and so on, helps to keep you more alert and to avoid outside distractions and daydreaming.

The efficiency scores you attain on this series will be a good indication of your success in mastering some basic techniques of self-recitation and applying them to your reading activities.

Nothing in this series will keep you from going back to reread in order to answer questions. There is nothing to keep you from going ahead and reading the questions first, then coming back to read the material. Either of these approaches takes extra time, however, and will keep your rate and efficiency scores down. Hard work and deep concentration should enable you to read materials at a maximum short-term reading rate and to achieve enough short-term retention to handle the questions adequately.

Note that asking and answering questions at intervals do provide additional study skill application to reinforce those ideas that you picked up in rapid reading and to plant them more firmly in your mind. This process reduces the dependence on high levels of initial comprehension and frees you to function at a more rapid rate of initial study reading—in short periods interrupted by the self-recitation activity.

Efficient reading in study situations is not merely word-by-word reading at any rate. Good study habits require other thought processes to back up the reading process and reinforce it.

Good reading habits cannot be defined in terms of rate and comprehension alone. They are characterized by an open mind, a wide range of flexibility in reading rate, a judgment as to relative importance of material being read, and a deep understanding of oneself as related to the reading project at hand. Reading rate as a reading tool is only part of the repertoire of a good reader.

Exercise VII–1

Szzzzzzz

TIM BRITT

(from *Wyoming Wildlife*, May 1967)

WAIT FOR SIGNAL TO BEGIN READING

One warm afternoon while working in eastern Wyoming, I dove to a nearby windmill to fill a water jug. As I slid out of the station wagon and my foot touched the ground, I heard it. Quickly, but quietly, I pulled my foot back into the vehicle and reached over the front seat for my .22 rifle. Taking but a second to eliminate the problem, I sat there and trembled for a few minutes.

It's not that snakes, even poisonous rattlesnakes, bother me so much, but I like to meet them on my own terms. Actually I think snakes are interesting critters, but again, I would rather be interested 100 in them, than have them interested in me.

Many people have a tremendous, unreasonable fear of snakes, such as one timid lady who turns her head whenever a snake is shown on television. The nearest I have ever come to losing my life was when I was about twelve and brought a garter snake into the kitchen. Mom didn't limit use of the broom to the snake; she used it on me, too.

The prairie rattlesnake, *Crotalus viridis,* rarely found at elevations above 8,500 feet, inhabits rocky open regions, grassy prairies, canyons, and agricul- 200 tural areas. Like many other reptiles, they are cold-blooded and derive their warmth from their environment. This is why it is quite common to see them basking on rocks, gravel roads, and other denuded areas, especially during the cool morning and evening hours. Prairie rattlers differ from other poisonous snakes in that they appear to be most active during the daylight hours while most poisonous snakes are nocturnal.

Warm-blooded animals are the preferred food of rattlesnakes. They feed to a great extent on field mice, small rabbits, gophers, prairie dogs, and occasionally birds.

Colorings of the Crotalus viridis 300

The ground color, or background color, of the prairie rattler varies from a light gray to "viridis," the species name for green in Latin. Actually, the most common color is a mottled grayish-green, with dark blotches, resembling solid figure-eights located down the center of the back from immediately behind the head all the way to the rattles. There may be from 33 to 55 of these blotches and they are normally outlined with white.

1. (T–F) The prairie rattlesnake is also known as the *Crotalus viridis.*
2. (T–F) The prairie rattlesnake is most commonly found in elevations above 8,500 feet.
3. (T–F) Most poisonous snakes are active during the daylight hours.

The prairie rattler is a common species

The prairie rattler, a species which inhabits a wide range over the western portion of North America, is one of the most widespread rattlesnakes in the United States.

When born, rattlesnakes with only a blunt "prebutton" at the tip of their tails, first shed their skin a few hours after birth and the rest of the first segment, or button is formed. Each time the snake 500 sheds its skin a new segment is added to the rattle. This occurs two to four times annually. A snake's age cannot be determined by counting the segments of the rattle and attributing one year for each segment. If the button is on the rattle, a snake's approximate age can be estimated. Simply count the segments of the rattle and divide by three, the average number of times a rattlesnake sheds its skin per year.

This system can only be used when the button is intact at the tip of the rattle. Since the terminal rattles often wear away until finally they are lost, a 600 string of nine rattles is unusual. The average lifespan of Wyoming rattlesnakes is seven or eight years, although some rattlers have been known to live up to twenty-five years. A twenty-year-old rattler would have 60 segments in its rattle at the three segments per year rate. Obviously, the rattles wear away, or are broken off much too rapidly to permit age estimation by this method except in the case of young snakes. The rattles are brittle and hollow and the segments fit together loosely; when the snake vibrates its tail the segments rub together and produce the "buzzing" or "rattling" sounds.

Prairie rattlesnakes vary in length

The stories involving five- and six-foot rattlesnakes usually refer to one of the diamondback species or the timber rattler, for the prairie rattlesnake varies only from two to four feet when mature.

Despite the terrible and frightening stories told around campfires on dark nights, the chances of being fatally bitten by a snake are more remote than being struck by lightning. More persons die annually from the sting of bees, hornets, wasps, and scorpions and from spider bites than from snakebite. According to a national survey, conducted by Dr. Henry M. Parrish, the danger of suffering from the 800 bite of a poisonous snake while hunting or fishing is very low. Of all the snakebite cases in the United States only about five percent involved hunters and fishermen. The same survey showed that about fifty persons in this country die from snakebite each year. Most of the fatal snakebites in this country result from imprudent handling of poisonous snakes. Statistics show that the greatest share of the victims are less than twenty years of age. Bites are usually sustained on the hands, arms, legs, and feet.

A poisonous snake doesn't always coil before it strikes. Rattlesnakes cannot strike more than two- 900 thirds or three-fourths of their body length unless they have a firm backing or they are striking downward from an incline. A rattlesnake does not always rattle before striking, however, and this warning should not be counted on by the outdoorsman.

4. (MC) The snake sheds its skin as often as:
   _____(1) once a month.
   _____(2) once a year.
   _____(3) once every season.
   _____(4) two to four times annually.
5. (C) If the _____ is present on the rattle, a snake's approximate age can be estimated.
6. (T–F) The prairie rattlesnake varies from two 1000 to four feet in length when mature.
7. (C) In this country about _____ persons die each year from snakebite.

Rattlesnake venom, yellowish in appearance and slightly thicker than water, is a completely taste-less and odorless substance, which disintegrates rapidly upon contact with the air. This fact casts a shadow of doubt on the validity of the old story about the fang stuck in a boot. As folklore has it, a man was fatally struck on the foot by a rattler about 20 feet long, or some such length. Years later the man's son, putting on his father's boots, immediately 1100 died from venom still in the fang, which had become embedded in the boot when the father was bitten.

The power of the strike embeds the fangs into the flesh of the victim and the muscles around the poison glands force the venom from the glands through the ducts and fangs into the wound. The action is similar to that which takes place in a hypodermic needle and syringe. The amount of poison ejected at any one time varies from part of a drop to two cubic centimeters, depending upon the size of 1200 the snake and the amount of time which has elapsed since the last venom ejection.

The prime reason everyone should know the poisonous snakes of their region, their habits, distribution, and abundance is that it will ease the mind of the individual in his outdoor pursuits. Most people have heard so many fantastic stories involving snakes that they have developed a fear, rather than a respect for snakes. In most cases snakes, even rattlers, are beneficial and of direct economic value. In instances where poisonous snakes present special hazards around campgrounds, fishing areas, and other recreational sites, perhaps their destruction is justified.

1300 8. (MC) The color of rattlesnake venom is:
   _____(1) slightly yellowish.
   _____(2) deep gray.
   _____(3) milky white.
   _____(4) mottled brown.
9. (T–F) The action of the rattlesnake bite is likened to that of the hypodermic needle and syringe.
10. (T–F) The author urges one to kill every 1350 rattlesnake he sees.

——STOP——ASK FOR YOUR TIME——

Record time immediately.

Time_____Sec.   RATE (from table on page 315):   R. _____

No. Correct:_____   COMPREHENSION (10% for each correct answer):   C. _____
(key on page 322)

VII–1   EFFICIENCY (R × C):   E. _____

Record on Progress Chart on page 299

Exercise VII-2

On Minding One's Own Business

WILLIAM GRAHAM SUMNER

(from the publication *In Brief;* material selected from William G. Sumner's
What Social Classes Owe to Each Other, 1883, Chapter VII)

WAIT FOR SIGNAL TO BEGIN READING

The passion for dealing with social questions is one of the marks of our time. Every man gets some experience of, and makes some observations on social affairs. Except matters of health, probably none have such general interest as matters of society. Except matters of health, none are so much afflicted by dogmatism and crude speculation as those which appertain to society. The amateurs in social science always ask: What shall we do? What shall we do with Neighbor A? What shall we do for Neighbor B? What shall we make Neighbor A do for Neighbor B? It is a fine thing to be planning and discussing broad 100 and general theories of wide application. The amateurs always plan to use the individual for some constructive social purpose, or to use the society for some constructive individual purpose. For A to sit down and think, "What shall I do?" is commonplace; but to think what B ought to do is interesting, romantic, moral, self-flattering, and public-spirited all at once. It satisfies a great number of human weaknesses at once. To go on and plan what a whole class of people ought to do is to feel one's self a power on earth, and to clothe one's self in dignity. 200 Hence we have an unlimited supply of reformers, philanthropists, humanitarians, and would-be managers-in-general of society.

1. (T–F) The author expresses the basic feeling that people find it more interesting to plan what someone else should do than to plan what they should do themselves.

The first duty

Every man and woman in society has one big duty. That is, to take care of his or her own self. This is a social duty. The matter stands so that the duty of making the best of one's self individually is not a separate thing from the duty of filling one's 300 place in society, but the two are one and the latter is accomplished when the former is done. The common notion, however, seems to be that one has a duty to society, as a special and separate thing, and that this duty consists in considering and deciding what other people ought to do. Now, the man who can do anything for or about anybody else than himself is fit to be head of a family; and when he be-

comes head of a family he has duties to his wife and 400 children, in addition to the former big duty. Then, again, any man who can take care of himself and his family is in a very exceptional position if he does not find in his immediate surroundings people who need his care and have some sort of a personal claim on him. If, now, he is able to fulfill all this, and to take care of anybody outside his family and his dependents, he must have a surplus of energy, wisdom, and moral virtue beyond what he needs for his own business. No man has this; for a family 500 is a charge which is capable of infinite development, and no man could suffice to the full measure of duty for which a family may draw upon him. Neither can a man give to society so advantageous an employment of his services, whatever they are, in any other way as by spending them on his family. Upon this, however, I will not insist. I recur to the observation that a man who proposes to take care of other people must have himself and his family taken care of, after some sort of fashion, and must have an as 600 yet unexhausted store of energy.

2. (C) According to Mr. Sumner, man's first duty is to take care of _____
_____.

3. (T–F) The author believes that man has an obligation to go beyond his duty to his family and to take care of others outside the family.

A twofold danger

The danger of minding other people's business is twofold. First, there is the danger that a man may leave his own business unattended to; and, second, there is the danger of an impertinent interference with another's affairs. The "friends of humanity" almost always run into both dangers. I am one of 700 humanity, and I do not want any volunteer friends. I regard friendship as mutual, and I want to have my say about it. I suppose that other components of humanity feel in the same way about it. If so, they must regard any one who assumes the *role* of a friend of humanity as impertinent. The reference of the friend of humanity back to his own business is obviously the next step.

4 & 5. (MC) The author says that the two dangers
of minding other people's business are:
_____(1) basic ignorance.
_____(2) political power.
_____(3) rash dictatorship.
_____(4) slandering gossip.
_____(5) voluntary servitude.   ← 800
_____(6) slighting one's own business.
_____(7) losing all one's friends.
_____(8) impertinent interferences.

Social quacks

The amateur social doctors are like the amateur physicians—they always begin with the question of *remedies,* and they go at this without any diagnosis or any knowledge of the anatomy or physiology of society. They never have any doubt of the efficacy of their remedies. They never take account of any ulterior effects which may be apprehended from the remedy itself. Against all such social quackery the obvious injunction to the quacks is, to mind their own business.

6. (T–F) The author believes that social doctors ← 900 are more concerned with remedies than with causes or effects.

The most needed reform

The greatest reforms which could now be accomplished would consist in undoing the work of statesmen in the past, and the greatest difficulty in the way of reform is to find out how to undo their work without injury to what is natural and sound. All this mischief has been done by men who sat down to consider the problem. What kind of a society do we want to make? When they had settled this question *a priori* to their satisfaction, they set to work ← 1000 to make their ideal society, and today we suffer the consequences.

Society, therefore, does not need any care or supervision. If we can acquire a science of society, based on observation of phenomena and study of

forces, we may hope to gain some ground slowly toward the elimination of old errors and the re-establishment of a sound and natural social order. Whatever we gain that way will be by growth, never by any reconstruction of society on the plan of some 1100→ enthusiastic social architect. Society needs first of all to be freed from these meddlers—that is, to be let alone. Here we are, then, once more back at the old doctrine—*Laissez Faire.* Let us translate it into blunt English, and it will read, "Mind your own business."

7. (T–F) The author believes that society needs some care and supervision in order to assure individual freedom.
8. (T–F) The basic need of society, as seen by Mr. Sumner, is to be left alone.

The root of dictatorship

We never supposed that *laissez faire* would give us perfect happiness. We have left perfect happiness 1200→ entirely out of our account. If the social doctors will mind their own business, we shall have no troubles but what belong to Nature. Those we will endure or combat as we can. What we desire is, that the friends of humanity should cease to add to them. Our disposition toward the ills which our fellowman inflicts on us through malice or meddling is quite different from our disposition toward the ills which are inherent in the conditions of all human life.

To mind one's own business is a purely negative and unproductive injunction, but, taking social 1300→ matters as they are just now, it is a sociological principle of the first importance. There might be developed a grand philosophy on the basis of minding one's own business.

9. (T–F) Mr. Sumner believes that a "laissez faire" system would bring us complete happiness.
10. (C) The basic idea of this article is that 1350→ people should _____.

——STOP——ASK FOR YOUR TIME——

Record time immediately.

Time_____Sec.   RATE (from table on page 315):   R. _____

No. Correct:_____   COMPREHENSION (10% for each correct answer):   C. _____
(key on page 330)

VII–2   EFFICIENCY (R × C):   E. _____

Record on Progress Chart on page 299

244

Exercise VII–3

The Enchantment with Enhancement

ERNEST SWIFT

(from *Wyoming Wildlife*, December 1962)

WAIT FOR SIGNAL TO BEGIN READING

An enticing connotation

Recently, two articles on super-highways appeared in *Conservation News*. They brought a mild protest to the effect that the editorials were of a negative nature, and that relations could be improved with the road builders if they were praised for having given some thought to beautification, the prevention of erosion, and the preservation of wildlife habitat.

In this regard the word enhancement has come into common use with reference to highways, high dams, and reservoir construction. Enhancement has an enticing connotation. It apparently lulls the less perceptive into the notion that more is being gained than lost.   100 ←

Realists know that such construction will continue. They are not being altogether enchanted by the word enhancement, but are insisting on a minimum of destruction.

1. (T–F) The word *enhancement* apparently lulls some people into the notion that more is being gained than lost.

A compromise

There are ever-increasing demands for the re-routing of highways where they would cut ugly gashes through a country beautiful. And, endless numbers of high dams are destroying the once mighty Pacific salmon runs. These problems have brought many a conservation group into a death struggle with these behemoths of progress.

The earth movers, the concrete builders and 200 ← the economists of both private enterprise and public bureaus have cared little in the past about the consequences of their programs. Techniques have reached a point of proficiency to alter drastically the face of the earth. Few if any of them want any truck with such philosophies.

To minimize the irritations caused by such dreamers, the road and high dam builders talk persuasively of enhancement. Talk does not increase construction costs. Nevertheless, there is insistent public demand for reducing needless damage.

Webster defines *enhance:* To raise, augment, increase, to increase worth or value, to beautify. 300 ←

Where highways level slum districts, the word enhancement might be correct. But where a farm

unit is split and becomes an uneconomical operation because of the highway, the owner sees no enhancement. It is also difficult to rationalize enhancement when waterfowl or fishing areas are drained or filled for road construction. Then, some miles further on, gravel pits are flooded and called enhancement.

A flooded gravel pit may minimize total destruction of some wildlife species in the region, but calling it enhancement is a misuse of the word. Nor 400 → can the relocation of a highway to save a park, a wilderness, a vista or a trout stream in any sense be termed enhancement. It is simply a compromise between two opposing ideologies.

2. (MC) Which of these phrases is *not* used by Webster to define the word *enhance?*
   _____(1) To raise.
   _____(2) To mitigate loss.
   _____(3) To increase worth.
   _____(4) To beautify.

3. (C) The term *enhancement* has been used as a _____ between two opposing ideologies.

A matter of interpretation

Inquiries and comments coming to the National Wildlife Federation have brought a great divergence of opinion. One state, with a natural resources committee of which the highway department is a 500 → member, has set up study committees. Their recommendations have resulted in the change of road specifications, rights of way maintenance, the creation of impoundments and shrubbery planting. This state also has a mandatory law that requires notification of the conservation commission on new road construction, or altering or discontinuance. This is certainly all to the good, and shows maturity and progress. Still, by close definition, it is more of a matter of mitigating losses than one of enhancement.

Storage reservoirs in some of the water-starved plains states create boating and fishing areas. There 600 → was a time when such flowages were one-purpose projects for holding water. Their worth for recreation has radically changed the thinking and increased the out-of-doors potential for their localities. Such projects have enhanced the communities recreationally and economically.

On the other hand, valuable timber, winter game yards, and fish spawning grounds are often destroyed by flooding, especially in the mountain country. Here is a case of attempting to mitigate losses of some salvage, where talking of enhancement is simply a play on words.

As the wetlands in the Dakotas are drained with taxpayers' monies, farm ponds have been built with money from the same source. The biggest $\overset{700}{\leftarrow}$ delusion of all is that they are enhancement to waterfowl. There are not enough of them to compensate for the drainage of natural ponds, and ducks do not like ponds with spoil banks that obstruct their view. That is the nature of the critter.

On the lower Mississippi where flood control is carried on by the army engineers, the loss of waterfowl habitat has been greater than any compensations. Again, enhancement becomes a myth.

What may happen to the Pacific salmon is brought to light in a speech by Mr. J. C. Swidler, chairman of the Federal Power Commission. Here $\overset{800}{\leftarrow}$ is a section of his address before the American Power Association on May 15, 1962. "By far the most troublesome problem is to reconcile the construction of dams with the preservation of a favorable environment for game fish. However, we cannot allow the fish problem to paralyze the Commission in acting on hydroelectric license applications."

Further on in the address is this statement: "If on the record in a particular case the fish problems are insurmountable and more would be lost than gained by approving the license, we shall of course deny the license application."

It is rather difficult to make these two state- $\overset{900}{\leftarrow}$ ments dovetail. Whether the latter one is crumbs for the peasants is a matter of individual interpretation.

4. (T–F) A state law requiring notification of the Conservation Commission on new road construction is a good example of true enhancement.
5. (T–F) The flood control on the lower Mississippi has resulted in more waterfowl habitat.
6. (T–F) J. C. Swidler made contradicting statements in reference to the fish problem and hydroelectric licenses.

A trick word

Since revolutionary times this nation has developed certain fixations regarding land-use. Time-honored priorities based on past economic standards $\overset{1000}{\leftarrow}$ have become quite deep-rooted. Testing their validity

under the present conditions of these fast-moving times has been a wrench to the traditional thinking of many people.

For decades agriculture had an incontestable priority over all land uses. As a result, millions of acres of sub-marginal land were farmed. Often valuable timber or grass cover was destroyed in the process.

Only land wholly unsuited for farming east of the Mississippi was left in forests until cut. Then followed sporadic farming efforts and tax delinquency. Producing techniques finally increased crop surpluses, and returned many an abandoned farm to $\overset{1100}{\rightarrow}$ regrowing timber. These methods also made possible a soil bank program, which on the prairies was beneficial to wildlife.

But looking back to original native game populations that once used the prairies, this respite in growing crops was hardly enhancement. Some would question going back that far, and so enhancement becomes a trick word.

7. (T–F) In the past, only land wholly unfit for raising timber was left to farming.
8. (MC) Which of the following was *not* a result of producing techniques in land use?
   _____(1) destruction of farms.
   _____(2) increased farm surpluses.
   $\overset{1200}{\rightarrow}$ _____(3) regrowth of timber.
   _____(4) soil bank program.

Realism versus fancy phrases

Is pollution control an enhancement? Or is it simply an abatement of industrial and municipal filth? A stump prairie replanted to trees comes under the accepted term of enhancement. But if the timber tract has been selectively cut with a residual stand left and protected from fire, the enhancement could be considered more valid.

Fancy phrases are no substitute for realistic thinking. In-roads of a destructive nature will continue on many resources. They will raise questions of gain or loss according to what values are considered paramount.

$\overset{1300}{\rightarrow}$ Let us not use the word enhancement unless it definitely fits the occasion. It is far more realistic to educate the public to demand a reduction of losses.

9. (C) Fancy phrases are no substitute for _____ thinking.
10. (T–F) The public should be educated to de- $\overset{1350}{\rightarrow}$ mand a reduction of losses.

——STOP——ASK FOR YOUR TIME——

Record time immediately.

Time____Sec.	RATE (from table on page 315):	R. ____
No. Correct:____ (key on page 322)	COMPREHENSION (10% for each correct answer):	C. ____
VII–3	EFFICIENCY (R × C):	E. ____

Record on Progress Chart on page 299

Exercise VII-4

Science and People

(from *The Royal Bank of Canada Monthly Letter*, February 1975)

WAIT FOR SIGNAL TO BEGIN READING

Research is work

Some persons are challenged by the mysteries of the moon and stars; others by the mysteries of living things, including themselves. Seldom do we find a person who is not, at some time or another, interested in one of these mysteries, who does not feel the challenge of the unknown.

Nonscientists tend to believe that a laboratory is swarming with eye-popping discoveries every week, but no knowledge is gained and no theory is developed without a great deal of labor. Both the "pure" scientist and the "applied" scientist work arduously.

Theoretical research seeks to know things bet-¹⁰⁰ ter; applied research seeks to learn how to do things better. In one case knowledge is sought for her own sake; in the other case the desire is to find ways of applying a newly discovered fact or theory to solution of practical problems.

Research workers in pure science are vastly enlarging our field of knowledge. In John Milton's memorable words they are "still searching what we know not by what we know, still closing up truth to truth as we find it."

Asking questions

Aristotle, son of a physician at the court of King Philip of Macedon, organized the first scientific inquiry in the world. He was so curious about nature that he had a thousand men collecting material for ²⁰⁰ his natural history.

A good scientist has a tidy mind that keeps thoughts and facts in their proper place; ability to discriminate so as to discern what evidence should be accepted and to discard what is irrelevant, paying attention to small details in research to prevent something vital from slipping away unnoticed; ability to recover quickly after work has been interrupted, keeping an eye on what neighbors are doing in the way of finding out and doing new things.

The most valuable of all the perceptions we ³⁰⁰ use in scientific research is the perception of cause and effect. Too often we say "in the beginning" and imagine that we have pinned down a vital point from which everything else follows, but before long we find ourselves asking: "What was there before the beginning to make it possible for the beginning to begin?"

Insofar as science accepts the principle of ⁴⁰⁰ causality, and inasmuch as the universe cannot be self-caused, we are led inevitably to the conclusion that there must be a causal factor not comprised within our present view of the universe. Thomas Aquinas put this principle in a nutshell: "No thing is its own cause, for then it would precede itself, which is impossible."

1. (C) The most valuable perception in scientific research is the perception of _____ _Causes_ and effect.

2. (MC) John Milton's memorable words:
   - ✗ (1) "Still searching what we know not by what we know, still closing up truth to truth as we find it."
   - _____ (2) "What was there before the beginning to make it possible for the beginning to begin."
   - _____ (3) "No thing is its own cause, for then it would precede itself, which is impossible."
   - _____ (4) "Necessity is the mother of invention."

3. (T F) Thomas Aquinas stated this principle: "No thing is its own cause, for then it would precede itself, which is impossible."

Science and progress

Science is one field in which progress should be measured and given credit. Therefore, we should not withhold praise from famous men and women of the past because their concepts have been outdated: our important duty is to improve on what they did.

Newton has been acknowledged as the greatest scientist in history: he discovered the law of gravita-⁶⁰⁰ tion, the laws of motion, the principles of optics, the composite nature of light, and with Leibnitz he invented the calculus.

There is not, however, any concept of Newtonian physics, believed at one time to be the whole truth, that has not been displaced. As Professor Alfred North Whitehead remarked: "The Newtonian ideas are still useful, as useful as they ever were, but they are no longer true in the sense in which I was taught they were true."

Icarus, whose airplane wings fell off and dropped him into the sea when the heat of the sun melted the wax that fastened them together, performed a useful service. $\underset{\leftarrow}{700}$

The first crude microscope was focused on the hidden minutiae of life by the Dutch microscopist Leeuwenhoek, in the 17th century. Three men, Professor E. Burton of Toronto University, James Hillier, and Albert Prebus, produced the electron microscope in 1936, opening up a whole new world to investigation. Roger Bacon discovered the explosive possibilities in a combination of saltpeter, sulphur, and charcoal and produced gunpowder in the 13th century. The present century saw the birth of the atom bomb.

4. (T-F) The concepts in Newtonian physics have not been displayed.
5. (T-F) Icarus had the wax melt on his airplane $\underset{\leftarrow}{800}$ wings.
6. (C) The first crude Dutch-developed microscope was in the __17__ century.
7. (T-F) Roger Bacon produced the electron microscope.

Important advances

Nobody can deny that science and invention have raised mankind to a higher level than the one occupied a hundred years ago. They have increased the output of work per man-hour, so that we are able to cope in some measure with the increased demands of a greatly enlarged population. Science has developed new products that cater to our comfort while increasing the number of occupations at which men and women may work. $\underset{\leftarrow}{900}$

Two of the greatest advances of our age are the production of drugs like penicillin, insulin, and sulpha, which have prolonged our lives by many years, and labor-saving machinery which has made work easier and provided more leisure.

Science has given nutrition, literacy, and health to people in the developed nations, and they are being extended, though slowly, to the developing peoples of the world.

Science and technology change not only our material environment but our institutions, and this is a good reason for everyone to keep up with what is happening, to learn about, or try to anticipate, the $\underset{\leftarrow}{1000}$ social implications of scientific discoveries and attainments. Every newly discovered process and every invention has brought with it unpredictable uses, created new obstacles to be overcome, and uncovered new problems and frustrations to be resolved.

The discoveries of science cannot be put to practical use without the services of the technologist who makes inventions by interpreting something, adding or taking away, or dividing or multiplying something. Every invention that proves useful stimulates further scientific studies which lead to improvements and to more inventions.

Nearly everyone has said at least once: "Neces- $\underset{\rightarrow}{1100}$ sity is the mother of invention," but it remained for Herbert A. Leggett, Vice-President of the Valley National Bank in Arizona, to say in one of his monthly letters: "We live in an era when invention is the mother of the unnecessary."

Automation is the technological revolution of the second-half of the 20th century, just as mass production was of the first-half. The late Norbert Wiener, distinguished mathematician of Massachusetts Institute of Technology, did much of the conceptual thinking that underlies the new technology. He predicted that automation will lead to "the human use of human beings"; that we shall experience a $\underset{\rightarrow}{1200}$ phasing-out of the type of factory labor which involves repetitive tasks. This will release men and women to use their specifically human qualities—their ability to think, to analyze, to synthesize, to decide and act purposefully—instead of wasting their talents on the dreary work that machines can do better.

These are fragments extracted from the score-sheet of science, typical of thousands of discoveries and developments that have contributed, alone or with improvement, to the advancement of human beings in peace and war.

8. (MC) The article mentioned two great advances of our age:
____(1) soil conservation and medicine.
$\underset{\rightarrow}{1300}$ ____(2) production of drugs and labor-saving machinery.
____(3) electronic discharge and technological revolution.
____(4) biological sciences and academic interests.
9. (T-F) Medical science is the technological revolution of the second-half of the 20th century.
10. (T-F) Norbert Wiener predicted that automation will lead to "the human use of $\underset{\rightarrow}{1350}$ human beings."

——STOP——ASK FOR YOUR TIME——

Record time immediately.

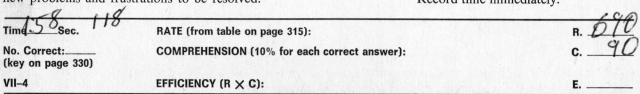

Time:____Sec.   RATE (from table on page 315):   R. ____

No. Correct:____   COMPREHENSION (10% for each correct answer):   C. ____
(key on page 330)

VII–4   EFFICIENCY (R × C):   E. ____

Exercise VII–5

Gardens under Glass

LILLIAN STROHM

(from National Wildlife, January 1975)

WAIT FOR SIGNAL TO BEGIN READING

More than a century ago, smoke belching from the factories of London led to the development of the miniature greenhouses now found in so many American homes, offices, and classrooms. Today, the glassed-in gardens are called "terrariums." Back in 1800s, though, they were called "Wardian cases," after Dr. Nathaniel Ward, an English surgeon and amateur horticulturalist.

Ward was dismayed to find that the bog ferns in his London garden were being killed by industrial pollution. Then, while inspecting a moth chrysalis he had covered with soil in a sealed glass jar, Ward found bog ferns actually thriving in their protected $\underset{\leftarrow}{100}$ environment. After experimenting with other plants in similar containers, he arrived at a remarkable conclusion. If plants had light, still air, and the proper amount of moisture, they could live encapsulated for years without care.

Subsequently, practical application of that discovery made it possible for countries to exchange plants that previously could not stand long ocean voyages. Sealed in glass cases, Shanghai sent new tea plants to India; Brazilian rubber trees were introduced into Ceylon; and botanical gardens exchanged rare and exotic plants from all parts of the world. More recently, ecology-minded home owners have found that modern Wardian cases can be made into $\underset{\leftarrow}{200}$ tables or hung from the ceiling in clear bowls of everything from antique bottles, old fishbowls, and brandy snifters to Steuben crystal cracker jars and various commercial plastic containers.

Used as classroom projects, terrariums demonstrate how a closed ecological system works. Energy supplied by sun or artificial light triggers the plants to use carbon dioxide from the air, plus water and plants food from the soil to produce plant sugars, a process called photosynthesis. The plant sugars take oxygen from the air and give off carbon dioxide, which is recycled back into the terrarium to make $\underset{\leftarrow}{300}$ more plant sugar, a process called respiration.

1. (T–F) Using a terrarium Shanghai sent tea plants to India.
2. (C) In the 1800s, glassed-in gardens were called _____ cases.

3. (MC) The process by which plant sugars take oxygen from the air and give off carbon dioxide is called:
   _____ (1) resorcinol.
   _____ (2) respiration.
   _____ (3) photosynthesis.
   _____ (4) photolysis.

The container

The possibilities are almost unlimited, from a traditional New England berry-bowl made with moss, tiny ferns, and creeping partridgeberry to a grouping of tropical plants, a woodland scene, or a $\underset{\rightarrow}{400}$ cultivated garden. Here are some pointers on setting up your own "Wardian case."

A glass container is preferable to plastic for creating a suitable micro-climate for house plants. Plastic has a tendency to retain water droplets instead of dropping them back into the soil. Clear glass is better than tinted because it will transmit all available light. A glass bowl with an opening large enough to accommodate your hand is as easy to plant as a rectangular aquarium tank and the lustrous glass is equally decorative on a table or hanging from a bracket. Clear glass strips leaded together make a beautiful container to use with antique furnishings, and a 20-inch glass globe on a metal stand blends $\underset{\rightarrow}{500}$ with modern furnishings.

The garden

Plants grouped in a terrarium should provide a contrast in color, form, texture, and growth habit; yet they need to be compatible enough to thrive in the same light, temperature, soil condition, and heavy humidity.

The woodland garden reproduces a natural scene in miniature by using native plants and rocks. Hemlock, spruce and laurel seedlings, wintergreen, club mosses, rattlesnake plantain, and partridgeberry are recommended for woodland scenes. Flowering plants might be violets, hepatica, bloodroot, or wild $\underset{\rightarrow}{600}$ strawberries; lichens and fungi give color and contrast, but they need to be watched for mold.

The bog garden needs acid soil and a cool location. Carnivorous plants that catch and eat flies and insects include: purple pitcher-plant, sundew, huntsman, born venus flytrap. Other bog plants are sheep laurel, swamp blueberry seedlings, and cranberry.

The cultivated garden is easiest for a city dweller to create since these plants come from a florist or department store. Among the most popular plants are:

Filtonia, a wild plant from Peruvian jungles, has pink or white veins. The *Club moss* or *rainbow moss* is difficult to grow outside a terrarium. *Hoya* 700←
wax plant has fragrant pink flowers. *Pittosporum,* of Japanese origin, is a shiny evergreen that can be trimmed into any shape. *Podocarpus,* an evergreen, will stay compact if pruned regularly.

The genus *Begonia* includes more than 1,000 species; for terrariums, the dwarf varieties are required. *Croton* is a tropical plant that needs bright light for best color. *Maranta* from Africa has beautifully marked leaves in shades of green, white, and pink. For ground cover, use *baby tears, philodendron, grape ivy,* or *moneywort.*

4. (T–F) Tinted glass will transmit light better than clear glass.
5. (T–F) Most materials for cultivated gardens 800← can be purchased from a florist.

The planting

First, wash the container in hot soapy water, rinse it thoroughly, and allow it to dry completely for 12 hours. To hide soil and roots, line container with sheet moss up to one-fourth the height of the container, placing top of moss toward glass. Then, add two inches of white pebbles for soil drainage, and spread a thin layer of hardwood charcoal bits over the pebbles to absorb chemical salts and decay gases. Next, use a layer of sphagnum moss to prevent the soil from washing into the drainage pebbles, or use 900← a layer of nylon net which serves the same purpose and will not decay. Now, add soil mix to fill the container one-fourth to one-third full. If you make your own mix, you will need one-third pasteurized garden loam, one-third builders' sand, and one-third milled sphagnum moss (moist but not soggy).

To make a bottle garden, the same materials are used but special tools are needed. A funnel made of rolled paper should reach almost to the bottom of the bottle to pour in the growing medium. A wire coat hanger can be fashioned into a plant placer by 1350→ using straight wire with an open loop on one end. 1000← Plant roots are washed then lowered into the bottle with this positioner.

Long tweezers made from split bamboo are needed to hold the plant in the bottle until the soil is tamped down with a cork attached to the end of a dowel.

To water a bottle terrarium, run the water down the inside of the glass, using a kitchen basket. The water level can reach the top of the drainage pebbles. Usually, no ventilation is needed. When 1100→ plants need trimming, a razor blade taped to a dowel makes clean cuts.

6. (T–F) Washed containers should be slightly damp for ideal planting.
7. (T–F) No special tools are needed for bottle gardens.
8. (T–F) To water a bottle terrarium, water is run down the inside of the glass.

The growing

Most gardens encased in glass do best with filtered light, not direct sun. If artificial light is used, special fluorescent tubes developed to simulate actual sunlight rays are more effective than regular tubes. A standard amount of light is 20 watts for every square foot of growing space.

Although sealed terrariums are possible, some 1200→ ventilation is usually needed to keep the glass from fogging and obscuring the plants inside. Inserting a small pebble between the lid and container is one easy way to ventilate. Use very little fertilizer to encourage slow growth and trim back plants that become overgrown. Mold is the most common terrarium plant disease. Remove all infected plants and treat the garden with a fungicide spray. Too much water, not enough light, or poor ventilation will encourage mold.

One final thing: *talk* to the plants in your terrarium. If you do, they will grow better—especially 1300→ if you remove the lid first. For as you talk, you will breath carbon dioxide into the container, and green plants thrive on carbon dioxide.

9. (MC) Standard wattage for light per square foot of growing space is:
——(1) 100
——(2)   80
——(3)   40
——(4)   20
10. (C) The most common terrarium plant disease is ——————.

——STOP——ASK FOR YOUR TIME——

Record time immediately.

Exercise VII–6

Totems under Siege

ALEXANDER K. CIESIESKI

(from *National Wildlife*, August–September 1975)

WAIT FOR SIGNAL TO BEGIN READING

With its teeth bared menacingly, the larger of the two figures has a fanciful likeness of a giant rock oyster. It was painstakingly carved into the base of an enormous totem pole during the mid-1800s by the Tlingit Indians of the Pacific Northwest. A smaller figure, on the right, represents an Indian fisherman. Together, the two objects portray the Tlingit legend of an angler who hooked a devilfish under a rock, only to have it tear loose. Against the better advice of his companions, the fisherman tried to capture his prey by reaching into a crevice, where the oyster seized him by the wrist. Despite heroic attempts to ↙100 rescue him—or so the story goes—the poor fellow drowned in the rising tide.

For decades, this famous arrangement stood in the Tlingit village of Cape Fox, Alaska. Then, in 1938, it was moved south to Saxman Totem Park near Ketchikan at the base of the Alaskan panhandle. Weathering has produced some definite decay in these figures, but they are among the healthier remaining specimens of Alaska's "endangered totems," some of which were carved more than a century ago.

Today, totem carving is almost a lost art. And ironically, the same damp coastal climate that favors ↙200 the growth of the western red cedars used for totems also provides excellent conditions for decay fungi that can destroy a pole in 50 years. Consequently, the few remaining totem poles of British Columbia and the Alaskan panhandle are under attack from wood rot and fungi. "Without protective measures, this unique heritage is doomed to slow deterioration," warns Dr. Joe W. Clark, wood products pathologist at the U.S. Agriculture Department's Forest Products Laboratory in Madison, Wisconsin.

1. (T–F) The Indian fisherman in the legend had been seized by a devilfish.
2. (MC) The paired totem arrangement is now ↙300 located at:
   _____ (1) Tlingit, Alaska.
   _____ (2) Cape Fox Village.
   _____ (3) Ketchikan Park.
   _____ (4) Saxman Totem Park.
3. (C) Decay fungi can destroy a totem in about ___50___ years.

The makers of the Alaskan totems, the Tlingit and Haida Indians, were fishermen and hunters in a land of dense rain forests, rugged mountains, and countless streams. Although their territory was more than 1,000 miles long, it was only 100 miles wide. Here, the golden age of totem carving flourished from 1830 to 1880, occasioned primarily by two ↙400 factors. The first and most obvious of these was the increased availability of iron tools. Secondly, and perhaps most important, a bourgeois class of Indian trappers emerged during the 1800s and commissioned craftsmen to create hundreds of totem masterpieces.

Interestingly enough, hardly any surviving totem poles stand today in the places where they were originally erected. Many were removed quite early from their original settings by private collectors and museums. By 1900, only about 600 remained. Some 40 years later, many of these had been all but destroyed by decay. Fortunately, the U.S. Forest Service and Indian Service transferred about 100 ↙500 poles from abandoned Indian villages to present-day totem parks.

In the late 1960s, Dr. Clark was working on a wood-bridge decay survey in Alaska when he was approached by Indians who wanted to prevent further deterioration of the poles in their totem parks. Surveying the condition of the poles, Dr. Clark found about one-fifth contained such serious internal decay that they were in danger of breakage or collapse. The outlook for many of the other totems, however, was—and still is—much brighter. "There are techniques we can use to slow the rate of deteriorations," Dr. Clark said. "Exterior decay—due to surface-↙600 invading fungi—can be controlled fairly easily by application of colorless wood preservatives."

It is much more difficult, though, to control interior decay. Seventeen of the poles at Sitka National Historic Park on Baranof Island have been treated by a double diffusion preservative process, Clark reports. Each totem was immersed in two preservative solutions.

"There's no doubt most of the remaining totem poles could be preserved for additional years of outdoor exhibition," Clark emphasizes. "It's a question of how practical it is to do it. Hopefully, all of the relatively sound poles will be treated with effective preservatives to halt any decay present and to pre-←700 vent new infections. However, funds for such work must be obtained and a systematic program must be organized if such procedures are to be effective. Some of the poles are too badly deteriorated to be maintained outdoors and should be moved to sheltered exhibit areas."

4. (T–F) Most of the totems were carved between 1830 and 1880.

5. (C) ___Fungi___ decay is the most difficult type to control.

6. (T–F) Many of the totems should be moved to indoor display areas for preservation.

Prior to 1900, totem maintenance was never part of the Indian tradition. Most totem poles lasted←800 satisfactorily for 50 years or longer. The expense and labor required to lower a large pole, repair it, and re-erect it was such that the same effort could be better used to create a new pole. And, restoring the pole of an ancestor brought little additional honor.

The totem pole is distinguished by its two-dimensional aspect, its use of distortions for special effect, and its usual symmetrical arrangement of figures and motifs. The style is uniquely symbolic of its abstract treatment of the subject and its emphasis on the subject's salient features. Thus, a woman is dis-←900 tinguished from a man only by a labret, a spoon-like ornament inserted in a slit in her lower lip.

Never a religiously significant idol, the totem pole generally represents images and symbols derived from legends and folk tales of the Northwest coastal Indians. Their world was full of wonders; nature dominated by supernatural powers; all creatures were in part spirit; and some animals were thought to have supernatural powers.

7. (T–F) Restoration of old totem poles is an ancient Indian tradition.

8. (MC) Totem poles are used primarily to preserve
___X___(1) legends and folk tales. ←1000
_____(2) family traditions.
_____(3) religious idols.
_____(4) historical events.

Some of the stories most commonly depicted on totem poles are those of Yethl, or Raven, creator of the world. The Tlingit and Haida believed it was he who freed the sun, moon, and stars from original captivity, released day light, caused the tidal waves of the sea, carried water to form lakes and rivers, and brought fire for mankind's use from a remote island. Although recognized as the great benefactor of man, he was pictured with something less than admirable traits: buffon, trickster, and philanderer.

1100→ Another rather frequent subject of "totemic" art is the story of Fog Woman. Associated with the run of fish when the mouths of streams are enveloped by low-lying fogs, she put all varieties of salmon in the Alaskan waters. When Raven fell in love with her, there were no salmon and he had to live on a meager diet of sculpins and cod. Once rich and secure, Raven became ungrateful and unfaithful to his wife. Abused and struck by Raven, Fog Woman started running toward the creek. Raven tried to catch her, but she slipped through his fingers like fog 1200→ and disappeared forever in the water. Fog Woman's daughters live at the head of every stream and to catch their glimpse is the last joy of a salmon on its final journey to die in the place of its birth.

Considering the unique and valuable role of the Alaskan totem parks in art and nature conservation, a visit to a site where totem poles were originally erected is still a highly moving experience. The villagers have long gone and the forest has reclaimed the clearing. The remains of fallen totem poles, too decayed to be moved decades ago, give birth to new 1300→ trees sprouting out of moss-covered trunks. Left in place, the old totem pole serves as a reminder to the modern-day visitor that nature is in a state of constant renewal.

9. (T–F) All totem carvings of Raven reflect deep respect.

10. (T–F) Fog Woman is portrayed as a bene-1350→ factor of the salmon.

——STOP——ASK FOR YOUR TIME——

Record time immediately.

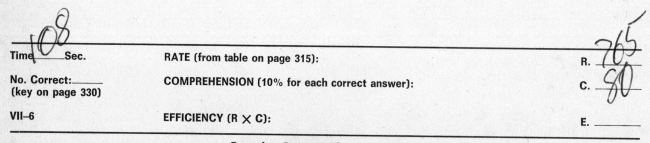

Time ___ Sec. RATE (from table on page 315): R. ___

No. Correct: ___
(key on page 330) COMPREHENSION (10% for each correct answer): C. ___

VII–6 EFFICIENCY (R × C): E. ___

Record on Progress Chart on page 299

Exercise VII-7

The Lady at the Bell

LON GARRISON

(from *Conservation Volunteer*, May–June 1967)

WAIT FOR SIGNAL TO BEGIN READING

In spite of their massive size and ancient hardware, the front doors of Philadelphia's Independence Hall swing easily and noiselessly. All of which added to the mystery, if it could be called that, of The Lady at the Bell.

She was just one of more than 2¾ million visitors who came to the Shrine in one recent year, and so "average" that after the incident no two observers were able to agree on her description. Just one of more than 2¾ million visitors? Not quite, for hers wasn't an "average" visit.

She pushed the big door open, one sunny afternoon last fall, and slipped quietly inside. Pausing 100 only long enough to let her eyes adjust to the darker interior, she walked straight to the Liberty Bell in the Tower Room at the end of the hall. Obviously acting from deep conviction, and a complete lack of self-consciousness, she dropped to her knees to offer a silent prayer. When she arose she leaned over, kissed the Bell, then walked out.

No flashbulbs popped. There was no fanfare, no publicity.

In her own way, The Lady at the Bell had chosen this as a fitting place to express to her Creator some significant personal message; then she dis- 200 appeared.

It is difficult for me to tell this story without developing a lump in my throat. But it has become a favorite because it illustrates a belief I've long held: the history of our land is important to our people because history belongs to the people.

A deep feeling for history

History is one of those good intangibles that spans everything from Federal preservation of major shrines of American history to individual concern for the events of local—or sometimes only family— significance. Occasionally these interests merge in surprising but understandable ways, as we realize anew the deep patriotism abroad in our land, and 300 the thoughtful respect our people have for historic places.

Throughout these United States, at different levels of time, I have seen the recognition of the worth of local history. The outcry appears to come from the same deep emotion—a determination that the symbols, the places, the concepts that shaped today's circumstances will be retained for patriotic reasons.

1. (C) The author stated that "History belongs 400 to the _____."
2. (T–F) The Lady at the Bell arrived at Independence Hall accompanied by a great deal of fanfare and publicity.

This is indeed a very deep wellspring of endeavor and pride. And, along with it is a surprising ingenuity in developing combinations of uses, of ways of finance, of preservation, and of restoration techniques.

Through most of my working years, having had some association with American events and memorialized landmarks, I have always approached these responsibilities with considerable humility, because I recognize that I come upon the scene only lately. Every historical park represents a chain that leads from the original event on through the subsequent recognition and labor of unselfish people with a vision, a gleam to follow, that saved these places for 500 Americans of today and for future generations.

Historic preservation

This very real and personal concern for history, so prevalent today, has united like-minded people across America into the National Trust for Historic Preservation. Historic preservation has been tied to urban renewal. The recent Historic Preservation Act, Public Law 89–665, establishes grants-in-aid programs. The whole preservation movement is today stronger, better organized, and more hopeful of success than ever before!

The President announced the creation of the 17-member National Historic Preservation Advisory Commission whose responsibilities, explicitly defined by the Act, include:

*Advising the President and the Congress on 600 historic preservation.

*Recommending measures to coordinate all public and private historic preservation programs.

*Advising on information programs about these activities.

*Encouraging public interest and participation in historic preservation efforts through the National Trust for Historic Preservation and other private agencies.

*Recommending studies dealing with adequacy of laws, regulations and statutes at all levels of government.

*Recommending studies dealing with the effects of tax policies on the general problems of historic preservation.

*Providing advice to states and local governments to aid them in drafting historic preservation legislation.

*Encouraging training and education in the field of historic preservation through private and public institutions.

3. (T–F) Urban renewal has been associated with $\underleftarrow{700}$ historic preservation.

4. (MC) The National Historic Preservation Advisory Commission has:
  ____(1) 17 members.
  ____(2) 10 members.
  ____(3) 82 members.
  ____(4) 50 members.

5. (T–F) One of the duties of the Advisory Commission is to encourage training in the field of historic preservation.

I see in the Historic Preservation Act signposts to two general fields of endeavor. The governmental sector of concern runs from the Department of the Interior to the individual state governments.

The extensive, privately owned and operated historic properties constitute the second field of endeavor. They, too, can qualify for assistance, but $\underleftarrow{800}$ through the independent National Trust for Historic Preservation, not through a governmental bureau.

Effectiveness of the historic preservation

A major thrust of the Historic Preservation Act is this grants-in-aid program. Here one fact is being overlooked. The Act did not appropriate any funds, but only authorizes Congress to make future appropriations for this purpose. Future appropriations will have to be considered in relation to the total appropriation needs of the Nation.

A common aspect of the program, for both the governmental and private preservation efforts, is that these funds will be made for planning acquisition $\underleftarrow{900}$ and restoration, but not for operation.

This exception—that funds cannot be used for operation—gets to the heart of one of the major concerns of all historic preservation programs: what can be done with historic properties? How many historic houses can the Federal Government, a State, a County, a Town, or a privately financed society afford to restore and operate?

This very practical problem arises when any property is being studied for the degree of restoration. Does every historic house get the years of painstaking research and careful craftsmanship that has gone into Independence Hall? Or is it possible $\underleftarrow{1000}$ to restore only the exterior in some cases, or only

one room of the interior and how can the rest of the building be used?

6. (T–F) The Historic Preservation Act appropriates money for their grants-in-aid program.

7. (MC) One exception of the preservation program is that the funds cannot be used for:
  ____(1) acquisition.
  ____(2) planning.
  ____(3) operation.
  ____(4) restoration.

Ingenuity in the use of restored structures

In many situations it is possible to establish standards for exterior restoration—creating or retaining a delightful and charmingly authentic community atmosphere. The best sites and buildings may $\underset{\rightarrow}{1100}$ be house museums, but the others can be restored outside and fitted for the utilitarian modern life of the community by contemporary use of the interiors.

Historic Districts are particularly good in preserving the flavor of a town's early history, its heritage, its character, without going overboard on the costs of total restoration, and without getting visitors intoxicated—or bored—on history.

Too many historic properties are actually dull for lack of attractive presentations of their "story." Too many are just bricks, mortar and fine furniture—these things do not speak for themselves; they need $\underset{\rightarrow}{1200}$ interpretation. This is the special art of park interpretive people, with their professional knowledge and standards.

There is no question that historians of today and of the future will laud the efforts being made today to preserve their historic scene.

The interweaving of life's personal values for an anonymous Lady at the Bell led to her identification of a Shrine of Liberty—Independence Hall—as a proper place for prayer. This was obviously a place for one of life's deeply expressive moments, yet this woman had an affection and friendship reaction to this major symbol of America that is deeply revealing.

$\underset{\rightarrow}{1300}$ 8. (T–F) Historic Districts are particularly good in preserving the flavor of a town's early history and heritage.

9. (C) Many historic properties, dull for lack of an attractive presentation, need interpretation to tell their _____.

$\underset{\rightarrow}{1350}$ 10. (T–F) Historians of the future will decry our failures to preserve their historic scene.

——STOP——ASK FOR YOUR TIME——
Record time immediately.

Time____Sec.

No. Correct:____
(key on page 322)

VII–7

RATE (from table on page 315):

COMPREHENSION (10% for each correct answer):

EFFICIENCY (R × C):

R. _____

C. _____

E. _____

254   Record on Progress Chart on page 299

Exercise VII-8

Winning Isn't Enough

PAUL H. GNADT

(from *Listen*, December 1973)

WAIT FOR SIGNAL TO BEGIN READING

The generation gap was obvious. He was 62, gray, and the shadow of retirement was creeping closer. They were young, restless with energy, the first payroll dollar far from the bank and farther from their thoughts. Yet they listened.

He was speaking about integrity, honesty, and sincerity, highlighting his reasons with rhyme. Strange ingredients at a basketball camp for boys in seventh through twelfth grades who traveled across the country to perfect their passing, dribbling, and shooting under the experienced eyes of college and prep coaches. But the basketballs lay bounceless, and 250 pairs of sneakers were silenced in attention as if what 100 their awed owners were hearing was gospel from a living legend. It was. He is.

John Wooden, head coach of the University of California at Los Angeles basketball teams since 1948, winner of seven straight NCAA championships (nine of the last ten), and currently fast breaking through opponents and the record book with a 75-plus game victory streak, was telling the attentive athletes that "winning the game isn't important."

Important to John Wooden is that while playing the game you try your best. "Try your best and you'll never lose," he declares. "You may be outscored, but you'll know you did the best you could 200 do." And that, according to the mentor whose 37-year coaching career totals 807 victories against only 196 losses, is success.

1. (T-F) John Wooden is now a living legend.
2. (T-F) John Wooden says "winning is important."

A life's philosophy

He continued to talk about building the foundations for success. The verbal blueprint included words like industriousness, enthusiasm, cooperation, alertness, and self-control. Additional support is supplied by skill, confidence, faith, patience, reliability, and sincerity. The completed structure is known as John Wooden's "Pyramid of Success."

Without notes he went on for twenty minutes. 300 They listened. John Wooden knows the pyramid. He lives it every day.

Living every day began in 1910 at Hall, Indiana, near Monrovia. Four Wooden brothers and their father, Joshua, formed the first of many quintets meaningful to John. The family farmed sixty acres, and there were plenty of chores for the boys to share. Joshua had a tremendous influence on his sons. He was hardworking, honest, and fair. He always made his boys' best interest his primary concern. He read the Bible daily and encouraged the 400 boys to read along. Today, next to photos of his grandchildren and memorabilia of seasons past, a Bible occupies a permanent and prominent place on Wooden's UCLA office desk.

The love that existed in the Wooden father-son relationship is best evidenced by the grade-school graduation gift John received from his dad. It was a piece of paper with this handwritten creed for John to live by:

1. Be true to yourself.
2. Make each day your masterpiece.
3. Help others.
4. Drink deeply from good books, especially the Bible.
5. Make friendship a fine art.
6. Build a shelter against a rainy day.
7. Pray for guidance, count and give 500 thanks for your blessings every day.

Long since worn out and transferred by typewriter to a small card, it travels in Wooden's wallet next to the torn pieces of a $2 bill Joshua gave to John on his first birthday in 1911. "There is no doubt that the father-son relationship between me and my players is a direct result of the love and guidance my father gave me," says a thankful Wooden.

Joshua believed in mixing work and fun; so in the classic tradition, he nailed a bottomless tomato 600 basket up on the hayloft wall for his sons to use. A few years later it was replaced by an iron ring, but progress with the ball wasn't as swift. Old rags stuffed inside a pair of Mrs. Wooden's black cotton hose substituted as the basketball.

3. (T-F) The University of California constructed the "Pyramid of Success."
4. (C) A *Bible* occupies a permanent place on Wooden's office desk.
5. (T-F) Joshua had little influence on John's values.

Success at basketball

Scrappy and tireless, John Wooden earned "all-state" basketball recognition for three years at Martinsville High, and was recruited by two colleges within Indiana—namely, Ball State and Notre Dame. 700 The opportunity that basketball gave Wooden to attend college became important since the family was forced to give up the farm prior to John's starting high school.

To everyone's surprise, John chose to attend Purdue University in West Lafayette, attracted by the basketball team's reputation and their fast-break style of play under Coach Ward (Piggie) Lambert.

Learning that if a student made the dean's list he received free tuition, Wooden studied especially hard.

He received some honors for hustling on the basketball court also, namely "All-American" for three consecutive years of varsity competition with recognition as "College Player of the Year" while a 800 senior. This resulted in a call from the U.S. Military Academy at West Point, which at that time was allowed to recruit top collegiate athletes for another four years of eligibility while studying for graduate degrees.

Wooden was ready to turn in his civvies and join the Long Gray Line when a feminine voice called a halt. Nellie Riley had been waiting back in Martinsville for John to graduate so they could be married. She wasn't about to postpone the wedding another four years while John dribbled along the banks of the Hudson. 900

Simultaneously, Wooden made another decision that would ultimately affect the lives of many people in general and the game of basketball in particular. George Halas, one of the founders of the National Football League, also had a basketball team for which he asked Wooden to play after graduation from Purdue. John's performance attracted the attention of the original New York Celtics, who offered him $5,000 for his services. When John discussed the offer with Piggie Lambert, the Purdue coach asked John why he had studied so hard and if he was ever going to use the knowledge he gained. 1000 Convinced that coaching was the direction to follow, John turned down the professional offer and accepted a job in Dayton, Kentucky, as high school athletic director, coach, and teacher.

6. (MC) Wooden attended a college at:

_____ (1) Notre Dame.
_____ (2) Ball State.
__X__ (3) Purdue.
_____ (4) UCLA.

7. (T-F) Although offered a professional basketball contract, Wooden never played professional basketball.

Wooden goes West

The acorn, however small, was now planted in the Midwest. Two unusual events would occur before its branches of influence and success would spread west to UCLA.

The first happened after the Woodens had 1100 moved to South Bend, Indiana, where John coached at Central High. The attack on Pearl Harbor prompted John to enlist in the Navy, where he was trained as a fitness officer and assigned to a ship in the Pacific. Returning to South Bend following his discharge, Wooden continued coaching; but he soon became disenchanted with the city. Eager to coach on the college level, he accepted the post at Indiana State University in Terre Haute. Two years produced a 47–14 record and a trip to the NAIA tournament for second place. John had always hoped to 1200 return to the Big Ten Conference as a coach, and the possibility became reality when Minnesota was one of two big-time schools to call with a firm offer. The other was UCLA. By prearrangement, on a specified evening Minnesota was to call for John's decision at 6 P.M.; UCLA, an hour later. A Minnesota snowstorm prevented the Minnesota athletic director from getting to a phone. When UCLA dialed on time, Wooden was headed for Westwood.

Wooden always carries a small cross in his pocket. He clutches it during times of tension. It reminds him to take care and beware of his reactions 1300 under pressure.

8. (MC) Wooden's first college coaching job was at:

_____ (1) Purdue.
_____ (2) Minnesota.
_____ (3) Ball State.
__X__ (4) Indiana State.

9. (T-F) Wooden was offered coaching positions at both Minnesota and UCLA at the same time.

10. (C) Wooden always carries a small _cros_ in his pocket.

——STOP——ASK FOR YOUR TIME——

Record time immediately.

Time __57__ Sec.

No. Correct: _____
(key on page 330)

VII–8

RATE (from table on page 315):

COMPREHENSION (10% for each correct answer):

EFFICIENCY (R × C):

R. __57__

C. _____

E. _____

Record on Progress Chart on page 299

Exercise VII–9

The White Monster

FRANK L. REMINGTON

(from *The Lion*, February 1963)

WAIT FOR SIGNAL TO BEGIN READING

A warning that came too late

One winter day several years ago four veteran skiers climbed a snow-laden slope in California's Sierra Nevada Mountains. Suddenly one of the men looked up to see a mass of snow roaring down upon them. "Look out! Avalanche!" he screamed. The snowslide thundered onward engulfing them in a furious white tide.

Although entombed under the snow, two of the sportsmen were able to carve an air space around their faces. The third skier, unconscious, was buried under four feet of snow, his face downward and one leg and a ski twisted under him.

Fortunately, the fourth man, his head barely 100 out of the snow, spotted another group of skiers and shouted for help. The rescuers, digging more than an hour to extricate them, saved the skiers who doubtless would have perished in a short time had they not been sighted.

Avalanches, or giant snowslides, are nothing more than large masses of snow and ice in swift motion down a mountainside. Indeed, avalanches, one of the most treacherous forces of nature, rank with earthquakes, tornadoes, and floods as great natural destroying forces. They are little recognized as killers because they usually occur in remote mountain areas where they seldom threaten man or his 200 property.

There are two fundamental causes of avalanches: terrain and climate. Acting together, plenty of snow and a mountain for it to slide on can produce an avalanche without any other assistance. If a slope is not at least of 25 degrees steepness, however, there is small chance of an avalanche. The shape of the slope, too, somewhat governs its snowslide potential. As a rule, convex slopes pose a greater avalanche hazard than concave ones because snow settling on a bulging surface builds up more instability.

Whether a snowbank can maintain its position 300 on a slope is determined by the weight of the snow and the angle of the slope. If these combined factors equal or exceed the snow's cohesiveness, they can precipitate a snowslide.

Each winter hundreds, perhaps thousands of avalanches cascade down the slopes of remote mountains.

The greatest avalanche disaster in United States history took place on a railroad, in March 1910, when a single slide swept three snowbound trains in Washington's Cascade Mountains to the bottom of the canyon. The resulting fatalities and over a million dollars in property damage forced the railroad to 400 build a tunnel which bypassed the slide area.

Avalanches in the U.S. reach only minor proportions compared to the devastating sizes they attain in other countries. Thousands of persons have been swept to their deaths and whole villages whisked away by giant waves of onrushing whiteness.

1. (T–F) Avalanches seldom pose a serious threat to individual lives or property.
2. (C) Avalanches are usually caused by the terrain or the _____.
3. (T–F) The greatest avalanche in U.S. history took place in a small mining town.

Avalanche tragedies

Indeed, only last year, in January, one of history's 500 worst avalanches occurred on Mount Huascaran, which rises 22,205 feet high in northern Peru. Rocketing down the mountainous slopes, the ponderous mass of ice, snow, rocks, trees, and mud traveled nine miles before it lost momentum. By that time it had entombed almost 4,000 residents of the two villages of Huarascucho and Ranrahirca. Very few villagers survived the icy wave which was 40 feet high and 1,000 yards wide.

Villagers who live in the Alpine valleys of Austria and Switzerland expect avalanches each year. Often these snow inundations occur at the same place and on the same date each year. Past experience 600 has taught residents to erect houses and barns in strategic positions. Frequently they build massive stone bastions, not to stop the white terror, but to divert its course. In the U.S., too, snow sheds and diversion walls are erected as an effective protective measure to confine a slide to a certain path or turn it away from the object to be protected.

Perhaps the most bizarre avalanche disaster occurred almost a century and a half ago when a group of adventurers attempted to scale the Alpine peak of Mt. Blanc on the French-Italian border. 700 Walking over a glacier, the party suddenly was swept

400 yards down the slope in a tobogganing mass of snow. Although several escaped, most of the climbers were dashed to death in the deluge and their remains later recovered.

Three of the bodies, however, fell into a vast glacier fissure and were entombed beneath an ocean of ice and snow. Forty-one years later, the slow-moving glacier disgorged the bodies in Chamonix, six miles away. One survivor of the party, now a wrinkled old man, identified the perfectly preserved and youthful-appearing remains.

Forest Service

The U.S. Forest Service's avalanche study commenced in 1937 when a solitary forest ranger was sent to Alta, Utah, in the Wasatch mountain ₈₀₀← range, about 30 miles from Salt Lake City. He spent his full time observing snow and studying avalanches. From this pioneer work grew the Forest Service's present avalanche control program.

Over a period of years the Forest Service studies have revealed and interpreted many of the snow's secrets. Today the Forest Service Snow Ranger's chief duty is to recognize the development of a hazardous avalanche situation in time to do something about it. In fighting avalanches the Snow Rangers observe the snow and weather conditions continuously so that danger can be immediately rec- ₉₀₀← ognized. In this work they consider 10 factors, all of which influence avalanche hazard: (1) depth of old snow; (2) old snow surface; (3) new snow depth; (4) new snow type; (5) new snow weight; (6) rate of accumulation; (7) wind force; (8) wind direction; (9) temperature developments; (10) snow settlement.

4. (C) An icy wave of snow, rocks, and ice entombed nearly _____ residents in two Peruvian villages.

5. (T–F) One avalanche on Mt. Blanc perfectly preserved the bodies of three victims for forty-one years.

6. (MC) The U.S. Forest Service's avalanche study was established in:
    ____(1) 1925.
    ____(2) 1937.
    ____(3) 1949.
    ____(4) 1958.

7. (T–F) The two primary forces influencing avalanches are wind force and direction.

1000 ←

Avalanche control techniques benefit not only winter sports areas but mountain highways and power and pipe lines at high altitudes. Some states like Colorado, where sliding snows present a constant winter hazard to motorists, have established their own highway avalanche protection services.

A person in the path of one of these tides of destruction, which often exceed a speed of 100 miles an hour, can do practically nothing to save himself. ₁₁₀₀→ Some fortunate ones have managed to stay atop the onrushing whiteness and ride it down the slope. Experienced mountaineers caught in a slide try to flop on their backs and make swimming motions with their arms and legs, attempting to maneuver to the edge of the avalanche. A victim buried in a mammoth slide has about as much chance for survival as a snowflake on a hot stove.

How to locate avalanche victims

One method involves a line of men advancing across the surface, probing the drift with long iron rods equipped with special hooks to catch in clothing. The other way makes use of specially trained Ger- ₁₂₀₀→ man shepherd dogs. These canines locate an entombed person by scent much quicker than probing with a pole, provided the victim is not more than 12 feet under the snow.

Today many ski enthusiasts equip themselves with an avalanche string, a thin red rope about 25 yards long which is slung around the waist and dragged along.

Most persons who have witnessed an avalanche agree that it's a beautiful and spectacular sight to see—provided they're not in its path.

8. (T–F) The state of Colorado has its own highway avalanche protection service as a safety measure.

₁₃₀₀→ 9. (MC) Specially trained German shepherd dogs can detect entombed persons providing they:
    ____(1) aren't under more than 12 feet.
    ____(2) leave some marks.
    ____(3) cling to the avalanche string.
    ____(4) are able to signal.

10. (T–F) The avalanche string, a flexible rope, ₁₃₅₀→ is about 25 yards long.

——STOP——ASK FOR YOUR TIME——

Record time immediately.

Time_____Sec.

No. Correct:_____
(key on page 322)

VII–9

RATE (from table on page 315):

COMPREHENSION (10% for each correct answer):

EFFICIENCY (R × C):

R. _____

C. _____

E. _____

Record on Progress Chart on page 299

258

Exercise VII–10

Old New Mexico

JOAN and MAX SCHUSSLER

(from *Adventure Road*, Winter 1966–1967)

WAIT FOR SIGNAL TO BEGIN READING

After driving through the limitless, level expanse of the vast American plains, we headed toward our destination—New Mexico. As we left the flat plateau we saw, far off beyond the prairies and rising out of the empty clear skies, a fantastic chain of snow-capped mountains.

This was truly the gateway to a new world. Climbing toward Taos we came to Cimmaron Canyon with its steeply rising wall of red and pink rocks forming Palisades which reminded us of some gigantic medieval fortress.

The surrounding forests abounded in game: deer, wild turkey, bear, and mountain lion, and to the south of us, on the plains, were vast herds of 100 antelope.

It was fall, and the golden-red of the shimmering aspens made it seem that the mountains were bathed in a halo of blood—hence the name the Spanish colonists gave to this last, bold spur of the Rockies, "Sangre de Cristo"—blood of Christ.

How wrong we were when we assumed that all American cities conformed to that convenient pattern of straight streets, neat and precise, all organized and numbered. In Taos where the streets wander off in all directions almost at random, the houses are all built of a reddish, golden mud, the adobe of Biblical 200 days. None of the walls of the buildings appeared to have been constructed with the aid of a carpenter's level, and the colors and forms blend perfectly with the landscape. Here the flowers make late fall seem like midsummer under a sky of such incredible blue that it looks as if someone had woven a magic canopy over the entire scene.

The people look Spanish

The darkskinned men and the haughty and lovely girls have rhythm in their walk as they promenade around the Taos Plaza. This lovely Spanish town square is the center of most of the activity in 300 Taos, and in the evenings the local citizens circle around it to the music of guitars, and an occasional mariachi band. The American flag flies 24 hours a day to remind citizen and visitor alike of the bravery of Kit Carson and his loyal followers who nailed the flag to a tree in this same Plaza during the Civil War,

and guarded it day and night to prevent the Confederate sympathizers from tearing it down.

The language in Taos is a musical patois of 400 Spanish; English is definitely the language of the minority. The visitor listening carefully to the sounds on a pleasant evening will also hear another language that isn't so easy to recognize—Indian, spoken in soft, deep voices by the colorfully blanketed people of the Taos Pueblo, located just north of town.

1. (T–F) The steeply rising walls of red and pink rocks are referred to as Vermillion Canyon.
2. (T–F) The Sangre de Cristo mountains were so called because the mountains appeared to be bathed in a halo of blood.
3. (T–F) In Taos the straight streets were all very 500 neat and precise.

Located far away from the closest railroad, and accessible only by highways (which until quite recently were pretty primitive) the town failed to fall in step with the so-called march of progress, and it has remained pretty much the way it was fifty or seventy-five years ago.

The town of Taos is, as is Santa Fe, at an elevation of 7,000 feet, and the climate is cool and pleasant in summer, and sunny in the winter. There isn't a lot of snow on the great plain that surrounds Taos, but to the north and east the mountains seem 600 to reach up and pull a heavy winter blanket over themselves, and the snow is abundant, providing some of the finest skiing conditions in the world.

We drove out to the famous Taos Indian Pueblo, a primitive village of mud and straw, virtually unchanged since its discovery by the bold Spanish explorer, Captain Alvarado in 1540. The very tasty Indian bread is still baked in the native adobe beehive-shaped ovens, found outside of each dwelling, and, generally, tightly closed to prevent the dogs from using them for shelters.

Ski Valley and the Rio Grande

700 Beyond the Pueblo and past its small herd of buffalo, we drove up a winding canyon, beside the lovely Hondo River, to a Swiss and French Alpine

village, the Taos Ski Valley resort, where a century ago the mining town of Twining had been.

We had also been advised to see the Gorge of the Rio Grande which bisects the vast Taos plain. In 1965 a new bridge had been built to span the Gorge. The approach to the fantastic bridge was no different from the rest of the country over which we had been traveling, relatively flat and covered with sagebrush and the yellow-flowered Chamisa, and 800← then, suddenly, we were on the bridge where we could see the river, 650 feet below us, with the sheer brownish-black walls of this fantastic gorge simply dropping away from the plain.

4. (T F) Taos, now a modern metropolis, has managed to keep pace with progress.

5. (C) The famous Taos Indian Pueblo is virtually _Unchanged_ since its discovery by Captain Alvarado.

6. (MC) The Taos Ski Valley resort was once a:
   __X__(1) mining town.
   _____(2) dude ranch.
   _____(3) conquistador campsite.
   _____(4) Indian village.

7. (MC) The famous bridge, spanning the gorge of the Rio Grande, was built in: 900←
   _____(1) 1956.
   __X__(2) 1965.
   _____(3) 1946.
   _____(4) 1962.

Traveling to Santa Fe

About a mile from the Picuris Pueblo, a very small Indian village, we drove through a remote, rural part of the country, inhabited entirely by the descendants of the Spanish colonists who first settled in these lovely valleys. As we approached the tiny hamlet of Truchas we noticed an ancient flume consisting of gigantic logs that had been hollowed out by the villagers, used to carry water from an irrigation ditch across a wide arroyo to the other side of the road. As we entered the village we saw the most 1000← beautiful old adobe church that we had yet come across—a church with great dignity, unmarred by any modern bric-a-brac, and with beautiful handmade beams and altarpieces. We later learned that

this was the country of the Penitentes, a secluded religious group that is still strongly represented in the remote mountain area of northern New Mexico. In earlier days the Penitentes acted out a Passion Play during Holy Week which involved the crucifixion of one of the members, and a procession wherein the other brothers indulged in self-flagellation.

Our road continued through this fascinating 1100← countryside to the village of Chimayo, long famous as the source of beautiful hand-woven blankets. The other industry seems to be the growing of chili, and we happened to be traveling through the area at a time when the chili was being hung outside to dry. Huge brilliant scarlet bunches of the plant, so coveted by the people of New Mexico, made impressive designs on the sides of almost every house and barn in the valley.

To our right, in the distance we could see the plateau on which is located the atomic city of Los 1200→ Alamos, as well as an amazing number of pre-Columbian Indian villages, such as Puye, and the long abandoned communities that are found in the area covered by Bandelier National Monument.

The highway led beyond the foothills, through the pinon and juniper forests, and finally, to the top of a series of hills where we looked down at Santa Fe below us. It was twilight, and the view was incredible—thousands of blinking lights, the startling red of the western sky, and, in the background, the majestic snow-capped mountains. New Mexico, rich in history and tradition, is nicknamed the Land of 1300→ Enchantment, and it would be difficult to think of a better description.

8. (T F) Picuris Pueblo was inhabited by descendants of the Spanish colonists entirely.

9. (C) A secluded religious group in the remote mountain areas of New Mexico is the _Penitentes_.

10. (T F) The small town of Chimayo is famous 1350→ for hand-woven blankets.

——STOP——ASK FOR YOUR TIME——

Record time immediately.

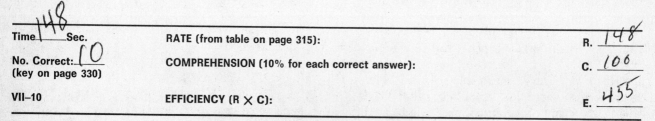

Time _148_ Sec. RATE (from table on page 315): R. _148_

No. Correct: _10_ COMPREHENSION (10% for each correct answer): C. _100_
(key on page 330)

VII–10 EFFICIENCY (R × C): E. _455_

Exercise VII–11

High Soars the Eagle

DICK KIRKPATRICK

(from *National Wildlife*, January 1963)

WAIT FOR SIGNAL TO BEGIN READING

Our national bird

When the Continental Congress chose the "American Eagle" as our national bird on June 20, 1782, their choice seemed a logical one. The native bald eagle is a strikingly handsome, regal-looking bird, and the eagle has been a symbol of freedom, valor, and strength dating back beyond the earliest historical records.

Surprisingly, his nomination met some stout resistance among the founding fathers—and an occasional detractor still takes a pot shot at his selection.

Despite all resistance, and against the arguments that the bald eagle is a thief (he is), a timid coward (sometimes), a carrion eater (partly right), 100 and a bully (right again), he became our national symbol.

The most dedicated eagle detractor, however, can not deny that he is a fine-looking bird. The dark-brown body and darker brown wings contrast sharply with the pure-white head and tail feathers, which glisten in the sunlight in flight and stand out strongly against the dark browns and greens of his native forest backgrounds. A large adult female bald eagle can weigh over 14 pounds with a flat-stretched wing-span of over 90 inches and a body length of over a yard. The adult eagle has few, if any, enemies other than man, and can prey on 200 almost any animal in sight at one stage of its life or another. Though their primary and favorite food is fish, eagles commonly kill and eat other birds and small mammals—chiefly rabbits and other small rodents—with occasional spectacular attacks on much larger animals.

1. (MC) The eagle's detractors have described him as:
   _____(1) a thief and a bully.
   _____(2) a symbol of the feudal system.
   _____(3) a homely, timid-looking bird.
   _____(4) an appropriate choice as national bird.

2. (T–F) An adult female bald eagle may have a wing span of over 7 feet. 300

3. (C) The primary and favorite food of the eagle is _____.

Symbol of might or overrated bully?

These are the source of many eagle legends, and the reason for much of the bird's reputation as a varmint. There are records of eagle attacks on almost every species of animal—even humans—and one impressive account of three bald eagles cooperating in bringing down, killing, and feeding on a three-quarters-grown pronghorn antelope.

There is record of a near-successful attack on a two-year-old Hereford heifer, and many records—mostly exaggerated—of attacks on human children 400 (including one ridiculous tale of an eight-year-old boy being lifted 75 feet and carried 200 feet). There are, however, authenticated records of attacks on children—logical in view of records involving larger animals where the eagle attempts to kill but not to carry off its victim.

The term "carrion-eater" is probably another unearned libel on the eagle's reputation, depending on your definition of the word "carrion." Like any predator, the eagle takes its food in the easiest way possible, certainly welcoming the windfall of a dead fish washed up on shore. Since most estimates of the 500 eagle's diet are made from analysis of stomach contents, it's hard to estimate the original freshness of partly digested findings. Such washed-up spawners are the main food of the northern bald eagle during the salmon spawning season.

Whatever the circumstances, the strike of the bald eagle can be a fearsome thing. He will follow and attack a diving duck under water, strike and kill a big Canadian goose in midair, and pick a mountain goat kid off a lofty crag. Even in his most unpopular hunting activity—robbing the smaller osprey of his hard-caught fish dinner—he is impressive.

Another shortcoming of the bald eagle, often 600 pointed out by scientists brave and agile enough to reach an occasional aerie, is the bird's apparent reluctance to defend his own nest. Though occasional individuals will attack an intruder, there are few records of their actually striking him. By far the more usual conduct is for the eagle to retire to a safe distance, perhaps crying out, but offering no resistance. Against other predators and the annoyances of smaller birds, however, the eagle will defend itself, and will sometimes put up a fierce struggle when cornered or trapped. At the same time, many eagles have been observed under attack by smaller birds and seen to retire in order with a dignified ⤺700 indifference. In general, however, in his conduct under pressure, the bald eagle is regarded by many authorities as a plain coward.

One really impressive feature on the eagle's side, however, is his nest-building capacity. Building in tall trees near water when possible, and returning to the same nest year after year, a pair will add another foot to the nest's height each season until it attains enormous proportions. Construction is mainly of sticks, branches and other available structural members in a sort of rampart, filled on the inside with smaller materials, then lined in the center with ⤺800 softer stuffs. The sheer bulk of the nest accounts for one of the eagle's few natural hazards—weather. High winds and structural failure can bring down the massive nest before the eggs are hatched or while the eaglets are still unable to fly.

4. (T–F) Records show that an eagle will not attack a human child.

5. (MC) Because the eagle sometimes feeds on dead fish washed ashore he has been termed a:
_____(1) scavenger.
_____(2) spawner.
_____(3) coward.
_____(4) carrion-eater.

6. (T–F) Despite other shortcomings, a bald eagle ⤺900 usually will defend his own nest against attack.

7. (T–F) One feature in the eagle's favor is his nest-building capacity.

Preservation of population

At the time of that debate by the Continental Congress, the bald eagle ranged over the entire North American continent, though most commonly around bodies of water that assured a good supply of fish. Since that time, however, man's depredations, both from hunting and from civilization's many changes in habitat, have greatly reduced their numbers. One new hazard is that of indirect poisoning through pesticides. However, the bird is not thought to be in danger of extinction anywhere. In ⤺1000

June of 1940, the "American Eagle" came under government protection under the Bald Eagle Act, though the then-Territory of Alaska was not included. The 34 years of bounty hunting in that territory are believed to have resulted in the killing of at least 100,000 eagles. After years of debate and the passage of much conflicting legislation, the Alaskan Territorial Legislature repealed its eagle bounty law on March 2, 1953. The birds may still be killed when "committing damage to fishes, other wildlife, domestic birds and animals." With the end 1100→ of bounty hunting, which had become an important source of income to many Alaskans, it is expected that the eagle population may return to "normal" within a few years.

Since the bald eagle is not a prolific breeder, it is hoped that protection throughout the continent will enable the population to achieve and maintain a balance. It may even increase, though not to a point of becoming an important predator again. A pair of eagles normally only produces two eggs—sometimes as many as three. They often manage to raise only one eaglet to maturity. The eggs have been described 1200→ as "ridiculously small for so large a bird"; consequently the eaglet takes quite a long time to develop into a self-sufficient individual. Often they mate and nest while still in their juvenile plumage. Even so, their slow rate of reproduction caused Alaskan ornithologists to fear that even inefficient bounty hunting could render them practically extinct.

Whatever his shortcomings, the loss of our bald eagle population would be a tragedy. Despite his detractors, he will remain our national bird, and the general public, ignoring his shortcomings and those detractions, will probably continue to regard him as an excellent choice.

1300→ 8. (C) The Bald Eagle Act of 1940 provided protection for "American Eagles" everywhere in the United States except
_____.

9. (T–F) Because the bald eagle is a prolific breeder, there is little chance of population depletion.

10. (T–F) A pair of eagles normally produces two eggs, often raising only one eaglet to 1350→ maturity.

——STOP——ASK FOR YOUR TIME——

Record time immediately.

Exercise VII–12

Egmont Key

THEODORE LESLEY

(from the *Congressional Record*, May 1, 1973)

WAIT FOR SIGNAL TO BEGIN READING

This legislation charges the Secretary of the Interior to preserve the historical, natural, and recreational values of Egmont Key (Coast of Florida) as a National Park. Many people have expressed enthusiastic support of this legislation, especially in light of the significant role the Key has played in Florida and U.S. history.

This informative letter came from Mr. Theodore Lesley, Hillsborough County, historian and resident of Tampa, Florida:

There are two examples of early Americana which fascinate me, both of which are fast disappearing from our skyline. They are the quaint "covered bridges," that formerly spanned the rivers of old, [100] and the coastal lighthouses. As with many others, I go a good many miles out of my way to visit either of these whenever they are known to be along my route of travel. Florida, to my knowledge, has none of its covered bridges left, but we do have several lighthouses whose long frontier histories are closely woven with the state's past, martime, and commercial development.

Undoubtedly you are aware [that] in our coastal waters Egmont Key is the first body of land one passes upon entering Tampa Bay. This little island of some 300 acres was the first strip of land sighted [200] by the early Spanish explorers of the sixteenth and seventeenth centuries. The pre-Dominican martyrs of America anchored off its shoreline, in 1549, and suffered death in an abortive attempt to establish an Indian mission on the Tampa Bay coast. This is but the first recorded touch that ties Egmont Key with the destiny of the Florida Indians, first with the Aborigines, the Timucuans and Caloosas, and later after their extension, with the Seminoles, whose descendants we know today.

During the early years when the Floridas were owned by Spain, the rivers, keys, and islands all bore Spanish names; however, when England came [300] into possession of the two provinces, East and West Florida (1768–1783), she sent her own map-makers into these lands and the majority of the old Spanish names gave way to those of English derivation. Espiritu Santo became Tampa Bay, the river emptying into it and on whose banks Tampa was later to be established became known as the Hillsborough, and the more important islands received like transformation. Among the latter, situated at the very entrance to the bay, was the one designated Egmont [400] Key. It was evidently named in honor of the second Earl of Egmont, whose served King George III as Lord High Admiral and Postmaster General.

1. (T–F) As they entered Tampa Bay, the first strip of land sighted by the early Spanish explorers was the little island of Egmont Key.

2. (MC) In its earliest years, Florida was owned by:
   _____ (1) France.
   _____ (2) England.
   _____ (3) Spain.
   _____ (4) Mexico.

3. (T–F) The small island of Egmont Key evidently was named in honor of King George III of England.

Here on the shores of Tampa Bay, January [500] 1824, the first permanent white settlement was made with the arrival of troops from Pensacola under command of Col. George Mercer Brooke. The encampment subsequently became known as Fort Brooke, and the small town of Tampa grew up next to its protecting walls.

A refuge from hostile Indians, it led a quiet existence until the outbreak of the Second Seminole Indian War. This conflict lasted from 1835–1842 and was the most costly of all the wars fought with the American Indians. Fort Brooke became the headquarters for the Army of the South, thus the residence of the commanders in the field, among them [600] Gen. Zachary Taylor, later President of the United States.

With hundreds of transports and supply vessels entering the harbor, the lighthouse was then erected on Egmont Key. At various times during this long struggle, Egmont Key was used as a gathering spot, or depot, where the captured Indians were camped until vessels arrived to carry them West. The lighthouse remained in use for commercial ships after this war was over. Several years later, in 1848, it was partially destroyed by a severe hurricane and inundated by sea water. Immediately rebuilt, it has remained in continuous use until this day.

4. (C) On the shores of Tampa Bay, January 700← 1824, the first permanent white settlement was made and became known as Fort _____.

5. (T–F) The Third Seminole Indian War, lasting from 1855–1858, was the most costly of all wars fought with the American Indians.

6. (T–F) At various times during the long Indian struggle, Egmont Key was used as a gathering spot, or depot where captured Indians were camped until vessels arrived to transport them West.

A distinguished American, Col. Robert E. Lee, later Confederate Commander in Chief, visited the coast and islands of Tampa Bay, in February 1849, 800← on a survey mission for the U.S. Government. This group in their report to the Secretary of War recommended that Egmont Key be reserved by the Government as a key to the defense of the area.

The Third Seminole Indian War, 1855–1858, again found Egmont Key a depot for captured Indians and those who came in peacefully for transportation to Western lands. The Chieftain in this uprising, Billy Bowlegs, with his war leaders and families, bid a final farewell to their nature land from here when the steamer, *Grey Cloud,* bore them away. This group of Indians which sailed from Egmont 900 Key, May 7, 1858, was the last to be deported from the State.

More peaceful years existed there until 1861 when Florida withdrew from the Union and joined her sisters in the Confederate States. The local militia, knowing full well they could not defend Egmont Key from the forces of the Federal blockade, dismantled the light from its tower and secreted it at Fort Brooke whose guns defended Tampa from a bay invasion. Thrice the town was bombed but not occupied. When Tampa was finally occupied by Federal troops in May 1864, the Egmont Key lights 1000← were found safe and carried, with other booty, to 1350→ Key West. They were returned in peace time and again mounted within the tower and continued in operation until replaced with more modern equipment years later.

During the war years of 1861–1865, a Federal detachment held Egmont Key. Small raids were made from there on the mainland, and it also served as a center for escaped slaves and Union sympathizers until a time they were able to be transported by ship to Key West. Lookouts were posted in its tall 1100→ tower, with glasses, searching the bay for Confederate blockade runners operating out of the Hillsborough River.

A peaceful existence again came to Egmont Key from 1865–1898. The latter year brought us war with Spain following the sinking of the American warship *Maine* in the Havana harbor. No less than three of the Tampa Bay keys were fortified against possible attack. Today on Egmont Key are to be seen the historic ruins of its fortifications, cannon, sandbagged dugout, munition magazine, post hospital, and long strips of paved roads, all dwarfed by the tall lighthouse on its isolated end of the key.

1200→ Peace finally reigns there as king. May it ever be so, free from commercialism, a wildlife refuge and a retreat for all the weary from the work-a-day world.

7. (T–F) The distinguished American, Col. Zachary Taylor, later Confederate Commander in Chief, visited the coast and islands of Tampa Bay on a survey mission for the U.S. Government.

8. (MC) The Chieftain in the Third Seminole Indian War, where leaders and their families were the last to be deported from the state, was:
   _____(1) Gray Cloud.
   _____(2) Red Cloud.
   _____(3) Billy Bowlegs.
   _____(4) Geronimo.

1300→ 9. (T–F) When Tampa was finally occupied by Federal Troops in May 1864, the Egmont Key lights were found safe and carried with the other booty to Key West.

10. (C) In 1898, peaceful existence at Egmont Key vanished, and war with _____ followed the sinking of the American warship *Maine* in the Havana harbor.

——STOP——ASK FOR YOUR TIME——

Record time immediately.

Time_____Sec. RATE (from table on page 315): R. _____

No. Correct:_____ COMPREHENSION (10% for each correct answer): C. _____
(key on page 330)

VII–12 EFFICIENCY (R X C): E. _____

Record on Progress Chart on page 299

Exercise VII–13

Free and Responsible People

(Excerpted from *The Royal Bank of Canada Monthly Letter*, November 1975)

WAIT FOR SIGNAL TO BEGIN READING

Everyone has the right to think and act and believe as he will, but also the responsibility to give an accounting sometime, somewhere, for what he chooses to think and believe and do.

The freedom one enjoys in a democratic country is not a matter of making absolutely free choice, but choice conditioned by a duty to act according to the trust reposed in one by fellow citizens. The foundation of a good nation is the sense of mutuality its people have.

Some pursue liberty in a frantic way, as if liberation from restrictions and laws were the greatest good in life. The legal basis of freedom is obedience ←100 to certain social and moral laws—a person may be free and yet under constraint; he can be both disciplined and free. "Doing your own thing" is not necessarily an evidence of freedom: it may be sparked by pride, or a feeling of incapacity to measure up in the customary environment.

The idea of freedom is not an abstraction—we have freedom *from* and freedom *to*. The good society gives its people the opportunity to realize ever greater human and spiritual values. Like other moral virtues, freedom can only be maintained by carrying ←200 out its duties.

A list of the liberties enjoyed by citizens would include religious liberty, political liberty, and the civil liberties: personal freedom, freedom of expression, and freedom of assembly and association. Every freedom has its correlative responsibility.

Whatever a person's position in society, laborer or executive, voter or politician, he has a duty to do his best. There are some who feel that if they obey the law they have done all their duty, but duty is not bounded by statutes. The sense of duty covers all cases of right doing where there is no law to →300 compel you to do it.

Duty is not a spectral figure, solemn and grim, stalking us and making notes of our delinquency. It is more like a guide, leading us to justify our existence by making the world a little better than we found it. If we had a hundred space platforms orbiting the earth, the human story would still be told in terms of individuals discharging their duty responsibly.

1. (C) The article stresses that freedom must be accompanied by _____.

2. (T–F) Duty is involved only where legal requirements exist.

Duty in a society

→400 There are in this world hundreds of things which are right but which cannot be legislated for— things that will never be done unless someone is prepared to do them for no reward except a feeling that he is contributing what is expected of him to society.

If a person is to walk with his head held high, he must make his contribution in duty done, fairness, sympathy, and good taste. He may stand aloof from another person or crusade that displeases him, but he should not therefore feel called upon to make life uncomfortable for people who differ from him.

→500 Acceptance of social responsibility means among other things not leaving others to do what we should share in doing. The world is so complex that we must inevitably owe much to our neighbors, but as far as possible every person should stand on his own feet.

Noblesse oblige is a beautiful concept which denotes the moral obligation to display honorable and charitable conduct. Human life depends upon a sense of obligation on the part of those people who are in a position to help others. Whether one be a capitalist, a worker, or a manager, he has this obligation to society.

→600 Entry into the group called "noble" is open to citizens of all classes. It requires only that we possess and practice traits that are common among those who are noble. This brings into being a new sort of aristocracy, made up of men and women from all levels and walks of life: sympathetic, enthusiastic, of clear vision and free thought, dedicated to greatness and bigness of service to mankind.

3. (T–F) Nobility is restricted to those in the upper classes.

4. (C) *Noblesse oblige* denotes a _____ obligation to others.

Increasing pressures

→700 In the last quarter of this century communities have had to take into account many features that did not trouble them in the first quarter—the proliferation of services combined with an unprecedented industrial growth; an urban concentration creating many new needs at the municipal level; urgent need to control air and water pollution; to conserve oil, coal, and natural gas and find substitutes; to develop low-cost housing, efficient urban transportation, and recreational facilities such as parks, green belts, and libraries.

All these involve responsible thought and work. Just as in family life, life in the community requires800← a mixture of dependence, sympathy, persuasion, and compulsion, and those who expect to reap the benefits of community life must undergo the fatigue of supporting it.

5. (T–F) Enjoying the benefits of a community requires some investment of work.

Living responsibility

What is it to live effectively responsible? It is to establish ourselves in the central undertaking of human life, in mutually fulfilling relationship with fellow humans. We need to remain human. Machines were introduced to be the extension of people's hands, but men are in danger of becoming an extension of the machine, functional robots, doing even good deeds mechanically.

Human beings are more and more refusing to900← be regarded as statistics. B. R. Sen, Director-General of the Food and Agriculture Organization of the United Nations, said: "What the world needs most today is not merely a wider exchange of material benefits, essential though it is, but also a conscious dedication to the right of man to grow to his full stature, regardless of the place of his birth, the color of his skin, or of the faiths and beliefs he might cherish."

6. (MC) In all responsibilities, the article stresses the importance of remaining:
    _____(1) independent.
    _____(2) active.
    _____(3) human.
    _____(4) adaptable.

7. (MC) The authority quoted was an officer of1000← 1350→ the:
    _____(1) United States.
    _____(2) United Kingdom.
    _____(3) United Nations.
    _____(4) Canadian government.

Act with sensibility

Liberty and duty are twinned with right reason, but shouldering responsibility does not mean carrying all the world's problems. The Golden Rule does not prescribe that a person shall take no care for his own interests and his own welfare. The person who wishes to remain free must continue to carry a very substantial load of personal responsibility for his own well-being.

Sir John Lubbock, writer of scientific works, 1100→ member of Parliament, and compiler of the first list of *The Hundred Best Books,* said: "We must be careful not to undermine independence in our anxiety to relieve distress. There is always the difficulty that whatever is done for men takes from them a great stimulus to work, and weakens the feeling of independence, and all creatures which depend on others tend to become mere parasites."

People need to be concerned about filling their role, about developing the "let's do something about it" attitude. Do-Democracy is democracy based on genuine participation through which a person answers 1200→ positively the question: "What duty do I owe to my country, to my neighbors, to my friends?" He will thus make history something more than a period to be lived through. He will be actively engaged in making history.

Acceptance of responsibility leads in business to the use of power and authority justly and sympathetically; in society it leads to a cooperative effort to improve the living conditions of all people wherever they live, and in personal life to the greatest fulfillment of an individual's capacity, large or small as it may be.

To act in that way is to assume responsibility 1300→ as a free human being and as a part of the universe.

8. (T–F) The article cautions the reader not to get carried away with good works.
9. (T–F) Sensible people become actively engaged in making history.
10. (T–F) The use of power and authority violates the principles of freedom and responsibility.

———STOP——ASK FOR YOUR TIME———

Record time immediately.

RATE (from table on page 315):

COMPREHENSION (10% for each correct answer):

EFFICIENCY (R × C):

R. _____

C. _____

E. _____

Exercise VII–14

Missing Matter

STEPHEN P. MARAN

(Excerpted from *Natural History*, January 1976)

WAIT FOR SIGNAL TO BEGIN READING

Studies with a space telescope show that iron and certain other common elements are in short supply in the thin gas that pervades our galaxy. Theorists disagree on where the missing atoms are, but suggest various possibilities: they may have condensed into microscopic dust grains, they may have accumulated into icy baseballs floating between the stars, or they may have become concentrated in the heads of interstellar comets.

In 1904, a German astronomer, Johannes Franz Hartmann, at the Potsdam Observatory, discovered a curious effect in the spectrum of the star Mintaka, located in Orion's belt. He reported that *"the calcium line does not share in the periodic dis-* 100 *placements of the lines caused by the orbital motion of the star."* Hartmann stressed the importance of this result by publishing these words in italics in *The Astrophysical Journal*. Hartmann concluded that the calcium vapor responsible for the spectral line must be located somewhere in space between the earth and Orion.

1. (MC) Hartmann concluded that the calcium he had observed was:
    _____(1) on the star Mintaka.
    _____(2) in the earth's atmosphere.
    __Y__(3) in the space between earth and Orion.
    _____(4) in his telescope lens.

Interstellar gas

Since 1904, astronomers have found other ele- 200 ments in space in addition to calcium, and have thereby identified a complex distribution of interstellar gas. With optical and radio telescopes, they have determined the spatial properties of this gas.

The importance of interstellar gas has grown over the years as new concepts of the origin of stars were formulated and it became clear to most scientists that stars are born by condensation from the clouds of the interstellar medium. At the same time it was accepted that much of the material of the stars is recycled back into space through the steady emanation of particles from the outer layers of stars. 300 If the stars are formed from the interstellar gas, however, then their chemical composition should resemble that of the gas. Unfortunately, some of the key elements in the interstellar gas cannot be detected by the conventional techniques of ground-based astronomy. Their identifying spectral lines are in the ultraviolet wave-lengths that are absorbed in the earth's atmosphere and thus cannot reach the observatories below.

It first became possible to attack this problem in recent years when ultraviolet instruments were launched for brief intervals of observation on rockets that attain high altitude in the atmosphere. But the 400 greatest progress has come since August 21, 1972, when NASA launched the *Copernicus* satellite, one of the Orbiting Astronomical Laboratories, carrying a 32-inch ultraviolet telescope. The satellite attained a virtually circular orbit at about 460 miles above the surface of the earth. At that altitude, *Copernicus* is outside the great bulk of our atmosphere and can observe the ultraviolet light from a great many celestial objects. Its onboard telescope was specially equipped by Princeton University astronomers to investigate the interstellar gas.

Among the key results of the *Copernicus'* observations was the discovery that the amounts of at 500 least ten elements are significantly smaller in the interstellar gas than in the stars. The measurements were made relative to hydrogen, known to be the most common substance in the stars and consequently used as a convenient standard of comparison when measuring the trace amounts in which most other elements are present in the universe. The "missing" matter in the interstellar gas includes carbon, nitrogen, oxygen, and iron. Estimates of the underabundance of iron, for example, range anywhere from a factor of 5 to a factor of 100. Where has all the iron gone?

2. (T–F) Interstellar gas is detected by ultraviolet wavelengths.

600 3. (C) The most common substance found in the stars and therefore used for measurement comparisons is _____.

4. (MC) *Copernicus* was:
    __X__(1) an Orbiting Astronomical Laboratory.
    _____(2) a NASA Space Flight.
    _____(3) a Princeton University telescope.
    _____(4) a Mars-bound space ship.

Dust grains

Astrophysicists believe that the missing matter is, in fact, present in the interstellar space but that it exists in a physical condition that does not allow it to absorb light in the spectral lines observed by *Copernicus*. The most obvious idea is that much of the gas has cooled and condensed into a solid state. Indeed, the presence of tiny solid particles in space 700 has been recognized since the 1930s. Although these "interstellar dust grains" do not produce spectral lines, they are responsible for a general diminution of starlight received on the earth—an effect that tends to block out more shorter, blue wavelengths than longer, red wavelengths. The situation is somewhat analogous to the reddening effect a large city's smog layer has on sunlight. This has led astronomers occasionally to refer to the dust grains of space as "interstellar smog."

5. (T–F) Interstellar dust grains produce definite spectral lines.

6. (T–F) Existence of tiny solid particles in space 800 has been known since the 1930s.

7. (T–F) Interstellar smog is caused by the disturbance of space ships and astronaut activities.

Dust balls

According to George B. Field, who directs the Center for Astrophysics in Cambridge, Massachusetts, the iron and other substances that are depleted in the interstellar gas are simply stored in solid form in the dust balls.

Field believes that the respective amounts of missing elements are precisely what you would expect from such a condensation process, and he has designed a model dust grain to account for the observations.

His picture is consistent with radio astronomy observations that have revealed clouds of hydroxyl 900 gas in our galaxy and with other studies made by the Princeton astronomers. Field goes on to compare his interstellar grain model to a microscopic world. "The interior of the grain, like that of the earth, is composed of iron and silicates. Its outer envelope, like the oceans of the earth, is water. The whole is immersed in a gaseous atmosphere, bathed in ultraviolet light and cosmic radiation."

8. (C) The outer element of Field's model is an envelope of _water_

Comets

1000 → Other scientists, however, disagree. They do not believe that all of the missing material can be stored in interstellar grains, and they suggest further the build-up of solid, icy structures much larger than a single microscopic grain. The theoretical dimensions of these icy objects range from those of a baseball to the size of a comet. Objects of this type would not contribute to the interstellar dimming and reddening of starlight in the manner of widely diffused dust, nor would they be observable from the earth by any known method. In fact, even the comets of our own solar system generally are invisible from 1100 → earth except when they come close enough to pass within the orbit of Jupiter.

The obvious objection to these theories is that they predict the existence of things in space which we cannot hope to record or measure, and which can only be checked by additional theoretical calculations. On the other hand, we do find comets in the solar system and they do appear to contain such materials as dust grains, ice balls, and molecules that include hydroxyl and possibly even molecular hydrogen.

Since there are comets in our solar system, presumably they also exist elsewhere in space. The 1200 → question is, "How many comets does each star have?" Are there enough in our galaxy to explain the great amount of missing interstellar matter?

It seems likely that the so-called missing elements are not truly lost, but can be accounted for by one or another version of these theories, or by a combination of them. Certainly some of the unaccounted-for material must be located in dust grains, while some of it may exist in the form of larger objects, including comets. The medium of interstellar space gives rise to the stars, and they, in turn, enrich 1300 → that same medium with their own gaseous and particulate emissions. The life cycle of the galaxy must thus include "gas to gas" in addition to "dust to dust."

9. (T–F) Comets appear to hold ice and dust grains.

10. (T–F) All of the missing material is probably 1350 → scattered around in tiny dust grains.

——STOP——ASK FOR YOUR TIME——

Record time immediately.

Time___ Sec.   RATE (from table on page 315):   R. ____

No. Correct:_____   COMPREHENSION (10% for each correct answer):   C. ____
(key on page 330)

VII–14   EFFICIENCY (R × C):   E. ____

Record on Progress Chart on page 299

Exercise VII–15

Bill of Rights

THOMAS I. EMERSON

(from *Public Affairs Pamphlet*, No. 489)

WAIT FOR SIGNAL TO BEGIN READING

The Bill of Rights embodies the ground rules of our democratic society. It guarantees the citizen basic rights that the government may not infringe, imposes obligations upon the government, and establishes the fundamental principles by which we as a people attempt to live together and govern ourselves. The provisions of the Bill of Rights are set forth in the United States Constitution and it is the special, though by no means the exclusive, responsibility of the courts to see that they are enforced.

The United States Constitution as originally drafted and ratified by the states in 1789 contained only a few provisions that guaranteed the basic rights 100 of the individual. But the citizens of the thirteen states who were called upon to ratify the Constitution forced the leaders in most of the state constitutional conventions to promise that a Bill of Rights would be added. That promise was fulfilled in 1791 when the first ten amendments were approved by the First Congress and quickly ratified by the states. These ten amendments are often referred to as the Bill of Rights. However, all provisions of the Constitution that guarantee individual rights, whether adopted before or after the first ten amendments, are usually 200 thought of as constituting the American Bill of Rights.

Origin for the Bill of Rights

Most of the provisions of the Bill of Rights had their origin in hard-fought struggles for human rights in England and in the colonies. The due process clause derives from the Magna Carta, the prohibition against infliction of "cruel and unusual punishments" from the English Bill of Rights, and the First Amendment protection of freedom of expression from both English and American pre-Revolutionary experience with suppression of political opposition. Other provisions have their roots in later periods of our history. The equal protection clause of the Fourteenth 300 Amendment, for instance, embodies a concept of human equality that grew out of the abolitionist struggle to eliminate slavery and the "badges of servitude" in America.

The growth of legal doctrine relating to the Bill of Rights dates primarily from the 1920s. Not until after World War I did the Supreme Court turn its attention from restricting governmental power over business enterprise to protecting the rights of individual citizens. The greatest expansion in interpretation of the Bill of Rights took place from 1954 to 1968, when Earl Warren was Chief Justice. Since 400 then, under Chief Justice Warren E. Burger, such expansion has slowed considerably.

1. (T–F) The 1789 U.S. Constitution had few provisions to guarantee the basic rights of the individual.
2. (MC) The due process clause is derived from the:
   _____(1) English Bill of Rights.
   _____(2) Pentagon Papers.
   _____(3) Declaration of Independence.
   _____(4) Magna Carta.
3. (T–F) The greatest expansion in interpretation of the Bill of Rights took place from 1850–1900.

The role of the Supreme Court

There has been a great deal of controversy over the approach the Supreme Court should take 500 in interpreting the Bill of Rights. Some people argue for "strict construction," others for "liberal construction." These terms are somewhat misleading. Actually, a "strict construction" of the Bill of Rights, which was designed to *limit* the power of government, could result in an interpretation that would restrict government authority and expand the rights guaranteed to the individual.

The real issue is whether the Supreme Court should construe the constitutional guarantees narrowly, confining them to the specific areas that the framers had in mind in drafting them, or whether it should apply them broadly to meet the problems of contemporary society.

600 The process of constitutional interpretation is not a sterile and legalistic construction of the literal words of the text. Most of the provisions of the Bill of Rights are couched in broad language, intended to express a fundamental principle, and do not contain specific instructions for dealing with a particular problem. But the specific abuse against which the provision was originally directed can be considered

only one manifestation of a wider problem that may change in form but not in essence.

Function of the Bill of Rights

The primary function of the Bill of Rights is to protect "minority members" of society. They may be in such a position because they are poor or power-⁷⁰⁰less, because they hold unorthodox ideas, because they belong to a minority religious, racial, political, or cultural group, or simply because they are opposing whatever "establishment" has power over them. The power structure, by definition, controls the major institutions. Those who wield the power are interested in getting results and tend to override or ignore the abstract rights of individuals who stand in their way. Protection of the minority right has been entrusted, in great part, to the one institution that stands somewhat apart from the battle, manned by persons trained in the application of general prin-⁸⁰⁰ciples, and authorized to act as the conscience of the community.

It must be remembered that the Supreme Court and the courts generally are not the only source of protection for the guarantees of the Bill of Rights. Other institutions, such as our churches and schools, play an important part. A nation beset by many problems and torn by dissension finds it difficult to maintain a healthy Bill of Rights. Nevertheless, courts remain the frontline defense of the Bill of Rights and must carry out that task in a generous, positive, and even aggressive manner. ⁹⁰⁰

4. (C) A _____ construction of the Bill of Rights would restrict government authority and expand individual rights.
5. (T–F) The author feels a real issue is how the people construe the constitutional rights guaranteed to the individual.
6. (T–F) The primary function of the Bill of Rights is to protect minority members of society.
7. (T–F) A troubled nation experiences difficulty in maintaining a healthy Bill of Rights.

Challenge of modern times

Few nations today have an effective Bill of Rights. Protection of the rights of the individual does not seem to be a natural tendency of a man as ¹⁰⁰⁰

a member of an organized society. It requires a conscious and deliberate effort over a long period of time.

The United States has been fortunate. A comprehensive system of individual rights was adopted at its founding and embodied in a written constitution. For a century and a half a natural balance of forces kept the ideas and practices of the system alive and relatively healthy. There were, of course, serious gaps and lapses—as in the case of black citizens or in many a police station; and in such ¹¹⁰⁰times of crisis as the Civil War, the growth of the labor movement, World War I, and the McCarthy era. Despite such lapses, the tradition of individual rights in this country has persisted and grown stronger.

In the last fifty years there has been a remarkable expansion of the legal doctrines that give substances to the Bill of Rights. At the same time, we face a very serious challenge to the existence of that system of individual rights.

Now we have learned that, left in purely negative form, the Bill of Rights is not always capable of achieving its goals: the equal protection clause has ¹²⁰⁰not succeeded in producing equality between the races; justice for the poor is not attainable through hands-off policies; and freedom of expression cannot be realized where the media of communication are controlled by a single economic interest. The system of individual rights today needs affirmative support. This support must come through governmental processes. Thus we are faced with the paradox of using governmental power to aid individuals in realizing their rights while curtailing governmental power when it seeks to restrict those rights.

8. (T–F) Owing to social lapses and gaps, the tradition of individual rights has diminished and grown weaker. ¹³⁰⁰
9. (MC) According to the article, in the last fifty years considerable expansion to the Bill of Rights has stressed:
   _____(1) political freedom.
   _____(2) rights of women.
   _____(3) legal doctrines.
   _____(4) freedom of expression.
10. (C) The system of individual rights today must secure some _____ support. ¹³⁵⁰

——STOP——ASK FOR YOUR TIME——

Record time immediately.

Time____Sec.	RATE (from table on page 315):	R. _____
No. Correct:_____ (key on page 322)	COMPREHENSION (10% for each correct answer):	C. _____
VII–15	EFFICIENCY (R × C):	E. _____

Record on Progress Chart on page 299

Exercise VII–16

Bring Me Men

C. A. STEVENS

(from *Frontier*, Summer 1974)

WAIT FOR SIGNAL TO BEGIN READING

The granite portal

BRING ME MEN TO MATCH MY MOUNTAINS,
BRING ME MEN TO MATCH MY PLAINS,
MEN WITH EMPIRES IN THEIR PURPOSE,
AND NEW ERAS IN THEIR BRAINS.

Those words, written by a poet named Sam Walter Foss, are etched into the granite portal that leads from the cadet parade grounds at the United States Air Force Academy, Colorado.

They also are etched into the hearts of the more than 8,700 young men who have marched by that portal and received their wings as second lieutenants in the Air Force.

The Air Force Academy, newest of the nation's service academies, was established April 1, 1954, by President Dwight D. Eisenhower. The first class entered in July 1955, at temporary facilities at Lowry Air Force Base, in Denver, Colorado. The Cadet Wing moved into the permanent facility north of Colorado Springs in August 1958, and the first class graduated the next June.

The Academy's 18,000-acre site is visited by more than one million tourists each year. All construction and landscaping are of native materials, such as "white Cherokee" marble from Georgia, granite from Minnesota, and trees and shrubbery from the Rocky Mountain area. The Academy is a major Air Force Command, and as a result is self-sufficient. It has its own support functions, including a hospital, housing areas for staff and their families, elementary and high schools (run by the El Paso County School District), chapels, and its own shopping center. Not all of its magnificent facilities came from taxpayer funds, however. The beautiful 50,000-seat Falcon football stadium, built at a cost of $3.5 million, was financed by private donations from Air Force families and interested civilians. The Cadet Farrish Memorial recreation area and the 18-hole Eisenhower Golf Course also were privately funded.

The Air Force Academy graduates young men after four rigorous years, with a Bachelor of Science degree in one or more of the 26 majors offered. Cadets are permitted to compete for scholarships and fellowships after graduation and have received a large number of these honorary awards. The Air Force Academy trails only Harvard, Yale, and Princeton in the number of Rhodes Scholarships awarded to U.S. universities since 1959. Cadets have won 17 of the coveted scholarships in fifteen years.

1. (T–F) Etched in the granite portal at the U.S. Air Force Academy are the words of the poet, Sam Walter Foss.
2. (T–F) Each year more than one million tourists visit the Colorado United States Air Force Academy.
3. (T–F) The Falcon football stadium was furnished from taxpayer funds.
4. (T–F) The Air Force Academy leads Harvard, Yale, Princeton in the number of awarded Rhodes Scholarships.

Purpose of the Air Force Academy

Since the Air Force Academy is a federal military institution, its goal is to graduate motivated Air Force officers with high ideals of duty, honor, and service to country. Its mission is to provide instruction, experience, and motivation to each cadet so that he will graduate with the knowledge, character, and qualities of leadership essential to his professional development as a career Air Force officer. Out of each graduating class, 85 percent of the new second lieutenants volunteer for pilot training, with the remainder going to graduate school or to directed duty assignments. Of the 8,700 graduates to date, more than 7,900 are still on active duty or are in Air Force Reserve assignments.

One of the latter happens to be a member of the *Frontier* family, and the story of Joseph P. Donahue III, a 1963 graduate of the U.S. Air Force Academy, is typical.

After leaving the "Sky Blue U" in 1963, Joe went to pilot training at Reese Air Force Base in Lubbock, Texas, and received his Air Force wings thirteen months later.

"There wasn't a tremendous need for fighter pilots when my class graduated," says Joe, "so most of us were assigned to large multi-engined aircraft. In my case, 'large' turned out to be the 500,000-pound, eight engined B-52 Stratofortress bomber!"

Pacific commander

Three years and 1,000 hours of flying time later, Joe was assigned to Pacific Air Force as an aircraft commander in the four-engined C-130 Hercules Troop and Cargo aircraft. The next two and a half years were to be the most exciting in his life, both from the viewpoint of "seeing the world" and because the 1968 and 1970 era was the most action-packed period of the Viet Nam conflict. In those 31 months, Joe flew 542 individual combat missions over the entire Southeast Asia area of conflict. He was shot down by hostile ground fire while trying to evacuate a beleaguered Army Special Forces group at Kham Duc, South Viet Nam, on May 12, 1968.

More than 5,000 North Vietnamese "Regulars" were estimated to be in the area, pouring rockets and mortar rounds into the camp.

"All we wanted to do was to get our men out," Joe recalled.

Unfortunately his aircraft was hit so heavily and rapidly by ground fire as they started their final approach, Joe had to shut down all four burning engines and crash-land with complete loss of engine power. A Marine Corps chopper responded by setting down amid a burning ammo dump to lift them out.

5. (C) _____ percent of the new second lieutenants volunteer for pilot training from each graduating class.

6. (MC) Immediately after graduation, Joe was assigned to the large multi-engined aircraft:
 _____(1) Convair 580.
 _____(2) B-52 Stratofortress.
 _____(3) C-130 Hercules.
 _____(4) Boeing 737.

7. (T–F) As an aircraft commander, Joe was assigned to the Atlantic Air Force.

Special awards

Joe was awarded the Distinguished Flying Cross for this voluntary attempt to rescue American troops, and later earned two Oak Leaf Clusters for subsequent combat actions at Song Be and Khe Sanh. He also was awarded the Air Medal with numerous clusters and the Viet Nam Service Medal with three stars.

Joe continued to further his education and earned a master's degree in Systems Management from the University of Southern California at Los Angeles.

After leaving active duty in 1970, he became Regional Director for the State of New Mexico in the Federal Law Enforcement Assistance Administration Program, aimed at helping all levels of the state's criminal justice system. He held that position for about a year and a half before being accepted by Frontier Airlines as a probationary pilot. Joe finished his 12-month probationary period successfully and was trained and qualified as both a first officer in the Convair 580 and as a second officer in the Boeing 737.

When Joe entered the Air Force Academy in 1959, he claimed Norristown, Pennsylvania, as his home. He now lives with his wife, Ann, a Colorado Women's College graduate, and three little daughters in Albuquerque, New Mexico. He commutes to Denver to fly his trips for Frontier, necessitating his being away from home about two-thirds of the time.

As a reserve officer in the U.S. Air Force, Joe's duties fittingly are those of an Air Force Academy Admissions Counselor, or "Liaison Officer." As the Deputy Commander for the State of New Mexico and West Texas, his work involves counseling young men of high school age so they are better prepared when they apply for admission to the Air Force Academy.

Does he still believe in the Academy's goals, methods and the demands it places on each cadet? In Joe's words:

"The Air Force Academy was the greatest experience I've ever had. It's been criticized occasionally, much to my chagrin, for being too *high and lofty* in its honor code, ideals and training goals. My feeling, however, is that only when honor, patriotism, and personal integrity become obsolete, will the high ideals of the U.S. Air Force Academy become obsolete."

8. (MC) Joe earned a master's degree in:
 _____(1) Law Enforcement.
 _____(2) Administration.
 _____(3) Credit Management.
 _____(4) Systems Management.

9. (C) Air Force Academy Admissions Counselor is the same as "_____ Officer."

10. (T–F) Joe still believes in the Academy's methods, and the demands it places on each cadet.

——STOP——ASK FOR YOUR TIME——

Record time immediately.

Time_____Sec.   RATE (from table on page 315):   R. _____

No. Correct:_____   COMPREHENSION (10% for each correct answer):   C. _____
(key on page 330)

VII–16   EFFICIENCY (R × C):   E. _____

Record on Progress Chart on page 299

Exercise VII–17

How to Produce an Idea

HELEN ROWAN

(from *Think*, copyright 1962)

WAIT FOR SIGNAL TO BEGIN READING

Degrees of creativity

The six-year-old child who succeeds in repairing his broken tricycle bell has a creative experience, New York University psychologist Morris I. Stein is fond of pointing out, but no one would claim that the repaired bell constitutes a "creative product" in the generally accepted meaning of the term.

It is possible, in other words, to differentiate roughly between individual creativity and social creativity. If you have an idea, it may be creative in comparison to all the other ideas you have ever had, which certainly represents individual creativity, or it may be creative in comparison to all the ideas *every-* 100 *one* has ever had; this represents social creativity of the highest order.

In short, the basic difference may be one of *degree* rather than kind. The highly creative person may be so because of the kind of problem he sets for himself and the quality of his response to it, but his creative process is not necessarily very different from what everyone goes through, or at least can go through.

It is necessary to bear this in mind because of the aura of mystery which has surrounded the creative process—a mystery which has been augmented rather than dissipated by the numerous accounts left 200 by the geniuses of history. Almost to a man—ancient or modern, writers, artists, musicians, scientists—they have gladly committed to paper accounts of how they did what they did and how they felt while they were doing it. The trouble with this kind of evidence, fascinating as it is, is that it is impressionistic, imprecise, and incomplete. Furthermore, one aspect has tended to overshadow all others in the public mind; this has to do with the role of "inspiration" in the creative process.

It is true that most highly creative individuals, 300 even those as different in temperament and field as Samuel Coleridge and Bertrand Russell, do report flashes of insight, of sudden "knowing," but when these bursts of inspiration are seen in the context of the entire process of which they are a part, they take on different significance.

1. (C) The basic difference between social and individual creativity may be one of _____ rather than of kind.

2. (T–F) The child who successfully repairs a broken tricycle bell has produced a "creative product" in the generally accepted meaning of the term.

The four stages

400 To most people who have studied the problem, it seems apparent that the creative process occurs in four (or five, as some would have it) stages, while others say that what knowledge we have of the various stages is of little help because it is sheerly descriptive.

But for whatever it is worth, many participants and observers have described the stages of the creative experience in the following terms:

Preparation.
Incubation.
Illumination.
Verification.

Some break the preparatory stage into two parts, saying that in a sense one's entire life—the 500 gaining of experience, education, the mastery of a medium, whether it be pigments or words or mathematical symbols—is preparation for the act of creating. Then next (or first) comes the stage of intensive preparation: The individual works, consciously and hard, on whatever problem he is trying to solve. This preparation involves enormous effort and eventually, in many cases, great frustration, with accompanying tension and anxiety.

3. (MC) The four stages of the creative process as described by many participants and observers are:

_____(1) preparation, incubation, illumination, variation.

_____(2) preparation, incubation, illumination, verification.

_____(3) preparation, experimentation, incubation, verification.

_____(4) preparation, incubation, experimentation, variation.

600 4. (T–F) Some people say that the preparatory stage may be divided into two parts, claiming that one's lifetime experiences, which are preparation for the act of creating, prelude the stage of intensive preparation.

The creator withdraws

Then the creator often withdraws from the problem, perhaps for a very short time, perhaps for a long period. There is no certain knowledge of what occurs during this period, but some psychologists believe that the subconscious is at work. Some believe that the period of incubation frees the individual of previous fixations, and that he is then able to see the problem with new eyes when he returns to it, while others would add to this hypothesis the $\overset{700}{\leftarrow}$ idea that during the withdrawal period the creator is receiving helpful cues from his environment and experience.

Whatever it is that happens, next comes the moment everyone yearns for: the burst of insight, an experience of the "Aha" or "Eureka!" type that we all have had in some degree. But when considered in the light of all that has gone before, it loses some of its mystery. Remember that the individual has already established an outside criterion against which he may check his idea or insight; he has been desperately looking for something; he sees it, recognizes it, $\overset{800}{\leftarrow}$ and cries, "Eureka!" (To give a homely example that has nothing to do with creativity, set yourself the task of finding a red-headed man who is speaking German and wearing green socks, and when you see him, you, too, will have an "Aha" experience.)

Following the illumination comes the period of verification or completion, in which time the individual applies all his skills and craft and intelligence to make solid the original insight and finish the creation.

A distinctive characteristic of highly creative individuals seems to be their ability to maintain an exceedingly delicate balance between the most in- $\overset{900}{\leftarrow}$ tense effort, on the one hand, and suspension of conscious effort on the other. Even though few would go as far as Edison did in saying that genius is only one percent inspiration, the other 99 percent being perspiration, all genuinely creative people do show that "transcendent capacity for taking trouble" that Carlyle said made genius. But other kinds of traits seem to be just as essential to their creativity. Many observers have mentioned the attitude of playfulness highly creative individuals reveal—the ability to get both enjoyment and amusement from juggling ideas or paints or words or whatever. They also show a $\overset{1000}{\leftarrow}$ certain kind of restraint: They are not driven to pursue their purposes implacably and directly at all times, nor to force a solution arbitrarily, but they seem to trust themselves to recognize *the* right solution when it emerges, and have enough confidence to wait for it.

5. (T–F) The period of withdrawal from the problem that a creator often experiences is referred to as the incubation stage.

6. (C) The stage of the creative process in which the creator experiences a burst of insight and recognizes his goal is $\overset{1100}{\rightarrow}$ called the stage of _____.

7. (MC) The stage of verification is the period of time in which the creative individual:

   _____(1) withdraws from the problem to gain a more objective view.

   _____(2) establishes some outside criterion by which to obtain insight.

   _____(3) recognizes the ultimate creation he has desperately been seeking.

   _____(4) applies his skills, craft, and intelligence to stabilize the original insight.

8. (T–F) A distinctive characteristic of highly creative individuals seems to be their inability to maintain a balance between the most intense effort and the suspension of conscious effort.

$\overset{1200}{\rightarrow}$ 9. (T–F) Creative individuals are driven to pursue their purposes implacably and directly at all times, showing little or no restraint.

No how-to-do-it books

The "how-to-do-it handbook of creativity" has never been written and probably never could—or should be. Nevertheless, it seems possible that all of us might increase somewhat the degree of creativity we show in our daily lives by making deliberate attempts to develop the kinds of attitudes, habits, and modes of operation that mark highly creative individuals. There is pretty general agreement that conscious effort alone cannot produce a creative achievement, but conscious effort may put us in a $\overset{1300}{\rightarrow}$ position where creative achievement is more likely.

10. (T–F) The author feels that all might increase the degree of creativity shown in their daily lives by attempting to develop the kinds of attitudes, habits, and modes $\overset{1350}{\rightarrow}$ of operation that are characteristic of highly creative individuals.

———STOP——ASK FOR YOUR TIME———

Record time immediately.

Time_____Sec.	RATE (from table on page 315):	R. _____
No. Correct:_____	COMPREHENSION (10% for each correct answer):	C. _____
(key on page 322)		
VII–17	EFFICIENCY (R × C):	E. _____

Record on Progress Chart on page 299

Exercise VII–18

The Myth of the Sacred Cow

MARVIN HARRIS

(from *Natural History*, March 1967)

WAIT FOR SIGNAL TO BEGIN READING

Among the popular myths of cultural anarchy, none is more widely accepted than that of the Indian sacred cow. Protected by Hindu taboo from being slaughtered and eaten, these supposedly useless animals wander about at will, impeding traffic and, it is reported, damaging crops. Indeed, in some parts of India, aged cattle are even housed in *gosadans*—bovine old-age homes.

But the myth of the sacred cow is part of a widespread overemphasis on the mismanagement of food production by primitive and peasant peoples. One often hears, especially in these times of vast aid programs for the underdeveloped countries of the world, that irrational ideologies and customs prevent 100 the effective use of available food resources.

In the case of the sacred cow, it must be admitted that the Indian dairy industry is among the least efficient in the world. In India, the average annual yield of whole milk per cow has been reported at 413 pounds, as compared with an average of over 5,000 pounds in Europe and the United States. Furthermore, of the 79.4 million cows maintained in 1961, only 20.1 million were milk producers. Among the 47.2 million cows over three years old, 27.2 million were dry and/or not calved. 200 If we go on to accept the proposition that India can make no profit from the negligible slaughter of its enormous cattle supply, we have completed the case for the great cattle bungle. Hence the conclusion of a recent Ford Foundation report on India's food problem:

"There is widespread recognition, not only among animal husbandry officials, but among citizens generally, that India's cattle population is far in excess of the available supplies of fodder and feed. . . . At least one third, and possibly as many as one half, of the Indian cattle population may be regarded as surplus in relation to feed supply." 300

This view is endorsed by government agronomists, and the Indian Ministry of Information insists that "the large animal population is more a liability than an asset in view of our limited land resource." Because of the perpetual food shortage for humans in India, refusal to slaughter cattle seems to prove that the mysterious has triumphed over the practical. Some would even have us believe that in order to preserve his cow the individual farmer is prepared to sacrifice his own life.

1. (C) The Indian _____ industry is one of the least efficient in the world.

2. (MC) In some parts of India aged cattle are 400 housed in "gosadans," meaning:
   _____(1) spacious corrals.
   _____(2) residences of the lower caste Indian.
   _____(3) bovine old-age homes.
   _____(4) neatly kept stables.

3. (T–F) In India the average annual yield of whole milk per cow is approximately 4,000 pounds.

4. (T–F) Cattle population in India far exceeds the food available for cattle.

A better understanding of the cow complex in India involves the answers to the following two questions: (1) Is it true that the rate of reproduction 500 and survival of the Indian population is lowered as a result of the competition between man and cattle for scarce resources? (2) Would the removal of the Hindu taboo on slaughter substantially modify the ecology of Indian food production?

Tractors not a realistic alternative!

The answer to the first question is that the relation between man and cattle—both cows and bullocks—is not competitive, but symbiotic. The most obvious part of this symbiosis is the role played by male cattle in cultivation. Indian farming is based on plow agriculture, to which cattle contribute up to 46 percent of the labor cost, exclusive of transport 600 and other activities.

Despite the existence of 96.3 million bullocks, of which 68.6 million are working animals, India suffers from a shortage of such animals. It is generally agreed that a pair of bullocks is the minimum unit for cultivation. But a conservatively estimated 60 million rural households dispose of only 80 million working cattle and buffaloes. This would mean that as many as two-thirds of India's farmers may be short of the technical minimum. Moreover, under existing property relations the bullocks cannot be shared among several households without further lowering the productivity of marginal farms. B. Desai, an Indian economist, explains why: ". . . over vast ⁷⁰⁰← areas, sowing and harvesting operations, by the very nature of things, begin simultaneously with the outbreak of the first showers and the maturing of crops respectively and especially the former has got to be put through quickly during the first phase of the monsoon. Under these circumstances, reliance by one farmer on another for bullocks is highly risky and he has got, therefore, to maintain his own pair."

We see then, that the draft animals, which appear to be superfluous from the point of view of what would be needed in a perfectly engineered society, turn out to be considerably less than suffi- ⁸⁰⁰← cient in the actual context of Indian agriculture.

No cows, no bullocks

Although the need for bullocks establishes the need for cows, it does not establish the need for 80 million of them. We are, however, coming closer to the answer, because we now know that to the value of the milk and milk products produced by the cows, we must add the value of the 69 million male traction animals also produced.

Among the other immediate and important contributions of the cow is the dung. In addition to the relatively minor value of dung as plaster in house ⁹⁰⁰← construction, this material is India's main cooking fuel because coal and oil are, of course, prohibitively expensive for the peasant family. India's grain crops cannot be metabolized by human beings without cooking. Thus, dung alone provides the needed energy, and cattle provide the dung on a lavish scale. Of the 800 million tons annually bequeathed the Indian countryside, the 300 million consumed in cookery amounts to the BTU equivalent of 35 million tons of coal or 68 million tons of wood, an impressive amount of BTU's to be plugged into an energy system.

Of the remaining 500 million tons of dung, the ¹⁰⁰⁰← largest part is used for manuring. It has been claimed that 160 million tons of this manure is "wasted on hillsides and roads," but it must be noted that some of this probably re-enters the ecological system, since as we shall see in a moment, the cattle depend upon hillsides and roads for much of their sustenance.

5. (T–F) The relationship between man and cattle is competitive.

6. (T–F) Bullocks are essential to the plow agriculture of the Indian farmers.

7. (C) The _____ of the
¹¹⁰⁰→ cow is India's main cooking fuel.

8. (T–F) A large part of the manure is used for fertilizer.

To the contribution of the cow as a producer of milk, we must add the production of meat, bullocks, manure, fuel, and hides.

In answer to the second question under consideration, it would thus seem that the basic ecology of Indian cattle production is not a mere reflex of the Hindu taboo on slaughter. The rate at which cattle are presently slaughtered in India is governed by the ability of the peasantry to slaughter them without impairing the production of traction animals, ¹²⁰⁰→ fuel, fertilizer, and milk. The least efficient way to convert solar energy into comestibles is to impose an animal converter between plant and man. The beef supply is now seen as one of the functions of the cattle complex, but this must necessarily remain a marginal or tertiary attribute of the ecosystem. As a matter of fact, it is obvious that any large-scale drift toward animal slaughter before the traction, fuel, and manure needs of the productive cycle were met would immediately jeopardize the lives of tens of millions of Indians.

¹³⁰⁰→ 9. (T–F) The supply of beef is now considered a major function of the cattle complex.

10. (MC) To slaughter cattle now would seriously impair the:

_____(1) religious concepts of the Indian.

_____(2) production of traction animals, fuel, milk, and fertilizer.

_____(3) Hindu doctrine of the sanctity of the cow.

¹³⁵⁰→ _____(4) Hindu expression of "ahisa," the sanctity of life.

——STOP——ASK FOR YOUR TIME——

Record time immediately.

Time_____Sec.   RATE (from table on page 315):   R. _____

No. Correct:_____   COMPREHENSION (10% for each correct answer):   C. _____
(key on page 330)

VII–18   EFFICIENCY (R × C):   E. _____

Record on Progress Chart on page 299

Will You Need a License?

(from *Occupational Outlook Quarterly*, May 1963)

WAIT FOR SIGNAL TO BEGIN READING

More than a hundred nonprofessional occupations are currently licensed by one or more states and a few others by the federal government. The trend is toward regulation of entry into more and more skilled and semiskilled jobs. Counselors, therefore, would do well to alert students to the license requirements of many occupations as well as the education and training needed. Licensing information for nonprofessional occupations is seldom available from a single authority and is difficult to gather. In order to provide counselors and teachers with some help in this field, the *Quarterly* presents the following article.

Questioned as to what kinds of jobs require a 100 license, most of us could readily count several professions. "Physicians," we might say, "and pharmacists, teachers, and certified public accountants." But what about skilled and semiskilled workers?

The Council of State Governments reported in *Occupational Licensing in the States* that nearly 75 occupations—both professional and nonprofessional—were licensed in one or more states. This was in 1952. Today the number has jumped to more than 100 for nonprofessional occupations alone. Job titles range from aerial prospecting to wild animal collector, and include beauticians, electrologists, guide-dog trainers, opticians, photographers, plumbers, and private detectives.

Purpose of licensing   200

A license has been defined as "authority to do some act or carry on some trade or business, in its nature lawful but prohibited by statute except with permission of the civil authority."

Occupational licenses are issued to safeguard the life, health, safety, welfare, and property of the citizen. These licenses permit only qualified members of an occupation to carry on their work. Regulation by license helps to shield the public from the incompetent worker or from fraud. At the same time, craftsmen are progressively challenged to meet the rising standards set by the governmental licensing bodies.

Growth of licensing

By the late 1800's, specialization of professions 300 and occupations was becoming the order of the day in the United States. This specialization, along with the increasing interdependence of all segments of society, made some occupational regulation a necessity.

Doctors and lawyers were among the first professional groups licensed. The quack doctor with his Indian herbs and the ill-qualified frontier lawyer were early targets for public disapproval. A demand sprang up for limiting entrance into these professions to well-qualified persons. The nonprofessional, too, was beginning to come under the critical eye of the public. "Handyman" plumbers were causing property damage 400 age through bungling assemblage of the new plumbing equipment just coming on the market. Measures to protect the public seemed necessary. Tragic mine cave-ins and explosions made clear that men of experience should inspect mining operations. Assurance that barbers would adhere to certain sanitary standards was greatly needed. In all these cases, some sort of government regulation seemed the answer. First entries in the list of licenses for nonprofessional workers were made in the 1880's and 1890's. That list is still growing. The fact that at least one state now considers licensing automobile mechanics is just 500 one example of the continuing interest in establishing skill and educational criteria for occupations affecting public safety and welfare.

Public demand has not been the only pressure behind the tide of license growth. Members of occupational groups, through their formal associations, have often been instrumental in getting licensure bills through their state legislatures.

These organizations, one after another, have worked to secure legislation which would establish educational and experience qualifications and would require the worker to pass an examination to qualify for a permit to enter an occupation. Although self-interest enters into this pressure—for the licensed worker does obtain a competitive advantage—the 600 public also benefits substantially by licensing.

1. (T–F) Occupational licenses are issued to safeguard life, health, safety, wealth, and property of the citizen.
2. (MC) Among the first professional groups licensed were:
   _____(1) nurses and judges.
   _____(2) lawyers and pharmacists.
   _____(3) doctors and lawyers.
   _____(4) nurses and plumbers.
3. (T–F) Public demand is the sole pressure behind the tide of license growth.

In most states, the licensing and regulation of the various occupations are under the supervision of boards of examiners or commissions. These agencies are small and independent, as a general rule. Their members—usually Governor-appointed—are, in most cases, members of the occupation regulated by the 700 ← board.

The functions of the boards are two-fold:
1. To control entrance into the occupations.
2. To support and enforce the work standards in the occupations.

This function is often accomplished through cooperation with trade associations. Since the members of the boards are members of the occupations their boards deal with, they are apt to be particularly responsive to the needs and desires of the licensed group. The licensing agencies sometimes cooperate with vocational schools in setting up educational standards and seeing that examinations match educational training.

In most states, the licensing agencies have the 800 ← following duties:

1. To examine credentials of applicants and determine whether their education and experience meet the requirements.
2. To investigate schools to determine whether they maintain standards which make them acceptable as training institutions for the occupation in question, and to draw up lists of approved schools.
3. To prepare the examinations used to judge the academic and practical qualifications of prospective licensees.
4. To grant licenses.
5. To issue regulations establishing approved standards of practice, to investigate charges of violations, and to conduct hearings. Where violations are proved, licenses may be suspended or revoked by the agency. 900 ←

4. (C) The licensing and regulation of the various occupations are under the supervision of the board of _____ or commissions.

5. (T–F) Supporting and enforcing work standards in the occupations is often accomplished through cooperation with trade associations.

6. (T–F) The members of the boards cannot be members of the occupation that their board deals with.

7. (MC) In most states the licensing agencies have five general duties. Which of the following is *NOT* one of the five?
_____(1) To examine credentials of applicants and determine whether their education and experience meet the require- 1000 ← ments.
_____(2) To investigate schools to see if proper textbooks are provided.

_____(3) To grant licenses.
_____(4) To prepare the examinations used to judge the academic and practical qualifications of prospective licensees.

Licensing and geography

The licensed occupations reflect the geography and history of our Nation. Where but in Wyoming would an airplane pilot need to register to engage in such occupations as horsehunting and prospecting? Rainmakers (or weather modifiers) are licensed chiefly in the western states, where weather is friend or foe of the rancher and forester. The fishing and 1100 → hunting guide must have a permit in a number of states where wildlife is plentiful. The harbor pilot is registered in the states along the seaboards and the Great Lakes. Maine, where sailors from the seven seas come ashore, licenses tattooers. And the mecca for American sightseers—Washington, D.C.—licenses tourist guides.

Licensed in all or nearly all states are practical nurses, barbers, beauticians, and embalmers. Some of the unique licenses that turn up are required in only one state (not all in the same state, of course). They are: cotton classer, transporter of horses, thresher, tattooer, and textbook salesman.

1200 → Many cities, towns, and counties have their own licensing provisions. Sometimes licensing authority is delegated by a state to municipalities. The booklet, *Licenses Required for Workers by the State of New York,* gives this information: "Towns or villages may regulate by license, specific occupations or occupational pursuits. Cities derive the majority of their licensing powers from their particular charters. The particular government unit should be consulted." Municipalities often require licenses for welders, electricians, plumbers, stationary engineers, bus drivers, taxi drivers, and similar occupations.

Besides state and municipal licenses, others are issued by federal agencies such as the Federal Aviation Agency, the Federal Communications Com- 1300 → mission, and the Atomic Energy Commission.

8. (C) Specific licensing requirements in many states reflect the unique _____ _____ or historical background of the locality.

9. (T–F) Maine, where sailors from the seven seas come ashore, licenses tattooers.

10. (T–F) Towns cannot regulate by license specific occupations or occupational pur- 1000 ← 1350 → suits.

——STOP——ASK FOR YOUR TIME——

Record time immediately.

Time_____Sec. RATE (from table on page 315): R. _____

No. Correct:_____ (key on page 322) COMPREHENSION (10% for each correct answer): C. _____

VII–19 EFFICIENCY (R × C): E. _____

Exercise VII–20

Wilderness

STEWART L. UDALL

(from *The Living Wilderness*, Spring–Summer 1962)

WAIT FOR SIGNAL TO BEGIN READING

Out of the wilderness—Mother of Resources—has come the raw material with which Americans have fashioned a great civilization. Our forbears molded the wilds: Trees became boards, prairies became pastures, iron became steel, and with such developments came the highest material standard of living yet known. Our ancestors were molded by the virgin continent in return—rugged, self-reliant, independent.

At first the effect of America on her new masters was less apparent than theirs on the land, but slowly Americans have come to realize that the wilderness has been an influence upon the national character, as well as a reservoir of abundance, and 100← is responsible for both the high spiritual and the material quality of American life.

The inspirational values of the American wilderness have moved an impressive roster of men to become advocates of wilderness preservation: Henry David Thoreau, Daniel Boone, John James Audubon, Jim Bridger, Theodore Roosevelt, and many others.

But not until the current decade did public concern about wilderness reach a crescendo.

We can no longer trust to the accidents of history to preserve for our enjoyment those few acres that have so far escaped exploitation. Inaccessibility will not be protection in the face of an increasingly 200← efficient technology.

Today the public has abundant leisure time, and more crowded living conditions than ever before in American history. People look increasingly to wilderness areas for recreation, for the renewal of routine-wearied bodies and jaded minds that have been deprived of once-familiar refreshing primeval influences.

Our society needs a benchmark, a check of natural conditions against which to measure the soundness of its values.

Wilderness preservation is the first element in a sound national conservation policy.

Preservation of wilderness is a tribute to "America the Beautiful," a demonstration of faith in her future and an ability to learn from her past. It 300→ demonstrates to the world that the United States is an inspired democracy, not exploiting every material resource in every cranny of the land, but wisely living on a sustained interest, not capital.

1. (T–F) Public concern about wilderness preservation has reached a crescendo in recent years.
2. (T–F) The first element in a sound national conservation policy is wilderness preservation.

Opportunity

The American wilderness heritage exists in some state and private areas but for the most part is in our federal jurisdiction. Wilderness areas occur in the National Park System, in wildlife refuges and 400→ ranges, and in parts of the national forests that are classified as wilderness, wild, primitive, or canoe areas. The uses of wilderness in all these classifications are compatible with, and essential to, the management objectives of the areas involved. . . .

Because of the rapid expansion of our society, our entire national land estate is facing competing, sometimes harmonious, sometimes conflicting, demands for usage of areas. The Constitution assigns to the Congress responsibility for public lands. Thus land administrators of the federal government have recommended to Congress legislation which emphasizes the proper responsibility of Congress to decide 500→ what areas may be preserved as wilderness for the American public. . . .

National status for wilderness lands in a National Wilderness Preservation System now can be achieved without having to acquire lands, without transferring areas from one jurisdiction to another, without establishing a new agency of government, or disrupting commercial or recreational enterprises. The option may not last long, if unused. It can be readily realized now, and at almost no cost in dollars and cents, or significant sacrifice.

3. (T–F) Most of the wilderness areas are restricted to state and local jurisdiction.
4. (MC) The Constitution assigns the responsi- 600→ bility for public lands to:
   _____(1) Congress.
   _____(2) the president.
   _____(3) state officials.
   _____(4) local authorities.

Requirements

The concept of wilderness that has been cherished by Americans is the idea of lands where man and his works do not dominate the landscape, where the earth and its whole community of life are untrammeled by man, where man himself is a visitor who does not remain.

Wilderness, therefore, is that condition of nature which affords man the ultimate opportunity for solitude and the kind of recreation that is primitive and unconfined. Any area of wilderness must be large enough to make practicable its preservation and use $\overset{700}{\leftarrow}$ in an unimpaired condition.

The United States Forest Service administers 29 "wild areas," and 14 "wilderness areas," in which primitive conditions are maintained. Designation of these areas has been based upon careful review of the multiple purposes of national forest lands. The Forest Service also administers 39 "primitive areas" which are under study to determine which portions are suitable for permanent designation, and which portions are not predominantly of wilderness value.

The National Park Service administers 48 units that contain wilderness suitable for preservation in a national program. Within the next ten years, the Park Service will need to take inventory of these units and $\overset{800}{\leftarrow}$ advise the Nation as to which parts of each unit should be developed for intensive visitor access, and which parts of the back country should be retained in wilderness condition.

Expansion of our society has made these appraisals of the national wilderness estate mandatory. At the same time a national wilderness program must continue to be sufficiently flexible to permit continued livestock grazing and the use of aircraft and motorboats where these are already well-established, as well as management provisions for dealing with fire, blight, and other emergencies. Commercial enter- $\overset{900}{\leftarrow}$ prises, roads, motorized equipment, and installations that would impair a wilderness environment should be precluded.

Requirements for national wilderness protection include definition of wilderness conditions and boundaries, and at the same time recognition of emergency or resource scarcity conditions which might make non-conforming uses of wilderness areas essential to the overriding national interest.

5. (C) Wilderness is that condition of nature which affords man the opportunity for _____ and recreation that is primitive and unconfined.

6. (T–F) The designation of lands as "wild," "wilderness," or "primitive" areas has been based on review of the multiple purposes of the lands.

7. (MC) Which of the following is *not* included $\overset{1000}{\leftarrow}$ as a requirement for national wilderness protection?

_____ (1) Definition of boundaries.
_____ (2) Recognition of emergency conditions.
_____ (3) Recognition of resource scarcity.
_____ (4) Realization of a national profit.

Prospect

The public has demanded assurance that the wilderness remnant will be protected for the recreation and re-creation of the American people.

A national program for wilderness preservation involves a great and enduring benefit at remarkably small cost. It calls for no new administrative agency, no transfer of jurisdiction over any public lands, no $\overset{1100}{\rightarrow}$ new lands, no new funds. It eliminates no established commercial or recreational uses.

A national wilderness program provides for specific study and appraisal of lands now managed as wilderness to determine their eligibility for a Wilderness System. It requires special specific action by Congress to extend Wilderness System protection to any new areas.

The National Wilderness Preservation System which is part of a national program provides protection as wilderness for some 2% of the United States, about an eighth of an acre per citizen by the year 2000. Future generations through this program will be assured the opportunity to experience the primeval which has contributed so much vigor to American character. Youth will be assured the opportunity to $\overset{1200}{\rightarrow}$ gain from the primeval the initiative, self-reliance, confidence, stamina which their forbears needed to accomplish their tasks—attributes which are needed equally today to perpetuate their achievements.

America has yet to prove that she is willing to balance material abundance with spiritual benefits. Our people deserve both. Through preservation of wilderness, there is within our grasp a lasting testament to the maturity of our society and a lasting legacy for the well-being of our people.

$\overset{1300}{\rightarrow}$ 8. (T–F) A disadvantage of a national program for wilderness preservation is that the great and enduring benefits are realized only at remarkably high cost.

9. (C) The National Wilderness Preservation system provides protection as wilderness equaling _____ acre per citizen by the year 2000.

10. (T–F) America has proved repeatedly that she is willing to balance material abundance with spiritual benefits.

$\overset{1350}{\rightarrow}$

——STOP——ASK FOR YOUR TIME——
Record time immediately.

Time_____Sec.

No. Correct:_____
(key on page 330)

VII–20

RATE (from table on page 315):

COMPREHENSION (10% for each correct answer):

EFFICIENCY (R × C):

R. _____

C. _____

E. _____

SERIES VIII
Critical Thinking Exercises

Purpose

Merely scanning for main ideas or more intensive reading for facts will not develop the critical reading skills demanded in so many situations in adult life today. In addition to the development of assimilation and retention skills, certain basic abilities of critical reading must be developed. You must be able to grasp literal and implied meanings and to relate to them by generalization. You must form evaluative reactions to what you read as you inquire about quality and accuracy of material. You must learn to judge rationally what you read. You must develop insight and understanding in applying the ideas you acquire from reading.

A whole book could be developed around the concept of critical reading skills. To some degree you began to apply them in your Study Reading Exercises. Although critical reading skills involve a different approach to reading that does not result in a measure of efficiency, you should recognize this type of reading as a part of your pattern of flexibility. Therefore, this book has been expanded to include some brief introductory exercises of this type.

Instructions

In this series, rate of reading is not considered as being of primary importance. You may read these little samples as fast or slow as you please, but you must take time to *think* about them carefully, either during or after the reading process—or both. The articles are all short excerpts presented with only a number and no identification of source. Each one is followed by a few questions to focus your thinking. Try to draw from the content clues that will help you to make judgments. Consider also the rest of the critical reading questions presented here:

1. What is the author's purpose?
2. When was this written?
3. To whom is this appeal directed?
4. What do you question in this material?
5. What key words were used to influence your emotions?
6. In what ways does the writer reveal a bias?
7. Who would have you believe this?
8. To which of your basic needs does the writer appeal?

After you have answered as many questions as you can, turn to the "KEY" materials on pages 323 and 331. There you will find an identification of the source of the material and a few comments about the purpose of the presentation. Judge for yourself the accuracy of your responses.

Suggestions

The process of critical thinking in relation to reading is a never ending life process. One is deluged with communications of all kinds, many of which are loaded with emotional appeal and propaganda techniques. Series VI–12 in this workbook includes an analysis of several basic propaganda techniques and may be worth rereading in connection with these exercises.

The exercises in this book are only a token of the continuing work that you must do to be a critical reader. The ultimate dimension of effective reading is the skill of *reading critically*. Can you differentiate fact from opinion? Can you evaluate the validity of opinion? Can you detect unsound reasoning and propaganda techniques? Can you keep these points in mind, even when you are functioning at some of your higher levels of reading efficiency?

You need to develop the ability to comprehend ideas that authors do not state specifically, but that they expect you to infer. You need to develop skill in extending your thinking about ideas to such concepts as making generalizations, perceiving relationships, predicting outcomes, and anticipating authors' purposes. You need to make judgments about authors and their ideas. They can try to influence you, but *you* have the final word. You can choose to reject an author and his ideas, and he has no recourse. Good readers try to develop skill in identifying and understanding the ideas they encounter in reading, but ultimate acceptance and application of these ideas depend upon many personal factors that have nothing to do with the reading process itself.

You can be a good reader if you seek to make a personal application of the skills you have learned and if you maintain an alert inquiring mind. But you will not be reading in the deliberate concept of reading that sets 800 words per minute as a maximum. Neither will you be a good reader because you whiz through all materials at some fantastic rate of speed reading. You can develop a flexibility that enables you to judge and to adjust your reading skills to the needs and purposes of the moment.

You will discover that reading makes a great difference in your life. As you seek the ideas behind the words, you will find that flexible and polished reading skills are keys to a vast reservoir of knowledge and stimulation. Only you can determine your ultimate potential in using reading as a tool for personal development.

Even the "great books" are not gods: they are only tools for you to use. They may even be dull tools if you approach them with less than the sharpest of your wits. Authors are often dry and boring to some readers. They do not have the advantage of observing your reaction—responding to your enthusiasm—clarifying, when you look confused. They must go on monotonously with their one-sided monologue in total ignorance of *your* enthusiasm or boredom. If you remember this, you may be more tolerant and more effective in applying your skills to get the most from their work.

But what you need is not patience, but really an impatience with yourself that forces you to decide what you are reading *for* and then to read *for it!* You need to be impatient enough to center the energy for effective reading in your own head. True concentration in reading is not the effort to "keep other thoughts out"; it is a by-product of having a goal challenging enough to attract the whole mind to the task of seeking it.

If knowledge is your goal, then you can attain it only when you think for yourself, not when you have merely understood what someone else thought. Knowledge is not something you learn or absorb: it is something you think and use and bring to life in your own ideas.

In short, you will become a part of the reading you do. You will be able to read and to know what it is all about and how it bears on other things you have read or done. You will read in a way that makes you think, and finally produce some ideas with the look and mark of your own mind upon them.

Exercise VIII-1

"They laughed when I wound up my shaver . . . " That's liable to happen to you when you first use it in front of anyone. A wind-up shaver may seem a plaything, or at best an emergency type of shaver (because it needs no cords or batteries). After all, how can a hand-cranked shaver rotate fast enough to do a clean and close job? And how many times do you have to wind the darn thing to finish one shave?

One answer at a time: The three-blade shaving head revolves at such a fast clip that it actually gives you seventy-two thousand cutting strokes a minute! Now, about the winding: the palm-shaped body is filled with a huge mainspring made of the same Swedish super steel used in the most expensive watch movements. You can crank the key just like a movie camera (about six turns) and the shaver shaves and shaves and shaves. From ear to ear, from nose to neck, without slowing down, it maintains its full shaving speed right to the end—and long enough to do the complete job. Hard to believe, but really true.

We have reason to believe that you will want to keep your shaver for the office, club, cabin or in a permanent place in your bathroom cabinet. Once you've tried it you won't let it go. The money that it leaves in your pocket; the dependability; the good, fast, clean shaves that you'll get—they'll give *you* the last laugh.

——— ——— ———

1. What is the author's purpose? _____
_____

2. To whom is this appeal directed? _____
_____

3. Who would have you believe this? _____
_____

4. To which of your basic needs does the writer appeal? _____

Exercise VIII-2

Once again the annual guessing game is already underway. It is a guessing game I first became aware of eight years ago. This is the ninth playing of the game.

The reason I mention this is that each year for the past seven years I have proposed devices, resolutions, propositions, and so forth, to suggest that perhaps the time has come for us to give thought to what has been happening to families in this very uncertain process.

Somehow, somewhere, the master planners of the schedules and dates have not yet managed to coordinate these schedules with the schedule of the school year. The net result is that most have found it impossible to spend any of the summer vacation time of their children with them in the spirit each of us would like.

I have contended that there is no reason in the world why we could not take one month off in the summer while the kids are out of school, in order to be with them and to enjoy them to the fullest, and then come back and continue the business at hand.

I hasten to point out that each year when this proposal has been made, I have been approached by those who say, "Well, next year it will be different. Next year we will do it."

So far as I'm concerned, this is "next year" for the ninth time. "Next year" is now. The time is at hand for us to give this matter serious thought.

——— ——— ———

1. What is the author's purpose? *1968*
_____ to say he was going on a month vacation this year

2. When was this written? *1968*

3. To whom is this appeal directed? *Parents*

4. In what ways does the writer reveal a bias?
_____ He believes that people should take time off.

Exercise VIII–3

Our life is frittered away by detail. An honest man has hardly need to count more than his ten fingers, or in extreme cases he may add his ten toes, and lump the rest. Simplicity, simplicity, simplicity! I say, let your affairs be as two or three, and not a hundred or a thousand; instead of a million, count half a dozen, and keep your accounts on your thumbnail.

In the midst of this chopping sea of civilized life, such are the clouds and storms and quicksands and thousand-and-one items to be allowed for, that a man has to live, if he would not founder and go to the bottom and not make his port at all, by dead reckoning, and he must be a great calculator indeed who succeeds. Simplify, simplify. Instead of three meals a day, if it be necessary, eat but one; instead of a hundred dishes, five; and reduce other things in proportion.

Why should we live with such hurry and waste of life? We are determined to be starved before we are hungry. Men say that a stitch in time saves nine, and so they take a thousand stitches today to save nine tomorrow.

Exercise VIII–4

So far, I had not opened my eyes. I felt that I lay upon my back, unbound. I reached out my hand, and it fell heavily upon something damp and hard. There I suffered it to remain for many minutes, while I strove to imagine where and *what* I could be. I longed, yet dared not to employ my vision. I dreaded the first glance at objects around me. It was not that I feared to look upon things horrible, but that I grew aghast lest there should be *nothing* to see. At length, with a wild desperation at heart, I quickly unclosed my eyes. My worst thoughts, then, were confirmed. The blackness of eternal night encompassed me. I struggled for breath. The intensity of the darkness seemed to oppress and stifle me. The atmosphere was intolerably close. I still lay quietly, and made effort to exercise my reason.

A fearful idea now suddenly drove the blood in torrents upon my heart, and for a brief period, I once more relapsed into insensibility. Upon recovering, I at once started to my feet, trembling convulsively in every fiber. I thrust my arms wildly above and around me in all directions. I felt nothing; yet dreaded to move a step, lest I should be impeded by the walls of a *tomb*. Perspiration burst from every pore, and stood in cold big beads upon my forehead. The agony of suspense grew at length intolerable, and I cautiously moved forward, with my arms extended, and my eyes straining from their sockets, in the hope of catching some faint ray of light.

___ ___ ___   ___ ___ ___

1. What is the author's purpose? _____
_____

2. When was this written? _____

3. To whom is this appeal directed? _____
_____

4. What key words were used to influence one's emotions? _____

1. What is the author's purpose? *show how someone reacts to the total isolation of unawareness*

2. When was this written? *1870's*

3. What key words were used to influence one's emotions? _____

4. Who would have you believe this? *Poe*

Exercise VIII-5

The summer soldier and the sunshine patriot will, in this crisis, shrink from the service of their country; but he that stands it now, deserves the love and thanks of man and woman. Tyranny, like hell, is not easily conquered; yet we have this consolation with us, that the harder the conflict, the more glorious the triumph. What we obtain too cheap, we esteem too lightly: it is dearness only that gives everything its value. Heaven knows how to put a proper price upon its goods, and it would be strange indeed if so celestial an article as freedom should not be highly rated.

I have as little superstition in me as any man living, but my secret opinion has ever been, and still is, that God Almighty will not give up a people to military destruction or leave them unsupportedly to perish, who have so earnestly and so repeatedly sought to avoid the calamities of war by every decent method which wisdom could invent.

The heart that feels not now, is dead; the blood of his children will curse his cowardice who shrinks back at a time when a little might have saved the whole and made them happy. I love the man that can smile in trouble, that can gather strength from distress and grow brave by reflection. 'Tis the business of little minds to shrink; but he whose heart is firm, and whose conscience approves his conduct, will pursue his principles unto death.

_____ _____ _____

1. What is the author's purpose? _____
_____

2. When was this written? _____
_____

3. To whom is this appeal directed? _____
_____

4. What key words were used to influence one's emotions? _____

Exercise VIII-6

Two elected high school student body officers from each of our 50 States and the District of Columbia are selected by their chief State school officers to come to Washington as delegates to the Senate youth program. Each delegate receives a $1,000 scholarship.

Young people such as these are our hope for a better tomorrow. We must do our best to get them involved in the political processes, take advantage of their ideas, their imagination, their social conscience and, yes, their dreams.

We must demonstrate to them that the system can work. Convince them by example that if you want to see government made more responsive to your wishes, you have got to get involved.

You cannot build a better society by dropping out . . . by standing on the outside shouting epithets and throwing rocks. You have got to come in and work at it.

Democracy is a living thing that must be constantly nurtured. You cannot expect it to survive if all you are willing to do is go to the polls in November.

These young people participating in the Senate youth program are more than sunshine patriots. They are the fabric from which a better America will be woven.

_____ _____ _____

1. What is the author's purpose? _____
_____

2. To whom is this appeal directed? _____
_____

3. What key words were used to influence one's emotions? _____
_____

4. In what ways does the writer reveal a bias? _____

Exercise VIII-7

We'd like to make your blood boil, to tell you things that will make you so angry you'll hardly see straight.

Just send us $10 and we'll guarantee to keep you angry for a whole year. (That's less than 94 angry cents a month!)

We've been studying for years the things that make any decent person's blood boil. Things like prejudice, injustice, and discrimination. Some of the things we publish aren't pretty. Some of our subscribers are upset when they read them.

That's too bad. But that's our job. There is always an element of outrage in telling the truth. And the materials you get from us are the most scholarly, hard-hitting, and factual to be found. We leave the namby-pamby social studies and the pat formula solution books to others.

Moreover, we'll get you mad four times a year. By sending you four shipments every year carefully selected in advance by specialists from our new publications. Next, we'll give you an opportunity to get madder yet, by letting you purchase additional material at a maddening 20 to 50% discount!

Wait till you read our publications on civil rights, civil liberties, black studies, Middle East tensions, books on race and politics, the radical right, the radical left, new works coming up on Israel and Jewish history, discrimination against women, plus some brilliant anthologies.

Wait till you read the publications on new developments in interfaith and interracial projects (OK, these particular things won't make you mad, they'll make you glad), an examination of some forgotten minorities, urban crisis, intelligence and race, to name a few.

Every year over 5,000 libraries trust us to get them mad. So do thousands of teachers and clergymen. And thousands of ordinary decent citizens, like yourself, fume because of us. What more can we do? Except to tell you to calm down. Relax. Slowly pick up your pen and fill out the enclosed coupon. Now mail it. We'll give you plenty of time to get angry once you get our first shipment of materials. Thank you.

——— ——— ———

1. What is the author's purpose? _____

2. What do you question in this material? _____

3. To which of your basic needs does the writer appeal? _____

4. What key words were used to influence one's emotions? _____

Exercise VIII-8

Okay, so you've had your automobile checked and you figure you are ready for winter. Not quite, for there are several more minor items that you can check yourself which are bits of knowledge that every motorist should carry with him from November through March.

In checking equipment items yourself, make sure your heater is working properly. Do you have a car jack in your trunk and a fully inflated spare tire? A flat tire on an isolated road during severely cold weather can mean serious trouble, if you suddenly discover that you don't have a jack or fully inflated spare.

Police and professional drivers experienced in winter driving say snow tires are far better than ordinary tires for both starting and stopping on snow and ice. Although heavy-duty chains are best of all, some motorists have been known to carry bags of sand in their trunks to give them extra traction. They suppose that the added weight gives the tires more pulling power on ice. Fact is, it doesn't, and if it's of considerable weight, it may even cause the rear end to sway severely. The only value of sand in the trunk is that it can be sprinkled on the ice for short-distance traction.

Health officers summed up advice to winter motorists with a warning to those over forty, those who are overweight, and those who have a record of heart problems. Go to great lengths to avoid overexertion in your efforts to free a stranded car.

——— ——— ———

1. What is the author's purpose? _____

2. What do you question in this material? _____

3. To which of your basic needs does the writer appeal? _____

4. What key words were used to influence one's emotions? _____

Exercise VIII-9

My strategy was to start a national war on apathy, to get people involved in community action in order to learn as well as help. For an educated person to think he is educated and pass the proverbial buck—well, you've had it. When you graduate, if you lack sensitivity, you are a vegetable. If the so-called educated don't become involved in the problems of the urban and rural poor, then they are going to become a part of our stale, stagnant power structure. Just another member of the status quo.

Our American colleges graduate two kinds of people: Those who memorize and swallow, and those who criticize and watch. I am critical of this intellectual, comfortable bull session attitude where one does an analysis of present American problems without getting his hands dirty.

You know, one of the most uncomfortable places to work in America is in middle-class America, because you are kind of worried about the peanuts and not the elephants. I think America is the sleeping giant. It isn't that we can't react to challenge; it's that we aren't challenging each other. We're in the land of the free, home of the afraid.

I want to draw people out, get them involved. When they become involved they become more inner-directed because the demand on the volunteer is to be creative, not to conform.

I want volunteers. We need field workers for the South this summer. They'll have to pay their own way, but we need them.

--- --- ---

1. What is the author's purpose? _____
_____

2. To whom is this appeal directed? _____
_____

3. What key words were used to influence one's emotions? _____
_____

4. In what ways does the writer reveal a bias? _____
_____

Exercise VIII-10

If one of your lesser women dare challenge the notion that there is a new American male, or worse, implies that you might not be one; here are some words which might dispose of the matter (and of her): Dr. Myron Brenton in his book *The American Male* says there are two traditional underpinnings for the concept of manhood: primitive contact with nature (the Marlboro Man) and the patriarchal duties and prerogatives conferred by being a breadwinner. Brenton goes on to point out that in an age of urban living and affluence, neither of these traditional bulwarks of manhood hold much water anymore. Result: The new American male has had to figure out ways of exercising his masculinity that don't depend on the old stereotypes.

The ways the new male finds are infinitely varied, of course. But some common characteristics, if not trends, seem to emerge: The new male sees the Big Picture, and relates his job to it; he is passionately involved in the times and applies himself where he feels most needed; he makes little distinction between work and play, and works at what he most enjoys doing; he wants to, and generally does, have an impact on society and/or his community; he relates to women as people, not simply as females.

So much for the new American male. Just remember this: If the woman bugs you about it, overpower her—preferably with rhetoric.

--- --- ---

1. What is the author's purpose? *To help males understand and overcome equality*

2. To whom is this appeal directed? *Males*

3. To which of your basic needs does the writer appeal? *Mental Stability*

4. What key words were used to influence one's emotions? *manhood, masculinity*

Exercise VIII–11

I give my pledge as an American to save and faithfully defend from waste the natural resources of my country—its soil and waters, its forests, minerals, and wildlife.

Conservation is a necessity in life today. The careful preservation and protection of our natural resources is the foundation of our country itself. But we are destroying these resources and they need help. The Great Plains and majestic mountains have provided sustenance for the human race since the beginning of time. Now I feel we should provide help and protection for them.

Man watches wildlife but he doesn't seem to realize that most animals rely on other species for survival. If one species becomes extinct, generally its dependent neighbor does too.

Our country is a country with more harsh punishments and beautiful rewards than any country in the world. Yet without a program to protect it from pollution and a generally worsening environment it will soon be destroyed—and all life with it.

Those concerned with conservation need help and support. The people are what make this whole thing tick. Those who realize the values of our rich natural resources and abundant wildlife must not be a silent majority. We cannot stand helplessly and watch waste products fill the sky and waters with ugliness like a victor over the defeated! Defeated? Not yet. But what about the future? We should start caring, not tomorrow, but today. We must be heard. Our pleas for clean air to breathe and clean water to drink have to be heard by the leaders of our great country; and they must echo in the heart of every citizen whether he be seven or seventy. This is vital not only for the preservation of our country's natural resources, but for our own existence as well.

_____   _____   _____

1. What is the author's purpose? _____

2. What key words were used to influence one's emotions? _____

3. In what ways does the writer reveal a bias? _____

4. To whom is this appeal directed: _____

Exercise VIII–12

The collecting of unusual rocks and semi-precious stones—rockhounding—is gaining momentum as a family sport in this country. One big reason: In addition to providing fun for everyone in the family, it also can be a "fringe benefit" for many, providing bonus adventures to their travel vacations. That's because rockhounding can be so easily combined with other outdoor sports—say, doing a bit of rockhounding while camping or fishing. (Or, maybe it's really the other way around—saving the fishing for when the rockhounding slows down.)

If you're interested in adding new variety and fun to your travels by graduating from the ranks of the "looker" to that of the real rockhound, you'll find the move much easier than you may have thought. A small rock pick, knapsack, a book or two, notebook, prospector's pan, a couple of small screens, plus a desire for a little adventure and a lot of fun are all you need to join the rockhounding clan.

Even the objects of your search often are much easier to find than many think. Today's rockhounds are, for the most part, content to search for materials which, though certainly far less valuable than gold or diamonds, are relatively abundant. Rocks like agate, jasper, petrified wood, chalcedony, onyx and sapphire are among the most popular and zealously sought after.

Join the mushrooming corps of rockhounds and you'll gain a hobby that promises rich bonuses in new adventures, some precious stones and a mother lode of fun.

_____   _____   _____

1. What is the author's purpose? _To stir up future rock hounds_

2. To whom is this appeal directed? _Outdoor families_

3. What key words were used to influence one's emotions? _"fringe benefit" gold diamonds zealously sought_

4. In what ways does the writer reveal a bias? _By not showing any cons_

Exercise VIII–13

Crime in the streets has become a cliché of our society. It is not a cliché to our citizens, many of whom are afraid to venture out after dark. It is not a cliché to those residents who work, shop, and socialize in large cities in the realization that they may be the next victim of a mugging, robbery, or rape.

At present, any person charged with a non-capital offense—and that means anything other than first degree murder or rape—must be released pending trial, unless release on specified terms will not reasonably assure presence at trial.

What this means, in brief, is that—no matter how dangerous such an individual may be to other persons or to the community in general—he must be released, as long as he is likely to appear at his trial.

It has been found that most of the "repeaters" tended to have long prior criminal records; and most of the crimes committed on bail were similar to the original charges brought. It seems that there may be some means of gauging which defendents pose a high risk to the community.

The judge who holds the preliminary hearing should decide how much of a danger the defendent poses to the community. If he poses a sufficient threat, the judge may impose tight restrictions on his freedom, including curfew, daily or even hourly reporting to specified officers, and limitations on companions and travel.

— —— ——

1. What is the author's purpose? _____
_____

2. To whom is this appeal directed? _____
_____

3. What do you question in this material? _____
_____

4. What key words were used to influence one's emotions? _____

Exercise VIII–14

When men cannot accomplish their goals in acceptable ways, they resort to shortcuts—and far too often, violence is the shortcut chosen.

Violence is self-defeating. It cannot result in true progress. But one of the tragic lessons of last summer's riots was that violence—the last alternative—often accomplished short-term results where reasoned approaches and orderly protest failed. Riots seemed to produce results—from sprinklers on fire hydrants to increased job opportunities.

Law and order must be maintained. But punishment alone is no answer. Orderly cities cannot be based on the passive order of a citizenry bowed into submission. They must be built on the order of a democracy working together for the common good.

Trucks, tanks, troops, and guns can restrain violence. But only citizens can maintain democracy—citizens with the self-respect that comes from participation in the society and the recognition of the rewards of initiative. Citizens denied the chance to achieve self-respect—economic, social, and moral—are denied fundamental justice.

Since we are dealing with people, since we must understand the forces at work in the city and our society, then we must look at the people, not the houses—at the individual, not the group—at what a man wants, not what someone else tells him he needs.

— —— ——

1. What is the author's purpose? _Non-Violent treatment of people looking for a better world_

2. When was this written? _Early 60's_

3. To whom is this appeal directed? _White Bearaucrates_

4. In what ways does the writer reveal a bias? _____

Exercise VIII–15

For many years, drug addiction from heroin was confined to hardened criminals in the big city ghettos of the United States. Today, however, this addiction is common among young people living not only in the cities but also in the suburbs and rural areas. No part of society, no neighborhood or family is immune from the disease and tragedy caused by drug abuse.

The drug problem is out of control; the number of addicts increases daily, and the number of crimes due to addiction increases proportionately.

Survival for an addict is expensive and hazardous. He needs about $40 a day for drugs, which the average user obtains by committing various criminal acts—usually assault and theft, sometimes murder. The drug addict is desperate and dangerous; obtaining his fix may impel him to violent action. In New York City, addicts steal more than $1.5 billion every year. Not only are people in New York and elsewhere being robbed, attacked, and killed because of the drug problem but the cities are losing their vitality, partially because of this disease. City dwellers, frightened by what might happen to themselves or their children, are moving away. The "smell of death," as Stewart Alsop recently called it, is becoming intolerable. Drug pollution is choking the country.

Unless the production of heroin can be curbed, unless we can confront the problem at its source, addiction will continue to pollute our cities, and our countryside as well. Almost 100 percent of the hard drugs being consumed in the United States today is produced abroad. Eighty percent comes from crops grown in Turkey and processed in France.

——— ——— ———

1. When was this written? _____
_____

2. What is the author's purpose? _____
_____

3. To whom is the appeal directed? _____
_____

4. What key words were used to influence one's emotions? _____

Exercise VIII–16

I rise today to pay tribute to a man who not only achieved greatness in his profession, but who also used his talents in the cause of freedom for all people.

His life exemplified all of the struggle of all black Americans to overcome racial injustice. As the first all-American black football player, as a graduate student at Columbia Law School, as an acclaimed performer on the stage and in Hollywood, he manifested throughout his life the courage to fight racism and to assert his rights as an American citizen. He helped to make black Americans proud of their heritage and to make all Americans proud of the achievements of their country.

He was a champion for the freedom of all individuals. By refusing to compromise his constitutional rights before congressional committees in the early 1950's, he embodied the spirit of American freedom. His life story will serve to remind us how important our constitutional rights are, and how zealously we must guard them.

The moving tones of his "Ol' Man River" symbolize the yearnings of all people to be free. We will not forget him for the lessons of his struggles against injustice.

——— ——— ———

1. When was this written? _____
_____

2. What is the author's purpose? _____
_____

3. About whom are these comments made? _____
_____

4. To whom are these comments directed? _____

Exercise VIII–17

We are all used to hearing the refrain: "If poor people showed some ambition and initiative, they could escape from poverty and the slums." There are many reasons for questioning the validity and relevancy of this assertion, but in one field its absurdity is obvious and distressing. No matter how great his aspiration and ambition, neither the poor Negro-American, nor the rich one, can choose where to live. Whether he is moving from a tenement into a city high rise, or from a high rise into a suburban garden apartment; or from a garden apartment into a country split level, the color of his skin bars him from access to a large part of the housing market. No matter how secure and successful he may be, he finds himself judged not on his financial responsibility, or even his personality or the number of children he has, but rather on his pigmentation.

Can there be any justification for this throw-back to slavery? Is there any rational basis for rejecting a man as a neighbor solely because of his color? I daresay no intelligent citizen can give these questions an affirmative answer, yet through ignorance and fear and prejudice the practice continues, and some people continue to defend it.

——— ——— ———

1. What is the author's purpose? _____
_____

2. To whom is this appeal directed? _____
_____

3. What key words were used to influence one's emotions? _____

4. When was this written? _____
_____

Exercise VIII–18

As regards my own education, I hesitate to pronounce whether I was more a loser or gainer by his severity. Much must be done, and much must be learnt, by children, for which rigid discipline and known liability to punishment are indispensable as means. It is, no doubt, a very laudable effort, in modern teaching, to render as much as possible of what the young are required to learn easy and interesting to them. But when this principle is pushed to the length of not requiring them to learn anything but what has been made easy and interesting, one of the chief objects of education is sacrificed. I rejoice in the decline of the old brutal and tyrannical system of teaching, which, however, did succeed in enforcing habits of application; but the new, as it seems to me, is training up a race of men who will be incapable of doing anything which is disagreeable to them. I do not, then, believe that fear, as an element in education, can be dispensed with; but I am sure that it ought not to be the main element; and when it predominates so much as to preclude love and confidence on the part of the child to those who should be the unreservedly trusted advisers of after-years, and perhaps to seal up the fountains of frank and spontaneous communicativeness in the child's nature, it is an evil for which a large abatement must be made from the benefits, moral and intellectual, which may flow from any other part of the education.

——— ——— ———

1. What is the author's purpose? _____
_____

2. When was this written? _____
_____

3. What do you question in this material? _____
_____

4. In what ways does the writer reveal a bias?
_____

Exercise VIII–19

Observe good faith and justice toward all nations; cultivate peace and harmony with all. The nation which indulges toward another an habitual hatred or an habitual fondness is in some degree a slave. It is a slave to its animosity or to its affection, either of which is sufficient to lead it astray from its duty and its interest.

The great rule of conduct for us, in regard to foreign nations, is, in extending our commercial relations, to have with them as little political connection as possible. Europe has a set of primary interests, which to us have none, or a remote relation. Hence she must be engaged in frequent controversies, the causes of which are essentially foreign to our concerns. Hence, therefore, it must be unwise in us to implicate ourselves by artificial ties, in the ordinary vicissitudes of her politics or the ordinary combinations and collisions of her friendships and enmities. Our detached and distant situation invites and enables us to pursue a different course. Why forego the advantages of so peculiar a situation? It is our true policy to steer clear of permanent alliances with any portion of the foreign world. Even our commerical policy should hold an equal and impartial hand; neither seeking nor granting exclusive favors or preferences, constantly keeping in view that it is folly in one nation to look for disinterested favors from any other; that it must pay with a portion of its independence for whatever it may accept under that character.

———   ———   ———

1. What is the author's purpose? _____
_____

2. When was this written? _____
_____

3. Who would have you believe this? _____
_____

4. To which of your basic needs does the writer appeal? _____
_____

Exercise VIII–20

A. Corrupt the young, get them away from religion. Get them interested in sex. Make them superficial, destroy their ruggedness.

B. Get control of all means of publication and thereby,

1. Get people's minds off their government by focusing their attention on athletics, sexy books and plays and other trivialities.

2. Divide people into hostile groups by constantly harping on controversial matters of no importance.

3. Destroy the people's faith in their natural leaders by holding them up for ridicule and criticism.

4. Always preach true democracy, but seize power as fast and as ruthlessly as possible.

5. By encouraging government extravagance, destroy its credit, raise fears of inflation, and general discontent.

6. Foment unnecessary strikes in vital areas. Encourage civil disorders, and foster lenient and soft attitude on the part of government toward such disorders.

7. By specious argument cause the breakdown of the old moral virtues of honesty, sobriety, continence, faith in the pledge and word, and ruggedness.

C. Cause the registration of all firearms in some pretext with a view to confiscating them and leaving the populace helpless.

———   ———   ———

1. What is the author's purpose? _____
_____

2. When was this written? _____
_____

3. Who would have you believe this? _____
_____

4. What do you question in this material? _____
_____

5. What key words were used to influence one's emotions? _____
_____

Vocabulary List

List all key words missed and all words underlined in error. *Look up* each word in the dictionary, *study* its meaning, see if it has different meanings in different contexts, *learn* some of its synoyms and *practice using* them in sentences. Many people find that "cue cards" are a valuable aid in vocabulary building. List the key word on the front of a small card and put definition and synonyms on the back. Carry a pack of these cards in your pocket to review at odd intervals.

Review this list periodically and check off those words you have added to your vocabulary.

1.

2.

3.

4.

5.

6.

7.

8.

9.

10.

11.

12.

13.

14.

15.

16.

17.

18.

19.

20.

21.

22.

23.

24.

25.

26.

27.

28.

29.

30.

31.

32.

33.

34.

35.

36.

37.

38.

39.

40.

41.

42.

43.

44.

45.

46.

47.

48.

49.

50.

Vocabulary List

List all key words missed and all words underlined in error. *Look up* each word in the dictionary, *study* its meaning, see if it has different meanings in different contexts, *learn* some of its synoyms and *practice using* them in sentences. Many people find that "cue cards" are a valuable aid in vocabulary building. List the key word on the front of a small card and put definition and synonyms on the back. Carry a pack of these cards in your pocket to review at odd intervals.

Review this list periodically and check off those words you have added to your vocabulary.

1.

2.

3.

4.

5.

6.

7.

8.

9.

10.

11.

12.

13.

14.

15.

16.

17.

18.

19.

20.

21.

22.

23.

24.

25.

26.

27.

28.

29.

30.

31.

32.

33.

34.

35.

36.

37.

38.

39.

40.

41.

42.

43.

44.

45.

46.

47.

48.

49.

50.

Vocabulary List

List all key words missed and all words underlined in error. *Look up* each word in the dictionary, *study* its meaning, see if it has different meanings in different contexts, *learn* some of its synoyms and *practice using* them in sentences. Many people find that "cue cards" are a valuable aid in vocabulary building. List the key word on the front of a small card and put definition and synonyms on the back. Carry a pack of these cards in your pocket to review at odd intervals.

Review this list periodically and check off those words you have added to your vocabulary.

1.

2.

3.

4.

5.

6.

7.

8.

9.

10.

11.

12.

13.

14.

15.

16.

17.

18.

19.

20.

21.

22.

23.

24.

25.

26.

27.

28.

29.

30.

31.

32.

33.

34.

35.

36.

37.

38.

39.

40.

41.

42.

43.

44.

45.

46.

47.

48.

49.

50.

Vocabulary List

List all key words missed and all words underlined in error. *Look up* each word in the dictionary, *study* its meaning, see if it has different meanings in different contexts, *learn* some of its synoyms and *practice using* them in sentences. Many people find that "cue cards" are a valuable aid in vocabulary building. List the key word on the front of a small card and put definition and synonyms on the back. Carry a pack of these cards in your pocket to review at odd intervals.

Review this list periodically and check off those words you have added to your vocabulary.

1.   26.

2.   27.

3.   28.

4.   29.

5.   30.

6.   31.

7.   32.

8.   33.

9.   34.

10.   35.

11.   36.

12.   37.

13.   38.

14.   39.

15.   40.

16.   41.

17.   42.

18.   43.

19.   44.

20.   45.

21.   46.

22.   47.

23.   48.

24.   49.

25.   50.

SERIES III (ODD NUMBERS—*continued*)

NO. 9

1. to mix confusedly
2. to be outstanding
3. a decisive moment
4. more than is needed
5. thought to be absurd
6. especially suitable
7. covering all phases
8. to comprehend
9. usual way of doing something
10. where one lives
11. the last in the series
12. boundary line
13. a sound like a moan
14. a scenic painting
15. not public in nature
16. to set back
17. a solitary existence
18. provide financial aid
19. a tidy person
20. an act of good will

NO. 11

1. a feeling of thirst
2. not certain to occur
3. to be obedient
4. that which is to come
5. showing hilarity
6. an acquired holiday
7. one who is a criminal
8. pass quickly from sight
9. to be in right accord
10. of his own free will
11. choosing from several
12. to come together
13. simplicity of style
14. roughly sketched
15. state of being strong
16. a short hurried view
17. only one of a kind
18. changed in appearance
19. to stand still
20. to be thankful

NO. 13

1. associated with the press
2. usual course of events
3. capacity of receiving impressions
4. one who displays strength
5. one who is not selfish
6. overwhelming amazement
7. an amiable person
8. an ample amount of anything
9. set apart from others
10. adhering to a set plan
11. all over everywhere
12. to anticipate the outcome
13. becoming more complex
14. that which is dispersed
15. thought to be significant
16. related to the truth
17. authorized by proclamation
18. to withhold a privilege
19. an act which is illegal
20. to be potentially obtainable

NO. 15

1. considered to be brilliant
2. a surface injury to flesh
3. that which is awarded
4. something awkward or unhandy
5. in a contrary or reverse way
6. a perplexing and frustrating experience
7. buildings for lodging soldiers
8. not capable of producing vegetation
9. a battle between two individuals
10. be reduced to a state of beggary
11. rise and fall of the voice
12. cancel out the effects of
13. the capital city of a state
14. a state of being careful
15. the cause of an event
16. taking a census of the population
17. that which is indisputable
18. a summons to fight
19. to assemble or accumulate together
20. to contend in rivalry

SERIES III (ODD NUMBERS—*continued*)

NO. 17

1. the monarch of a kingdom
2. that which is relatively low
3. to enlarge either in fact or appearance
4. a representation of the surface of the earth
5. a martyr for the sake of principle
6. using the faculty of remembering
7. reproduced on a miniature level
8. the sixtieth part of an hour
9. which is within reasonable limits
10. a system of teaching morals
11. a moderately feeble-minded person
12. a complex situation or mystery
13. to have very narrow limits
14. quality or state of being neutral
15. a state of being nominated
16. does not deviate from the average
17. that which stands in the way
18. counted as obsolete in style
19. to vindicate or justify an act
20. under the oppression of a tyrant

NO. 19

1. the earth upon which we live
2. to develop and cultivate the mental processes
3. the practice of referring overmuch to oneself
4. to be envious of the other person
5. to be equal in quantity or degree
6. an error in the way a person thinks
7. that which becomes extinct
8. to be supported by evidence based on facts
9. to have a prescribed or set form
10. terror excited by sudden danger
11. to be full or complete in quantity
12. the accumulation or increasing or profits
13. a gesture used to enforce an opinion
14. to give a gift to someone
15. the act or action of gliding
16. the goal to obtain in winning the race
17. a meeting face to face with a client
18. to supply water to the land by canals
19. that which is regarded as an island
20. January, named after the Latin deity, Janus

KEY FOR INCREASING READING EFFICIENCY

SERIES IV (ODD NUMBERS)

	NO. 1	NO. 3	NO. 5	NO. 7	NO. 9	NO. 11	NO. 13	NO. 15	NO.17	NO.19
1.	S	D	S	D	D	S	D	S	S	S
2.	D	D	D	S	S	D	S	D	D	D
3.	S	D	S	S	S	S	D	D	D	D
4.	D	S	D	D	S	D	D	D	D	S
5.	D	S	D	D	D	S	D	D	S	D
6.	S	D	D	S	D	D	S	D	D	S
7.	D	S	S	D	D	D	D	S	S	S
8.	D	D	D	D	D	D	D	D	S	S
9.	D	D	D	D	D	S	S	D	D	D
10.	S	D	S	S	D	S	S	S	S	D

SERIES V (ODD NUMBERS)

	NO. 1	NO. 3	NO. 5	NO. 7	NO. 9	NO. 11	NO. 13	NO. 15	NO. 17	NO. 19
1.	F	T	T	F	T	F	F	T	T	F
2.	2	4	3	1	3	1	2	1	3	4

SERIES VI (ODD NUMBERS)

	NO. 1	NO. 3	NO. 5	NO. 7	NO. 9	NO. 11	NO. 13	NO. 15	NO. 17	NO. 19
1.	T	Automation	T	light	F	Philadelphia	T	T	T	F
2.	F	T	magma	F	Wilkinson	F	physical	4	2	1
3.	T	math	2	gas	1	3	3	Sandstone	T	T
4.	decibels	T	F	T	T	F	T	F	environment	1
5.	1	F	T	T	T	T	F	T	3	T
6.	F	F	F	2	F	T	F	F	F	14
7.	swim-bladder	2	F	3	Llewellyn	4	F	1	T	F
8.	F	T	Iceland	F	F	F	T	T	F	F
9.	T	F	1	F	4	museum	4	springs	F	municipal
10.	2	3	T	T	T	T	psychosomatic	F	activity	T

SERIES VII (ODD NUMBERS)

	NO. 1	NO. 3	NO. 5	NO. 7	NO. 9	NO. 11	NO. 13	NO. 15	NO. 17	NO. 19
1.	T	T	T	people	F	1	responsibility	T	degree	T
2.	F	2	Wardian	F	climate	T	F	4	F	3
3.	F	compromise	2	T	F	fish	F	F	2	F
4.	4	F	F	1	4,000	F	moral	strict	T	examiners
5.	button	F	T	T	T	4	T	F	T	T
6.	T	T	F	F	2	F	3	T	illumination	F
7.	50	F	F	3	F	T	3	T	4	2
8.	1	1	T	T	T	Alaska	T	F	F	geographical
9.	T	realistic	4	story	1	F	T	3	F	T
10.	F	T	mold	F	T	T	F	affirmative	T	F

In this series there are no exact or "right" answers. You were asked to read critically in an effort to understanding underlying purpose, emotional appeal, bias and propaganda techniques. You were asked to try to identify time and place of appeal.

As a key to checking on your own critical thinking, this key section consists of the identification of the source of the material and a few comments about the setting from which it was taken.

See how close you were to identification of basic factors. Think about those which you missed, and go back and read the material again to check out your own sensitivity to key words and ideas.

VIII–1
(an advertisement by the Haverhill's Company of San Francisco, California, in *Natural History,* February 1968, p. 22)

The purpose of this article is to sell the Haverhill's new shaver, which the company claims will give the consumer dependable, fast, and economical service for some time. The advertiser appeals to the reader's need for quick, convenient shaves.

VIII–3
(an excerpt from *Walden* by Henry David Thoreau. Boston: Houghton Mifflin Company, 1893, p. 32)

Henry David Thoreau was a transcendentalist who believed that simplicity is the key to a happy life. He went to Walden Pond to live for several months to "suck out all the marrow of life and to live deep." In his book *Walden,* Thoreau is trying to sell appreciation for the simple life as he experienced it in his Walden experiment.

VIII–5
(an excerpt from "The Crisis" by Thomas Paine, as it appears in *The Great Works of Thomas Paine.* New York: D. M. Bennett, 1878, pp. 382–383)

Thomas Paine wrote "The Crisis" to attract, interest, and involve people in the causes of the Revolutionary War. In this particular passage, he is condemning those who give up when the going gets rough. He warns that they will live to regret their "cowardice."

VIII–7
(A general mailing advertisement for a subscription service offered by the Anti-Defamation League of B'nai B'rith, 315 Lexington Avenue, New York, New York 10016)

The writer's purpose is to convince the reader that the firm that he represents will stir him up by exposing many of the shortcomings of today's society through hard-hitting and provocative articles, which the reader can obtain by subscription to the firm's series of studies. Words such as "blood boil," "angry," "prejudice," "discrimination," "upset," "outrage," "namby-pamby," and "fume" are used to sell the reader on the author's materials. His appeal is directed to the reader's intelligence by indicating that the studies are not the usual clichés generally available, but are exposés written by some of this country's best authors. Thus, the appeal is also to one's sense of honesty and integrity.

VIII–9

(taken from "Slum Lord, Sunny Side Up," by Marlise James and Ned Coll, the *Moderator*, April 1968, p. 51, with permission of the editor)

The author is the founder and director of the Revitalization Corps, which seeks to combat the problems of the poor through community action. The purpose of the selection is to make the educated aware of their obligation to help with the War on Poverty, and the author is making a particular plea for help the following summer.

VIII–11

(an article from the September 1970 issue of *Wyoming Wildlife*, reprinted by permission of the editor)

This article was prepared from a contribution by a 13-year-old schoolboy from Ranchester, Wyoming, David Seibert, and is an appeal to the readers to take some positive action to support conservation activities and to preserve some of the beauties he enjoys for the use of future citizens.

VIII–13

(taken from the *Congressional Record,* Vol. 113, No. 6, January 18, 1967, p. S441, by Senator Brewster, Maryland, Democrat)

The senator from Maryland, situated next to Washington, D.C., which has an extremely high crime rate, made these comments in support of a bill that would provide that at the first hearing of a defendant charged with a felony, the judge be empowered to consider the safety of the community as well as the likelihood of the defendant's appearance at trial, in setting conditions for bail. An appeal is made for public health and safety.

VIII–15

(Taken from the *Congressional Record,* Vol. 117, No 15, February 10, 1971, p H626, by Representative Monagan, Connecticut)

In his speech to the House, Mr. Monagan is urging the passage of a bill that would curtail the traffic of illegal drugs into the United States. Mr. Monagan is very concerned with the effects that drugs are having on our society and points out that the illegal use of drugs is not confined to the criminals in ghettos, but is spreading through our whole cultural system. By reducing the supply of narcotics illegally entering the United States, the Congress can make a much needed contribution toward controlling the growing menace of drug addiction and related crime.

VIII–17

(taken from the *Congressional Record,* Vol. 113, No. 198, December 5, 1967, p. S1789, by Senator Edward Kennedy, Massachusetts, Democrat)

Senator Kennedy urges the Congress to pass an open housing bill to bar racial discrimination in certain housing developments. The senator feels that the color of a man's skin should not bar him from access to a large part of the housing market. There is an appeal made for fair play and the communality of man.

VIII–19

(an excerpt from George Washington's *Farewell Address to the People of the United States.* Boston: Old South Leaflets, General Series, V. I, number 4, 1888, p. 15)

Before leaving office as the first president of the United States, George Washington made a speech to the people in which he offered advice on how to preserve the new nation. In this passage, he suggests that our country should refrain from interfering in any way with foreign countries.

SERIES II (EVEN NUMBERS)

NO. 2	NO. 4	NO. 6	NO. 8	NO. 10
1. cot	glimpse	cook	keen	humiliated
2. polite	charlatan	house	ministers	headland
3. mount	settlement	fish	eat	boast
4. falsehood	steps	gutter	empty	dominion
5. resin	hamper	blaze	pork	deny
6. predicament	cry	grass	jangle	incompetent
7. memory	sharp	level	lose	enrage
8. dromedary	sop	affront	medicine	inflexible
9. measure	hat	braid	concerning	possessions
10. conceal	afflict	intended	cutlery	muffler
11. contaminate	killer	weep	levy	stalks
12. green	melt	saving	disgusting	bag
13. dabbler	salary	plant	gas	biological
14. price	friendship	prayer	brush	see
15. shell	child	chest	vanquish	cheat
16. doctrine	short	inlet	pigeon	divinity
17. dart	drop	revise	holder	hasten
18. fortunate	struggled	scowl	pawn	dealer
19. contract	practice	assert	smaller	concept
20. tidy	ignited	chance	trap	hash
21. gait	cornucopia	western	harbor	resound
22. dwell	choose	advance	fury	restoration
23. pat	answer	part	furtive	form
24. befall	exhausted	relieve	coagulate	wooer
25. pocketbook	taut	ripped	squander	useless

NO. 12	NO. 14	NO. 16	NO. 18	NO. 20
1. embarrass	plentiful	wrong	obscure	covetous
2. testimony	stake	bearer	assemble	rustic
3. morn	teach	heal	consider	naive
4. outbreak	industrious	guide	homemaking	robin
5. temerity	plume	crepe	penalty	cloth
6. ask	listen	angry	nose	inscrutable
7. weighty	succulent	spite	vegetable	elevation
8. foreign	wet	path	immunity	grateful
9. adventure	tormentor	wisdom	tolerable	manufacture
10. elder	depend	secure	fanciful	gratify
11. element	site	adhered	person	acknowledge
12. compassion	compassion	below	esteem	base
13. receive	oscillate	foolish	competency	road
14. injured	change	perplex	watch	disaster
15. staff	wife	perimeter	law	science
16. delve	official	relate	closet	producer
17. cringe	bureau	get	beguile	trade
18. tools	anticipate	chasm	final	thankfulness
19. house	useless	jewel	statement	consultation
20. ray	probable	accident	teacher	fair
21. aspect	torment	confined	degraded	hunter
22. director	bag	denial	buyer	mend
23. manifested	quit	tray	unite	depression
24. expanded	drench	shrewd	grand	exist
25. conquer	flung	unaffected	confusion	omnipresent

SERIES III (EVEN NUMBERS)

NO. 2

1. to recognize again
2. precious metal
3. a high polish
4. to empty out
5. a belief held
6. prose fiction
7. of little breadth
8. to belong to
9. infinite in size
10. entertains another
11. surface of earth
12. to poke something
13. made independent of
14. to make peace
15. leave it out
16. possessing dignity
17. an enormous animal
18. administer justice
19. not correct
20. one who expects

NO. 4

1. correct position
2. gentle animal
3. a gradual decline
4. diminish in size
5. abundant harvest
6. be flustered
7. upright position
8. to be stable
9. rather sleepy
10. ruinous condition
11. neglect of duty
12. expressive of pain
13. marked boundary
14. to annihilate
15. this very instant
16. ramble along
17. most valuable part
18. being clumsy
19. to collapse
20. to complicate

NO. 6

1. hurrying for aid
2. nearly as easy
3. more than needed
4. very small quantity
5. one or the other
6. a great error
7. plain to see
8. not interested in
9. scandalous conduct
10. just the opposite
11. at the beginning
12. a surviving part
13. obviously clear
14. about dawn
15. he who is a criminal
16. craving something
17. offer your service
18. avoiding something
19. being historical
20. dislike to work

NO. 8

1. rising in power
2. should be allowed
3. according to facts
4. to dispose of
5. to reach the peak
6. brought about by
7. prepared to go on
8. exclusive of others
9. not very busy
10. death by violence
11. decent in character
12. free from reproach
13. keep from falling
14. a great outcry
15. very necessary
16. completely exhausted
17. place for vacations
18. one who is punctual
19. one who is courageous
20. shattered to pieces

SERIES III (EVEN NUMBERS—*continued*)

NO. 10

1. punishment for an offense
2. an act of entering
3. in complete contrast
4. to pronounce guilty
5. to complicate matters
6. free from blame
7. to throw with violence
8. from this time forward
9. a military foe
10. to come to an end
11. the art of carving
12. a large river barge
13. to have an aversion to
14. to be part of an audience
15. anything very old
16. rough in countenance
17. pleasant salutation
18. one mad dog
19. to rush some place
20. to be in a safe place

NO. 12

1. consecrated as sacred
2. betray a trust
3. not according to facts
4. bottom of the scale
5. training for an event
6. that which is immense
7. an act of teaching
8. prove to be right
9. an orderly arrangement
10. one of the seasons
11. a table in a room
12. in a close-by vicinity
13. to answer yes
14. to be against
15. one noble in spirit
16. lack of attention
17. that which is interior
18. retain ownership of
19. to present for acceptance
20. to pause undecidedly

NO. 14

1. possessed with a severe handicap
2. soon to be indispensable
3. as often as necessary
4. an annual event or happening
5. the appendix of a book
6. to engage with close attention
7. close to correctness
8. to submit to arbitration
9. a military organization
10. something made without skill
11. to assault another person
12. the acceptance of an assumption
13. quality of being atrocious
14. to make trials or experiments
15. sale of goods to highest bidder
16. that which is authentic
17. to establish by authority
18. that written by his own hand
19. feeling of aversion toward something
20. a belief of some sort

NO. 16

1. to have and to keep
2. that which is tormenting
3. that which is done instantly
4. a confusing predicament
5. be on your guard
6. the part that is taken away
7. having gone astray
8. to arrange into chapters
9. idle chat in a conversation
10. the leader of the organization
11. to clarify the issue or report
12. to group or segregate in classes
13. instrument such as a clock
14. any system of rules or principles
15. that which is beyond
16. that which lies next to
17. to receive with intention or returning
18. that which is the bottom
19. to apply a brake to
20. characterized by brevity

SERIES III (EVEN NUMBERS—*continued*)

NO. 18

1. to make plain by means of interpretation
2. closely acquainted or familiar with
3. that which is in fashion
4. that which is without strength or solidity
5. a kind of a watertight structure
6. the foot of an animal or a person
7. to be eternal or infinite in duration
8. that which happens or occurs
9. a person who gives evidence as to what happened
10. extremely good of its kind
11. that which exceeds what is usual
12. personal conduct motivated by expediency
13. something considered as abnormal
14. living under false pretenses
15. sequence with no interval or break
16. in the nature of an enchantment
17. consecrated to a noble purpose
18. a habitual course of action
19. that which has a deceptive appearance
20. that which happens early

NO. 20

1. an allowance to one retired from service
2. that which is perplexed
3. pertinent to the present condition
4. formative in nature as clay or plastic
5. quality or state of being popular
6. the duties of a porter
7. within the powers of performance
8. a precaution taken in advance
9. a query relative to a problem to be solved
10. safeguarded by divine care and guidance
11. to puzzle out a mystery
12. a vessel holding one quart
13. to ramble or wander with no set goal
14. a place where anything is kept in store
15. a long loose outer garment
16. a part presented for inspection
17. to separate in different directions
18. coming first in logical order
19. to be slow or tardy in action
20. the guard going the rounds

SERIES IV (EVEN NUMBERS)

	NO. 2	NO. 4	NO. 6	NO. 8	NO. 10	NO. 12	NO. 14	NO. 16	NO. 18	NO. 20
1.	D	D	D	S	S	D	D	S	S	S
2.	D	S	S	D	S	D	D	D	D	D
3.	S	S	D	D	S	S	S	S	S	D
4.	S	S	S	D	S	S	S	D	D	D
5.	D	D	D	D	D	S	S	D	D	D
6.	D	D	D	S	D	S	D	D	D	D
7.	D	S	D	D	D	D	S	S	S	D
8.	D	D	D	D	S	S	D	D	D	S
9.	S	D	D	S	D	D	D	S	S	D
10.	D	D	S	D	D	D	D	D	D	S

SERIES V (EVEN NUMBERS)

	NO. 2	NO. 4	NO. 6	NO. 8	NO. 10	NO. 12	NO. 14	NO. 16	NO. 18	NO. 20
1.	F	T	T	T	F	F	T	T	F	F
2.	1	2	1	4	3	1	4	4	2	2

SERIES VI (EVEN NUMBERS)

	NO. 2	NO. 4	NO. 6	NO. 8	NO. 10	NO. 12	NO. 14	NO. 16	NO. 18	NO. 20
1.	T	sudden	T	F	F	individual	T	F	apathy	1
2.	2	F	quarreling	F	community	F	3	T	F	T
3.	F	neurotic	1	T	T	T	4	2	F	T
4.	F	T	F	jetport	F	propaganda	F	T	3	F
5.	3	2	F	T	mind	4	Colorado	4	T	F
6.	distinctive	F	F	photographs	1	T	T	intent	F	economic
7.	special	F	emotions	3	T	F	turnout	T	ecological	T
8.	T	1	T	T	3	F	F	environment	T	F
9.	T	T	2	F	T	T	T	F	4	north-south
10.	F	T	T	2	F	1	F	F	T	4

SERIES VII (EVEN NUMBERS)

	NO. 2	NO. 4	NO. 6	NO. 8	NO. 10	NO. 12	NO. 14	NO. 16	NO. 18	NO. 20
1.	T	cause	F	T	F	T	3	T	dairy	T
2.	himself	1	4	F	T	3	T	T	3	T
3.	F	T	50	F	F	F	hydrogen	F	F	F
4.	6	F	T	Bible	F	Brooke	1	F	T	1
5.	8	T	interior	F	unchanged	F	F	85	F	solitude
6.	T	17th	T	3	1	T	T	2	T	T
7.	F	F	F	T	2	F	F	F	dung	4
8.	T	2	1	4	T	3	water	4	T	F
9.	F	F	F	T	Penitentes	T	T	Liaison	F	1/8
10.	mind their own business	T	T	cross	T	Spain	F	T	2	F

In this series there are no exact or "right" answers. You were asked to read critically in an effort to understand underlying purpose, emotional appeal, bias, and propaganda techniques. You were asked to try to identify time and place of appeal.

As a key to checking on your own critical thinking, this key section consists of the identification of the source of the material and a few comments about the setting from which it was taken.

See how close you were to the identification of basic factors. Think about those which you missed and go back and read the material again to check out your own sensitivity to key words and ideas.

VIII–2
(taken from the *Congressional Record*, Vol. 113, No. 7, January 19, 1967, p. S558, by Senator Gale McGee, Wyoming, Democrat)

The purpose of the speech is to persuade the Senate to recess for the summer, although no formal measure is proposed. The appeal is made to the legislators' feeling for family unity by keeping families together at their homes in the summertime.

VIII–6
(taken from the *Congressional Record*, Vol. 117, No. 13, p. S1003, by Senator Hubert H. Humphrey, Minnesota, Democrat)

Senator Humphrey, through his use of such words and phrases as "hope for a better tomorrow," "their social conscience," "Democracy . . . must be nurtured," and "fabric from which a better America will be woven," is pointing out to the Senate that it is within the power of the youth of today to insure a lasting Democracy in America in the future. He pleads for recognition that America has responsible youth who are concerned and that, contrary to some, not all youth are radicals and irresponsible.

VIII–4
(an excerpt from "The Pit and the Pendulum," Edgar Allan Poe, as it appears in *The Works of Edgar Allan Poe*, Volume II. New York: A. C. Armstrong and Son, 1902, pp. 465–466)

Poe's story, "The Pit and the Pendulum," tells of the terror invoked upon men by the Spanish Inquisition. The character in this story has been arrested and thrown into the dungeon for heresy. The terror he feels upon awakening is a very real part of this story.

VIII–8
(taken from "Weathering the Winter," by A. R. Roalman, *Americana: The American Motors Magazine*, November/December 1967, p 15, with permission of the editor)

Appealing to the reader's need for knowledge of driving safety hints, the purpose of the article is to advise readers of some precautions for winter driving and car maintenance. The author of the article represents an automotive company which has an interest in making driving as pleasurable and safe as possible.

VIII–10

(taken from "The New American Male" by Sherman B. Chickering, in the *Moderator*, February 1, 1968, p. 2, with permission of the editor)

The author's purpose is to show how the modern American male has changed along with the changes in society. The "new" American male seeks to exercise his masculinity through a greater devotion to his job and working at what he must enjoys doing. The author makes an appeal to American men to defend their new image.

VIII–16

(from the February 4, 1976, issue of the *Congressional Record*)

In this excerpt from a speech of Hon. Harold A. Ford of Tennessee on January 29, 1976, Mr. Ford recognizes the recent death of Mr. Paul Robeson and pays public tribute in the House of Representatives to Mr. Robeson's distinguished life.

VIII–12

(taken from "Rockhounding" by Pete Czura in *Americana: The American Motors Magazine*, November/December, 1967, p. 17, with permission of the editor)

The author, who represents a motoring magazine, appeals to the reader's sense of adventure and desire to make traveling more enjoyable and interesting by collecting rocks.

VIII–18

(an excerpt from John Stuart Mill's *Autobiography*. New York: P. F. Collier and Son, 1909, p. 39)

John Stuart Mill's education is unique in many ways. He was a genius who was educated by his father. Although he received no formal education from an institution, Mill makes some comments on education that are meaningful to educators today. He believes the old "brutal and tyrannical" system was not effective, but he also condemns the new system for being too easy.

VIII–14

(taken from the *Congressional Record*, Vol. 113, No. 8, January 23, 1967, p. S709; by Senator Abraham Ribicoff, Connecticut, Democrat)

The senator, in an effort to curb violence in the cities, proposes the addition of a new title VIII, entitled "Urban Redevelopment Areas," to the Public Works and Economic Development Act of 1965. The need for job opportunities could be met by providing financial assistance to public works and business loan projects. The senator makes a plea that citizens, not guns, can restrain violence.

VIII–20

(taken from the *Congressional Record*, July 19, 1968, p. H7114, by Representative Saylor, Pennsylvania, Republican)

Representative Saylor, having been given permission for extraneous remarks, brings to the attention of the House, the Communist Rules for Revolution, as he took them from the Scottish Rite Masons' publication entitled "Youth: Have We Failed Them?" These Rules were among the captured papers taken in Dusseldorf, Germany, in May 1919. The Florida State Attorney recently obtained a new copy of them from a known Communist party member, who admitted that these Rules were a part of their unit plans.

SUGGESTED SEQUENCE FOR A TWENTY-HOUR READING PROGRAM

All basic series and numbers refer to basic exercises in this book. Pretests, posttests, and the supplementary exercise book, *Maintaining Reading Efficiency,* may be ordered from Developmental Reading Distributors, 1944 Sheridan, Laramie, Wyoming 82070.

(Schedule is designed for ten two-hour periods. For a 50- to 60-minute class, plan only about half the material scheduled. The "5-minute break" divides the material in two sections requiring approximately the same amount of time.)

FIRST PERIOD

Use a standardized, 10-minute reading test such as the *Maintaining Reading Efficiency Tests.*

(Score and collect.)

Discuss potential goals and materials to be used.

SERIES #	EXERCISE #
I	2, 4, 6

Explain Charts

5-MINUTE BREAK

II	2
V	2
VI	2
VII	2

SECOND PERIOD

I	8, 10, 12, 14
II	4, 6, 8
III	2

5-MINUTE BREAK

V	4
VI	4
VII	4

THIRD PERIOD

I	16, 18, 20
II	10, 12, 14
III	4, 6

5-MINUTE BREAK

V	6
VI	6
VII	6

Supplementary Reading Exercises from *M.R.E.*

FOURTH PERIOD

II	16, 18, 20
III	8, 10, 12, 14
IV	2, 4

5-MINUTE BREAK

V	8
VI	8
VII	8

Supplementary Reading Exercises from *M.R.E.*

FIFTH PERIOD

III	16, 18, 20
IV	6, 8
V	10

5-MINUTE BREAK

VI	10
VII	10

Supplementary Reading Exercises from *M.R.E.*

SIXTH PERIOD

IV	10, 12, 14, 16
V	12

5-MINUTE BREAK

VI	12
VII	12

Supplementary Reading Exercises from *M.R.E.*

SEVENTH PERIOD

IV	18, 20
V	14
VI	14

5-MINUTE BREAK

VII	14

Supplementary Reading Exercises from *M.R.E.*

EIGHTH PERIOD

V	16
VI	16
VII	16

5-MINUTE BREAK

Supplementary Reading Exercises from *M.R.E.*

NINTH PERIOD

V	18
VI	18
VII	18

5-MINUTE BREAK

Supplementary Reading Exercises from *M.R.E.*

TENTH PERIOD

V	20
VI	20
VII (If time allows)	20

5-MINUTE BREAK

Use a final, standardized, 10-minute reading test such as one of the *Maintaining Reading Efficiency Tests.*

(Score in class and discuss comparisons with beginning tests.)

	RATE TABLES	KEY ODD	EVEN	PROGRESS CHART
SERIES I	307	NONE NEEDED		297
SERIES II	307	317	325	297
SERIES III	309	318	326	297
SERIES IV	311	321	329	297
SERIES V	313	321	329	299
SERIES VI	315	322	330	299
SERIES VII	315	322	330	299
SERIES VIII	NONE NEEDED	323	331	NONE NEEDED